The End of an Era

Also By Curtis Carroll Davis

Chronicler of the Cavaliers: A Life of the Virginia
Novelist, Dr. William A. Caruthers

The King's Chevalier: A Biography
of Lewis Littlepage

John Sergeant Wise as candidate from Virginia for the
United States Congress, 1883.

The End
of an Era

by John Sergeant Wise

Edited and Annotated by
Curtis Carroll Davis

New York · Thomas Yoseloff · London

Special Contents of this Edition
© 1965 by A. S. Barnes and Co., Inc.
Library of Congress Catalogue Card Number: 64-20273

Thomas Yoseloff, *Publisher*
8 East 36 Street
New York 16, New York 10016

Thomas Yoseloff Ltd
18 Charing Cross Road
London W. C. 2, England

6071
Printed in the United States of America

Opening Remarks

The supporting material for this new edition of a widely praised, much plundered, oft damned volume of Civil War reminiscence will concentrate on elucidating the volume rather than describing the author. This is because the central facts of the author's life may be surveyed at a glance in Appendix 2 or consulted in detail via the titles in Bibliography 1, and because the access allowed me to the author's papers has made available such a wealth of matter on the provenience of the volume as to constitute almost a story in itself. This story is a rewarding one alike for the study of the creative process and of American social history. Because, however, the author's career was so varied and so fruitful, certain aspects of it still not on the record will be touched upon here in order to offer as illuminating a portrait as possible of a man too often condemned in his home territory. He attracted the condemnation primarily because, at the worst possible time, he turned Republican!

A lawyer of the articulateness of John S. Wise needs no one to plead a "brief" for him. Nevertheless, for enabling me to do so from my special point of view, I should like to acknowledge the assistance and good will of the following: Francis L. Berkeley, Jr., ex-curator of manuscripts at the University of Virginia Library; the late Demaree Bess, contributing editor, *The Saturday Evening Post;* William Couper, late Executive Officer and historian of Wise's *alma mater*, the Virginia Military Institute; Milton C. Russell, head of the Reference and Circulation section in the Virginia State Library; and J. Russell Wiggins, executive editor, *Washington Post and Times-Herald.*

Let me next pay tribute to those without whose approval the appearance of this book would not have been possible: the Wise family. All five of Wise's surviving children have been generous in their cooperation. Each has written me at length about memories of their father, and each memory has proved a special contribution. I would thank his daughters, Mrs. James P. Barney of Princeton, New Jersey, and Mrs. Charles L. Moore of Charlottesville; his sons, Byrd D. Wise of New York City, Henry A. Wise of "Clifton," Accomack County, Virginia, and Jennings Cropper Wise of Hampton, author and one-time Acting Commandant of the Virginia Military Institute; his grandsons, Henry A. Wise IV of Watertown, New York, and John S. Wise of Charlottesville. Jennings C. Wise has been steadily helpful in, among other things, supplying the rare photographs which illustrate this edition.

My chief obligation goes out to Mr. Henry A. Wise, his father's law partner, executor, and owner of his papers. For granting me unrestricted and exclusive access to these papers, and then enduring months-long queries about problems they elicited, I am fundamentally indebted to him. For their easy exploitation at Farmington during a sultry June sojourn I thank Mr. Wise's son, John S. Wise, who, in company with his wife, showed once again that the venerable traditions of Virginia hospitality are still green as the rhododendron at Goshen Pass in springtime.

CURTIS CARROLL DAVIS

Baltimore, Maryland
April, 1964

Contents

Illustrations

A Brief for John Sergeant Wise

A Brief for John Sergeant Wise

> Like most authors, Mr. Wise has the highest regard for
> that one of his books which is not the popular favorite.
> He says his head may have been best in "The End of an
> Era," but his heart was in "Diomed" and his soul in
> "The Lion's Skin," which has been least noticed.
>
> J. H. Lindsay in the *Library*
> *of Southern Literature*, XIII. 5,939

The best work of Wise's head was begun some time
during the latter half of 1897 and concluded by April
1, 1898. From his law offices in the Edison Building at
44 Broad Street, New York, on January 21, 1898,
during the course of a letter about *Diomed* to his long-
time friend, the Mississippi Congressman John Sharp
Williams, Wise declared:

I have nearly completed another book which is the life
of a boy, on lines like those of Diomed. The boy tells what
he saw from 1846 to 1865. Then he died. Everybody he
ever knew died. Everything he ever saw disappeared. And
he began a new life, in a strange land. When that comes
out I hope you will read it, & I think it will get a little
closer to you than the dog.

On April 1 of the same year Wise informed Richard
Watson Gilder, editor of the *Century Magazine*:

I have just finished a book called 'The End of an Era.' It begins in 1846 and ends in 1865. It is a narrative of the experiences of a slave-holden boy. It is really my own autobiography as a boy and winds up at the surrender of Johnson's [sic] army . . . after being a man and an officer, I became a child again and went back to school in boy's clothes.

If it had ever been Wise's intention, as the Williams passage suggests, to write an allegory or an historical romance about the War, he changed his mind. This was very good. The leading student of Southern literature, Professor Jay B. Hubbell of Duke University, has observed of Wise's fellow Virginian, novelist John Esten Cooke: "Of the seven books which he wrote dealing with the war not one is the book he should have written—a plain, straightforward account of what he had experienced. . . ." Conversely we may say that *The End of an Era* (1899) is exactly the book Wise should have written, *i.e.*, about what he had experienced. Yet it is something richer than plain or straightforward.

During a speech about the Cavaliers and Puritans at the Congregational Club, Chicago, in 1894, Wise had stressed the value of folklore as "that part of human history more valuable than any other," in that formal histories were only "deductions of writers from facts they may not understand" and in any event had been filtered through the writer's personality. In his article, "The Open Season," for the *Saturday Evening Post* in 1905, he confessed that the three delights of his life remained hunting, military battles, and love-making: "I became deeply involved in all three before I was a voter, and although I have since tried many other things these three still bear the palm."

From this pair of opinions, flanking in time the creation of *The End of an Era*, we may induce two things about that volume before so much as opening it: the book will be one man's personal interpretation of "history"; it will have the taste of life. It is in fact a consciously literary performance which, by utilizing from time to time someone else's experiences (the author's brother, Dr. Richard A. Wise), falls into a few errors. Let us look at the artistry first.

At the outset it may be asserted, repeating Sir Winston Churchill, that John S. Wise had in his head "the essential structure of the ordinary British sentence," which "is a noble thing." Having it, he knew how to use it. We can tick off various literary devices he employed: the flash-back (p. 1), suspense (pp. 7–8), the anecdote (p. 68), total-recall dialogue (pp. 83–87), and deft characterization (President Buchanan, p. 72; General Scott 103–14; Secretary Benjamin, pp. 176–77; General Mahone, pp. 325-26). For an example of the felicitous use of exposition, look at the passage beginning at the top of page 21. To see the effects of Wise's oratorical experience, try counting the words in the sentence commencing at the bottom of page 222. From time to time we are offered set pieces constituting independent essays in themselves. Three of them comprise a panorama of the Virginia scene: the Eastern Shore in "The Kingdom of Accawmacke,"

Chapter II; the Piedmont in "How the 'Slave-Drivers' Lived," Chapter X; and the West in "Presbyterian Lexington," Chapter XVI. Wise can be epigrammatic, too. Consider his simile on John Smith (middle of p. 12), a personality who continuously attracted him and about whom he had delivered an address before the Mayflower Descendants at Delmonico's in New York on November 23, 1896. Read his phrase about the *Monitor*, at the top of page 203, or about the sound of rifle fire, at the top of page 319.

Like all writers Wise had his favorites among the writers who had gone before him. In speech and article he rarely failed to summon forth a quotation from prose or verse. In *The End of an Era* his literary allusions or quotations are moderately numerous and interestingly varied.

Two of the more enduring virtues of *The End of an Era*, then, are its style and its comprehensiveness. Fortunately it is no mere military chronicle. Wise was far more interested in people than in places, and in delineating people he had, by 1899, become a perceptive, unprejudiced reporter. A Virginia Military Institute cadet who had survived his tour of duty as "Mr. Rat," Wise had had the privilege of mounting guard over the bier of Thomas J. Jackson (see p. 270); and he contributed an extensive, ancedotal sketch of that General—"as grim as a pot on a fire"—to *The Circle* in 1908. Yet it is significant that *The End of an Era* opens and closes with vignettes of Union officers.

Wise never agreed to the rightness of the Fifteenth

Amendment on Negro suffrage, but that he detested slavery any reader of Chapter VI can see. Like that of all Southerners from slave-holding families of the better sort, his attitude toward the Negro was paternalistic. He knew him thoroughly as an individual, and he understood the nuances of the ante-bellum slave hierarchy. From his father he had learned to pinpoint, almost at a glance, the African origin of the blacks: Congolese, Guinean, Senegambian, or West Indian. Such knowledge, based on good will, inevitably brought sympathy. When the Union League Club of New York had resolved to release its Negro employees as a post-bellum gesture of liberation, and hire whites, it was Wise—said to be the Club's first Confederate member—who, at the plea of Monroe Davis, his former valet whom he'd placed in a good job there, spoke out so eloquently against the plan at a called meeting on April 24, 1901, the membership proceeded to vote it down 286–109. The result is that the Union League is today the only important Manhattan club retaining Negro help.

In a McKinley campaign speech in the Opera House at Atlanta on October 31, 1896, Wise felt he had the right to turn to James Longstreet, sitting nearby, grasp the feeble old soldier's hand, and as the audience burst into cheers, declare: "General, you and I have waited long for this day. We rode out far in advance of our lines. There was more danger, in times past, that we would be killed from the firing of our own troops, than from those in our front. But this night and this scene is our best recompense. The troops are up, and ready for the charge!"

Yet it was also Wise who, selected to deliver the Memorial Day oration at Grant's Tomb on Riverside Drive in 1891, had observed of his and Longstreet's mortal enemy:

There is to-day an Arab stroking his steed under shady palms by the solitary fountain, reflecting on the greatness of Grant. There are gentle Chinese and Japanese reading, in their own language, the story of his life, with wonder and admiration. There are American Indians, crouching by desert fires, picturing to themselves, in rude imagination, the sort of man he was. There are Egyptians, floating on the Nile, dreaming of Grant, and Vicksburg, and the far off Mississippi. There are Russians, with half illumined minds, struggling to reconcile the strength and tenderness, the power and mercy, to them so strangely blended, in his great character. There are Frenchmen learning pertinacity. There are Spaniards and Italians on whom his forgiveness and magnanimity will not be lost.

Hypocrisy? Not at all. No less than twenty-two Wises, including John and his father the ex-Governor, served in the War: this is spelled out in a large "Confederate Roster of the Family of Henry A. Wise," dated January 31, 1908, which the family presented to Lee Camp No. 1, Confederate Veterans. John S. Wise had been a good Confederate. He grew up into a better American. The fact that he is able, in *The End of an Era*, to describe the process of transition not only with a natural gift for narrative, but also without prejudice and without rancor, is perhaps the

John Sergeant Wise in the uniform of a second lieutenant, Provisional Army, C.S.A., 1865.

chief reason why his book ranks as a permanent contribution to American belles-lettres.

II

> The North can scarcely comprehend how bitter was
> the abuse visited upon Wise, Longstreet, and a few
> other Southern leaders when they became Republicans
> after the war. Though Wise was in Congress for a brief
> time, his new political faith closed his public career,
> drove him from the leadership he practically inherited,
> and finally compelled him to seek a livelihood by
> curbing his hot temper to the tedium of a New York
> law office. No braver act was ever done in battle than
> Wise performed in the Virginia of the new era when
> he turned from all his friends and took his post in pol-
> itics by the side of his freed slaves to seek the right as
> he saw the right.
>
> "The End of an Era," editorial,
> *New York World*, May 14, 1913 (8/2-3)

The fact that our author induced his brother
Richard A. Wise, M. D. (1843–1900), Professor of
Chemistry at the College of William and Mary, to
"stand for me in several episodes" certainly does not
"mar the narrative." From the antiquarian point of
view it does, however, blur the picture. A chapter-by-
chapter credit rating for *The End of an Era* is therefore advisable. Supplied on very good authority, it
may be found as Appendix 1 to this edition. A few
minor errors of fact are pointed out in the Notes to the
text. Two passages embodying problems of larger
significance will be discussed here.

The first is the Tabb-Rutherford wedding (p. 397
following). Neither the Jefferson Davises nor Varina

Howell Davis' sisters attended it. In reacting to an attack from Mrs. Davis on this score, Wise makes about as persuasive a defense as a writer can for the sins of creative reminiscence.

From her residence at the Girard Hotel on West 44th Street, New York, Mrs. Davis sent Wise a bitter eleven-and-a-half page missive on mourning stationery (see p. 21, below). She was incensed about *The End of an Era* in general and, in particular, about its author having labelled her sisters as "large." Wise responded February 8, 1900, with a fourteen-page epistle:

"You say truly [he told the Confederate President's widow] that this was not at the Rutherford's, and that neither Mr. Davis nor they nor yourself were in fact there. I remember distinctly that the Von Boercke episode occurred at Mr. McFarland's. In the endeavor to make a composite portrayal of Richmond society as it existed then, I did bring into the Rutherford entertainment a number of persons who were not present. I thought such license legitimate, and that it did not fall under the head of falsehood. Feeling that the presence of the Presidential party would add eclat, and that in view of your public position specially, it would not be an unwarranted liberty to do so, I did introduce you all.

What may or may not be a more significant error occurs in the fourth paragraph of page 429. This is General Lee's reaction to the Sayler's Creek engagement. As reported by Wise (who always misspelled it Sailors'), it sounds defeatist. According to the *Publications* of the Southern History Association, this dialogue immediately "aroused much attention in the Southern press" upon its advance appearance in the *Atlantic Monthly* for April-May, 1899, and should be discounted as contrary to all other knowledge of Lee's character. One such reaction was a lead editorial in the Richmond *Times* for April 11, 1899, captioned "John S. Wise on General Lee." While not impugning Wise's sincerity, the paper concluded that after thirty-four years he had "dreamed" this conversation so persistently he now took it for gospel. The *Times* was confident "there is not a Confederate soldier alive who will not believe that his memory has served him a wretched trick."

The day after this editorial appeared the *Times*'s owner and publisher, Joseph Bryan, from a sick bed at "Laburnam," his big house on the northern outskirts of Richmond, dispatched a letter to Wise in New York. He had not heard of the editorial in advance, said Bryan, but had read the *Atlantic* article with the greatest interest and found it splendidly narrated. "I thought the Times article most uncalled for & have so written the author & I wish to express my real regret that it appeared." Nor was he astonished to read of Lee's frankness, for the General often took people by surprise in this way, "& I certainly would not, in my paper, put a presumption against your direct statement."

At once Wise retorted to the effect that this apology should in justice be made as public as the words that had caused it. Then he proceeded to the broader issue of the *Times*'s long-standing animus against himself and his brother, Dr. Richard A. Wise. From the time of Joseph and his brethren, Wise declared, to call a man a dreamer "has been about synonymous with a liar"—and then to see this copied all over the country! He knew very well the motive lay in the fact that the *Times*'s editorialist, like all Virginians, could attribute no possible good to a Confederate veteran who had turned Republican. He, Longstreet, Mosby, and Mahone, had all suffered from this imputation of dishonesty. The correspondence between the two men ended huffily, but they remained friends.

For the rest of his life Wise never ceased to maintain the authenticity of Lee's reaction to the Sayler's Creek engagement. On October 26, 1909, for example, the Virginia novelist Constance Cary Harrison wrote him from her home at 1607 I Street, N. W., Washington, D. C. In an old album of Confederate souvenirs she had come upon the transcript of a telegram from Lee to President Davis date-lined "Headquarters, Rice's Station, Southside Railroad, April 6th, 1865." It read: "I shall be tonight at Farmville. You can communicate by telegram to Meherrin, and by courier to Lynchburg." Mrs. Harrison sent the transcript to Wise with the query if this was the one he had carried? "Such was my understanding from my husband, but I have wished to make sure about this most interesting relic of our débâcle." (She was composing her own War reminiscences.) "You who have already done this so cleverly and with such authority, will know how absorbing I find my task."

From his offices in the Commercial Cable Building at 20 Broad Street, New York, Wise replied at once, as was his custom in correspondence. "It is more than forty four years since I reported to General Lee at Rice's Station, April 6th, 1865. I bore from him to Mr. Davis a brief dispatch but cannot swear to the identity of this." All he could recall was that Lee had told him he felt it imprudent for security reasons to put in writing more than a terse statement of his whereabouts. Wise assured Mrs. Harrison that he had discussed the Sayler's Creek passage with Colonel Charles Marshall, Lee's personal secretary throughout the War, and with Colonel Walter Taylor, Assistant Adjutant General of the Army of Northern Virginia, and that both had told him they did not find Lee's statement surprising. When he entered President Davis's presence at Danville, Wise added:

Burton Harrison was very kind to me. He saw I was more dead than alive and helped me to get something to set me up. In those days it didn't take long for me to revive. He was present at the long examination to which I was subjected, and in one of the last interviews I ever had with him he told me he had still in his possession the dispatch I bore, and that he would give it to me. After his death I had half a mind to ask you for it, but I did not think you should part with it and do not blame you for not doing so. In fact I think he told me once that he would have complied with his promise but that you would not permit him to do so.

Wise venerated Lee without worshipping him. There are among his papers three typescript drafts, with as many titles, of a speech he delivered on Lee from time to time. Their text has been substantially published by the Montclair, New Jersey, *Times*, January 25, 1908 (pp. 1–2), in its account of Wise's oration the preceding day at the local Outlook Club. Exactly one year earlier the *New York Times* in its issue for January 22, 1907, under the caption "Lee As a Fighter," had published a long letter from Wise taking to task certain passages in the paper's anniversary editorial on Lee for January 19. It was not Lee who was Fabian in his tactics, Wise declared, but Johnston. Lee was more the Parthian. He was by nature aggressive, particularly at the Second Manassas (Bull Run)—"the boldest in conception and most aggressive in execution of all the battles fought by Lee"—and it was only logistics that prevented his engineering more such victories. ". . . it seems a pity that such a man should never have had the opportunity to be seen at his military best." Wise recalled Lee's hazel eyes with their web of crow's-feet at either side, revealing that here was a man who could laugh as well as frown. When speaking on Lee, he liked to quote a martial passage from "The Burial of Dundee" in W. E. Aytoun's *Lays of the Scottish Cavaliers*.

In his historical novel, *The Lion's Skin* (pp. 259–62), Wise provides a striking portrait of Lee during the course of his evocation of the 1869 season at the Greenbrier White Sulphur Springs. This has been called the most brilliant in the annals of that resort, and both Wise and his father attended (the Governor sitting for a group photograph with Lee, Beauregard, Magruder, and other Confederate paladins.) In June, 1911, Wise corresponded with Houghton, Mifflin Co.

about a biography of Lee. The firm said that, though they were about to release Mary Johnston's novel, *The Long Roll*, and were negotiating with Gamaliel Bradford for book publication of his Lee articles running in the *Atlantic*, they were interested. As it turned out, Wise's declining health prevented further action.

A year and a half later when Wise, in Bryn Mawr Hospital with the heart ailment that would mark the beginning of the end, was passing his hours holding court for friends and, of course, reading widely, he went through Thomas Nelson Page's recent *Robert E. Lee: Man and Soldier*. Though flat on his back, Wise got off an eight-page letter in pencil to his old friend, dated December 18, 1912, pointing out minor errors and faulty emphases in the volume. Toward its close he had, he observed ruefully, detected a resemblance between the General and himself in that they both had the same type of heart trouble with attendant suffering. Page's reply of December 23 from his residence at 1759 R Street, N.W., in Washington, went partly as follows:

I am glad you liked my Lee. I did the best I could with it. . . .

For example, I gave your father's brigade the credit for the defense of Petersburg, to which I felt it was entitled. If you had written me your letter before that book came out, I would have bodily copied and quoted just what you have said, in it, about that brigade. I shall copy the letter, and if I ever publish another edition, I will put it in as you wrote it. You never wrote a better

page in your life than that, and you have written many
ringing pages. Your 'End of an Era' is, in my judgement,
one of the few books relating to the war, that will live,
and from it will be taken, not only the color and the
flavor; but the substance of the times, when the defini-
tive history shall be written. Your 'Diomed' has much of
the same color in it, and will be an authority on the old
Virginia life; and maybe from that and from some of the
Virginia writings of one who was your young Lieutenant
when you were the Captain of the old Richmond Light
Infantry Blues, will be taken the picture of Virginia life
which will finally stand as the portrait of that courageous
prime.

III

> I did not know or appreciate, when I wrote The End
> of an Era, that I was doing the things you mention.
> Neither side in the great Civil war was as bad as the
> other pictured it, & neither, I may add, was as good
> as it pictured itself. If I held up to any one, in his
> true light, the character of my grand brave old father,
> I feel that I am amply repaid. For he was, in truth,
> the bravest, the most incorruptible, and simplest old
> Roman I ever knew.
>
> Wise, "Kiptopeke," Cape Charles,
> Va., Sept. 18, 1911, to John Jay Chapman

In his letter to Richard Watson Gilder, of April 1,
1898, Wise had said: "Two publishers are after me
for this book, but I would rather publish it serially in
the Century than in any other way, even if I also publish it as a book." For some reason the negotiation did
not materialize. Instead the last two chapters ran in
the *Atlantic Monthly* the following spring, and on

June 3, 1899, Wise wrote editor Walter Hines Page of that magazine as follows:

I do not know how the book will succeed, but certainly the two chapters which have been published seem to have met with a very cordial reception. I have endeavored to meet the wishes of the last reviser by 'shortening sail' as much as possible, and am fully aware of my verbosity, but I have taken the liberty of restoring a few of my slaughtered innocents which he murdered in platoons and I think you will sustain me in the wish I cherish to indulge now and then in a little sentiment and in a few touches of philosophical reflection, and not compel me to launch our craft double reefed, close hauled and almost under bare poles, as if we expected to sail right out into a tornado.

They sailed instead into such favorable weather that over the years, according to the files of Houghton, Mifflin Co., *The End of an Era* passed through twenty-seven printings to a total sale of 12,329 copies. As he had done with his dog book, *Diomed*, and would do with *The Lion's Skin* and *Recollections of Thirteen Presidents*, Wise did not relax upon completion of the manuscript and permit his publishers to take over. Instead he conducted a genteel but brisk personal propagandizement by distributing gift copies of the book to influential friends and appropriate institutions in various parts of the land. These he would usually autograph with an individualized sentiment that seemed to make a hit with recipients—such as the one given General John E. Roller of Harrisonburg, Virginia, "my friend for thirty-seven years" (now in the Vir-

ginia State Library), or that sent to the Poe Alcove
of the University of Virginia Library (gratefully
acknowledged by Professor James A. Harrison).

Further distribution occurred through the good offices of acquaintances, kin, and enthusiastic readers.
Wise's friend E. P. McKissick, proprietor of the Battery Park Hotel in Asheville, vowed he had given away
eighteen copies, with such delightful response he was
preparing to leave the hotel business and go into book
selling! The Richmond attorney J. Preston Carson en-
closed two dollars, asking for an autographed copy he
wanted to send a Union General he knew. A wealthy
Philadelphia matron, Mrs. William J. Latta of Wissa-
hickon Heights, had her book store forward a copy
for autographing so that she might auction it off at a
benefit for the Germantown Hospital. The wife of the
ex-Mayor of Charlotte, North Carolina, mailed a copy
to her friend Grace King, the New Orleans novelist.
The volume was read *by* a hundred Union veterans
at an Old Soldier's Home in Maine and *to* a class of
forty-five young ladies at a private school on Prairie
Avenue, Chicago.

Resultant from this activity *The End of an Era*
found itself being perused in such unlikely places as
the United States Consulate at Dundee, Scotland, or
the Palazzo Barbaro at Venice. When the author's
cousin, John C. Wise of "Wonwell," near Warrenton,
Virginia, returned from Portugal in May, 1906, he
told how he and his wife had dined in Lisbon with the
American Minister, Colonel Charles P. Bryan, at a
large banquet also attended by the King and Queen.

As the Wises prepared to advance and be presented to Their Majesties, John C. Wise suddenly felt someone tugging furtively at his coattails. An unknown voice whispered in his ear: "Have you read 'The End of an Era'? . . . so my thoughts flew from the House of Braganza to the Kingdom of Accomac."

Over the years letters of this sort poured in on the author. They came from friends as close as B. A. "Duck" Colonna of Washington, D. C., or from total strangers. They came from Union veterans and Confederate veterans. They came from prominent people —Mayor Seth Low of New York, Secretary of the Navy John D. Long, ex-General G. Moxley Sorrel, C. S. A., German Minister the Baron Speck von Sternburg—or from ordinary citizens. All of them asked questions, proffered opinions, requested genealogical assistance, sent reviews, praised the author, or took him to task. Several said the book read just like a novel. Many said, write a third book. Others said, we were so glad you stopped where you did. Still others said, what a pity you didn't carry it on into Reconstruction. Some called it *The Last of an Era*, some *The New Era*. Those who knew Wise well addressed him as Captain; those who didn't, as "Hon.," "Colonel," "General," or "Governor." (Throughout life he was so steadily confused with his father, Governor Henry A. Wise, that his "public disclaimer," he assured the editor of the Petersburg, Virginia, *Index-Appeal*, "has been made so often that my doing so has become ridiculous and elicits laughter.")

The proprietor of Blue Ridge Springs, Virginia,

assured Wise he had eminently fulfilled James Barron
Hope's prophecy in his "Portsmouth Memorial Poem"
about the coming of "some historian both strong and
wise." Another correspondent was gratified that here
at last the North might view an authentic Southern
gentleman on display, instead of having to swallow
the stereotype in F. Hopkinson Smith's *Colonel Carter
of Cartersville*. From The Homestead at Hot Springs,
Virginia, Mary Pegram Alexander wrote on behalf of
her sister and herself to say thanks "for your beautiful
and discriminating tribute to our brother Col. 'Willie'
Pegram. . . ." A woman in New York City wanted to
know the repository of the shipping list for 1635? A
gentleman down at Memphis expressed strong doubts,
as a native of good old Accomac, that the distinguished
John Custis had ever been a Rotterdam tavern-keeper.
A man in New York wanted the exact day and hour
Wise had reached Danville since he was preparing a
monograph on the subject, "Lincoln in the Telegraph
Office." A member of The Century Association in
Manhattan, Charles Collins, stated he had failed to find
that either Whittier, Emerson, or for that matter Long-
fellow had in fact written panegyrics on John Brown:
"If I am wrong kindly indicate the verses in question."

When Federal troops overran "Rolleston" early in
the War, a Freedman's School for ex-slaves was set up
in the carriage house under the auspices of the American Missionary Association. Presently the story got
about that General Benjamin F. Butler, U. S. A., as a
smirking salute to the memory of the plantation's
former owner, had induced Annie Brown, daughter

of the notorious Kansan, to come and teach there. The report was accepted even by the scrupulous Barton H. Wise in his biography of the Governor. On December 1, 1908, however, from his Vesey Street offices Oswald Garrison Villard, editor-in-chief of the New York *Evening Post*, sent Wise a deposition taken down recently by one of his agents out in Petrolia, California, from Annie Brown effectively refuting the allegation. The preceding June 10, Villard had queried Wise on the same general subject. In connection with his researches into Brown's life he wished to ascertain Governor Wise's true reaction to Brown's personality. The author of *The End of an Era* replied the very next day:

I was with him constantly from the date of Brown's affair at Harper's Ferry until his death, September 12, 1876, literally in my arms at Richmond, and I think I know his feeling as thoroughly as anybody but himself . . . . I have frequently heard him say concerning John Brown that he was impressed with his truthfulness, his sincerity and his absolute fearlessness, but he did not regard him as our friend [George T.] Downing evidently does, nor do I believe that he said it 'depressed him to think of the part he had taken in depriving so good a man of his life.' That would have been maudlin feeling, and there was nothing maudlin about my father. He thought that John Brown was a homicidal maniac, whose mind was unbalanced on the subject of slavery, and whose plans for attacking it were those of a crazy man.

Two other passages from *The End of an Era* that evoked special response from readers were the account of hog-killing time and the portrait of Colonel "Bob"

Preston. Few people wrote in about General Lee. Here is a sampling of the things that moved them enough to cause them to address the author over a period from November, 1899, through December, 1909. The consensus was almost uniformly favorable. From reading them one can comprehend how crucially the Civil War had penetrated the American psyche.

1899

Nov. 14 Wholesale saddler Sherwood Hall, Grand Rapids, Mich:
Your account of making the shot was, oh! So natural. How many nights (Friday), I have sat up making those drop pellets and then cutting the ends off, to go shooting Saturday; and then, there was no fear that the shot were not heavy enough . . . in fact, these self, home made shot were the most deadly charge I ever fired if they did sometimes cut the Game up badly.

Dec. 28   Archie Aiken (aged *ca.* 13), Danville, Va:
Some time this winter I will read it through   papa says a year from now I will understand it better.

1900

Jan. 4   Mrs. Jefferson Davis, New York City:
You are not true to yourself or the traditions of our country when you begin your book with a panegyric upon Genl Sherman who marched through our battle riven country with a horde of creatures who took everything movable from the helpless women and children and cursed and maltreated them for resisting arson and theft. . . .

This was not a man to submit to the domination of the "Gray Mare" because he was thinner in flesh than his wife. I think I see your inspiration is from "The Secret

History of the Confederacy" by Pollard, and the files of Daniel's Examiner—The character of these two men was so low and their sins of commission were so many that I hoped you never could be ranged on their side, even in dealing with an enemy. It grieves me to know that the son of my dear old friend Gov Wise and the brother of the stalwart young hero Jennings Wise . . . could call the struggle in which he fell "Vanity Fair". . . .

I perfectly appreciate that you did not willingly lampoon my husband or hold up his sorrow stricken widow to the derision of this generation intending to be offensive, but only to give a jocular turn to a phrase which would attract attention, and I forgive it freely, but I am grieved over your book and should gladly see it burned as were those of old in the presence of the Apostles of truth.

Your friend,
V. Jefferson Davis

January 22   Banker William C. Seddon, Baltimore, Md:
It . . . will do an immense deal of good in fostering good feeling between the North and South. In no book which I ever read, is brought out the real position of the master towards his slave, as is accomplished in this book.

February 19   John T. Dickson, New York City:
Your criticism of the Presbyterian style of people of Lexington, was amusing in the extreme, but what convulsed me more was your own experience at the "Tabb Rutherford" wedding. . . . as I knew Miss Rutherford, I can realize the whole affair as one of supreme ridiculousness.

May 19   Attorney General of Virginia A. J. Montague, Richmond, Va:
Every chapter is good, but your hog killing is so true to nature it made me feel like a boy again and wish for a

broiled pig tail. Your description of Gen. Fitz. Lee does you great credit under the circumstances.

May 29   Henry Bolling, Richmond, Va:
introducing myself as . . . the body-servant of Gen'l Jno. B. Preston [Colonel "Bob"] whose Orderly you were. . . .

Please excuse the length of this letter and my presumption, which you may attribute to the fact that I may feel some little importance attached to myself because my name is in print. . . . I must speak of the red leather boots Gen. Preston had made for you and the three days I spent in trying to get them black. It was about the hardest and most unsatisfactory job I ever undertook. I am pretty old now and just manage to get along.

1901

August 9   James H. Wilson, Wilmington, Delaware:
. . . notwithstanding the digs you give me on account of the speed I made from Reams' Station to the neighborhood of Fort Powhattan, I wish to think you for writing the book and to compliment you on the good taste and the good feeling which pervades it from cover to cover. . . .

One word more. Of course I was as fast as I could and if your people had laughed less and rode faster—in short if they had been the great and incomparable leaders you describe and evidently believed them to be, I should not have got away with my command comparatively intact as I did. The fact is there is something more in the history of Wilson's Raid in South Virginia than appears to the superficial observer—but let that pass!

1902

January   Alexander Hunter, Department of the Interior, Washington, D. C:

Your criticism of certain of our officers is just only they did not go far enough. . . . About Huger—to him McClellan owes the salvation of his Army. . . . Napoleon would have shot Huger the next morning, tho' I am glad the old fellow was spared for I have spent many happy days as his guest at Gordonsdale, the family seat of the Peyton family at Fauquier Co., Va., which Genl Huger bought.

February 3   William Waldorf Astor, 1st Viscount Astor of Hever Castle, "Cliveden," Taplow, Bucks:

Your story is so well told, that it is a pity there should remain upon future editions the blemish of any inaccuracy, however trifling. I therefore invite your attention on page 330 to the word "petite" which, being feminine, is not applicable to General Beauregard; and on page 290 to the attribution of a crossbow to the naked boy, which is an anachronism. The crossbow was a weapon in use only during the Mediæval Period & is not properly in the hands of Cupid who, in any figure of speech, should have only the surrounding of the Ancient World.

February 10   H. P. Finley, Ann Arbor, Mich:

Your very full, correct (as I saw it) and graphic account of the Sailor Creek fight brought vividly to my remembrance incidents of that fight, which was, as you say, a hot one.

In riding over the field early in the morning after the battle I picked up official orders bearing your Fathers signature as "Gen Commanding." I regret to add that I was foolish enough to show these to my Brigade Commander later and that a *request*—which you will readily understand amounted to an order, transferred them from me to him.

June 17   Lawyer Wm. Allen Butler of Butler, Notman, Joline & Mynderse, New York City:

There is such a striking coincidence between the record of your feelings on visiting the slave auction at Richmond in 1859 and my own experience on a visit to the same spot in 1858, as expressed shortly afterwards, that I am sending you my volume of poems [*Nothing to Wear,* new ed., 1899], in which you will find on page 76 what is in some respects a transcript in verse of your description of the slave sale you attended.

1904

May 12   Eugene R. Youngs, Connecticut Mutual Life Insurance Co., Hartford:

I am a Connecticut young man with a passionate fondness for the South, and a great desire to locate there, and your book has added to my already great admiration for the brave and gallant people within its boundaries.

October 5   C. C. Kinney, Dallas, Texas:

When I read your political will at the end of the book I made up my mind to write you & tell you of an incident I have never mentioned to any one, but which made a life time impression upon me. Twenty odd years ago, when I was quite a lad you were taking tea at my fathers house in Staunton, and during the meal, you & father were discussing politics, & you remarked to him that you were a republican or had joined the Republican party, because it would support Mrs. Wise & and the little Wise's while the Democratic party would not. My political ideals were shattered right there. . . . I spoke to father about it next day, & he said don't you repeat that my son. Some years later I understood.

1905

February 9   [Mrs.] E. C. Crim, New Market, Va:
I always feel that you are so near and dear to me, as you are one of my youthful heroes. How well I remember the eventful day as you came in line of battle down Shirleys hill. I saw the terrible shell that nocked you down as you came down the hill. I *will never forget you.*

November 1   Attorney E. W. Spangler, York, Pa:
... I should like also to possess a copy of your "The End of an Era," and in return will send you a copy of my "Little War Experience," a book of 270 pages profusely illustrated. I enlisted in the Union Army in 1862 when sixteen years of age, and may have met you on the field of battle. Of course, at this late day, I cannot remember all the faces I saw in the opposite ranks.

My father-in-law was . . . so ardent a Confederate that my wife inherited $5,000.00 worth of Confederate Bonds. Perhaps you can advise me of their present value.

1906

March 19   Attorney John G. Paxton, Independence, Mo:
Some years ago I read with pleasure your book. . . . Later I read it aloud to my boys with the result that one of them was made to study more than he ever did in order to enter the V.M.I.

1908

March 25   Student John H. Summers, University of Cincinnati Law School:
Indeed I felt a great pride throughout the narrative on account of knowing that you were a member of my college fraternity Beta Theta Pi. . . . If anything is pleasing to me it is for the signal success of a Beta. . . .

1909

February 12   Journalist Stephen Bonsal, Bedford, N.Y:
I should like very much to go to Accomac and before
going I should like above all things to meet the writer
who has made an epoch of our history live again and as
I think for all time.

December 10   Author Constance Cary Harrison, Washington, D.C.:
By the way, let me say that if all the books on the war
were written with the spirit of youth and military ardor
yours carries on every page, they would be much more
convincing to the general reader, and more agreeable to
the veteran!

Professional reviewers gave *The End of an Era* just
as favorable a reception, and for as varied reasons. The
Home Journal and the *Book Buyer* lauded the author's
moderateness of tone. Both the *Home Journal* and the
Dial felt the portrait of General Scott was specially
striking. The *Dial* thought Wise's account of Accomac
life at least as good Virginiana as his friend Tom Page's
The Old South, while the *Book Buyer* drew a general
comparison with Page's novel, *Red Rock*. The *Nation*
had over-all praise, but drew attention to one error:
the author's assertion on page 132 that most Virginians
were like himself in hating slavery. The *American
Historical Review*, while it believed "the student of
American history will not dwell long" on the book,
admired such vignettes of the Old Régime as those of
the way a plantation mistress supervised her domain,
the slave auction, and the anti-democratic mores of

Richmond society. (For the War period, Cocke's one-man currency office was singled out.)

Though the libraries of both William and Mary College and the Virginia Historical Society received copies of *The End of an Era*, neither the *William & Mary Quarterly* nor the *Virginia Magazine of History & Biography* deigned to review it. By contrast the widest-read Virginia author of them all, one of the best-known American women writers, handed down a flattering verdict from her syndicated column in the Philadelphia *North American*. Answering a reader's query for the best published authority on the War, "Marion Harland" (Mary Virginia Terhune) had this to say:

One of the most readable and altogether the fairest story of the civil war is "The End of an Era," by John Sargent [sic] Wise, an able lawyer and the son of an ex-governor of Virginia. . . . I consider the work a very valuable addition to the literature of that period. I have read no other history that treats the delicate and painful subject with more skill and candor.

IV

Speaking of his literary work, Mr. Wise said it was his great pastime. He likes nothing better than to write rambling reminiscences. "The remuneration for the articles is like the stories the Irishman read in the dictionary—too short," he remarked.

"'The End of an Era' is going much better than I expected a book of its kind would. . . ."

Baltimore *Sun*, October 12, 1905 (12/5)

By the time he delivered this opinion in the lobby of the Hotel Rennert at Baltimore, where he was conferring on a case arising from the reorganization of the Maryland Trust Company, Wise was recognized perhaps less as a lawyer who wrote books than as an author who happened to practice law. As author, the War and its aftermath had been good to him. When he traveled to Watertown, New York, in July, 1902, to address the officers of the 9th U. S. Infantry (in which his son Hugh was a Captain) on the subject, "The North and South in the Spanish War," he told his listeners he had decided not to discuss the North and South after all. ". . . that is ancient history [cheers]. I had more fun getting licked." Just the preceding month he had elaborated those passages in *The End of an Era* about the *Great Eastern* into an article on Lord Kelvin for *The Electrical Age*. In 1906 in *Bob Taylor's Magazine* he would evoke the shades of Generals Ashby, Rosser, and Early in "A Modern Greek," his affectionate sketch of Jimmie Thomson, the V.M.I. cadet from Jefferson County, in the Scotch Presbyterian country (related to the youth of the same name described on pp. 229–30, below), who as Major James W. Thomson met death valiantly just before the War ended. He would retell the story of Sisson's Kingdom (Chapter XXIII, *The End of an Era*) in a *Putnam's* article of 1909. The fact that Wise wrote from personal experience, and wrote deftly, rescues even the humblest of these efforts from inanity.

Meanwhile *The End of an Era* had entered American historical annals. As a glance at Bibliography 2

will show, it has stayed there. This busy man of affairs
had contrived to produce an item of authentic Americana and, simultaneously, of Virginiana. And here was
irony to spare: partly because of his espousing the
Republican cause in the Old Dominion during Reconstruction, a leading Confederate chronicler had had to
leave the South—then found fame and fortune in the
North.

In March, 1905, on the appearance of his only published fiction, *The Lion's Skin: A Historical Novel
and a Novel History*, Wise's interpretation of the Reconstruction in Virginia lacerated afresh the wound of
animosity separating him from his native State. For
years the Virginia Society of the Cincinnati refused to
admit him within its select circle, though he was gene-
alogically qualified. (Not until the autumn of 1908,
when publisher Joseph Bryan staged a love-feast at his
Richmond mansion, did resistance crumble.) Over the
years this attitude had been sufficiently widespread—
especially among certain of the more influential alumni
of the University—to cause Wise untold grief. Yet he
was charitable enough to inform Northerners, shortly
after his appearance at Richmond in November, 1902,
as counsel for a Negro group contesting the legality of
the new State Constitution:

Virginians, while they have strong feelings and strong
prejudices, are not as a rule socially intolerant or vindictive. The State was always divided nearly evenly in public
sentiment. The old political antagonisms between Whigs
and Democrats were very intense, but seldom invaded the

realm of social intercourse, and accustomed the upper classes not to confound the two.

His last public speech, delivered at a Confederate monument-raising on the Eastern Shore of Virginia in the autumn of 1912, was a plea for intersectional tolerance. "It is true," he told the assembled veterans, "that [Virginia] has been made to tread the wine-press of humiliation alone in many ways." But it was certainly not true that she is decadent, as some claim. And in any event let us have a truce to this eternal prating about Northern "hypocrisy" and a Lost Cause.

Just one month before the appearance of *The Lion's Skin* Wise was asked to address a fund-raising banquet of the Colonial Dames at Richmond on February 21, 1905. In view of the redoubtableness of this counterpart to the Cincinnati, he might never have been asked if any of the members had had a chance to peruse his novel. Yet his appearance before such a gathering may be said to symbolize the fact that the Commonwealth had decided to swing open the gate. Certainly one passage the old battler now uttered is a memorable statement of the workings of Virginianism:

Something, I know not what, makes the heart's tendrils of the Virginian sink so deep into his native soil that death alone detaches them. With other people and in other lands, be they ever so hospitable and we ever so successful, we know but one standard by which to gauge them and judge them good or bad, delightful or the reverse, as they approach our ideals of Virginia and Virginians. In Egypt we measure the fecundity of the valley of the Nile by the standard of James River low grounds.

We calculate the height of the Rocky Mountains by reference to our recollections of the peaks of Otter. The Hudson and the Rhine only suggest to us the James, the York and the Rappahannock, and until the hand of the iconoclast destroyed our Grecian temple of a Capitol and replaced it with a hay shed beween two tobacco barns, the Acropolis on the Capitoline Hill in Rome was only suggestive to us of the Capitol in Richmond.

In part, the speaker himself subscribed to such provincialism. The fact that he could not—and never did —go whole hog remained the poniard among the posies that were his memory of Virginia.

It is a truism that good writers are often bad speakers. Not so, John S. Wise:

No matter where he went [his son Byrd recalls] a crowd would gather round to listen to his conversation. When I was with him at a dinner where he and Chauncey Depew spoke, I heard Mr. Depew say that he wouldn't have dared to come if he had known my father was to be there, because of contrast. And Job Hedges spoke up to say, 'They think I'm funny, but they know John Wise is more truly humorous.'

As awareness of his ability grew, Wise worked his way up the seating lists on a banquet circuit extending from Bay City, Michigan, to Atlantic City, New Jersey —from Riverton, Maine, to Memphis, Tennessee. Over the years he ascended from mere guest, to toast responder, to honored guest, to featured speaker. Several times he was toastmaster and at least once Story Teller. Most of these stints he performed gratis; many paid his expenses; some brought fees ranging from $50 to

$150; several were handled by the J. B. Pond Lyceum Bureau in New York. Everywhere he made an impression.

You might expect one Virginian to say of another, as did the toastmaster of the Bankers' Association banquet at the Hotel Chamberlin in 1909: "In the City of New York, where he lives, when he is booked for an occasion of this kind, Senator Depew and General Horace Porter are stricken dumb as they see their fame waning before this rising star." It meant more when a Rhode Island master of ceremonies had introduced him in 1908 as a person of "genial countenance, happy temperament, and colossal intellectuality. . . ."

The background against which Wise's declamation resounded varied from the Colored Men's branch of the YMCA, at 252 West 53rd Street, New York, to the Transatlantic Society of America in the Academy of Music at Philadelphia, with the Philadelphia Orchestra as accompaniment and a twenty-seven-part programme. The topics he chose might be "The Hotel Man in Literature," before the City Hotel Association at Delmonico's; "What Lawyers Hope for from Automobiles," before the National Association of Automobile Manufacturers at the Waldorf-Astoria; "Books from the Authors' Standpoint," before the Aldine Association at 111 Fifth Avenue; on Robert Emmet, before a group of Irish-Americans; on "Abraham Lincoln— from a Southerner's Standpoint," before the Lincoln Association of Jersey City at the Jersey City Club; and of course, every now and then, on Robert E. Lee.

The groups Wise addressed might be the Third

Panel Sheriff's Jury of New York City; the Silver Grays of Beta Theta Pi (he'd pledged it at Charlottesville); the Corn Exchange Bank on its fiftieth anniversary; the Lafayette College Alumni Association, other toast responders being President Seth Low of Columbia, journalist Murat Halstead, and raconteur Job E. Hedges; the Canadian Camp, Wise introducing Ernest Thompson Seton, George Shiras, and Commander Robert E. Peary; the first Gridiron Club banquet at Washington (in 1885); or the Princeton Alumni of New York, other toast responders being novelist S. Weir Mitchell and Harvard professor Bliss Perry. He sat at table with such diverse personalities as General Sherman, the Japanese Minister, Baron Kaneko, or President Woodrow Wilson of Princeton University. Clubs and associations to which he belonged as regular or honorary member included the Clover in Philadelphia; the Lotos, Pleiades, and Aborigines in New York; and the Kiptopeke Club in Richmond, named for his home on the Point of Cape Charles, Wise being "King" Kiptopeke.

From this panoplied series of personal appearances some stood out more than others. Wise's lawyerly discussion of "New Litigation on Highways" at Albany in 1891 is said, by the *National Cyclopaedia of American Biography*, to have attracted such wide attention it was used as a text in American and European universities and cited in the Reichstag during debates on German electrical franchises. That same year it was the ex-Virginian who was selected to deliver the Memorial Day address at Grant's Tomb on Riverside Drive before a thousand military personnel and five thousand civilians. His 1898 speech at New Market, Virginia, on the fallen at that battle, was an enormous local event. In 1900 it was this native Southerner who gave the Memorial Day oration at Gettysburg National Cemetery before GAR and Spanish-American war veterans, patriotic societies, and four hundred school children. In 1903 his address, "New Market Day at V.M.I.," on the occasion of the unveiling of his fellow cadet Sir Moses Ezekiel's statue, *Virginia Mourning Her Dead*, became and remains one of the classic speeches of that institution.

What were the ingredients of this magic?

The first was platform presence. Wise's natural vanity ripened into that serene self-control most outstanding orators exhibit. As he matured and grew stout, his bouncing, boyish appeal yielded place not to ponderosity but to a commanding portliness. Where tall, thin Governor Wise had had an occasional tendency to slouch on the hustings in any old garb and dribble tobacco juice, the son was a spotlessly groomed, stand-up-straight declaimer. Here is the reaction of three thousand Philadelphians, as reported next day by the *Inquirer*, when Wise delivered a Fourth of July oration in 1887 at Independence Square. His speech climaxed ceremonies that included a parade of two thousand soldiers, a choir of two hundred and fifty voices, fireworks, two balloon ascensions, and a regatta on the Schuylkill:

As the well-known Virginian stepped forward, he was greeted with rounds of applause. His clean shaven face

moved not a muscle as he waited for the applause to subside. Then he began his speech. He had not spoken five
sentences before it was apparent than an orator had
arrived. As he progressed in his speech the people became
warmed up, and at almost every sentence he was applauded. From the very first he carried his audience with
him. . . . Men and women stood in the broiling sun and
strained their ears for every word. He has a good voice
and a clear enunciation, and made a very favorable impression.

The second ingredient was an extraordinary memory
and an unusually well-stocked mind. Wise had the
requisite information for any topic. He also knew precisely how he wanted to say it. When checking proofs
on a speech he had given at Delmonico's in 1896 to the
Society of Mayflower Descendants on one of his favorite subjects, Captain John Smith, Wise scribbled on the
back of the typescript—"Mr. Edward Carroll Jr.: Dear
Sir, This is the speech as I made it & want it reported.
Your notes are *horrid*. J.S.W."

The third, perhaps most seminal, ingredient was
personal commitment to his topic. Like his brother
Jennings before him, Wise became Captain of the élite
Richmond Light Infantry Blues. When he had to resign
to assume the U.S. District Attorneyship, and the Company turned out en masse to tender him a silver punch
bowl, his speech of thanks and farewell was so moving
many of the outfit were in tears—including himself.
During New Market Day at V.M.I. in 1903 Wise, who
was not the orator of the occasion, was detected standing among cronies at the back of the room. Begged to

John Sergeant Wise as captain of the Richmond Light
Infantry Blues, about 1881.

come forward, he did so and spoke extemporaneously. Another alumnus present, Major General E. W. Nichols, recalled what ensued:

In the Jackson Hall he took the platform and held his audience spell-bound; in tears himself, at times, he had all of us weeping; and then again through our tears we were roaring with amusement at some of his sallies. As a raconteur Captain Wise had no equal, and as a speaker from a public platform he was most impressive. At the banquet his name did not appear as one of the speakers! *** Of all the addresses I have ever listened to, and I have listened to a great many, I have never listened to its equal. On this occasion Captain Wise's heart was involved, and his head and his tongue were both equal to the heart's promptings. The whole surrounding, and the very atmosphere, appealed to every fibre of his being.

He arose quickly and quietly began; warming up to his task he passed from peroration to peroration, and there were at least three or four occasions when his hearers thought he had concluded. But, no, he passed on by greater flights to greater heights and finally reached a climax that brought his auditors to their feet in frenzied acclaim and congratulation.

Another ingredient was Wise's ability at story-telling. It had made him at least the equal in Virginia of Tom August, a Richmond lawyer Wise himself acclaimed as a wit. Where appropriate, he could be divertingly vulgar or impressively profane (but never obscene). He had the actor's gift for dialect stories. Though fond of Irish anecdotes—probably because of the family's beloved nannie, Eliza Happer, called Idie or Mammy Liza—Negro tales were his favorite. One of the best (during the course of an article on the conditions of Virginia slavery before the War, in the *Saturday Evening Post*, January 27, 1906) concerned the Hon. John Y. Mason, American Minister to France in the 1850's, when Jennings Wise was his Secretary of Legation. Mason and Napoleon III were poker-playing cronies; and while the Emperor was rather a dour type, he derived amusement out of trying to introduce Mason to the Haitian Minister. A Greensville County, Virginia, slave owner, Mason knew exactly where the place of a black man was; so Napoleon met with repeated failures. One night during a ball in the Tuileries the Emperor came up to the American Minister:

"Ah, Monsieur Mason! May I not introduce you *now* to ze Haitian Minister?"

"No, thank you, Sire," said Mason icily.

"Mais, Monsieur Mason! Have you seen heem tonight? Is he not magnifique in his reebons and medals?"

Mason gazed reflectively across the hall at the ebony Minister in his resplendent uniform.

"Sire, I think that, clothes and all, he'd fetch $1,000."

Then there was the time Fitzhugh Lee was running for some office in Virginia after his tour of duty as Major General, U.S.A., in the Spanish-American War. Orating in far western Carroll County, Lee noted that a local mountaineer, whom he recognized as one of his ex-Confederate troopers, was skulking at the edge of the crowd. After his speech was finished, Lee approached the old fellow and inquired why he had not paid closer attention to a former commander's words?

"Ah'm jest a-standin' hyar hopin' to die some day an' git to Heaven afore you do, Jin'l."

"Why is that?"

" 'Cause, Jin'l, ah got my heart set on seein' whut ol' Jube Early's face is gonter look like when you come a-struttin' in wearin' *thet* uniform!"

With the approach of the Presidential election of 1908 Wise was impaired physically. He had also acquired a low opinion of Taft, the Republican nominee. But he liked Bryan even less, and wanted to assist some of his sons in their political ambitions. So he permitted his name to be placed on its list of speakers by the Republican National Committee, and stumped doggedly through Massachusetts, New York, Pennsylvania, Ohio, and Virginia.

At the Academy of Music in Norfolk, October 21, he let out the stops for George Nelms Wise, a cousin, who was running for Congress from the First District, and the Hon. C. Bascom Slemp from the Ninth. A Norfolk monthly, the *Galaxy*, though pro-Bryan, thought the sixty-two-year-old speaker had never been more effective. Its reporter would have put his age at forty-five, maximum. As Wise warmed to his topic, one of the newsmen covering the event—a pale-faced young cynic sporting a red necktie and chewing hard on gum—presently forgot his nonchalance and began to hearken.

We have heard and read of audiences being 'held spellbound' by oratory, but never until this night has the writer been a unit in such a gathering; it was our first experience, and as such is worthy of commemoration upon these pages. So complete was the spell that Mr. Wise wove around his hearers that when he bowed his head in conclusion and turned to his seat, not only the master of ceremonies, but the gentlemen on the platform and the audience as well, were thrown into momentary confusion. The very band that should have relieved the tension broke into belated and momentarily uneven music. From his first utterance it was very clear that this speaker was no public pretender to fame nor a poacher on the preserves of others. Here was originality and initiative of a sure and certain quality. Wit of flashing brilliancy, eloquence, pathos, poetry, the whole shot through with scintillations of the finest humor, flowing in a torrential stream through considerably over an hour and a half. The Hon. John S. Wise is a fat man, and fat men are proverbially prosaic, ofttimes dull, but here was a fat man of unfailing virtuosity, with the daintiness, the deftness, the facility of the courted Apollo of the Forum who once had aroused the best of Rome to mad enthusiasm.

V

> "Take hold, John, of the biggest knots in life, and try to untie them—try to be worthy of man's highest estate—have high, noble, manly honor. There is but one true test of anything, and that is, is it right? If it isn't, turn right away from it."
>
> Father to son: from Barton
> H. Wise, *The Life of Henry A. Wise*, p. 422

Probably the main reason John S. Wise was such a winning orator was because his radiant personality was the projection of a spirit utterly at home in its world. He lived the "Good Life" lovingly. He had two residences from which to do so. His summer home was "Kiptopeke" on the Point of Cape Charles, Virginia, named for the Indian chief who had bade John Smith welcome. It was formally house-warmed in October, 1899, as a subscription sports club called the Cape Charles Venture. When this failed at the close of 1903, Wise assumed sole ownership. In Manhattan the family lived first at 21 East 76th Street, but by the end of 1898 had settled at 154 West 76th, between Ninth and Amsterdam Avenues, in sight of the Hudson River. This house, declared the author in *The Lion's Skin*, was "as distinctly Virginian as if a bit of the old soil, with everything upon it, had been transplanted bodily to New York. Black domestics serve them; not the ashen travesties of the race who have lived in the North until all the grease is gone out of their skins, and they look unhealthy, say, 'I guess,' and feel it necessary to be insolent in order to assert themselves. . . ."

Though Wise's income began to fall off after 1901 or so, and he never saved anything, his valiant energy enabled him to give all the children good educations and generally maintain a sparkling social life. (His wife, Eva, headed the cotillon club of the Southern Society.) For Sunday night suppers there were always at least ten guests. An excellent cook, Wise relished doing his own shopping at the Washington Market, often accompanied by his oldest daughter, Eva, who thought him "a real epicure and to market with him was a liberal education for a future housewife." Browne's Chop House, an actors' hang-out on 28th Street, was a rendezvous. Within two years of coming to Manhattan, Wise's weight shot up to 225 pounds.

He was a fair judge of wine, but preferred hard liquor. Egg nogg and mint juleps were favorites, and Wise knew exactly how the latter should be concocted: with brown brandy, and the gum still clinging to the leaves. Taken before breakfast, here was nectar indeed, "old John Custis up yonder at 'Arlington' [Northhampton County, Virginia] used to say. I've got one of the finest mint patches you ever saw—roots right from Mount Vernon. I'll make you one tomorrow."

Thus he assured Charles Francis Adams, whose visit to "Kiptopeke" in April, 1912, Wise turned into a regional event. Early next morning, as Adams sat on the porch absorbing the superb Bay and ocean panorama and munching fresh figs, he saw his host puttering around the mint patch, under the eaves. When, however, the King of Kiptopeke bore down upon him extending a frosted glass, the Bostonian refused point blank.

"You don't wash the mint, you say? Well, thank you, none for me. I'll take mine straight: I've seen at least a dozen of your hounds in that mint patch this morning."

Wise was rarely without his cigar, and chewed a plug or took a pipe occasionally. "When he felt inclined," his son Byrd recalls, "he would forego any one or all of his regular habits for a year or more at a time. Cigarets, gin, and whistling were abuses he would not tolerate. He insisted no man could whistle and think at the same time and no man should be

unthinking while awake. Gin, he said, was for loose
women and irresponsible darkies to keep them from
thinking. Cigarets were evidence of mental paucity."

For Wise the "Good Life" would have been un-
thinkable merely indoors. Though no more than a
fair sailor, he was an inveterate open-water fisherman.
Though far from an expert horseman, he loved riding
and entertained important people at it. Field sports
were his central avocation. When he was running for
Governor of Virginia, *Harper's Weekly* felt it should
inform readers that he "enjoys the distinction, too, of
being one of the best judges of dogs in the Union, and
he prides himself on the record he has made as a
sportsman." Wise perfected his own dog remedy—
"Sergeant's Condition Pills"—and bred, sold, doc-
tored, and corresponded about dogs with people all
over the nation, from officials of the Dayton Pointer
Club in Ohio to near-illiterates everywhere. The
felicitousness of his "Reminiscences of a Sportsman"
in the *Chicago Field* (1880) was recalled by a California judge as late as 1911. He strove mightily to get
his monumental, illustrated series, "American Pedigreed Pointers," published in book form. This did not
eventuate; but his novel, *Diomed* (1897), the first dog
book by an American, had gone into four editions by
1908.

For if Wise was passionately fond of flowers and
something of a gardener—he called the orchard at
"Kiptopeke" his collection of family trees—small-
game hunting was his ultimate love. By mid-1889
he could inform President Harrison, when inviting

him down for a shoot below Richmond, that in the
last decade he had bagged five thousand birds. During
his Virginia politicking days he regularly went hunting after a campaign—for "jollification" if he won, for
"consolation" if he lost.

But the "Good Life" was lived indoors, too. Wise's
cultural responses were keen and various. As artist
he enjoyed drawing impromptu sketches of animals,
birds, and flowers for the delectation of his children.
As music lover he was fond of old ballads, Italian
opera, and especially Gilbert and Sullivan. His taste
in drama ran to the Irish musical plays of Chauncey
Olcott or comedies starring Frank Daniels. His antiquarian urge would prompt him to treasure a letter
by the English poet, Thomas Haynes Bayly, for its
autograph; berate editor R. A. Brock of the Southern
Historical Society *Papers* for misspelling the given
name of orator Seargent Prentiss (which Wise proceeded to misspell); engage in a controversy over the
Virginia Convention of 1858 with a young newsman
from the *Richmond Evening Journal* named Douglas
S. Freeman; or swap an epistle of Governor Wise's
with the Indiana collector, Jesse W. Weik, for a legal
plea written by Lincoln.

His facility with the pen ranged from a squib playing on Grover Cleveland's employment of "innocuous
desuetude"—which Whitelaw Reid used as an editorial filler in the *Tribune* on March 5, 1886 (p. 4, col.
4)—to his letter writing. This, in range of subject
matter, variety of recipients, and projection of personality may fairly be termed a distinct phase of his

literary activity. As a competent judge of correspondence, President Theodore Roosevelt, told Wise,
in acknowledging from Oyster Bay in December,
1908, the gift of some oysters and terrapin: "The
oysters I began on at once and can certify that they
are most delicious. But the letter—that is the best,
richest, and spiciest of all: I think of putting a clipping
from it into the terrapin stew to add to its flavor."

So there lies John S. Wise—lawyer, duellist, orator,
genealogist, gardener, politician, sportsman, raconteur,
author, combat veteran. Take him all in all, there was
a man. Take him part by part, a virtuoso. The fullest
introduction to most of the parts is that "best work of
his head"—*The End of an Era.*

The End of an Era

PREFACE

THIS book needs this much of an apology. It is to a great extent the autobiography of an insignificant person. If it were that alone, it would have no excuse for publication, and would possess little interest for those outside the immediate home circle. But it is not an autobiography alone. It introduces views of Southern life and feelings and civilization, prior to and during the war, which possess an unflagging interest for the American people; and it tells the true story of several striking events which preceded our civil strife, and many episodes of the great war. Besides these, it gives accurate descriptions not heretofore published of the appearance and actions and sayings of many distinguished participants on the Confederate side.

When I first concluded to print the book, I made an honest effort to construct it in the third person. It was a lamentable failure, and made it appear even more egotistical than in its present form. Having returned to the narrative in the first person singular, I found myself a participant in several scenes in which I was not actually present. How to eliminate these, and at the same time preserve the continuity of the narrative, was a serious problem. I solved it at last by the consent of my only living brother that he would stand for me in several episodes, having told me all I know.[1] I will not mar the narrative by pointing out the places in which my brother is myself. This confession redeems the book from being classed either as an autobiography or a romance; and whenever anybody shall say to me, "Why, you were not there?" I will answer, like the Israelite gentleman, "Yes, I know. Dot vas mine brudder." The reader gets the facts as they were, and that is all he ought to expect.

I dedicate it to my old Confederate comrades, the bravest, simplest, most unselfish, and affectionate friends I ever had.

J. S. W.

NEW YORK, September 10, 1899.

[1] Hon. Richard A. Wise, Williamsburg, Va.

CONTENTS

THE END OF AN ERA

CHAPTER I

A LONG WAY FROM HOME

It was the day after Christmas in the year 1846.

Near sundown, two young officers of the army of the United States sat upon one of the benches on the promenade of the great reservoir which supplies the city of Rio de Janeiro with water.

Both were lieutenants, — one of engineers, the other of artillery. Any one half acquainted with the United States would have recognized them as West Pointers; and their presence in this far-away spot was easily accounted for by a glance downward from the coign of vantage where they sat, at a fleet of United States men-of-war and troop ships riding at anchor in the bay.

Nowhere in all the world is there a scene more beautiful than that spread out before them. Below, falling away down the mountain side to the silver sands of the bay, were the palms and gardens, and orange and olive groves, surrounding the residence of the Cateti suburb. To seaward, the southern boundary of the mile-wide entrance to the bay, loomed the bald, brown peak of the Sugar Loaf Mountain, with the beautiful suburb of Botafogo nestling near its base. Huge mountains, their dense foliage lit by the sinking sun, ran down to the water's edge upon the opposite or northern shore. Far beneath

them was the Gloria landing for naval vessels. To westward, sweeping out into the bay with bold and graceful
curves, and spread beneath them like a map, was the peninsula upon which the city of Rio is built, and beyond
this, gleaming in the evening sunlight, and studded with
islands of intense verdure, extended the upper bay until
it was lost in the distance, where, on the horizon, the blue
peaks of the Organ range closed in the lovely picture.

The ships bearing the commands to which the young
gentlemen were attached were bound to California around
Cape Horn. The troops were to take part in the war
then flagrant between the United States and Mexico. A
short stop had been made at Rio for water and provisions,
and these two youngsters were among the first to apply
for and obtain shore leave.

The dusty appearance of their dress, and other evidences
of fatigue, showed that they had not failed to sustain the
reputation of their countrymen as investigators of everything new and strange. In fact, they had, in the morning,
exhausted the sights to be seen in the city. After amusing
themselves in the shops of the Rua Direita, and replenish-
ing their stock of Spanish books in the Rua do Ovidor,
and wandering through several churches and residence
streets, they had become very much interested in the remarkable aqueduct which supplies the city of Rio with
water.

Our young soldiers, in their engineering zeal, had followed the aqueduct back to its source of supply; and
now, bound for the Gloria landing, were resting, deeply
impressed by the great work, and by the genius and skill
of its builders. But both the youths, recalling the fact
that it was the Christmas season, felt, in spite of all the
tropical novelty and strange beauty surrounding them,
as evening closed in, a yearning for an American home

and voice and face; and their conversation naturally enough fell into conjecturing how the Christmas was being spent by their own loved ones in the United States, or in bemoaning the good things they were missing.

While thus engaged, they saw two men approaching. One was in civilian dress; the other wore the uniform of assistant surgeon in the United States navy. The new-comers were engaged in animated conversation; and, although the civilian was a man of forty, while his companion was a youngster of twenty-five, there was little if any difference in the alertness of their steps.

The faces of the young officers lit up with pleasure as, upon the near approach of the two pedestrians, they caught the sound of genuine United States English. They had observed the American flag floating from a residence in the Cateti, and had no doubt that the persons who were now passing were in some way connected with the lega-tion. Accordingly, with that freedom which fellow coun-trymen feel in addressing each other in foreign lands, the West Pointers arose at the approach of the two gentle-men, and, catching the eye of the elder of the two, ad-vanced, announced their rank and service, and made some inquiry as a groundwork of further conversation. They were not mistaken in their surmises. The gentleman addressed was the Envoy Extraordinary and Minister Plenipotentiary to the Empire of Brazil from the Republic of the United States. A title like that was well calculated to paralyze the familiarity of two young military men; and when they realized that, unannounced and covered with dust, they had of their own motion ventured into conversation with the bearer of such an august title, their first impulse was to apologize for their temerity and to withdraw. Even from an officer of no higher grade than captain in their own service, they were accustomed to a

greeting strictly formal, usually accompanied by the inquiry, " Well, sir? state your business; " and, having
done so, they were generally glad enough to salute and
withdraw. Here they were, without any business, standing in the presence of a high official, with nothing more
to say, and with no excuse to give for what they had said.
But before their embarrassment could grow more annoy-
ing, the minister put them completely at their ease.
" Well met! " he exclaimed; " we are just returning
homeward from the city. Come! The more the merrier:
you shall dine with me. I still have some Christmas
turkey and plum pudding, and we will drink the health
of the good angel who sent my countrymen to me at this
blessed season."

During the course of their walk to the American legation, the young fellows had opportunity to observe their
newly found host more carefully. To them he was a
revelation. His name and position in politics were not
unknown to them; for although still young, he had for
many years been a conspicuous figure in national politics
in the United States. The echoes of his eloquence, as
well as accounts of his game-cock courage, had penetrated
even into the isolated world of the Academy at West
Point. In fact, he had been absent from the United
States but two or three years upon this mission, which
had been accepted partly on account of failing health,
and partly from a desire to strike a blow at the infamous
African slave-trade. He had accomplished much towards
breaking up the slave-trade, and derived great benefit to
his health.

Brilliant at all times in conversation, he was, on this
occasion, unusually interesting. The sight of his country's ships in the harbor, and the news of the struggle
with Mexico, so excited and elated him that he was seen

at his best by his visitors. The two boys studied him as if he had been some great actor. Tall and thin, he was nevertheless exceedingly active and muscular. His dress consisted of simple black, with spotless linen. He wore the open standing collar and white scarf affected by the gentlemen of that period. The only ornament upon his person was a large opal pin confining the neckerchief. His head gear, suited to the climate, was one of those exquisitely wrought white Panama hats which is the envy of men living beyond the tropics. Beneath this was a head exquisitely moulded, with a noble brow, and large hazel eyes, the ever-changing expression of which, coupled with a full, rich voice, charmed and fascinated his guests. His silken blond hair was thrown back and worn long, as was the custom of the day. A nose too handsome to be called Roman, yet too strong to be designated as Grecian; a mouth wide and mobile, filled with even, white teeth; and a strong chin with a decided dimple, — completed the remarkable face which turned in ever-changing expression, from time to time, towards its companions, as they strode homeward in the twilight.

Such was the American minister; and, according to the mood in which one found him, he impressed the stranger as the gentlest, the tenderest, the most loving, the most eloquent, the most earnest, the most fearless, the most impassioned, or the fiercest man he had ever met. Nobody who saw him ever forgot him.

They reached the legation just as it was growing dark, and as the full-orbed moon was rising from the distant sea. Seeking the veranda, and seating his guests in the wicker easy-chairs with which it was well supplied, the minister excused himself, and left them for a few minutes to their own observations and reflections.

As the soft sea-breeze came up to them, laden with

garden perfumes; as they watched the golden highway of
the moon's reflection on the sea; as they saw the twinkling lights of the ships in the deep shadows of the bay
below them, — they felt as if they had indeed discovered
an earthly paradise; and when a fair blond girl in filmy
apparel glided through the drawing-room and joined them,
speaking pure English, it seemed as if their paradise was
being peopled by angels. Everybody here spoke in English. Everything spoke of home. The pictures on the
walls, the books on the tables, yes, the dishes at table,
were all American.

The visitors were conducted to their apartments to
make necessary preparations for dinner. Soon after their
return to the drawing-room, the minister reappeared with
a look somewhat troubled, as he apologized for his long
absence and the non-appearance of the lady of the house.

A moment later the folding-doors rolled back, and the
English butler announced that dinner was served. Oh,
what a contrast with the ward-room of the man-of-war in
which our two lieutenants had been dining for a month or
more!

Dinner over, the company once more sought the cool
veranda, where coffee and cigars were served. There they
were joined by Baron Lomonizoff, the Russian minister,
who had called to be informed of all the recent developments in the controversy with Mexico, and who spoke
English perfectly. Later, just as the baron was bidding
adieu, in fact, at what seemed to our young friends to be a
very late hour for visiting, the oddest imaginable specimen
of Brazilian humanity was introduced as Dr. Ildefonso.

His efforts at English were startling. They nearly
convulsed our two young friends, and reconciled them to
their own failures at Portuguese.

As the little doctor showed no signs of leaving, and

as, by one or two indications, the young visitors began to suspect it was time for them to go, they reluctantly took their departure, thanking their host a thousand times for the pleasure he had given them, and chatting joyously, on the route to the ship, about the good fortune which had given them such a Merry Christmas.

The little Brazilian doctor and the surgeon in the navy had remained because there was work on hand for them. I entered my name on the docket of humanity that night; and, as the lawyers say, my cause was continued until the further order of the court.

How do I know it? I will tell you.

Forty-five years later, at a great banquet in New York, I was sitting beside an aged, grizzled general of the armies of the Union.

Said the old general cheerily, " Did I ever tell you of my visit to your father in Rio?" Receiving a negative response, he proceeded in his inimitable way to recount every incident above set forth, omitting the hour of his own departure from the legation. The memory of the struggles of the little Brazilian doctor with the English language still amused him immensely. He was recalling some absurd mistake of Dr. Ildefonso, when I looked up, and, with a merry twinkle in my eye, said, " General, at what hour did you leave the Cateti that night?" " Oh, I should say about eleven or twelve o'clock," said the general. " Well, now, do you know, my dear general, I deeply regret you left so early. I arrived myself that night about two hours after your departure, and would have been so delighted to meet you under my father's roof." This sally was met by a hearty laugh from the listening company, and was followed by a glass of wine to the memory of those olden days, since when so many things have happened.

The young lieutenant of artillery, and the old general above described, was no other than William Tecumseh Sherman, commander of the armies of the Union. His companion was the officer who afterwards became famous as General Halleck. Neither of them ever met again their host of that evening.

In later years, he also became a distinguished general, but on the Confederate side. He never knew that Sherman and Halleck, the great Union generals, were the young officers he entertained at Rio the night I was born ; for he died many years before the general revealed his identity as above related.

Forty years after this meeting, when I was in Congress, I received a letter from a dear old retired chaplain of the navy living in Boston, Rev. Mr. Lambert, asking my assistance in some public matter, and concluding with the remark that this demand of a stranger sprung from the fact that the writer had held me in his arms and baptized me at the American legation in Rio, April 14, 1847.

In the spring of 1847, my father asked the President for a recall ; and, his petition being granted, the United States frigate Columbia was placed at his disposal for the return to America.

I was a tried seaman when, for the first time, I set foot upon the soil of my country, and took up my residence where my people had lived for over two hundred years. I was not born on the soil of the United States, but nevertheless in the United States; for the place where I was born was the home of a United States minister, and under the protection of the United States flag, and was in law as much the soil of the United States as any within its boundaries. Descended from a number of people who helped to form the Union, born under the glorious stars and stripes, rocked in the cradle of an American man-of-war, and taught to love the Union next to my Maker, little did I dream of the things, utterly inconsistent with such ideas, which were to happen to me and mine within the first eighteen years of my existence.

CHAPTER II

THE KINGDOM OF ACCAWMACKE

OUR voyage terminated in the kingdom of Accawmacke, the abiding-place of my ancestors for two and a half centuries. Although within eight hours of New York and six hours from Philadelphia by rail, the region and its people are as unlike those of these crowded centres of humanity as if they were a thousand miles away.

John Smith tells us, in his memorable narrative of his earliest American explorations, that when Captain Nelson sailed in June, 1607, for England, in the good ship Phœnix, he, John, in his own barge, accompanied him to the Virginia capes; and there, after delivering his writings for the company, he parted with him near the southernmost cape, which he named Cape Henry. Sailing northward, Captain Smith first visited the seaward island, which he named Smith's Island, after himself. It is still called Smith's Island, and is owned by the Lee family. Then he returned to the northernmost cape, at the entrance to the Chesapeake Bay, and named it Cape Charles, in honor of the unfortunate prince afterwards known as Charles I. Upon the point of this cape Smith encountered an Indian chief, whom he describes as " the most comely, proper, civil salvage " he had yet met. The name of this chief was Kictopeke. He was called " The Laughing King of Accomack," and Accomack means, in the Indian tongue, " The Land Beyond the Water." He bore in his hand a long spear or harpoon, with a sharp-

ened fish-bone or shell upon its point; and he it was who
taught John Smith and his companions to spear the
sheepshead and other fish in the shallow waters hard by.
John Smith and The Laughing King have been buried
for well-nigh three centuries, but the people about Cape
Charles still spear sheepshead on the shoals in the same
old way.

Smith and his companions cruised along the western
shore of this Peninsula of Accawmacke, which is the eastern shore of the Chesapeake Bay, until they reached what
is now called Pocomoke River, the present boundary between Virginia and Maryland. The distance is probably
eighty miles. The reason assigned for the long cruise
was that they were searching for fresh water. To those
who know the abundant springs of the Peninsula, this
statement is surprising. Overtaken in the neighborhood
of Pocomoke by one of those summer thunder-storms
which are so prevalent in that region, they were driven
across the bay to the western shore, and thence they
cruised down the Chesapeake until they turned into what
is now called Hampton Roads. Passing the low sand-
spit where the ramparts of Fortress Monroe now frown
and the gay summer resorts are built, they stopped at
the Indian village Kickotan, located upon the present site
of Hampton. Obtaining there a good supply of food
from the Indians, they returned to the Jamestown settlement, about forty miles up the river, then called Powhatan, now known as the James. In this as in all things,
the Englishman appropriated what belonged to the Indian, and King James supplanted King Powhatan.

It was on this return voyage that Smith, while practicing the art acquired from the King of Accawmacke,
impaled a fish upon his sword, in the shallow waters about
the mouth of the Rappahannock River. Unaware of the

dangerous character of his captive, he received in his wrist
a very painful wound from the spike-like fin upon the
tail of the fish. This wound caused such soreness and
such swelling that he thought he was like to die, and his
whole party went ashore and laid Smith under a tree,
where he made his will. " But," says he, " by night time
the swelling and soreness had so abated that I had the
pleasure of eating that fish for supper." The next morning the journey was resumed, and the place, in remembrance of the incident, was named Stingaree Point. To
this day, that point at the mouth of the Rappahannock
is called Stingaree Point; and that fish is still called
Stingaree by the people along the Chesapeake Bay.

After this famous cruise, John Smith, who was as active and restless as a box of monkeys, made his map of
Virginia, which is still extant, — and a pretty good map
it is, showing his capes and his islands, and his points and
his rivers, and what not, — in which map the Kingdom
of Accawmacke bears a most conspicuous part.

On that historic document, old John at certain points
printed little pictures of deer, to show where they most
abounded ; and at other points he designated where the
wild turkeys were most plentiful. The author of this
humble narrative has, in his day, hunted every variety of
game which abounds at the present time in Old Virginia ;
and just where the deer and turkeys were most abundant
in 1608, according to John Smith's map, there are they
most abundant now. In the counties of Surry and Sus-
sex, upon the south side of the James, run, doubtless, the
descendants of those very deer whose pictures adorn the
map of John Smith, published three centuries ago ; and
within the past twelve months the writer has followed
the great-great-great-grandchildren of the identical turkeys, no doubt, from whose flocks were captured, in 1616,

the twenty birds sent by King Powhatan to his brother
the King of England.

But to return to our Kingdom of Accawmacke.

After the Jamestown colonists had tired of poor old
John Smith, after he had blown himself up with his own
powder while smoking in his boat, upon one of his return
trips to Jamestown from the present site of Richmond;
after he had returned to England, broken in health and
spirits, — the colonists who remained found, among their
other miseries and tribulations, that they were sadly in
need of salt.

Bearing in mind stories brought back from the coast
by Smith, Sir Thomas Dale, governor, in the year 1612
detailed a party from the Jamestown settlement to go to
the Kingdom of Accawmacke and boil salt for the settlers
at Jamestown.

We may well imagine that such a task was far from
grateful to those to whom it was allotted. It was looked
forward to by them, no doubt, as the equivalent of solitary confinement in a dangerous locality. At Jamestown
the settlers were located upon an island. This fact and
their numbers gave them comparative security from the
savages. In Accawmacke the party assigned to salt-
boiling was placed upon the same land as the Indians;
and its numbers were so small, and the position so isolated from the chief settlement by the Chesapeake Bay
between them, that their situation would have been most
perilous in case of attack. It was therefore, doubtless,
in the spirit of satire that the party named the place at
which they first located upon the eastern shore, Dale's Gift.

Thus came about the first settlement of the white man
upon the eastern shore peninsula of Virginia; and, recog-
nizing its separation from the other settlements, the kings
of England for many years addressed all their decrees to

the Virginia colonists to their "faithful subjects in ye Colonie of Virginia and ye Kingdom of Accawmacke."

Like many another venture undertaken reluctantly and in ignorance, this settlement upon the eastern shore proved to be anything but an irksome and dangerous transfer. The party at Dale's Gift found the Accawmacke Indians totally unlike the warlike and treacherous tribes across the bay; and from that time forth there never was, not even at the time of the general outbreak of the savages in 1629, any serious trouble between the whites and the Indians of the eastern shore. The climate also was much more salubrious than that of the swampy region where the brackish waters at Jamestown bred malaria. As for sustenance, they found the place an earthly paradise. In the light and sandy soil corn, vegetables, and many varieties of fruit grew with little care of cultivation and in great abundance. Fish and shell-fish of every kind abounded in the ocean, bay, and inlets. Wild fowls of many sorts, from the lordly wild goose to the tiny teal, swarmed in the marshes and along the coast. Game in great abundance, furred and feathered, could be had for the shooting of it upon the land; the fig and the pomegranate grew in the open air. And the influence of the Gulf Stream, which in passing these capes approaches to within thirty miles of the coast and then turns abruptly eastward, made, as it still makes, residence upon the eastern shore of Virginia most charming and delightful. The eastern shore men were the epicures of the colony. A hundred years before New York knew the terrapin, it was the daily food in Accawmacke.

We may be sure that the less fortunate settlers at Jamestown, Smithfield, Henricopolis, Flower de Hundred, and the Falls of the James were not long in finding out the delights of this, at first, despised settlement in Accawmacke. History tells us that when, twenty years later, the colony of Virginia was divided into eight colonies, "to be governed as are the shires in England," the Accawmacke settlement was of sufficient importance to constitute of itself one of these eight counties; and in 1643, when the whole colony had a population of but fifteen thousand, one thousand of these were upon the eastern shore. When Captain Edmund Scarburgh, presiding justice, opened the first County Court of Accawmacke at Eastville, the county seat, in the autumn of 1634, The Laughing King of Accawmacke had no doubt ceased to laugh; for he, like many another savage chief before and after him, had by this time felt the fangs of the British bull-dog sink deep into the vitals of his kingdom, and became sensible of the fact that it was a grip which, once fastened upon its prey, never relaxed its hold.

Rare old records are those of Captain Edmund Scarburgh and his successors, and very curious reading do they furnish. You may see them, reader, if, instead of flashing and dashing over every other country in search of novelty, you will seek the things which are interesting in your native land, within a stone's throw of your door. There they are, preserved to this day, in the little brick court house, and are continuous from then until now, without a break, preserving the history of their section intact through a period of nearly three centuries.

The Peninsula is no longer a single county. About 1643, ambitious Colonel Obedience Robins, from Northamptonshire, England, succeeded in changing the name of the Peninsula to Northampton. It was not until 1662, when the eastern shore of Virginia was divided into two counties, that the upper portion resumed the old title of Accawmacke, which it retains to this day. The lower part of the original Accawmacke is still called Northampton.

Nowhere is the type of the original settler in Virginia so well preserved, or are to be found the antique customs, manners, and ways of the Englishman of the seventeenth century in America so little altered, as in the Kingdom of Accawmacke. No considerable influx of population from anywhere else has ever gone to the eastern shore of Virginia since the year 1700. The names of the very earliest settlers are still there. Everybody on the Peninsula knows everybody else. Everybody there is kin to everybody else. Nobody is so poor that he is wretched ; nobody is so rich that he is proud. The majority of the upper class are stanch Episcopalians, just as their fathers were Church of England men ; and the remainder of the population are for the most part Methodists, Baptists, and Presbyterians.

The vices of the community, as well as the virtues, are equally well-recognized inheritances from their progenitors. Fighting and drunkenness are by no means absent, but theft is rare among the whites. The kinship and sociability of the population are such that the fondness of the Englishman for sports of all kinds is freely indulged. No neighborhood is without its race-boat; no court day without its sporting event of some kind ; and no tavern without its backgammon board, quoits, and, in old times, its fives-court. The poorhouse has fallen into decay. When a man dies, his kin are sufficiently numerous to care for his family ; and while he lives, there is no excuse for pauperism in a land where earning a living is so easy a matter.

The citizen of Accawmacke may begin life with no other capital than a cotton string, a rusty nail, and a broken clam, and end it leaving a considerable landed estate. With his string for a line, his nail for a sinker, and his clam for bait, he can catch enough crabs to eat, and sell enough besides to enable him to buy himself hooks and lines. With his hooks and lines he can catch and sell enough fish to buy himself a boat and oyster tongs. With his boat, fishing-lines, and oyster tongs he can, in a short while, catch and sell enough fish and oysters to enable him to build a sloop. With his sloop he can trade to Norfolk, Baltimore, Philadelphia, and New York, sell fish, oysters, and terrapin, and carry fruit and vegetables, until he has accumulated enough to buy his own little patch of ground, and build his house upon it. Then, from the proceeds of his fruit, berries, and every variety of early vegetable, for which he will find excellent markets, he is sure of a comfortable living with easy labor; and he will be happier in his simple home than many who are far more pretentious, and whose incomes are far greater.

Such has been for three centuries, and still is, the place and people among whom my lot was cast when I arrived from Brazil, — descendants of the families of Scarburgh, Littleton, Yeardley, Bowman, Wise, West, Custis, Smith, Ward, Blackstone, Joynes, Kennard, Evans, Robins, Upshur, Fitchett, Simpkins, Nottingham, Goffigan, Pitts, Poulson, Bowdoin, Bagwell, Gillett, Parker, Parramore, Leatherbury, Cropper, Browne, and the rest of them, who were there when Charles I. was king, and who gave the name of Old Dominion to Virginia because they refused to swear allegiance to the Pretender Cromwell, and made the colony the asylum of the fugitive officers of their lamented sovereign.

Poor enough pay they got for their loyalty; for, when Prince Charlie came to his own, although Sir Charles Scarburgh, son of old Captain Edmund of blessed memory, was Court Surgeon, and although Colonel Edmund Scarburgh, his brother, was made Surveyor-General in

Virginia, in recognition of his fidelity, the reckless sovereign gave away the devoted Kingdom of Accawmacke to his favorites, Arlington and Culpeper. To this day, one of the loveliest places upon the Peninsula, on Old Plantation Creek, bears the name of Arlington, bestowed upon it by John Custis, in honor of one of the proprietary lords of the eastern shore.

A famous local celebrity in his day was this old John Custis, — feasting and junketing at lordly Arlington. When, in 1649, Colonel Norwood, seeking asylum in Virginia after King Charles's defeat, was shipwrecked upon the coast of the eastern shore, he first secured abundant clothing from Stephen Charlton, a minister of the Church of England, and his sufferings were atoned for, he says, by finding John Custis at Arlington. He tells us how he had known him as a tavern-keeper in Rotterdam, and of the high living he had with Custis in his new home until he put him across the bay to Colonel Wormley's, more dead than alive from hospitality.

From the point of Cape Charles to the Maryland boundary, the coast of the Peninsula on sea side and bay side is indented with inlets, which are called " creeks " in this section. On the bay side, going northward from the cape where the oldest settlements were made, the names of these creeks are English, such as Old Plantation, Cherrystone, and Hungers. Higher up the bay side, the names given by the Indians before the white settlements seem to have been retained; for we have successively Occahannock, Nandua, Pungoteague, Onancock, Chesconessex, Annamessex, and Pocomoke as the names of the beautiful and bold inlets on the bay side. On the sea side, they rejoice in such titles as Assawamman, Chincoteague, and the like. These numerous inlets, many of which are navigable for vessels of considerable size, are but a few miles

apart, and divide the · Peninsula into many transverse
" necks." Thus it often happens that neighbors living
on opposite sides of these creeks, within hailing distance
of each other, find it necessary, in order to visit each other
by land, to travel miles around the head of the creek divid-
ing them. Small boats are, therefore, as much in use as
means of intercourse between neighbors, and for visiting
the post-offices and little towns at the wharves, as are
horses and vehicles; and an eastern shore man is as much
at home in a boat as upon the land. The public roads of
the counties are called Bay Side and Sea Side roads, and
their general course is up and down the Peninsula, just
inside of the heads of the creeks. The only transverse
public roads are those to the wharves, and an occasional
cross road from the Bay Side to the Sea Side road.

It by no means follows, from the general use of boats,
that the travel by land is diminished; for in no place is the
proportion of wheeled vehicles to population greater than
upon the eastern shore. Poor, indeed, is the citizen who
cannot own, or cannot occasionally borrow, an animal and
a vehicle of some kind. Strangers, visiting that section
for the first time, get the impression that at least half the
population is continually driving back and forth upon the
highways; and the number and variety of animals and
vehicles collected at the county seat on court day is something truly astonishing. The speed at which the driving
is done is likewise a matter of comment and observation
by many visitors to the eastern shore.

People from the Blue Grass regions, where size and
bone and symmetry count for so much in horseflesh, are at
first disposed to look contemptuously upon the Accomack
type of horse; and, indeed, it must be confessed that he
is not the highest expression of physical beauty. But
never was the Scripture saying, that " the back is fitted

to its burden," better exemplified than in the tough and wiry little animal which you will sit behind, if you ever make a visit to this far-away kingdom. Small in stature, inclined even to those homely features known as ewe neck and cat ham, often higher behind than in front, and with great length of stifle, he is not, I admit, imposing to look upon. We must carefully scan the cunning little fellow before we condemn him. Note, if you please, in the first place, that the close, shiny coat bespeaks a strong infusion of the thoroughbred; observe the large, gazelle-like eyes beaming beneath the foretop, which is fluffy and shaggy from the constant influence of salt sea air; watch the nervous playing of the pointed ear, and see how the broad forehead tapers away to the muzzle, with its wide and flexible nostrils; observe the clean, straight legs and flat knees before, and bent stifles, well muscled, behind; run your hand over those pasterns, long, limber, and without a windgall; and do not overlook the cup-like, often unshod, hoofs. What say you to those sloping shoulders, that deep chest, and those well-rounded ribs, close coupled to the heavy hips? When you have finished, you will not ridicule a moving machine like that, if you know good horseflesh when you see it. You may call him pony if you like. Many of them do, indeed, possess a cross derived from the wild pony of Chincoteague Island. Now, I see you turn to look at the light conveyance, with its almost fragile harness, and know you are wondering whether such an outfit, drawn by such a horse, will take you to your destination. One drive will dissipate every doubt. You are starting for a journey in a country where there is not a hill twelve feet high within fifty miles, over light, well-packed sand roads, on which, in many places, you could hear an egg-shell crush beneath the wheel.

Come, mount with me. Never fear that our vehicle and harness are frail. They are light, but not fragile. In the matter of our driving we are exquisites, and we buy the toughest and the best. Never fear that we shall be overturned, or that we shall hurt the horse. Hurt him? I love him as the apple of my eye; and he knows me as the Arab steed knows his rider. See how the little rascal snuffs for a caress, as I loosen him from the fence where he and a long line of his companions are made fast. Now we have backed him out into the roadway. Gentle as a lamb, quick as a kitten, see the little bundle of nerves start the instant the reins are gathered, and how, with that squat between the shafts, and spraddle, and over-reach in the hind legs, known to every horseman as the surest sign of going, he is settled to his work, and spinning us along at a slashing gait. Before long, twenty miles lie behind us, and when we pull up at Belle Haven or Horn Town, not a sign of weariness or punishment does the little beggar show. All that he asks — and he asks that in a way that no one can mistake his wish — is that we loosen his check-rein and let him stretch that bony neck, and give a long, deep heave, before he takes thirty swallows from the roadside water-trough. Then he rubs his neck against my sleeve, and his unclouded eye says, " Come, I am ready. Let us go again."

Let me tell you, also, that the horse is not the only thing which you will find better than it looks in the Kingdom of Accawmacke. The pretty little white-painted, red-roofed houses are better than they look, as you will learn when you enter their hospitable portals, and find them the abodes of refinement and virtue and hospitality. The quaint, flat farms are better than they look, as you will learn when you see the bountiful crops of fruit and high-priced early vegetables and berries which they pro-

duce. The sea side and the bay side are even better
than they look, as you will know when you learn the
wealth of fish and shell-fish and sea food and game of
which they are the storehouses. The people themselves
are better than they look; for, beneath their unassuming
and oftentimes provincial appearance, they possess great
shrewdness, great powers of observation, strong character, decided opinions, refinement, and considerable education ; and, without one tinge of false pride, they are of
a lineage as old and as honorable as any of which America can boast.

Two things, also, you will find in this locality which
can be no better than they look. One is the daybreak
and sunrise from the sea, and the other is the exquisite
sunset which lights land and ocean as the orb of day sinks
out of sight to the west beneath the waves of the Chesapeake. Not sunny Italy, with all her boasted wealth of
color, can surpass the many-tinted loveliness of evening
in the ancient Kingdom of Accawmacke, to which, for
some years to come, my residence was now transferred.

CHAPTER III

OUR FOLKS IN GENERAL AND IN PARTICULAR

OUR folks have been in Old England since the days of Alfred, and in America since Thomas West, Lord de la War, was governor of the Virginia colony in 1608, when numerous brothers, cousins, and relatives followed him hither in search of the treasures of the still undiscovered South Sea.

There and here, for centuries, in peace and in war, they have never failed to be mixed up in the thick of whatever game the English stock has played.

They have lived and died in Devonshire and Somersetshire for nearly ten centuries. Until its recent destruction to make way for the government buildings, the old family nest at Plymouth was almost as well known to Englishmen as the banks of the Tamar itself. Burke tells us the name is among the oldest in England.

The first American ancestor of our name was a younger son of these old Devonshire people, and came to the Virginia colony in the reign of Charles the First. The ancient shipping-lists show that he sailed from Gravesend, July 4, 1635, after first taking the oath of allegiance to king and church. He was a lad of eighteen, who, yielding to the spirit of adventure which then prevailed in England, joined his friends, the Scarburghs of Norfolk, in the Kingdom of Accawmacke.

Two hundred and sixty years of separation ordinarily works considerable estrangement, and difference in characteristics, between the separated branches of a family. Not so with our people. If they possess one predominant trait, it is their faith in and attachment to anybody and everybody bearing the name, or springing from the old stock. But for the evidence it gives of stanchness in love and loyalty, the way in which the old ties are kept up, to this day, between the English and American branches would seem absurd. Descendants in the eighth degree since the separation recognize the kinship; and the English cousins welcome the Americans to hearth and home, taking no note of the two and a half centuries which have elapsed since the American immigrant wandered off from his English home, and placed the Atlantic Ocean between himself and his family.

And let me tell you, you boys of America, that there is no higher inspiration to any man to be a good man, a good citizen, and a good son, brother, or father, than the knowledge that you come from honest blood. Few who have it scorn it, and many of those who are loudest in belittling it would give all they have to possess it. And, boys, let me tell you another thing. When you are hunting for that honest blood, when you are looking back into the wellsprings of your existence for the source of the virtue, the courage, the manhood, the truth, the honesty, the reverence, the family love, the simplicity of life, which will make you what true men ought to be, believe me, you are more apt to find it in the progenitors who came from "the right little, tight little island" than anywhere else on this rolling planet.

Don't deceive yourselves with the notion that England did not furnish the best of us. We have had our troubles with her in the past, it is true. But it is hard for the mother to realize that her boy is grown, and accord him his rights as a man. She sometimes makes it very

uncomfortable for him by failing to recognize that he is
no longer in his swaddling-clothes. But there is not a
true-hearted boy in the world who, in spite of his mother's shortcomings, does not feel in his heart that there
is no other like her.

Don't take my word for it, if you think I am an old
fogy. Wait until you grow up and see the world for
yourselves. Travel through Russia, or Turkey, or Austria,
and you will never see a thing to stir your heart with a
desire to be one of them. Stand in the shadow of the
Pyramids, and you will be untouched by one wish that
your blood were Egyptian. Go through Germany, and,
while you will find there much to admire, there will still
be something lacking. In the home of the fickle Gaul,
even at Napoleon's tomb, the American boy is not in
touch with his surroundings. Spain and Italy, while possessed of a wealth of antique beauty, are to us only echoes
of a decayed and different civilization.

But, some sunny day in London, wander through Westminster Abbey and read the names. Some misty morning
in Trafalgar Square, cast your eye upward to the form of
Nelson, as he stands there in the fog, with the lions sleeping at the base of his column. In some leisure hour, visit
the crypt of St. Paul's, where the car that bore Wellington
to his rest still stands. Then, perhaps, you will appreciate the meaning of an old fogy when he tells you,
"There's nothing outside America which tugs at an
American's heart-strings like the names and deeds and
monuments of Old England."

Don't let us deceive ourselves about it, either. Don't
think or say that it is a better country than our own.
Don't let us be Anglomaniacs. That is not at all necessary. America is good enough for us. In many things
these blessed United States already equal any nation on

the globe. In almost everything, time considered, they
are a marvel. Within the past seventy years, American
inventive genius has contributed more to make life easy,
and to advance civilization, than all the world beside in
many hundred years, if we except the inventions of printing and gunpowder. In future we may, and probably
shall, become in all things the greatest nation that ever
existed. But it is not disloyalty to your own country,
and no disparagement of its greatness, to thank God that
the people from whom we sprang were Englishmen, and
that we have part and lot in England's glory.

In all America, there is no spot more emphatically English than the Kingdom of Accawmacke. Nay, more: there
is many a spot in England to-day where the manners and
customs of the population have changed more from what
they were in the seventeenth century, than those of that
little peninsula in America. Of the twenty-five thousand
white people in the two counties of the eastern shore of
Virginia, it is safe to say that four fifths of them are descendants of the earliest English settlers, and that there
has been less infusion of foreign element there within the
last three centuries than in many parts of England itself.
But a few years ago, this writer sat in the old church at
Bishops Lydeard, Somersetshire, and looked over the
congregation. The resemblance in appearance between
the people assembled there and the congregations he had
often seen in the Episcopal Church at Eastville, the first
county seat of Accawmacke, and in the Bruton Parish
Church at Williamsburg, was striking.

The first John Wise married Hannah, eldest daughter
of Captain Edmund Scarburgh. In 1655, we find him
locating his grant from Governor Diggs on Nandua Creek,
and in 1662, he was one of the first presiding justices of
the newly formed county of Accawmacke. In this year,

also, the Indian chief Ekeekes, for "seven Dutch blankets" sold him the two thousand acre tract on Chescones-
seck, named "Clifton" by its new purchaser, — a tract of
which the greater part descended without deed from father
to son for six generations, until sold to pay the debts of
the seventh heir, who was killed in 1864 in the American
war between the States.

John, eldest son of the emigrant, married a Matilda,
daughter of Lieutenant-Colonel John West, and died in
1717. Their son John married a Scarburgh, daughter
of Colonel Tully Robinson, and died in 1767. Their son
John married a Margaret, daughter of Colonel George
Douglas, and died in 1770. Their son John married first
a Mary, daughter of Judge James Henry, and then a
Sarah, daughter of General John Cropper, and died in
1813; and their son Henry, a younger son, was my father.
Related to a great number of the people of his county;
known to all; honored and respected for his high character; and beloved for his widely known talents and eloquence, which had reflected honor upon the community, —
father's return from Brazil to his home in Accomack was
the occasion of great rejoicing and festivities upon the
eastern shore.

No more beautiful spot for a dwelling-place can be
found anywhere than his home named "Only." It is
located upon a bold estuary of the Chesapeake, called
Onancock Creek, which comes down westwardly from its
source, and, upon reaching Only, makes a graceful turn,
first southward, then westward, then northward, and,
curving like a horseshoe, incloses within its bend five
acres of ground, with banks high above the stream and
level as a table, on which stands a grove of noble oaks of
the original growth.

In the neck of the horseshoe, with the grove behind it

and a fan-shaped lawn of greensward before it, stood the
mansion house. It was not a stately structure. There
are few such among the simple folk of this Peninsula.
But it was a model of scrupulous neatness, every way fit
for the residence of an unpretentious country gentleman,
and, outside and inside, gave evidence of taste and refinement. On the eastern side of the lawn, a terraced garden
ran down to the water's edge; and about the porches,
roses, cape jessamines, and honeysuckles climbed in great
luxuriance. Adjoining the house were the kitchen and
quarters of the household slaves, and outside the lawn,
beyond the terraced garden, were the barns, carriage-
houses, stables, and cattle-pens. Still further away were
the quarters occupied by the plantation slaves. Looking
upstream, other pretty points were visible, on which, in
groves, the picturesque dwellings of the neighbors were
seen; and in the further distance was the village of
Onancock, with its steeples, and sandy streets, and red-
topped houses, and wharves swarming with boats of all
sizes from the schooner to the skiff. Westward from
Only, the stream courses broad and shining between sloping banks, on which, here and there, their greensward
often coming down to the water's edge, stood other homes,
which looked smaller and smaller in the distance. Far
away, beyond a dim point of pines marking the mouth of
Onancock Creek, the sparkling whitecaps of the bay are
visible, with the sails of commerce passing up and down,
or turning in and out of the entrance to the creek.

On the beautiful November morning determined upon
for welcoming my father on his return to the United
States, relatives, neighbors, friends, clients, and political
adherents began to assemble at Only.

Bright and early, activity was visible on the plantation.
Under the wide-spreading oaks, long tables were impro-

vised, covered with snowy linen, and groaning with everything good to eat. At several points under the bluffs, pits
were dug where beeves and sheep and pigs were bar-
becued, and oysters and clams and crabs and fish were
cooked by the bushel. Great hampers of food, sent from
the village, or from the homes of neighbors, stood about
the tables, ready for distribution when the feast should
begin. The house itself, decorated with flowers and
evergreens, was thrown wide open to the guests, and in
the rooms of the first floor was spread a collation for the
more distinguished visitors.

By eight o'clock in the morning, the earliest of the
guests hove in sight. By ten o'clock, the grandees of
the county began to arrive.

There were Colonel Joynes, the county clerk ; Lorenzo
Bell, the county attorney ; the Arbuckles, the Custises ;
the Finneys, the Waples; the Corbins from near the Maryland line ; the Savages from Upshur's Neck ; the Crop-
pers from Bowman's Folly on the seaside ; the Sneads
from Mount Prospect ; the Upshurs from Brownsville ;
the Baylys from Mount Custis ; and the Yerbys, the
Nottinghams, the Goffigons, the Kennards, and Smiths,
from Northampton. But why enumerate ? Their name
was legion.

By midday the stables and stable-yards were filled ;
and the horses, fastened to the front-yard fence, formed a
continuous line ; while the creek about the grove was literally filled with small craft ranging from canoe to "pungy,"
and a steamboat had arrived from Norfolk with a great
company and a band of music. This band, playing in the
grove, was an endless source of wonder and delight to
many of the primitive people, who heard a brass band
that day for the first, and no doubt, in some instances,
the last time in their lives.

Within the house, father and mother held a long levee, welcoming old friends, and stirred to their hearts' depths by the simple ovation of which they were the recipients.

Without, under the shade of the trees, hundreds of visitors, after paying their respects to the host and hostess, walked or sat about and chatted with each other.

We may be sure that not the least theme of their conversation was politics; for not only was it in Virginia where everybody talked politics everywhere, but it was just at the period when Americans were carrying all before them in Mexico, and the Whigs were about to elect old "Rough-and-Ready," and snatch political control from the Democracy. Nor was there lack of party differences among the assembled guests, to give spice to the discussions. Hot and heavy was the argument between "Chatter Bill" Nottingham and "Monkey" Johnson, as to which national party was entitled to the honors for the American triumph in the Mexican war. Everybody had his nickname in these days.

Colonel Robert Poulson, the county representative in the legislature, had his group around him, as, red in face and solemn of mien, he ventilated his views on the best method of protecting the Virginia oyster-beds from Maryland poachers. Captain Stephen Hopkins, the largest vessel-owner of the county, had his admiring coterie, who insisted upon hearing his opinion, which he gave modestly, as to the prospect of a rise in the price of corn in the Baltimore market. Not far away, a noisy group of youngsters were bantering each other as to the respective merits of two saucy centreboard skiffs that rode proudly near the shore, and it was not long before a race between the Southerner and the Sea-Gull was a fixed event of the future.

As the day wore on, and when the multitude had been

fed, a movement from the house to the grove indicated that something important was about to occur. The host and hostess and the distinguished guests moved out to an improvised platform under the oaks, and there began the formal ceremonies of welcome.

Colonel Joynes, the venerable county clerk, as of course, called the gathering to order, when the stragglers had all drawn near. Then came the introduction of a young fellow from Hampton, afterwards somewhat known as a poet, who read an original poem lauding Virginia and her honored son. Then followed a brief address of welcome from young Bell. And then father stood up, facing, for the first time after years of absence, the people among whom he was born ; the kin who had loved him from his infancy ; the constituency who had made his brilliant career possible ; the people who still had faith in him, and had come so far to do him honor.

It was an impressive scene. Restraining himself, and laboring under the deep emotion such interest in himself was well calculated to arouse, he drew his audience to him with the simple speech which the skilled orator so well knows to be the most effective at the outset. Then, gradually warming up to his theme, he pictured the yearning of his heart for these old scenes during his long exile in foreign lands ; reviewed his work abroad in the interest of humanity ; his desire to see the infamous slave trade abolished ; his hope for some scheme by which the curse of slavery might ultimately be removed without wrong to the owner ; his realization of the glorious work accomplished by the Union arms in Mexico during his absence ; his deep sense that, with restored health and the youth remaining to him, there was still much of his life's work before him ; his gratitude to God for this restoration to his own people ; his deep emotion at this evidence of their continued trust; and his abiding faith in their further confidence in him. He concluded with a brilliant and genuine tribute of affection for a constituency so true and so confiding. His audience were wrought into a burst of thunderous applause, which was renewed and renewed as the band played, "Carry Me Back to Old Virginia."

The formal ceremonies over, the visitors gradually dispersed, and quiet reigned once more at Only.

It is the death of that era — a death which begun with my birth, and was complete before I attained manhood — that is to be chronicled in the following pages.

CHAPTER IV

MY MOTHER: FIRST LESSONS IN POLITICS

THE autumn of 1850 brought an event freighted with deep significance to me. My mother died. Although I was but four years old, it made a profound impression, and it exercised an incalculable influence upon my after life. My mother was a Northern woman, daughter of Hon. John Sergeant, a distinguished lawyer, and for many years representative in Congress from Philadelphia. Her people were of New England blood, identified with the earliest and most important events of the Plymouth Colony.

She had been taught to practice economy, simplicity, and scrupulous neatness and order. She was deeply religious, charitable, sympathetic, highly sentimental, and withal ambitious. She was one of those beautiful, refined creatures for which the City of Brotherly Love is famous. Hers was one of those extraordinary natures whose physical comeliness seems to make no injurious impression upon loveliness of character. Indeed, both in herself and with those about her, consideration of her appearance was subordinated to appreciation of her moral and intellectual beauty.

It was seven years after her marriage before she fully realized the vast difference between the life in which she had been reared and that into which her marriage had brought her. For, prior to their departure for Brazil, father, being in Congress, had resided for the most part in

Washington, and had no fixed establishment in Virginia.
In Brazil, social conditions had been strange to herself
and husband alike.   It was only on my father's return
from Brazil — when the Virginia establishment was resumed — that she realized the vastly altered terms of her
existence.   It is fortunate it was so.   It gave time for her
wifely love to become fixed and deepened beyond disturbance ; and residence in Brazil undoubtedly took away
the shock of slavery as it existed at home.   Coming now
to a knowledge of Virginia slavery, it was much less repulsive than it would have been if she had been transplanted direct from Philadelphia.   Notwithstanding this
gradual change, the contrast was strong enough to make
her fully realize the difference between the duties and the
pleasures of her new home and those to which she had
been accustomed in girlhood.   Of the society about her,
she had nothing to complain.   The good old people were
of excellent social position, and Philadelphia was their
social rendezvous.   Many of them were acquaintances of
her family.   They were neighborly and congenial enough,
and the means of intercommunication were excellent.
One of lighter tastes, and less serious purpose and sense
of duty, could easily have found, in her new surroundings,
all the social enjoyment she desired, and might have been
quite happy and free from care.

But it was not so with the mistress of Only.   She had
too much of the old Puritan blood in her to ignore the
word "duty."   She adored her husband, and was as ambitious as himself, which is saying a great deal.   She knew
that, if he was to maintain his professional and political
prominence, she must assume her share of the duties of
their domestic life ; and when she fully realized what that
meant for her, she doubted her ability to bear the burden
it imposed; but, asking God to sustain her, resolved to try.

With the abundance of servants at her command, the care of her children was a task comparatively easy. But it was these very servants who were the chief cause of her anxieties. They were slaves. When she had consented to marry her husband, she had not fully considered, perhaps, the difference between conducting a Philadelphia household and being mistress of a Virginia plantation. At the former place, an impudent or sick or worthless servant might be discharged or sent to a hospital, and the place supplied by another. Here, a discharge was impossible. Beside the necessity for discipline, every requirement, whether of food or clothing, or care in sickness, had to be supplied to these forty servants, who were as dependent as so many babies. In those days, slavery was not looked upon, even in Quaker Philadelphia, with the shudder and abhorrence one feels towards it now. It had not been a great while since it existed in Pennsylvania. A few slaves were still owned in Delaware, and Maryland and Virginia were slave States. The time had come, it is true, when it was abolished in Pennsylvania; but its existence was a fact so familiar that it produced no particular protest or expression of abhorrence, and, by all save a small coterie of abolitionists, was regarded as probably permanent. Slave-owners mingled with non-slave-owners upon terms of mutual regard and respect, unaffected, apparently at least, by any consideration of the subject of slavery.

Even if my mother had no qualms of conscience concerning ownership of negroes, her sense of duty carried her far beyond the mere supplying of their physical needs, or requiring that they render faithful service. Forty immortal souls, as she viewed it, had been committed to her guidance. Every time one of these gentle and affectionate creatures called her " mistress," the sense of obliga-

tion resting upon her, to keep their souls as well as their
bodies fit for God, echoed back to her tender heart with
alarming distinctness.   And in time, sweetly and humbly
as she performed her task, it became very irksome.   She
sleeps to-day in Laurel Hill, on the banks of the Schuylkill, having died at the early age of thirty-three, and no
one knows how much that sense of duty to her slaves
contributed to her death.

Ah, you who blame the slaveholder of the olden day,
how little you know whereof you speak, or how he or she
became such ; how little allowance you make for surrounding circumstances ; how little you reck, in your general
anathemas against the slave-owner, of the true and beautiful and good lives that sacrificed themselves, toiling to do
their duty to the slaves in that state of life to which it
pleased God to call them !   There is not a graveyard in
Old Virginia but has some tombstone marking the resting-
place of somebody who accepted slavery as he or she
found it, who bore it as a duty and a burden, and who
wore himself or herself out in the conscientious effort to
perform that duty well.   Mark you, I am not bemoaning
the abolition of slavery.   It was a curse, and nobody
knows better than I the terrible abuses which were possible and actual under the system.   Thank God, it is
gone.

All that I am saying to you now is, you who fought
slavery, as well as you who have heard it described in the
passionate denunciations following its death, realize that
the name of slave-owner did not always, or even in the
majority of cases, imply that the slave-owner was one whit
less conscientious, one whit less humane, one whit less
religious, or one whit less entitled to man's respect or
God's love, than you, who, because, perhaps, you were
never slave-owners, delight to picture them as something

inferior to your precious selves. After all, it was not you, but God that abolished slavery. You were his mere instruments to do his work.

In the case of my mother, her task was somewhat lightened by the character of her possessions, for the slaves were of more than usual intelligence, and were, for the most part, family inheritances.

This was no abode of hardship and stony hearts. No slaves were sold from that plantation. The young ones might have eaten their master's head off before he would have taken money for their fathers' and their mothers' children. No overseer brandished the whip that is so prominent a feature upon the stage, or in the abolition books of fiction.

Back to me, through the mists of nearly half a century, comes once more the vision of the young Puritan mother, who followed the man she loved into this exile from every association of her youth, and yet was happy in that love because she worshiped him next to her God.

Now I see her upon a Sabbath afternoon, with all her slaves assembled in the hallway, dressed in their Sunday clothes. Young and old, her own children and her servants, are gathered about her to listen to the word of God.

I have heard many great orators and preachers in my day, but never a voice like that of my mother, as she read and expounded the Holy Word to her children and her slaves.

In later years, I have heard great voices and great melodies, but never sweeter sounds to mortal ear than those of my mother and her children and her slaves, singing the simple hymns she read out to them on those Sabbath afternoons at Only, in the days of slavery.

Then came the lessons in the catechism taught to chil-

dren and slaves in the same class, where, before God, the
two stood upon equal terms, the blacks sometimes proving
themselves to be the quicker scholars of the two.

Such was my childhood's home; and such was many
another home in that land which, year by year, is being
more and more depicted by ignorance and prejudice
as the abode of only the brutal slave - driver and his
victim.

The beautiful month of October, 1850, with its wealth
of color and its exquisite skies, rolled round. All seemed
well at home. My father, once more immersed in political life, was absent in Richmond, a delegate to a great
constitutional convention, where all his energies were
directed towards adjusting the true basis of representation
in the legislature between the sections of Virginia where
slavery existed and those where no slaves were owned.
It was a difficult question, on which he had taken ground
in favor of a manhood suffrage as opposed to suffrage
based upon representation of the property owners. Nearly
every mail brought letters to mother announcing the progress of the fight, in which she seemed deeply absorbed.
The reputation which her husband was making resulted
five years later in his election as governor, and she clearly
foresaw that result. This prospect reconciled her to the
separation, and made her look bravely forward to an
expected event.

One day I missed my mother, and was told that she
was ill. Servants were hurrying back and forth, and
soon the doctor arrived. Bedtime came, and Eliza, the
white nurse, took me away from the nursery adjoining
my mother's chamber, and put me to bed in a strange
room. There, after undressing me, she made me kneel,
and, in saying my prayers, ask God to bless mamma.
When I was tucked away in bed, she sat beside me, and

stroked my long tresses, and sighed. It was all very
strange. "Mammy Liza, is mamma very sick?" I asked.
"No, my child, I hope not," said she, and then bade me
go to sleep, and soon I closed my eyes.

It was not for long, for in an hour or two I heard
voices in the hall, and hurrying footsteps, and, awakening
and sitting bolt upright in bed awhile, I finally slipped
down to the floor, and made my way, in my thin night-
clothes, into the hall, where I found the servants assembled, and weeping as if their hearts would break, uttering
loud lamentations. "What is it, Aunt Mary Anne?"
said I, cold, and shivering with fright. "Oh, my po'
baby, yo' mamma is dead, — yo' mamma is dead! Oh,
my po', po' mistis is dead — dead — dead!" she screamed,
at the same time seizing me, and wrapping me in her
shawl, and bearing me back to the warmth.

Night wore away mournfully enough, until at last, with
a faithful slave beside me, I sobbed myself asleep, crying more because others about me wept, than because I
knew the real cause for my grief. Morning came, and
when I awoke, I could not yet fully understand the solemn
silence of all about me, or the meaning of the strange
black things I saw. Breakfast over, the old nurse came
to me to go with her and see mamma. In silence, and amid
the sobs of every servant on the place, I and my little brother and sister were led into a darkened room. There,
on the bamboo bedstead which she had brought as her
favorite from Rio, lay mamma, apparently asleep, a tiny
baby resting on her breast. By her side, his head buried
in the pillow, and sobbing as if his heart would break, was
my oldest brother, — not her own child, but one who had
loved her as his own mother, and who now mourned a
second mother dead. Gazing out of the half-opened window, dressed in solemn black, stood the physician who had

sought in vain to save her. I was frightened and awed beyond utterance.

The next day the Fashion, Captain Hopkins's best vessel, lay to at the Only landing. A fearful-looking black box covered with velvet was borne aboard the Planter with solemn steps. Her sails were hoisted. With the freshening breeze she bore away, and, as the evening sunlight made a shining pathway on Onancock Creek, the vessel pursued her course westward until she became a tiny speck and disappeared. They told me that my mother was in heaven. Since that day, whenever the route to heaven arises to my mind, I see the white sails of a vessel gliding westward in the golden pathway made upon dancing waters by the brilliant sinking sun of a clear autumn evening.

The home-coming of father, some weeks after this sad event, was pitiful indeed.

He had been advised of my mother's death by a messenger, who rode forty miles down the Peninsula, crossed the bay to Norfolk, and thence telegraphed to Richmond. Such were the difficulties of communication, even at that recent date. When the news first reached him, the body was on its way to Baltimore, and thither he repaired to meet it, and accompany it to its last resting-place. After this, he had been compelled to return to his duties in the convention at Richmond, a widowed relative having meanwhile assumed charge of his family, and holding them together until he could return.

In the darkness of a drizzling winter evening, after a long, cheerless ride, he drew near his desolate home. A chill nor'easter storm, which had lasted for two days, made the passage across the Chesapeake, in the stuffy little steamboat Monmouth, exceedingly disagreeable. The few friends he met at the wharf expressed their sympathy more by subdued speech and close grasp of the hand than in actual utterance. A storm-stained gunner, clad in oilcloth, who had just made his landing from his goose-blind to ship his game to market, came up to the carriage and handed in, as tribute of his interest, a beautiful brace of brant. As he shook the rain from his tarpaulin, remarking that it was a great day for shooting, he uttered no word of consolation ; but his manner and his act were as delicately suggestive of his reasons as if he had been bred to the manners of a court.

Although the vehicle sent for father was amply supplied with curtains, aprons, and robes, the rain beat in upon him as he drove facing the storm, its cool moisture not ungrateful to his fevered cheek. Ordinarily, the homeward ride on such occasions was relieved by cheerful conversation between master and man concerning domestic matters and the progress of farm work. To-night, the weeds of mourning and the sunken cheek and eye had awed the faithful slave into respectful silence, which the master seldom saw fit to break. Homeward they sped in silence, with little to vary the monotonous pitapat of Lady Ringtail's hoofs in the shallow pools with which the storm had filled the level roads.

He lay back with folded arms and half-closed eyes, resentfully brooding upon the hard fate which had twice made him a widower. At a turn of the road they passed a silver maple, whose faultless form and beautiful coloring in springtime and in autumn had so excited the admiration of his wife that the children had named it " mamma's tree." It was leafless and bare to-night. A scurrying blast, shaking it as they passed, blew down from it a shower of raindrops, as if in mockery.

At the outer farm-gate the driver alighted, and, as father walked the mare slowly through the open gate, he

caught sight of the twinkling light which shone from the
chamber where mother had died. It had ever been a
beacon to him in days gone by. There, many a day, had
she sat and watched for his return; and many a night
had she drawn back the curtain that he might see her
signal first of all. The sight of it had always warmed
his heart. Now, he almost shuddered at the thought of
returning home. As they entered the yard, and drove
around the circle leading to the doorstep, he turned his
face away from her terraced garden, only to look upon
the arbor, where, in days gone by, she had delighted to
sit and watch the sunsets.

Before the vehicle drew up at the door, news of the
father's and the master's arrival had spread through all
of the household. Wide open flew the doors, and down
the steps, bareheaded and heedless of rain or wind, we
children rushed, shouting "Papa— papa— papa!" and
springing into his arms with rapturous kisses. One by
one we were snatched and hugged and kissed, and pushed
backwards up the steps, with orders to run in out of the
rain, while he busied himself for a moment giving directions concerning his luggage and the care of Lady Ringtail.

Poor little ones! How insensible they were to the great
calamity that had befallen them! How little they realized his loss or their own! In the short weeks since our
mother's death, — weeks filled with deep affliction to him,
— our mourning-clothes had become familiar to us; our
kind old aunt had taken mother's place in all our thoughts
and for all our wants; our mamma was only a beautiful
vision of the past. We laughed and romped, and greeted
papa with joyous faces; unconscious alike that we had
cause for sorrow, or that his heart was bleeding afresh at
sight of us.

The welcome awaiting him within was different from the joyous babble of the little ones outside. There, almost dreading to meet him, was the half-grown daughter of his first marriage. She was old enough to know and feel what a deep, irreparable loss had come upon her just when she most needed the love and care and guidance of the one now dead. It was not, and yet it was, her own mother that had died. And there was the tender-hearted woman who had come to keep together his little flock until his return. She had truly loved his wife, and now, herself a widow, she had seen him twice bereft.

As these two twined their arms about him, and buried their faces upon his shoulder sobbing, the prattling motherless children paused in their merriment to wonder why their grief should give itself new vent upon an occasion so joyous as papa's return.

But let us not dwell longer upon a scene so mournful.

Before leaving Richmond, father had written home directing that a chamber should be prepared for himself as far as possible from his former apartment. He could not brook the thought of living surrounded by the familiar objects of her chamber. Although he had been much absent of late, and much engrossed in other ambitions, he was a man devoted to his family, and deeply interested in his home. He knew, whenever he reflected upon the facts, that his apparent neglect of these duties of late was because of political objects he could not abandon, and that his course had been taken with his wife's approval; but ever and anon the thought came back to him that she had been alone when she died, and, in spite of all philosophy, the memory of that lonely death distressed if it did not actually chide him. He determined that, even at the sacrifice of ambition, he would henceforth devote himself to the duties he owed to his children and his home, and

make to her memory the atonement for what he could not
help regarding as neglect of her when she lived.

To this resolution I was indebted for four or five of the
very happiest years of my life. To this day, my fancy
takes me back to that great chamber where father made
me his bedfellow and constant companion; to that high
tester bedstead where, many a night, tucked away amid
comfortable linen, I watched the great hickory logs flicker
and sputter upon the andirons, and closed my eyes, at
last, lulled by the never-ceasing scratching of father's
goose-quill pen at a great writing-table in the centre of
the room; to the delightful half-consciousness of being
folded in his arms when, late in the night, he joined me,
and hugged me to his heart.

We were early risers, we two chums and companions.
By daybreak, the servant came in and built a roaring fire.
By sunrise, father and I were dressed, and out upon the
farm, or at the stables or the cowpens, followed by Boxer
and Frolic, our Irish terriers. The fashionable folk of
to-day affect the Irish terrier, and imagine that they have
a new breed. Father had a brace of them over forty
years ago, and they were sure death to the rabbits of
Only. Many and many a day we came back to breakfast
with one, two, or three molly-cottontails caught by Boxer
and Frolic in our morning excursions upon the farm.

Then there was hog-killing time, when, long before day,
the whole plantation force was up with knives for killing,
and seething cauldrons for scalding, and great doors for
scraping, and long racks for cooling the slaughtered
swine. Out to the farmyard rallied all the farm hands.
Into the pens dashed the boldest and most active. Har-
rowing was the squealing of the victims; quick was the
stroke that slew them, and quicker the sousing of the
dead hog into the scalding water; busy the scraping of

his hair away; strong the arms that bore him to the beams, and hung him there head downward to cool; clumsy the old woman who brought tubs to place under him; deft the strong hands that disemboweled him. And so it went. By the time the sun was risen, how bare and silent were the pens where hogdom had fed and grunted for so long a time!

How marvelous to youthful eyes the long rows of clean-scraped hogs upon the racks; how cheerful the blazing fires and boiling pots, and how sweet the smell of the hickory smoking in the cold air of daybreak; how merry and how happy seemed every one upon the place, old and young, men and women, girls and boys, in the midst of this carnival of death and grease! Up with the earliest, I was one of the busiest men in all the company, — now frying a pig-tail upon the blazing coals beneath the scalding-pots; now claiming a bladder to be blown up for Christmas; now watching the wonderful process of cleansing, or lard-making, or sausage-grinding. My! what tenderloins and spare-ribs were on the breakfast-table! my! how, for a fortnight after hog-killing, what sausages and cracklin, and all sorts of meat, we had! The skin of every darkey on the place shone with hog's grease, like polished ebony; and even Boxer and Frolic grew so fat they lost their interest in rabbit-hunting.

Then came the lovely springtime, when the ploughing began, and I followed him about the farm until my poor little legs were ready to give way beneath me. And the great red-breasted robins and purple grackle lit in the new-ploughed ground, from which such sweet aroma rose. And the golden plover, sweeping past, fell to father's unerring gun, I scrambling after them through the crumbling loam.

Then followed the harvest time, when birds'-nests and

young hares were in the stubble, and when the children
rode upon the straw-loads. And the summer days, when
father took me sailing in the Lucy Long, and sea-trout
fishing at the lighthouse, or built and rigged and sailed
for me such boats as no other boy ever had !

After that came the autumn time, when my uncle, a
famous Nimrod, appeared with dog and gun, and taught
me the mysteries of quail-shooting, so that I could tell
how Blanco the setter stood, and how Bembo the pointer
backed, and how Shot retrieved, and talked about these
things like a veteran sportsman.

And there, also, was our annual visit, in charge of
Eliza, the white nurse, to our grandmother in far-off Philadelphia. This was the period of good behavior and
restraint, neither of which I always practiced ; and, as I
viewed it, it bore hard upon my other engagements. A
short city residence was not altogether distasteful to me ;
but there were so many horses to ride, and so many boats
to sail, and so many dogs to work, and so many fish to
catch, and so many things to do at Only, that I looked on
the Philadelphia trip as time wasted from more entran-
cing employments. I felt that I was growing rapidly,
and that there were a great many things which I might
grow past, if I did not keep going all the while ; and thus
it was that at seven years old I was regarded as what we
call an enterprising youth.

Nor was I too young to detect that there were marked
differences between methods of life and thought at home,
and those which prevailed in Philadelphia.

My mother's family, especially the dear old grandmother, to whom my mother's death had been a great
blow, were exceedingly kind, and did everything to make
the visits enjoyable ; but there was a something in their
treatment of us little orphans which approached to pat-

ronizing, and, young as I was, my pride rebelled against
the idea that any one could condescend towards us.

One day, when I heard an aunt refer to me as her "little savage," I grew furiously angry; and another day,
when the white servant referred to me as a slave-owner, I
let her understand that I did not own a slave who was
not her superior in every quality, good manners and
good looks included. These were only episodes in what
were otherwise, on the whole, very happy visits; but,
young as I was, I early learned that between the people
of my father's and my mother's home there was brewing
a feeling of deep and irreconcilable antagonism, the precise nature of which I could not altogether comprehend.

As early as the autumn of 1852, I was made very happy
by being sent to school. As was the case in almost every
section of the South, the village school-teacher at Onancock was a Northern man. My brother Richard, three
years older than myself, was my companion. We were
furnished with red-topped boots, red neckerchiefs, warm
overcoats, warm caps with coverings for the ears, and tin
luncheon-pails, and never were we more elated than on our
first triumphal march to Onancock, a mile away. As we
passed the farmyards and the fields where our old friends
the slaves were at work, many were the cheery words
spoken to us.

"Dat's right," said saucy Solomon; "I spec' you'll be
as big a man as Mars' Henry hisself when you is done
school."

"You'd better not pass through Mr. Tyler's yard.
He's got a pow'ful fierce dog," shouted Joshua.

And the last thing said by old George Douglas, who
was something of a tease, was, "Don't you let none of
them Onancock boys lick you, for you comes of fightin'
stock."

Thus began our education, and a good beginning it was ; for we were blessed with a conscientious teacher, a school at a healthy distance, and at once entered the class with a red-headed girl, clever as she could be, with whom I fell in love, and who put me to my trumps every day to keep her from " cutting me down " in the spelling-class.

Thus passed away the happy days of childhood, — days unlike those which come to any boy anywhere nowadays ; days belonging to a phase of civilization and a manner of life which are as extinct as if they had never existed.

Yet in those times, but nine years before war and emancipation came, there was no thought that either was near at hand. My brother and I, on our return from school, were put across the creek at Onancock wharf. One sunny evening, we found father at old Captain Hopkins's store at the wharf, the spot where the village post-office was kept. He had been rowed up to the village in his yawl, the Constitution, and was waiting to take us home with him. The mail had just arrived, and an eager throng was listening to the news of the presidential election. The old captain read the returns, which told that Franklin Pierce was to be the next President, and the crowd cheered vociferously. Father was called upon for a speech, and briefly expressed his gratification at the result. The thing which most struck my ear was father's congratulation of his friends that the election of Pierce set at rest all fears as to slavery and secession, or concerning the abolitionists. He told how Pierce, being a Northern man, must prove acceptable to the North ; and how, being sound upon the slavery question, his administration would allay the fears of the slave-owner, and quiet the threats of secessionists. Everybody agreed that this was so, and everybody hurrahed for Pierce and King ; and, as the Constitution rushed homeward on the placid waters,

under the strokes of two sable oarsmen, I puzzled myself
to guess what were the fears of the slaveholder, and what
were the threats of the secessionist, and who were the
abolitionists.

Now, I was a young gentleman who, when athirst for
knowledge, held not back. Accordingly, I opened my
inquiries in a series of questions, and received answers
much after the following order : —

" What are the fears of the slaveholder ? "

" Why, my son, there is a small number of fanatics in
the North who demand that slavery be abolished immediately, and the slaveholders are apprehensive of them."

" What is a fanatic, and what is an abolitionist ? "

" A fanatic is a wild enthusiast, who will listen to nothing which interferes with his demands ; and an abolitionist is one who demands that the slaves shall be
freed."

" Are there many people of that kind in the North ? "

" Yes ; more than we know about."

" Is Pierce that sort of man ? "

" Oh, no. He is not in favor of freeing the slaves."

" Well, now I know what the slaveholder fears, tell me
next what is the threat of the secessionist."

" Young man, you listen too closely. Secession means
that a State, like our Virginia, being dissatisfied with the
way the Union is managed, would withdraw from the
Union, and establish an independent government of her
own, or form a new one with other States which withdrew
with her. Secessionists are men who threaten to do
that."

I paused a minute, and thought over all this ; then,
looking up, said : —

" Well, if we secede, we shall not be the United States
any more, shall we ? "

" No."

" And if we shall not be the United States any more,
we shall not have the stars and stripes for our flag, and
the Old Constitution and the Columbia frigates won't
belong to us any more, will they?"

" No, not if we secede."

" Well, now, papa, don't let's secede. No, sir; don't
let's secede. You are not for secession, are you, papa?
Think of what a horrible thing it would be to give up the
government grandpa and General Washington made, and
the flag, and the ships, and all that, and start another
thing all new, without any history or anything. You are
not a secessionist, I know, because you said you were not.
Are you, papa?"

"No, no, my boy. Far from it. Nobody loves the
Union better than I do. Nobody has better cause to love
and honor and cherish it. I was reared in the home of a
grandfather who fought for it by the side of Washington;
I was taught from my earliest infancy to venerate the
flag of the Union. My manhood, at home and abroad,
has been dedicated to its service; and God grant that
the Union may never be rent asunder in my day by the
fanaticism of the North or the passion of the South.
Heaven be praised, the election of Mr. Pierce seems to
put at rest all fears on that score from any direction."

We were nearing the landing. The autumn sun had
sunk into the distant bay. The long shadows of the
grove at Only were thrown towards us across the pooly
waters. Earth, air, and sky were bathed in the glories
of an Italian sunset, as these fervid words fell from
father's lips; and never in all his life had he spoken
more eloquently or more truly. What he had said
soothed and comforted me, to whom the thought of the
possibility that Virginia could be aught but part of the

American Union, or that we might lose the American flag, had never come before.

Thus it was that I learned my first lesson in politics, and was well and firmly assured that that could not possibly happen which did actually happen within the next nine years.

CHAPTER V

THE KNOW-NOTHING CAMPAIGN AND LIFE IN RICHMOND

DURING the next three years, we had things pretty much our own way at home, as far as female control was concerned. The dear old aunt who presided over father's household, although we loved her very much, was too indulgent to be a successful manager of children; and while Eliza, the Irish nurse, was firm and strong enough, we were rapidly growing beyond her control.

Then there was my aunt's son, a most attractive fellow, just entering upon manhood,— a thorough-paced child-spoiler. It was no uncommon thing for him to take me to the county seat, or the neighboring villages, where, while he pursued his amusements, I found companions and playmates that were improving neither to manners nor ideals of life. The association was delightful, nevertheless. On these excursions, there was no whim of fancy which that partial young relative was not more than ready to gratify. Our attachment was lifelong, and in after years the deep and abiding interest of my old-bachelor cousin in all that concerned me never abated until he died. At home, I had a thousand things to make boyhood happy. With the grown-up slaves I was a great favorite; and, as was often the case in plantation life, the little darkeys near my own age were my playmates and companions, and accepted me as their natural leader and chief. By the time I was eight years old, I could shoot, and ride, and fish, and swim, and sail a boat; I had a yoke of yearling

oxen broken by myself; my own punt in which to go fishing; fishing-lines and crab-nets; a dog and a colt; and
had become a breeder of most prolific chickens. Nothing
pleased me more than dropping corn in planting-time, or
hauling wood and straw with my own team. For months
at a time I would go barefoot, during the summer season,
dressed in brown linen and a straw hat. All this laid in a
store of health and strength that was of great value in
after years. In truth, I was a most bustling, energetic lad,
with no end of vitality, but lacked the parental government and care of a mother; and it was a blessed day for
me when my father married again.

My father's third wife was a refined and cultivated
woman, of suitable age, and possessed a most lovable disposition. It was not long before she established her
dominion in our household, — a dominion of love.

I was taught to observe meal-times; to appear with
hair brushed and face and hands washed; to attend family prayers; to spend less time at the negro quarters; to
account more precisely for my nomadic wanderings; to
devote regular hours to studies; and in many ways
to adopt much more orderly methods than I had been
accustomed to pursue of late. All which came in good
time, for I was soon to become a city boy.

In 1855, a great political contest occurred in Virginia.
A faction known as the Know-Nothing party, or the
American party, had sprung up suddenly, and had tri-
umphed in a number of the Northern States. It was a
secret organization, with oaths and grips and passwords.
Its rallying cry was that Americans should rule America.
Incidental to this watchword was a real or fancied hostil-
ity to foreigners, particularly the Irish, and to the Catholic
Church. Until it reached Virginia, it had been success-
ful everywhere. Father believed in the teachings of

George Washington that secret political organizations
were dangerous to republican liberty, and in the teachings
of Thomas Jefferson that no man should be proscribed on
account of his religion. He maintained that neither Irish-
men nor other foreigners should be oppressed or ostracized
by reason of their religious faith or their nationality.

The result of the approaching conflict seemed exceedingly doubtful when he was chosen as the Democratic
candidate for governor of Virginia. The circumstances
of his selection were not altogether flattering or hopeful.
Many of his political associates preferred him as the man
in their opinion best fitted to make the desperate fight,
but there were others who preferred him because they
believed the struggle was hopeless and secretly desired
his defeat. He accepted the nomination; and although,
at the outset, the Know-Nothing party had an enrolled
majority of ten thousand of the entire voters of the State,
he entered upon one of the most remarkable campaigns
in Virginia politics, and after a brilliant canvass was
elected by ten thousand majority.

It is seldom a boy nine years old is deeply interested
in politics, but this campaign was one that enlisted the
intense enthusiasm of young and old.

In American politics, we have recurring periods of political "crazes." Of late years we have witnessed several
such. The Greenback craze, the Granger craze, the
Silver craze, have each in its turn arisen, and, for the
time being, made whole communities drunk with excitement. Friends of many years are estranged by these
ephemeral issues. They are carried into business, into
church, into the household, everywhere, until entire com-
monwealths are so wrought up that even women and children take part until election day, and after that we hear
no more about them. Such commotions are like brush-

fires, which, igniting instantly, burn and crackle and fill
the whole heavens with smoke, as if the world was on fire,
and then die out as suddenly as they sprung up.

The Know-Nothing craze of 1855 was just such an excitement. Our community was divided into factions. Everybody took sides. Men who had never been known to show
an active interest in politics became intense partisans, and
political discussion went on everywhere. One of the first
results experienced by me was a black eye and a bloody
nose, received in a hard fight with the son of the village
blacksmith. Exactly how the row began, neither of us
could clearly explain; but we were on opposite sides, and
that was sufficient. It was a drawn battle, for the blacksmith interfered, having no intention of losing a valuable
trade by reason of political differences. In the little village of Onancock, the rival organizations found vent for
their enthusiasm by building and flying two immense
kites, with the names of their respective party candidates
emblazoned on them conspicuously. Many an evening,
after school was dismissed, I saw half of the villagers of
the place out on the green flying their Know-Nothing and
Democratic kites, as if the result depended upon which
flew the highest.

In due course came election day. Father being absent,
the young cousin above referred to represented him at
the polling-place, and took me with him. In those days,
voting was done openly, or *viva voce*, as it was called, and
not by ballot. The election judges, who were magistrates,
sat upon a bench with their clerks before them. Where
practicable, it was customary for the candidate to be present in person, and to occupy a seat at the side of the
judges. As the voter appeared, his name was called out
in a loud voice. The judges inquired, " John Jones (or
Bill Smith), for whom do you vote ? " — for governor, or

for whatever was the office to be filled. He replied by proclaiming the name of his favorite. Then the clerks enrolled the vote, and the judges announced it as enrolled. The representative of the candidate for whom he voted arose, bowed, and thanked him aloud; and his partisans often applauded.

All day long I sat upon my cousin's knee, or played about the platform. Nobody smiled more broadly, or applauded more vigorously, at votes cast for father; and nobody was more silent or haughty when votes were cast against him. At sundown, the polls were closed, and, to my infinite mortification, the majority at the precinct was announced as in favor of the Know-Nothings. The craze had simply taken possession of the place and run away with it. The ignorant and the vain had all been captured by the signs and grips and secret passwords of Know-Nothingism. For the first time in his life, father was defeated at his home. I thought we were done for. When we were safely bundled in the vehicle, and headed for home, I felt like crying, and the Know-Nothing cheers still rung in my ears most depressingly. What mortified me most of all was the fact that I knew of a bantering compact between the owners of the rival kites that the victorious party should own the kite of the vanquished, with the privilege of flying it tailless and upside down. The thought of seeing our beloved kite in such ignominious plight nearly prostrated me. As a matter of fact, the result at this precinct had been fully anticipated by the grown folks, and gave them no serious concern as to the general result. The Know-Nothing majority was really less than they had claimed. Seeing how I was cast down, my cousin, holding me between his legs in the one-seated buggy, endeavored to explain that there was no cause for alarm. Long before he finished, he discovered that, worn out by the fatigue and disappointment of the day, I was fast asleep, and in that condition he bore me into the house in his arms, laid me on the broad settee in the hall, and covered me with the lap-robe.

More cheering news from other places came thick and fast in the next few days, and it was not long before I was delightedly watching the Know-Nothing kite sailed tailless and upside down by father's friends.

Then came the preparations for removal of our residence to Richmond for four years.

No life could have been more in contrast with that at Only than the one to which I was now introduced. January 1, 1856, father took the oath of office as governor, and we proceeded to establish ourselves in the Government House, as it was called.

It is a fine old structure, simple in exterior, very capacious, surrounded by pleasant grounds, fronting the Capitol Square at Richmond. The house at Only seemed like a wren-box contrasted with this great residence. With play-grounds, and stables, and conservatory, and outhouses, it was indeed a most attractive place. Young gentlemen nine years of age are not apt to underestimate their own importance in such a situation, and I was no exception to this rule. The legislature was in session in the Capitol, and as a large majority of the members were in political sympathy with father, I received a great deal more attention and petting from them than was good for me. My bump of reverence never was over-developed, and under the influence of this sort of thing, I rapidly became very pert. But there were other directions in which I did not find life " all beer and skittles."

A school was selected where, beside a decided lack of enthusiasm for any school, I found this particular one not altogether a bed of roses. Being the best school obtainable, it was attended by the sons of the most prominent people of the place. And therein lay the trouble. If their fathers' views had controlled the election of governor, our residence at Only would have been undisturbed. The city was the stronghold of Know-Nothingism in Virginia. In a vote of nearly four thousand, father had not received exceeding nine hundred votes, and they were for the most part from the humbler classes. The Richmond Democrats were so few in numbers that they were called the "Spartan Band." The rural votes gave father his majority, especially in the splendid yeomanry of the Shenandoah Valley, among whom very few slaves were owned. They were the men who afterwards, drawn into the war to fight the slave-owners' battles, won with their valor the immortal fame of Stonewall Jackson.

Father had notions about manhood suffrage, public schools, the education and the elevation of the masses, and the gradual emancipation of the slaves, that did not suit the uncompromising views of people in places like Richmond. It was the abode of that class who proclaimed that they were Whigs, and that "Whigs knew each other by the instincts of gentlemen." The slave market was a flourishing institution in Richmond, fully countenanced if not approved and defended. The majority of Richmond people hated the name of Democracy, and, almost always defeated by it, were willing to unite with the Know-Nothings or any other party to defeat their enemy the Democracy.

At school, I very soon discovered that the Richmond city boys were disposed to turn up their noses at me, not only as a country boy, but because I was my father's son. I had several fistic encounters with them, and after that, things went on more smoothly, but not very pleasantly.

There never was such a place as Richmond for fighting

among small boys. The city is built over a number of
hills and valleys, and in those days the boys of particular
localities associated in fighting bands, and called themselves Cats. Thus there were the Shockoe Hill Cats, the
Church Hill Cats, the Basin Cats, the Oregon Hill Cats,
the Navy Hill Cats, etc.

About this time we were seized with the military fever.
In those days, the State of Virginia had a large armory
at Richmond, and a standing army of a hundred men!
The command was known as the " Public Guard," but
the Richmond boys called them the " Blind Pigs." The
syllogism by which this name was reached was unanswer-
able. They wore on their hats the letters P. G., which
certainly is P I G without the I. And a pig without an
eye is a blind pig. Q E D.

The public guard was as well drilled and cared for
as any body of regulars in the United States army. It
guarded the penitentiary and public grounds, and was a
most valuable organization in many ways.

Captain Dimmock, commanding officer, was a West
Pointer, I think, and the beau ideal of a soldier. His son
Marion and my brother, three years my senior, conceived
the idea of forming a boy's soldier company. Father en-
couraged the idea, and caused a hundred old muskets in
the armory to be cut down to the proper size for boys.
Captain Dimmock entered heartily into the scheme. The
boys were drilled assiduously. Their uniform was neat
cadet gray; and for several years the " Guard of the
Metropolis " was one of the most striking institutions of
Richmond. It always paraded with the Public Guard,
and the precision of its drill astonished and delighted all
beholders. Seven years later, William Johnson Pegram,
the first lieutenant of that company, attained the rank of
brigadier-general in Lee's army before he was twenty-one

years old, and although killed in battle, is still remembered as one of the bravest and most brilliant artillery commanders of the civil war. Many other members were utilized as drill-masters at the outbreak of the war, and subsequently became excellent officers.

Too young to carry a musket, I was made marker of this famous company, and was as proud of my uniform and little marker's flag as a Frenchman of the Cross of the Legion of Honor.

CHAPTER VI

BEHIND THE SCENES

THE present generation finds it difficult to realize the position in the Union occupied by Virginia, even as late as 1856–60, to which period our narrative now brings us. People recall, in a general way, that Virginia was once the theatre of many historic events ; that she gave birth to many great men in the early days of the Republic ; and that she was the chief battle-ground in the civil war.

A romantic interest attaches to her in consequence, and there is a certain tenderness for Virginia felt towards no other State, even in sections which were once arrayed against her.

But from many causes, a decline in her social and political importance has occurred within the last forty years, which, in its rapidity and in its extent, presents one of the most remarkable instances in history. Let us not stamp it as degeneracy. The day when she produced men of the type of Lee and Jackson is too recent to justify despair.

It is made doubly difficult to judge her by the character of the writings concerning her. On the one hand, we have extravagant eulogiums and fond laments of those who laud her old-time history and people, and admit no defects in them ; on the other, the always unfair and often ignorant denunciations of the anti-slavery folk, who are unwilling to admit, even at this late day, that any good could come out of the Nazareth of slavery. Both are wide of the mark. The social and economic conditions of Virginia were neither utopian, as the one loves to depict, nor bad and vicious, as the other would represent them.

It is undeniably true that, between the two extremes of society, as it existed there prior to 1865, was an awful gulf, upon one side of which were green pastures and still waters, and on the other noisome bogs filled with creeping reptiles. It was a condition incompatible with every theory of republican equality among men, and beyond question repugnant to the ideas and sensibilities of free communities.

Whether what has followed will ultimately result in a better civilization is as yet far from settled ; but whether for better or for worse, it is certain that a social, economic, and political earthquake, never surpassed in suddenness and destructive force, burst upon that people, working changes that have left little trace of what was there before.

If the Virginian who died forty years ago could revisit his native commonwealth, he would find it difficult to recognize the place where he lived. If he located it by the streams which still flow to the sea, and the mountains still standing as sentinels through the centuries, he would soon learn, even concerning these, that many are no longer landmarks of Virginia, but, snatched from her in the hour of her weakness against her will, are now possessions of an alien State. For the less enduring things, — for men such as he knew, for their very habitations, their mode of life, the fashion of thought of his day, for its wealth, its refinement, its culture, for its lofty incorruptibility and high-mindedness, — he would search sadly and in vain.

In the day of which I write, Virginia, among the States of the Union, was, in territorial area, second only to

Texas. Her western boundary was the Ohio River; northward, her Panhandle projected high up between Ohio and
Pennsylvania. Her wealth made her credit at home and
abroad above question. Her bonds sold higher in New
York and London than those of the federal government.
Her political importance placed her sons in commanding
positions in the cabinet, on the bench, and as representatives to many important foreign governments. In every
national assemblage her voice was hearkened to as that of
a potent and conservative and reliable guide.

Richmond was admittedly the centre of a society unsurpassed in all America for wealth, refinement, and culture.
Nearly every distinguished foreigner felt that his view of
America was incomplete unless he spent some time in the
capitol of the Mother of States and Statesmen. Soldiers,
authors, sculptors, artists, actors, and statesmen sought
Richmond then as surely as to-day they visit New York
and Boston.

The actual population of the city was small. It is difficult to realize that in 1860 Richmond had but thirty-eight
thousand inhabitants. But the truth is, that its real constituency was much greater; for it was the assembling-
point of a large class of wealthy persons who resided on
their plantations upon the upper and lower James, and in
Piedmont, Tidewater, and the South Side.

It is not uncommon nowadays to see references to
Southern society of that period as uncultured, and rather
sensual than intellectual in its tastes. This historic falsehood, like many others assiduously told for a long time,
may find permanent lodgment in the belief of the future.
No statement was ever more unjust. With inherited
wealth, with abundant leisure, with desire to excel in
directing thought, and to attain that command of men
which knowledge affords, with an innate passion for ora-

tory, a thorough education was the natural ambition of a
Virginia gentleman. True, his efforts were not directed
towards acquiring practical or scientific knowledge; for
these were in those days possessed, for the most part, by
men who expected to apply them to earning a livelihood.
But in education in the classics, in the study of ancient
and modern languages, in history, in philosophy moral
and political, in the study of the science of government,
in the learned professions, no men in America were better
equipped than the wealthy Southerners of that period.

It is true, there was no public-school system, and the
reason for it was very plain. The wealth of the upper
classes enabled them to have private tutors. The paucity
in numbers of the lower classes of the whites, and the distances at which they lived apart, rendered public schools
impracticable for them. Education of the blacks was,
of course, contrary to all ideas of slavery. Suppose we
depended upon the wealthy to inaugurate public schools,
— how many should we have? Yet nobody suspects that
they are indifferent to education. The best proof of the
care of the slaveholding Southerner for education may be
found in the lives of distinguished Northern men who
grew up fifty years ago. In many instances, they record
the fact that their first employments were as tutors in
wealthy Southern families. The private libraries of Virginia destroyed in the war, or burned in the old Virginia
homesteads, would have filled every public library in the
North to overflowing. Every current periodical and publication of that day, American and foreign, was upon the
library table of the Virginian not later than it was in
the Northern reading-room.

Conversation at social gatherings did not run to games
and sports, and dress and dissipations, and gossip and
amusements, but to the great events of the day, to the

latest productions in literature and art, and to things
worthy of man's noblest thought and discussion. It is an
insult to the memory of those most intellectual people to
describe the men as a breed of swearing, drinking, and
gambling fox-hunters, and the women as pampered, candy-
eating dolls. The per cent. of youth educated at foreign
universities was greater in proportion to white population,
at the outbreak of the war, in Virginia than in Massachusetts. This was natural, in view of the greater individual wealth.

It is true that every enterprise dependent upon what
is known as public spirit, or originating in the demand
or desire of common use, was sadly lacking. Wealthy
people seldom coöperate. Each buys, for private use,
things which all might well use in common if the price
was an important consideration ; and none, perhaps, have
as much, or as good, as all might more cheaply obtain if
they acted conjointly.

In times of slavery, there never was a decent hotel or
public livery in the South. The private establishments
were so large that their hospitality was deadly to the success of public houses, or other provision for the public
comfort. Of a thousand or two thousand visitors to the
city of Richmond, not one hundred would seek public
accommodation. They either had town residences of their
own, or were taken in charge by friends and relatives as
soon as they reached the city. Everybody was kin to
everybody. Visitors were ushered into vacant chambers
that were already yearning for them, attended by the servants that were idle in their absence, furnished with equipages and horses that needed use and work, and fed of an
abundance that had been wasted before they came. All
this was repaid by their mere presence, which banished
ennui, in those days when public amusements were rare
and inferior.

The domestic luxury and comfort of these people was all that heart could wish for. Their houses were furnished sumptuously in every detail. From drawing-room to chamber, everything was provided which wealth could wish. Mahogany, rare china and glass ware, massive silver, and the choicest of damask and linen were found in the dining-room, which was an important feature of every home. But there was a singular lack of the elaborate ornamentation and gilding so prevalent at present. The servants were in numbers, in thorough knowledge of their duties, in considerate care of their guests, and in respectful deference to their superiors, such as never were surpassed anywhere, and such as are now found on no portion of the earth's surface, unless, perhaps, it be in England. The Virginia cook and the Virginia cooking of that time were the full realization of the dreams of epicures for centuries. They also have passed away, like many of those precious gifts which are too delightful to be of long continuance. The dress of the period was, considering the opulence of the people, remarkable for its simplicity. Of diamonds and precious stones and jewelry there was abundance, and they of the most costly kind, and in quality the costumes of the women were of the best; but neither in number nor in extravagance of make-up was there any such display, especially in public, as later times have developed.

Male attire was exceedingly simple. As late as 1858, several of the old gentlemen wore the queues we see in pictures of Washington and his contemporaries, but those instances were exceedingly rare. Among elderly men, no such thing as a beard was admissible. The clean-shaven face was almost without exception. Young dandies began to wear hirsute adornments about the time Ned Sothern appeared in "Our American Cousin," and made "Lord

Dundreary " side-whiskers the fashionable fad. Elderly gentlemen wore broadcloth, with tall silk hats, high standing collars, and white or black stocks. This was varied among country gentlemen by broad slouch hats of felt or straw, and expansive white or nankeen waistcoats. During the heated term, a fashionable attire was an entire outfit of white or brown linen duck.

Until the year 1858, there was little difference between the costumes of old and young men, except in neckwear. Among youngsters, colored cravats were worn. About that year came, among the ultra fashionables, a remarkable outfit, consisting of short, double-breasted reefing jackets, trousers immense at the hips and tapering to the ankles, Scotch caps, and " Dundreary " whiskers. But a country youth would have scorned such wild imaginings of tailors. A city man thus equipped, walking beside a woman in hoops and a broad-faced bonnet, would give Fifth Avenue a genuine sensation if he reappeared to-day.

The private equipages were handsome. Rogers, of Philadelphia, and Brewster, of New York, built nearly all of the carriages in use among the Virginians, and the horses were Virginia or Kentucky thoroughbreds. There was rivalry to possess the handsomest teams, and the equipages on Franklin Street compared favorably, in number and style, with those in any city in this country. One remarkable old lady, a Mrs. Cabell, had a vehicle swinging upon immense C-springs, drawn by large Andalusian mules of her own importation, with liveried coachman and footmen. But that was never adopted as a model. Even at that late day, a few people drove to the White Sulphur in their private vehicles, and a drive of forty miles to visit friends in the country was a mere episode. The sociability of the period was great.

Concerning the mode of life, there were but two important meals daily. Breakfast, except for business people or
schoolchildren, was rather late. Morning visiting among
the ladies was from one o'clock until three P. M. The
dining hour was generally at three P. M. From dinner
time until about 7.30 P. M. came a leisure period for
driving ; and then an informal repast, consisting of tea,
coffee, chocolate, biscuits, sandwiches, and light cakes,
served in the drawing-rooms. At this hour the family, its
guests and visitors, were generally assembled in their best
dress. The meal, if such a light repast could be so designated, was served by butlers bearing great trays. Every
drawing-room had its "nest" of tiny tables on which
to place the plates and cups. The repast did not even
interrupt the flow of conversation. In pleasant weather,
many of the guests sat upon the porticoes and were served
there. This was the time when young folks, male and
female, interchanged visits.

Music, vocal and instrumental, and dancing varied the
enjoyment of those charming evenings. The wit of the
time was brilliant and refined. There was Littleton
Tazewell, remembered as having declined a proffered cup
of tea by dryly saying : " No, thank you, I would be azwell
without the T." There was Tom August, whose wit was
like Sheridan's. He it was who refused to bet on the
great four-mile race between " Red Eye " and " Revenue "
because, as he said, the result was already certain. When
asked why it was certain, he replied, " The first legal
maxim I ever learned was, ' Id certum est, quod certum
Reddi potest.' " On another occasion, responding to the
frightened inquiry, " Who is that ? " when a neighbor
heard him falling downstairs, he promptly replied, " 'T is
I, sir, rolling rapidly." Sweet Tom August, — courtly
to dames, loving to friends, brave in war, brilliant at the

bar, gentle and loving to the last, — green be the grave
that covers thee! Dying July 31st, he laughed, an hour
before he died, and remarked, " For once, the first and
last of August have come together."

And then there was mincing and primping John R.
Thompson, the poet, and young Price, now a grave professor of Columbia, and handsome, dashing Willie Munford, to-day a white-haired minister ; and Jennings Wise,
and Brandfute Warwick, and John Pegram, — the last
three dead in the battle front before five years had rolled
by. And there were young Randolph Barksdale and
Randolph Harrison, twin Apollo Belvideres in youthful
beauty. And red-faced George Pickett, in his army
clothes, before Gettysburg immortalized him, leading
his charming petite sister to the piano to flood the house
with melody like that of the mocking-bird. There, too,
was the brilliant Lucy Haxall, whose exuberant wit made
all the welkin ring ; and sweet Mary Power Lyons, who
made men better for beholding such exquisite refinement
and maidenly beauty ; and the rich Penn heiress from
New Orleans ; and the gentle Morsons ; and Pages and
Carters and Lees by the score.

In the quiet corners sat matrons smiling on this scene
of pleasure, — Dame Scott, of Fauquier, with her great
white turban, her intellectual face looking like a queen's ;
Mrs. Judge Stanard, handsome and charming; Mrs.
James Lyons, young and beautiful as the most blushing
débutante ; stately Mrs. Fowle, of Alexandria, and, by
her side, hospitable Mrs. McFarland, and beautiful and
accomplished Mrs. Seddon, of Goochland. Last, but
by no means least, were the middle-aged and elderly
representative men of the city and State, engaged in
courteous attention to the ladies, or grouped in drawing-
room, library, or veranda, discussing the living issues of

the times. There was James Lyons, one of the leaders
of the Virginia bar, the handsomest man of his day; and
noble-looking John B. Young, who, in the forefront of
his profession, still found time to read Dickens until
he was a walking encyclopædia of Dickens's wit; and
William H. McFarland, Richmond's king of hospitality,
portly and imposing, in ruffled shirt and spotless black;
and Judge Robert Stanard, whose very presence was
suggestive not only of the bench, but of a certain weakness he had for whist and "Lou" and "Bragg;" and
George W. Randolph and Roscoe B. Heath, the rising
men of the bar; and the Reverends Joshua Peterkin and
Charles Minnegerode, spiritual doctors; and Doctors
Deane and Haxall, doctors of the flesh, — all mingling in
most delightful and refined exchange of courtesy and
thought.

Once or twice a week the public band played in the
Capitol grounds. The park was illuminated. The citizens generally promenaded up and down the great parade
and enjoyed the music. Our home was opened on such
occasions to father's friends, and with clean-washed face
and most approved attire, I flitted in and out: now petted
in the drawing-room; now stealing away with a biscuit or
a cake for some little pet darkey; now out in the public
square with my boy acquaintances.

School occupied our mornings, and three afternoons of
the week were allotted to our French. When older, I
should never have begrudged that time to so charming a
companion as Mlle. Vassas, the *institutrice*, but we looked
upon her then as our natural enemy. Afternoons and
Saturdays were left to us to indulge in boyish diversions.
At first, these were harmless and domestic enough. In the
spacious grounds about the Government House, we had
pet pigeons, tame squirrels, a rabbit-warren, an improvised

gymnasium, and other things to make home happy. Old
Harry, our slave coachman, often accompanied us on
horseback rides; and the boys of our acquaintance were
glad to avail themselves of the attractions at our home.
We were warned against playing in the streets, or wandering into other portions of the city, and for a long time
obeyed such commands very well. But in time, I found
many excuses for absence. Between the visits to the
state barracks, where our soldier company drilled, and to
the Penitentiary, where ingenious convicts, without regular employments, built us boats, and engines, and cannon,
and wagons, and all sorts of toys, there were always plausible excuses for frequent and long absences, the real
nature of which were never very closely investigated.

Then came the excitement of another presidential
election. I hear you exclaim, " Now what possible interest could a presidential election possess for a boy ten
years old ? " You ask that question because you do not
know the society I am describing. Not a day passed that
I did not hear something about the dangerous condition
of the political situation. Long before James Buchanan
was nominated by the Democrats, I knew that Stephen
A. Douglas, " the little giant," with his views of squatter
sovereignty, could not command the vote of the Southern Democracy. Father was a warm supporter of Mr.
Buchanan as the representative of the conservative element
of Democracy. Accordingly, when Buchanan was nominated, largely through the influence of the Virginians,
I felt a personal interest in the success of " Buck and
Breck," and was their avowed advocate in all places.
Richmond was still unreconciled to Democracy; and the
American ticket, headed by ex-President Fillmore and
Andrew Jackson Donelson, was a hot favorite in Vir-
ginia's capital. As for the new and third party, known

as Republican and led by Fremont and Dayton, it literally had no following there. Out of the 160,000 votes cast in Virginia in the presidential election of 1856, only 1800 votes were cast for the Republicans, and they were nearly all cast in the Panhandle.

But the supporters of Buchanan and of Fillmore made a great noise in Richmond. They were united in ridiculing Fremont, but divided in all else. Nearly every night, open-air political speaking took place, with parades, banners, red lights, and bands of music, and great orators visited the city. From these, and from the political cartoons, which were very plentiful, I learned a great deal about Buchanan and Breckinridge, and about Fillmore and Donelson; but I was led to regard the candidacy of Fremont as a political farce, and chiefly heard of him as finding woolly horses in the Rocky Mountains, and running away with Jessie Benton, daughter of Missouri's great senator. I did not realize that, although the storm of abolition had not yet assumed full force, it was rapidly gathering, with its centre in this Republican ticket; nor appreciate that, in many Northern States, Fremont was drawing to his support a great following, which, with its " wide-awake " processions and other demonstrations, excited an enthusiasm not seen in politics since the time of " Tippecanoe and Tyler too." Even when the election occurred and Buchanan was chosen, I did not know that the real battle had been between Buchanan and Fremont, and that, for the first time, a solid North had been arrayed politically against a solid South.

No; however seriously a scrutiny of the returns may have affected older and more thoughtful people, young folks, and many older folks than I, looked only at the results, and regarded the election of Buchanan as once more putting at rest the plans of the abolitionist and the fears of the slaveholder. Little did I foresee that within eight years from the time I was hurrahing for "Buck and Breck," I should be led in battle by Breck in an assault on Buck, and upon everything that Buck and Breck stood for in the great election of 1856.

The result of the election of 1856 gave great satisfaction at our home. In the year 1857, passing through Washington on our return from the annual visit to Philadelphia, I had the distinguished honor of visiting a President for the first time. In company with a friend of father's, we children were taken to the White House. The President was a charming old gentleman, of very distinguished appearance. His greeting was cordial and simple. I looked him over carefully, and wondered why he had one hazel and one blue eye, and why he had never married. Then I reflected that perhaps that was the real reason, for the dear old fellow seemed exceedingly fond of children, and perhaps, after all, would have had a wife and children, if he could have found a lady who would be content with a pair of misfit eyes. Very sweet and tender eyes they were, however. After looking through the President's conservatory and receiving some pretty flowers, and eating a fine piece of President's cake, and being intrusted with some kind messages for father, we felt that we had not made any mistake in supporting Buchanan for President.

Soon after this, we had an opportunity of seeing an eminent representative of the other side in politics. Personal animosities did not enter so largely into politics in those days as they do now, although the stakes of the political game were greater, and the issues really more vital.

An abolitionist in the abstract, as conceived by us, under the teachings surrounding us, was a very frightful creature. We had heard much of past negro insurrec-

tions inspired by secret Northern emissaries. It was part
of my early education to learn of a fearful massacre, led
by a desperate negro named Nat Turner, in the county of
Southampton, a few years before I was born. I had been
taught to believe that Nat Turner and his deluded followers had really had no cause of grievance, but that secret
abolition emissaries had gone among them, and with devil-
ish malignity had stimulated them to rise in the night, and
put to death a number of innocent people who had been
good to them all their lives, to whom they owed every debt
of gratitude for becoming their masters here and making
Christians of them, instead of leaving them savages in
Africa. All this seemed reasonable, with no argument on
the other side; and the fact that Nat Turner and all who
joined him were wiped off the face of the earth seemed a
natural result of Nat's lack of appreciation of the good
state in which he lived. In a general way I had heard,
and heard it with regret, that the real culprits, the abolitionists, who had made Nat Turner do these horrid things,
had escaped, and from time to time contemplated the possibility that such fiends still existed, and still prowled at
night about negro quarters, and induced them to run
away. Of course, I had no idea that such a thing as a
negro insurrection could occur in our community with
a body of troops present like the Public Guard. But why
talk of such possibilities? Were not the negroes perfectly content and happy? Had I not often talked to
them on the subject? Had not every one of them told
me repeatedly that they loved " old Marster " better than
anybody in the world, and would not have freedom if he
offered it to them? Of course they had, — many and
many a time. And that settled it.

   All this being true, I looked upon an abolitionist as, in
the first place, a rank fool, engaged in trying to make

people have what they did not want; and in the next
place, as a disturber of the peace, trying to make people
wretched who were happy, and a man bad at heart, who
was bent on stealing what belonged to his neighbor, or
even inciting the murder of people for slaveholding, as if
slaveholding were a crime, when it was no crime, but a
natural and necessary condition of society.

With views like this concerning abolitionists in general,
my curiosity was greatly excited when I heard that one
William H. Seward, the acknowledged leader of the Republican party in the North, was not only in the city of
Richmond, but was visiting and being entertained by the
Hon. James Lyons, a connection and supporter of my
father.

When I was presented to Mr. Seward, I was greatly
surprised to find him a natural-looking person, with most
attractive manners, genial, bright in companionship, laughing in his talk, and actually going so far as to call his
host Lyons, and the other gentlemen by their given names.
Mr. Seward surprised me also by eating and drinking and
smoking, and having a good time generally ; and I watched
him long and in vain to see some distinguishing mark by
which I might thereafter recognize an abolitionist. I discovered none, except it be a wonderfully large nose, which
was also a characteristic of John Brown and Abraham
Lincoln, his brother abolitionists.

I listened in vain for some utterance of abolition views
from Mr. Seward, but the party seemed more interested
in a decanter of old Madeira, and a discussion of some
passing social event, than in the all-absorbing question of
slavery, and so Mr. Seward's convictions were reserved
for future expression. I thought he might possibly give
money to Austin the butler, with which to escape from
slavery, but, so far as was ever discovered, nothing like

that occurred. Mr. Seward came and went. He enjoyed
his visit, and his host enjoyed his company. But neither
made much impression on the political views of the other.

Many other things were happening which drew my
attention to the subject of slavery. During our next
visit to Philadelphia, everybody was talking about a book
and a play called "Uncle Tom's Cabin." I had heard
mention of the book at home, as a very powerful but
very "pernicious" book. More than once the subject
had come up in conversation in my presence ; and I had
heard the work spoken of as a cruel travesty upon Southern life, disgusting in its sentimental sympathy with the
negro. I was surprised to find that everybody in the
North was reading "Uncle Tom's Cabin," and pronoun-
cing it a remarkable production ; and when it was proposed, on our next visit to Philadelphia, to take me to
a theatre to see this wonderful play of "Uncle Tom's
Cabin," I was delighted. Never did theatrical performance open to any one more gratifyingly than that wonderful drama. In my heart I had a feeling that our Northern kinsfolk thought their homes were finer than those
in our beloved South. I did not think so. When,
in the opening act, I saw the beautiful Southern home,
with its flowers and bowers and sunshine, I said to myself,
"Now they will see how we live, and will envy us." Yes,
old Uncle Tom and all his family were just such darkeys
as were in Virginia. And as for Eva, there she was,
looking like a hundred little girls I knew, and infinitely sweeter in voice and eye than the prim Northern
girls surrounding me. And Eva's father! I knew a
hundred charming young fellows just like him. Her mother ? Well, there was no denying it that now and then
we saw one like her, but she was not a common or attractive type. And Topsy ? Yes, there were darkeys just like

her, even within my limited knowledge. I laughed and enjoyed myself along with the others over Topsy's queer antics.

The play moved on. In time the slave auction came, and the negro-buyers, and the terrible domestic tragedy to Uncle Tom, and the fearful Mississippi River trip, and the whipping of Eliza's husband, — her flight, the blood-hounds, and all the ghastly story which thrilled a nation. I was too young to grasp the moral of that story, yet old enough to feel my heart rebel against things which I had never before seen laid at the door of the people I loved and among whom I lived. I believed that many of them were the mere creations of a malignant enemy, who had conjured them up out of her own imagination to prejudice the outside world against my kith and kin, and I indignantly denied, when questioned concerning the play, that such scenes were possible. I had never wit-nessed them, or heard of them, in the home of my father. I resolved to denounce and forget this new phase of sla-very which that night had revealed to me, and the anger and the pity which I heard expressed by the people about me confirmed me in the belief that they were sentimental-ists on subjects of which they were ignorant, and that the denunciation of slavery by Northerners sprang from pre-judices engendered by just such outrageous exaggerations as those of " Uncle Tom's Cabin."

But the play made a deep and lasting impression upon me. The sweet vision of little Eva, the inexpressible pathos of Uncle Tom, the freaks of Topsy, came back to me time and time again. Alas! they returned yoked in my memory with the wretched figure of Legree, the blood-hounds, and the misery of the other scenes, and the possi-bility that it all might be true revealed itself to me in a way that I little expected. I knew there was such a thing

as a negro-buyer. On one or two occasions I had had
such men pointed out to me. I had been taught to regard
them as an inferior class of humanity; but this knowledge
came principally from the negroes themselves, for the
grown people of my own class seldom referred to them,
and they received no sort of social recognition. I had, in
fact, seen in the newspapers advertisements of the sale of
negroes, side by side with little figures of a man with a
pack on his back, and the offer of a reward for a runaway.
But never until my return from the North was my curiosity sufficiently aroused to make me locate the place of selling negroes, or determine me to see a sale.

Among my Northern kinsfolk was a young uncle, a
handsome, witty fellow, much younger than my mother.
Notwithstanding her death, he had kept up his affection
and intimacy with father. Influenced partly by his regard
for father and partly by pride as a Pennsylvanian, he had
become an ardent supporter of Mr. Buchanan. He occupied a rather prominent position as a Democratic member
of the Pennsylvania legislature. Controlled doubtless by
his warm attachments in the South, he had no squeamish
feelings about slavery. He loved the Union, and sincerely
believed that the only way to preserve it was by recogniz-
ing the existence of slavery, and by protecting the slaveholders in all lawful ways. He believed also that men like
his brother-in-law were convinced that slavery ought to
be abolished; and that the best way to bring that result
about, without disunion and conflict, was to trust to its
gradual accomplishment by the slave States themselves,
acting under the influence of men such as he knew, instead
of attempting to coerce them by outside influence, which,
as he believed, would arouse their antagonism and defiance, so as to defeat or delay the end desired. This was
the honest feeling which made many a Northern man a

Democrat in those days. It may have been an error in judgment, but it was an error, if error at all, on the side of Union and fraternity, springing from a knowledge of their Southern brethren, a respect and regard for them, and a desire for the peaceful solution of a most perplexing problem. Let no man at this day denounce that feeling as cowardice or lack of principle. The man of whom I write felt that way and acted that way to the last. But when the "irrepressible conflict" came, he laid down his life with a smile for the Union, while many a man who had precipitated the struggle never went to the front. And he was but one of thousands.

It was he who had taken me to see "Uncle Tom's Cabin;" and it was he who had petted me, and taken me about the streets of Philadelphia, and spoiled me in many ways; and it was he who had taken me to visit the President; and now he had come to visit us, and spend a week of leisure with his favorite brother-in-law.

My oldest brother had recently returned from Paris. He had been absent as Secretary of Legation in Berlin and Paris for nearly six years. He and my uncle were nearly of the same age, and devoted friends. Father loved this oldest son as the apple of his eye, and the feeling of that son for his father was little short of adoration. The relations between these three — father, son, and brother-in-law — were of the most intimate and beautiful kind. Together they conferred, as if they were men of the same age, and, being in full accord on public questions, their views were always harmonious, whether looking to some social pleasure, or some coöperation for the advancement of their political plans. Father had higher ambitions than he had yet realized. He was becoming prominent as a possible candidate for the presidency. Both from a natural inclination and a desire to promote his candidacy, my

brother had become editor of the "Richmond Enquirer,"
the leading Democratic journal of Virginia ; my uncle was
heart and soul enlisted in securing support for father
among his own constituency. It was believed that his
well-known conservatism on the subject of slavery, and
his intense devotion to the Union, would make his prospects very good for the nomination.

I had unrestrained access to the library, where this trio
frequently assembled ; and, without being admitted into
their graver conversation, heard it, and understood its general tenor. The occupations of my father and brother left
their visitor to find his own amusements until the evening
hour, and he diverted himself at such times by reading or
sight-seeing, or in diversions with the children, of whom
he was very fond.

One Saturday, thus left alone with me, the subject
of "Uncle Tom's Cabin" came up. He asked if I had
ever seen a slave sale. "No," said I, all alert, for since I
saw the play I had resolved that I would some time see
a slave auction ; "but I know where they sell them. I
saw the sign a few days ago. Let us go and see what it
is like." So off we started. Out of the beautiful grounds
and past the handsome residences we went, turning down
Franklin Street towards the great Exchange Hotel, which
was at that time the principal public place of Richmond.
Beyond it we passed a church, still used as such, although
the locality had been deserted by residences, and stables
and little shops surrounded it. As we proceeded, the
street became more and more squalid and repulsive, until
at last we reached a low brick warehouse, with its end
abutting on the street and running far back. Over the
place was the sign, with the name of an owner and
the words "Auction House" conspicuously painted. At
the door hung a red flag, with an advertisement pasted on

its side, and up and down the street a mulatto man walked
with another flag, ringing a large bell, and shouting, "Oh,
yea! Oh, yea! Oh, yea! Walk up, gentlemen. The sale
of a fine, likely lot of young niggers is now about to
begin." To these he added, in tones which were really
merry, and with an expansive smile, that they were " all
sorts of niggers, belonging to the estate of the late ———,
sold for no fault, but to settle the estate; " and that the
lot embraced all kinds, " old ones and young ones, men
and women, gals and boys."

About the door, and on the inside, a few men were
grouped, some in their shirt-sleeves. For the most part,
they had the appearance of hostlers. The place itself
looked like a livery stable within the building. For a
long distance back from the street, there were no side-
lights or skylights. In the rear only was it light, where
the structure projected beyond those on either side of it,
and there the light was ample, and the business in hand
was to be transacted.

We moved cautiously through the dark front of the
building, and came at last to the rear, where a small platform occupied the centre of the room, and chairs and
benches were distributed about the walls. Another large
mulatto man appeared to act as usher, standing near a
door, through which from time to time he furnished a
fresh supply of slaves for sale. A large man, with full
beard, not a bad-looking fellow but for the "ratty" appearance of his quick, cold, small black eyes, acted as
auctioneer. A few negroes sat on the bench by the door,
they being the first "lot" to be disposed of. The pur-
chasers stood or sat about, smoking or chewing tobacco,
while the auctioneer proceeded to read the decree of a
chancery court in the settlement of a decedent's estate,
under which this sale was made. The lawyers represent-

ing different interests were there, as were also the cred-
itors and distributees having interests in the sale. Besides
these were ordinary buyers in need of servants, and slave-
traders who made a living by buying cheap and selling
for a profit. We took seats, and watched and listened
intently.

After reading the formal announcement authorizing
the sale, the auctioneer became eloquent. He proceeded
to explain to his auditors that this was " no ordinary sale
of a damaged, no-'count lot of niggers, whar a man buyin'
a nigger mout or mout not git what he was lookin' fur,
but one of those rar' opperchunities, which cum only once
or twice in a lifetime, when the buyer is sho' that fur
every dollar he pays he 's gittin' a full dollar's wuth of
raal genuine nigger, healthy, well-raised, well-mannered,
respectful, obejunt, and willin'." " Why," said he, " gentlemen, you kin look over this whole gang of niggers, from
the oldest to the youngest, an' you won't find the mark of
a whip on one of 'em.   Colonel ———, for whose estate
they is sold, was known to be one of the kindest marsters,
and at the same time one of the best bringers-up of niggers, in all Virginia. These here po' devils is sold for
no fault whatever, but simply and only because, owin' to
the Curnel's sudden death, his estate is left embarrassed,
and it is necessary to sell his niggers to pay his debts, and
for distributin' some reddy monny amongst numrus 'aars.
Of these facts I assure you upon the honor of a gentleman."

Having thus paved the way for good prices, he announced that among the slaves to be offered were good
carriage-drivers, gardeners, dining-room servants, farm
hands, cooks, milkers, seamstresses, washerwomen, and
" the most promisin', growin', sleek, and sassy lot of
young niggers he had ever had the pleasure of offerin'."

The sale was begun with some " bucks," as he facetiously called them.   They were young, unmarried fellows
from eighteen to twenty-five.   Ordered to mount the auc-
tion-block, they stripped to the waist and bounced up,
rather amused than otherwise, grinning at the lively bidding they excited.   Cautious bidders drew near to them,
examined their eyes, spoke with them to test their hearing
and manners, made them open their mouths and show
their teeth, ran their hands over the muscles of their
backs and arms, caused them to draw up their trousers to
display their legs, and, after fully satisfying themselves on
these and other points, bid for them what they saw fit.
Whenever a sale was concluded, the successful bidder
was announced, and the announcement was greeted by the
darkeys themselves with broad grins, and such expressions as " Thank Gord," or " Bless de Lord," if it went
as they wished, or in uncomplaining silence if otherwise.
It was surprising to see how thoroughly they all seemed
to be informed concerning the men who were bidding for
them.

The scenes accompanying the sales of young women
were very similar to those with the young men, except
that what was said to them and about them was astonish-
ingly plain and shocking.   One was recommended as a
" rattlin' good breeder," because she had already given
birth to two children at seventeen years of age.   Another, a mulatto of very comely form, showed deep embarrassment when questioned about her condition.

They brought good prices.   " Niggers is high " was the
general comment.   Who bought them, where they went,
whether they were separated from father, mother, brother,
or sister, God knows.   Let us hope the result was as
humane as possible.

" I am now goin' to offer you a very likely young chile-barin' woman," said the auctioneer. "She is puffectly helthy, and without a blemish. Among the family, she is a universal favorite. I offer her with the privilidge of takin' her husban' and two chillen with her at a very rejuced price, because it is the wish of all concerned to keep 'em together, if possible. Get up here, Martha Ann." A large-framed, warm, comfortable-looking, motherly soul, with a fine, honest face, mounted the block. "Now, gentlemen," said he, continuing, "ef you'll cast yo' eyes into that corner, you will see Israel, Martha Ann's husband, and Cephas and Melindy, her two children. Israel is not what you may call a raal able-bodied man. He broke his leg some years ago handlin' one of the Curnel's colts, and he ain't able to do heavy work ; but I am asshoed by everybody on the place that Israel is a most valuable servant about a house for all kind of light work, and he can be had mighty cheap."

"Yes, sir," spoke up Israel eagerly, "I kin do as much ez ennybody ; and, marsters, ef you'll only buy me and de chillun with Martha Ann, Gord knows I'll wuk myself to deth fur you."

The poor little darkeys, Cephas and Melinda, sat there frightened and silent, their white eyes dancing like monkey-eyes, and gleaming in the shadows. As her husband's voice broke on her ear, Martha Ann, who had been looking sadly out of the window in a pose of quiet dignity, turned her face with an expression of exquisite love and gratitude towards Israel. She gazed for a moment at her husband and at her children, and then looked away once more, her eyes brimming with tears.

"How much am I offered for Martha Ann with the privilidge ?" shouted the auctioneer. The bidding began. It was very sluggish. The hammer fell at last. The price was low. Perhaps, even in that crowd, nobody wanted them all, and few were willing to do the heartless act of taking her alone. So she sold low. When the name of her purchaser was announced, I knew him. He was an odd, wizen, cheerless old fellow, who was a member of the Virginia legislature from one of the far-away south-side counties adjoining North Carolina. Heaven be praised, he was not a supporter of father, but called himself an Old-line Whig, and ranked with the opposition. He seemed to have no associates among the members, and nobody knew where he lived in the city. He was notoriously penurious, and drew his pay as regularly as the week rolled around.

"Mr. —— buys Martha Ann," said the auctioneer. "I congratulate you, Mr. ——. You've bought the cheapes' nigger sold here to-day. Will you take Israel and the young uns with her?"

Deep silence fell upon the gathering. Even imperturbable Martha Ann showed her anxiety by the heaving of her bosom. Israel strained forward, where he sat, to hear the first word of hope or of despair. The old man who had bid for her shuffled forward, fumbling in his pockets for his money, delaying his reply so long that the question was repeated. "No—o," drawled he at last; "no—o, I'm sorry for 'em, but I railly can't. You see, I live a long way from here, and I ride down to the legislatur', and, when I get here, I sell my horse and live cheap, and aims to save up enough from my salary to buy another horse and a 'chile-barin' woman' when the session's done; and then I takes her home, ridin' behind me on the horse. Thar ain't no way I could provide for gittin' the man and the young uns home, even if they was given to me. I think I'm doin' pretty well to save enough in a session to buy one nigger, much less a whole fambly." And the old beast looked up over his spectacles as he counted his money, and actually chuckled, as if he expected a round of applause for his clever business ability.

A deep groan, unaccompanied by any word of complaint, came from the dark corner where Israel sat. Martha Ann stepped down from the platform, walked to where he was, the tears streaming down her cheeks, and there, hugging her children and rocking herself back and forth, she sobbed as if her heart was breaking.

My companion and I looked at each other in disgust, but neither spoke a word. I was ready to burst into tears. The old creature who had bought the woman lugged out his hoarded money in sundry packages of coin and paper, and, as he counted it, said, " Martha Ann, cheer up; you 'll find me a good marster, and I 'll get you a new husband." He might well have added, " and the more children you have, the better I 'll like you."

Thank God, the scene did not end there. The silence was oppressive. The veriest savage on earth could not have witnessed it without being moved. "Let us go away," I whispered. At last the suspense was broken. A handsome, manly fellow, one of the lawyers in the case, exclaimed, " By —— ! I can't stand this. I knew Colonel —— well. I know how he felt towards Israel and Martha Ann and their children. This is enough to make him turn in his grave. I am unable to make this purchase ; but sooner than see them separated, I 'll bankrupt myself. Mr. ——, I will take Martha Ann off your hands, so as to buy her husband and children, and keep them together."

" Well, now, you see," drawled the old fellow, pausing in his work, with trembling hand, " if you feel that way, the time to speak was when the gal was up for sale." His eye glittered with the thought of turning the situation to advantage. " You see she 's mine now, and I consider her a very desirable and very cheap purchase. Moreover, if you want her, I think you ought to be willin' to pay me something for the time and trouble I've wasted here a-tryin' to git her."

The proposition was sickening. But the old creature was so small himself that his demand of profit was likewise small, and the matter was soon arranged. Whether he remained and bought another " chile-barin' " woman is unknown; for, sick at heart at the sights we had witnessed, we withdrew, and walked slowly back in the glorious sunlight, past the neighboring church, and up to the happy abodes of Virginia's best civilization, little inclined to talk of the nightmare we had been through. From that hour, the views of both of us concerning slavery were materially modified. Throughout the day, the horrors we had witnessed came back and back again to me ; and, recuperative as I was, I was very, very unhappy.

That night, the experiences of the morning were the subject of a long and anxious and earnest conversation between father, my brother, and my uncle. At its close, I felt much relieved and proud of them, and better satisfied, because they were all agreed that a system in which things like that were possible was monstrous ; and that the question was, not whether it should be abolished, and abolished quickly, but as to the manner of its abolition.

Within seven years from that time, my brother and my uncle were both dead, — killed in battle on opposite sides, in a struggle resulting from slavery. Father's fortune and happiness were engulfed in the horrible fraternal strife which grew out of this cancer on the body politic, — a cancer which all three of those men were honestly anxious to destroy.

Virginians ! you who in our day were led by Lee and Jackson ! have you read this chapter ? Is it true or untrue? Ask yourselves calmly. The time has now come when you ought, in justice to yourselves, to try to satisfy yourselves wherein your old system was wrong and unjustifiable, as well as wherein it was right. One who loves you wrote this story; one who was your comrade in the fight we lost; one who has no word of blame for you, but, on the contrary, believes that we had every provocation to fight; one who, as long as he lives, will glory in the way we fought, and is proud of his own scars, and teaches his children to believe that the record of Confederate valor is a priceless heritage.

It is not written when the truth can do you harm. It is not written by an alien in feeling, or an enthusiast for an abstract idea. It is written to make you think, — to make you ask yourselves whether you can, before God, claim that all was as it should be when we had slavery. It is written to reconcile you to your loss by showing you from what your children were delivered.

It is penned in the firm belief that some day, while brooding upon the happiness, the wealth, the culture, the refinement then possessed by the South, and to so large an extent lost to her now, you may realize that all these, delightful as they were, did not justify the curse and misery of human slavery. I seek to make you realize, if not admit, that its abolition was a greater blessing to us even than to the slaves, and that emancipation was worth all we surrendered, and all the precious lives that were destroyed; to bring you to confess, the brave and generous men I know you to be, that the time has come at last when, through our tears, and without disloyalty to the dead, in the possession of freedom and union and liberty, true Confederates, viewing it all in the clearer light and calmer atmosphere of to-day, ought to thank God that slavery died at Appomattox.

CHAPTER VII

MY BROTHER

IN the last chapter I spoke of the return of my brother Jennings from France. After graduating at Bloomington, Ind., and studying law at William and Mary College, and before he attained his majority, he had received from President Pierce an appointment in the diplomatic service, and was sent to Berlin as attaché of the American Legation. He spent three years in Berlin and Heidelberg, and was thence transferred to Paris as Secretary of Legation, where he further improved himself by study, and by contact with the most polished society in Europe. When he returned to Virginia in 1857, at the age of twenty-five, he was well equipped for a brilliant career. His home-coming after a long absence was the occasion of great rejoicing in our family. It was as if a new light had sprung up in the household. My brother was so modest and unaffected that his acute intellect and varied information were not always revealed to strangers. His disposition was so amiable that in all his life he never had a boyish quarrel with any one. Of singularly mature and sedate nature, he had been his father's loved and trusted companion before his departure for foreign parts ; and now that he had returned and was about to assume life's serious responsibilities, they became inseparable companions. He at first entered upon the practice of law; but although he secured reasonable employment, and was thoroughly trained in common, civil, and international law, he found the practice irksome, and lacking in excitement. His ambition was for political distinction, and very soon he quit the law, and became editor of the " Richmond Enquirer," the Democratic organ of Virginia. The touch of a master hand was quickly revealed in that journal. His familiarity with foreign politics, and the new lights shed upon them by his knowledge and criticisms, attracted widespread interest on the part of his fellow-journalists, as well as the public. In domestic politics, his ardent nature was soon made manifest upon every page. Since the death of Father Ritchie, its once famous editor, the " Enquirer " had lost ground, and descended to the level of a staid and humdrum commonplace newspaper.

Within a short time the paper again stood foremost among Southern journals, and my brother's name became as well known as that of his father. His social successes were not less marked than his professional triumphs. Women and children idolized him. And well they might, for he preferred their society to that of men. Passionately fond of music and of dancing, it was his delight to steal away from the sombre circle of his own sex, or leave the after-dinner cigar and wine, to join the ladies in the drawing-room. There he would linger with unsatisfied delight, listening to the music, or dancing until all others were exhausted. An accomplished linguist, with all sorts of interesting knowledge of the world, delightful in conversation, he possessed an indescribable charm for women. Yet, although he was brought into daily contact with exquisite creatures, whom it was almost impossible not to love, his fondness for the other sex seemed altogether platonic.

If a child saw him once, it never forgot him. Children flocked about him as if he had been the Pied Piper of Hamelin. He rejoiced in this sovereignty, and ever went prepared with trifles to surprise and delight them.

One of the most remarkable things about him was his unaffected piety. He never made a profession of religion, yet he was as punctilious in church attendance as an elder; and in the silence of his chamber, where no one saw him, he prayed every night before retiring. Unlike the many blasé youths who are spoiled by residence in France, a long life in Paris had produced no visible effect upon his purity of life or childlike faith. Whoever was thrown with him, young or old, superior or inferior, first wondered at his sweet simplicity, and then loved him for his unaffected naturalness, sincerity, and gentleness. This charming young brother, returning after so long an absence as if from the dead, was a revelation and a source of wonderment from the time I awoke in the morning until I closed my eyes at night. This was literally true, for until his coming, I had never seen anybody open the day, winter and summer, with a plunge into an ice-cold bath; likewise, until his arrival with his Parisian love of the theatre, I had never closed the day at the playhouse with a companion always glad to go, be it ever so bad a show.

My brother Richard, near my own age, had been sent off to boarding-school, leaving me sole occupant of our sleeping apartment. The chambers of the Government House were large and lonesome, and it was with unspeakable pleasure that I obtained consent of the newcomer that my little bed should be placed in his chamber. From this association sprung pleasures innumerable. The marvelous things from Paris and Berlin were sources of unending interest and information. There were the great German Schlagers, or dueling-swords, used by the Heidelberg students in the contests among their fighting corps, and in time I was fully informed about the habits of the German universities. How it tickled me to hear the story of young Sidney Legare, of South Carolina, who joined the Saxon Corps, and, armed with one of these selfsame Schlagers, fought and won his battle with a German baron! The inscriptions on the hilt bore the names of the young Americans who maintained the pluck of the United States among the Continental youth.

There also were fencing-foils and masks, with which he had become so expert in beautiful Paris that he was known in every *salle d'armes*. With these we had many a friendly bout, until I considered myself quite a rattling blade with the foils. Then at times our conversation was in French; especially when I required cash, or proposed some amusement, I plunged away at him with all the French I could command, until I really improved in speaking. From him also I learned much of Parisian court life in the time of Louis Napoleon, and many a day laughed at the stories of the intimacy between Napoleon III. and the Hon. John Y. Mason, of Virginia, the American Minister to France, in whose house my brother had been regarded almost as one of the family.

My bright and joyous room-mate, bustling about o' mornings, making his toilet after his exhilarating bath, often sang snatches of Parisian operas, or repeated long passages from Shakespeare, Byron, and Walter Scott, for he was full of romance. Thus I became familiar with operatic airs, and could repeat many of the striking poetical quotations. And there were the Parisian clothes and toilet articles and preparations, — wonderful French waistcoats and cravats and neckerchiefs, and boots and shoes, and eau de quinine for those curly locks, and pomade for that downy mustache; every one of them strange and new and very captivating to me. I would rub my own frowsy mop of hair, hitherto only half brushed, with that eau de quinine, until my scalp was as red as a lobster, and sighed that I had no mustache on which to test the perfumed stick pomatum. What is there on this earth more delightful to the small boy than rummaging among the toilet outfit and dress of a grown-up brother? And he told me wonderful stories of knights and ladies and tournaments, and put me to reading Sir Walter Scott; and gave me a famous copy of "Charles O'Malley, the Irish Dragoon," and laughed with me over "Handy Andy;" and in the evenings, when lessons were difficult, lifted me along with Cæsar and Virgil or mathematics, that we might go together later to the show. Then there were the German wines he had brought home, four hundred varieties; for, while he was abstemious, and cared little for spirituous or malt liquors, he loved to sip the Rhine wines with his cigar; and I, who was by no means averse to them, was soon an expert in Niersteiners, and Laubenheimers, and Moselle Auslice, and Liebfraumilch, and Johannisbergers, and all the rest; but above all, I loved the sparkling Moselles, which have all my life reminded me of that beloved companion of those happy days. Oh, never had boy a friend and mentor like him, — so lovable, so affectionate, so considerate, so pure, so stimulating to honest work, so willing, so resourceful in innocent amusement.

One night we attended the play of "East Lynne" at the old Richmond Theatre. The performance was poor enough, to be sure, to a young man fresh from Paris, but I thought it was great. On our way home, he remarked that the only performer of merit in the caste was the young fellow, John Wilkes Booth. In him, he said, there was the making of a good actor. The criticism made an impression upon me, who remembered the man and the name. Little did I imagine then that in seven years my beloved companion would be one of the victims of our great national tragedy, or that, at its close, the callow stripling who played before us that night would shock the civilized world with the awful assassination of the President.

And now we come to the antithesis of all these happy incidents. I have dwelt upon him at length with a purpose, — he illustrated a peculiar phase of that civilization. Gentle as was that brother, — tender and loving as he was to every one, devoted as a slave to his father, deferential to his mother as if she had been a queen, courteous and considerate towards the humblest servant who ministered to his wants, honored and beloved by everybody with whom he was thrown, — he was nevertheless as fearless and uncompromising in certain things as the fiercest knight who ever entered the lists. He was, more emphatically than any man I ever knew, the type of the class to which he belonged. He had been educated in a school, at home and abroad, which not only recognized the code duello, but accepted it as the most rational mode of settling private differences.

Of private differences personal to himself, my brother had none. But father's reputation was the object of his care above all others. On one occasion, when asked if his heart had not yet been touched by woman, he replied, " No. My love for father — my desire for his advancement — is the absorbing passion of my life. It leaves no place for other deep affection. Female society is indeed most attractive, but beside the other feeling, it is a mere passing thought. I have no time for other serious love." What an odd speech for the latter half of the nineteenth century ! Does it not sound mediæval ?

In the course of public discussion of public men, there were criticisms of his father, — some facetious, some severe. Concerning such, he had determined upon a line

of action. Quick and hot and insulting came the reply
to every comment of this kind. Then followed, in due
course, the inquiry as to authorship, the avowal, the demand of a retraction, the refusal, the challenge, the duel.
To the young editor, there was nothing alarming in
all this, there was nothing improper, there was nothing
unexpected. He had resolved that whoever criticised
his father should do so at his peril, should be insulted,
should be fought if it was so desired, and that to this
line of conduct he would adhere until such criticism
stopped, or he himself stopped a bullet.

How absurd, how utterly Quixotic, such a course seems
to us to-day! Yet, in that time, not only was it deemed
no absurdity, but a great number of the community, in
fact a majority, regarded it as natural and manly, evincing
chivalry of the very highest order.

Now, whatever other commodities may have been scarce
in Virginia markets of that time, fighting was as easily
obtainable as blackberries in June. Not many young
Virginians were his peers in intellect and accomplishments, but there were many who were as brave and no
more intimidated by the danger of a duel. Many such
were opposed to him in politics, and were unwilling to
forego, from any fear of fighting, the decided expression
of their opinions on politics in general, or of his father
in particular.

The result was that he had all the dueling the most
enthusiastic advocate of the sport could desire, for the
next two years. A cabal of father's political antagonists
held a conclave, if reports were true, and determined that
the son was an obstacle in their way, to be disposed of,
in furtherance of their arrangements to defeat the father.
Under these refined, humane, and highly civilized conditions, my brother Jennings actually fought eight duels in

less than two years. It all seems ludicrous to us, in our prosaic, commonplace, and common-sense way of looking at things nowadays; but it was no joke to me, when every two or three months I missed my beloved companion from his room and bed for several days, only to learn that he was engaged in fighting another duel. Pitiful and anxious indeed were the days and nights passed on such occasions, waiting to know the result. To me it was an enigma past my comprehension. What it was all about, I could not understand. I would read, and read again, the publications leading to these fearful duels; and for the life of me I could not comprehend what there was in them to drive men to seek each other's lives. I could not conceive the mental or moral processes by which my sweet brother, who never quarreled with anybody, could bring himself, without anger, to shoot at another man with deadly intent. And when he returned, laughing at the eagerness of my embraces and welcome, and apparently bearing no ill-will towards anybody or anything on earth, and when I saw him say his prayers at night, and go to church, and mingle in gay society, just as he had done before, the mystery only deepened.

My brother most certainly seemed to bear a charmed life, for no one ever hit him in these many encounters. On the other hand, it was no mystery to me that he hit nobody himself, for I knew that a more execrable shot never went afield. Sometimes, after this abominable dueling began, we practiced with dueling-pistols. His foreign education had trained him only in the use of the broadsword and the foils, and these were not American weapons. On several occasions, I saw enough of his bad marksmanship to know that if he hit anybody it would be by accident; for he was both inexpert and inapt with firearms, and I easily outstripped him in marksmanship.

The thing went on; duel after duel occurred. In one of them, the gallant fellow, after his opponent fired, discharged his pistol in the air, because his adversary was near-sighted and at his mercy. In another, after ineffectual exchange of shots and the customary palaver, matters had been adjusted. At last, on another occasion, the antagonists had actually started to leave the field, when his adversary demanded another shot. His demand was acceded to, and at the next fire my brother succeeded in hitting him, and seriously wounded him. Little credit he deserved for marksmanship; it was another instance like that of the shooter portrayed in " Punch," in which a sportsman, hitting a bird after many failures, appealed to the Scotch game-keeper: " Ah, Sandy, I hit that one." " Yes, sir," was the reply, " they will fly into it sometimes." But whether designed or accidental, this last performance, after making a great hubbub for a few days, resulted in giving him a breathing-spell, and he had no more duels prior to the outbreak of the war.

CHAPTER VIII

UNVEILING OF WASHINGTON'S STATUE, AND REMOVAL OF
MONROE'S REMAINS, 1859

In all her history, from the formation of the federal
government until the hour of secession, no year stands
out more prominently than the year 1858 as evidencing
the national patriotism of Virginia. To one participating
in the scenes enacted in Richmond, and listening to the
speeches of her leaders, the statement that within three
years the old commonwealth would renounce allegiance to
the federal Union would have seemed preposterous.

The State, at great expense, had reared a noble monument to the memory of George Washington. It consists
of a central shaft surmounted by an equestrian statue of
Washington, with six smaller plinths, on which are placed
heroic figures of Virginians, representing different periods
of her greatness.

Not one of these men was famous for deeds done on
behalf of Virginia alone. The fame of each and every
one of them rests upon public services, or sacrifices for the
nation.

Among such, Virginia finds her greatest names.
There was Washington, her son, father of his country ;
there, too, Andrew Lewis, who penetrated the unexplored
wilderness of the Northwest and made it hers. Yet she
joyously ceded all claims upon it to the nation, as her
contribution to perpetual union and fraternity, imposing
only the conditions that slavery should never exist there,

and that alternate sections of land should be dedicated to public education. There was also Patrick Henry, who roused thirteen colonies to revolution with his immortal eloquence; and George Mason, who drafted a bill of rights epitomizing the aspirations and safeguards of republican institutions in language which, from then until now, has furnished the substance of the written charts of government of all the newly admitted States; and Thomas Jefferson, sage, philosopher, and seer, author of the Declaration of Independence, the Statutes of Religious Liberty, and founder of Virginia's university; and General Thomas Nelson, who devoted his fortune to the Continental struggle, and trained an American cannon upon his own house when it was the headquarters of Cornwallis at Yorktown; and John Marshall, who began his public career as captain in a Virginia regiment, served at Valley Forge and Monmouth, and afterwards, as Chief Justice of the United States, was the peerless expounder of that Constitution which he had fought to establish.

Oh, what a galaxy of men, encompassing the very heavens of our national life! What other commonwealth could produce its like then? What other can produce it now?

Is it surprising that the Virginians, whose State was mother of the nation's father, whose great Chief Justice, the youngest of the immortal group, was the lodestar of constitutional construction, loved that Union and rejoiced in it, and honored it from their hearts' inmost depths?

In other States, jealousies and animosities against the Union may have existed, but, up to that time at least, such sentiments found little lodgment in the breasts of the Virginians.

With beating hearts and honest pride, they assembled from every section, February 22, 1858, to unveil the equestrian statue of Washington. The figures of Henry and Jefferson had preceded that of Washington, and were on their appropriate plinths. Poor Crawford, the sculptor in charge of the work, had died from over-exertion in Rome after the Washington figure was cast and shipped to America. The presence of his widow lent an additional and pathetic interest to the scene about to be enacted.

The vessel bearing the statue arrived at Richmond from Italy some weeks before the unveiling. The male population of the city, men and boys, dragged the statue through the streets from the wharves to the Capitol grounds, a distance of over a mile. Enthusiasm was unbounded on every hand.

Of all these new sights I there beheld, that which captivated me most was the corps of cadets of the Virginia Military Institute. The State owned an arsenal at Lexington, in the valley between the Blue Ridge and the Alleghanies. Prior to 1839, she kept a guard at this arsenal. In that year, she established there a military school, in charge of Captain Francis H. Smith, a distinguished graduate of West Point. It was organized strictly on the lines of the United States Military Academy, as to drill, discipline, tuition, and all else. At first the number of cadets was limited to a few, who received board and tuition free, and in return guarded the property of the State, and agreed to teach school for a certain period after graduation. By degrees, a large number of cadets were admitted upon condition that they pay for board and tuition. The school grew; extensive buildings were erected; and in 1858 the Virginia Military Institute had over three hundred cadets, and was the best establishment of the kind in the United States, except the United States Military Academy. It resembled the latter in everything but in the liberality of appropriations, and the assurance of an appointment to the army. Its original superintendent remained in charge, and he continued to hold the office for fifty years. To this uniformity of administration much of the high reputation of the school was no doubt attributable.

The appearance of the corps on the above occasion, the first on which I ever saw it, was sufficient to excite the wildest enthusiasm of a small boy. Never before had I seen such trim, alert figures; such clean, saucy-looking uniforms; such machine-like precision and quickness of drill; such silence and obedience. From the first day my eye rested on the cadet corps, the height of boyish ambition was to be a cadet. Four companies of infantry and a section of artillery drawn by " rats " constituted the cadet outfit.

The " rats " referred to were not genuine rats like those attached to Cinderella's coach, but "plebes," or new cadets, who, until they remain a year and hear " Auld Lang Syne " played at the graduation exercises, are called "rats." The only thing about this fine body that struck me as in any way lacking in soldierly appearance was the commandant of the infantry battalion. He was not my ideal of a soldier, either in military bearing, or in the manner in which he gave his commands. His uniform was not new; his old blue forage-cap sat on the back of his head; and he stood like a horse " sprung " in the knees. His commands were given in a piping, whining tone, and he appeared to be deeply intent upon his business, without paying much regard to the onlookers. On the other hand, the officer commanding the section of artillery was the model of a martinet. He was petite, quick as a lizard, straight as a ramrod, and his commands were delivered like the crack of a whiplash. I thought him a perfect commanding officer.

The cadets were quartered in the Richmond Lyceum. When the ceremonies were over, the small boys collected about the corps like flies about molasses, and, when the cadets marched off to their quarters, followed them, I among the foremost. I knew several of the cadets. When the command was halted near its quarters, we boys crowded around it in such a way that we inconvenienced the officer in charge. He passed along the line, tapping us back with the flat side of his sword, exclaiming in a deprecatory voice, " Get away, little boys! Get away — get A–W–A–Y ! " It was ludicrous, and I could detect smiles, even on the faces of the thoroughly disciplined cadets ; but something in the manner of the officer made the boys get away, and get away in a hurry.

When the parade was dismissed, on inquiring about the officers, I learned that the odd-looking commandant was familiarly called " Old Jack ; " that his real name was Major Jackson ; and that the cadets, while disposed to make light of him for his eccentricities, dared not trifle with him. As to the other officer, Major Gilham, all agreed that he was the best drill-officer and tactician they had ; that he was far superior to Major Jackson ; and they spoke with profound respect of the infantry tactics of which he was the author.

At the grand reception given that night by my father, I again saw both these officers, and their bearing confirmed me in the judgment that there was no question which was the superior soldier. Major Jackson was plainly dressed, wore coarse shoes, had a weary look in his blue eyes, took very little part in conversation, seemed bored by the entertainment, neither ate nor drank, and, after paying his respects to the governor, and to General Winfield Scott, commander-in-chief of the armies of the United States, quietly disappeared. Colonel Gilham, on the other hand, was urbane, ubiquitous, and remained until the close of the entertainment.

In after years, I had occasion to revise my opinion of the relative ability of these two men, for Major Jackson was none other than the immortal Stonewall; and Major Gilham, while brave enough, never rose beyond the rank of colonel, and retired from active service in 1862 to resume his professorship at the Institute.

And "Old Fuss and Feathers!" — bless his colossal old soul! was ever a name more appropriately bestowed? — I saw him also that day, for the first time. What a monster in size he was! Never was uniform more magnificent; never were feathers in cocked hat more profuse; never was sash so broad and gorgeous. He was old and gouty, keen for food, quick for drink, and thunderous of voice, large as a straw-stack, and red as a boiled lobster. His talk was like the roaring of a lion, his walk like the tread of the elephant. No turkey-gobbler ever strutted or gobbled with more self-importance than did the hero of Lundy's Lane. The women flattered him, and he liked it. The men toasted him, and he never refused to join or to respond. As long as he remained, he was the cynosure of all present. When he withdrew, a characteristic incident occurred. In the great hallway, he called for his wraps and his galoshes. The servants were quick to hurry forward with them. Several cadets had been invited to the entertainment, and were standing about awestruck in the presence of the commander-in-chief.

As the servants offered him his cloaks and overshoes, he waved them away imperiously, and in his commanding voice thundered out, "No, no! Let the cadets attend upon me. Here, you cadets! Help me with my overshoes and wraps. It is not every day that I can get such orderlies, and it is not every day that you can wait upon the general of the armies." The boys leaped forward to his assistance, delighted at such distinguished condescension, and soon had him fully caparisoned. With his arms about their shoulders, he laboriously descended the sleety marble steps, shouted back some cheery words to those watching on the portico, entered the fine carriage which awaited him, slammed the door, and drove away, snorting and puffing, in all his majesty.

What a wonderful mixture of gasconade, ostentation, fuss, feathers, bluster, and genuine soldierly talent and courage was this same Winfield Scott of blessed memory! A great smoking mass of flesh and blood! So devoted to epicurean enjoyment that, even when he was candidate for President, he lugged into his public papers allusion to his " hasty plate of soup." But for all that, a splendid soldier in the service of his country for over fifty years. What a contrast he presented to his favorite companion, — gentle, quiet Colonel Lee!

It was days after this glorious celebration before its excitements subsided sufficiently to enable me to concentrate my reluctant mind upon Latin, French, and mathematics.

Delightful, inspiring to patriotism, exhilarating, as were the ceremonies at the unveiling of the Washington statue, the scenes enacted in Richmond in July of that same year outstripped them far in gorgeousness, and in the display of fraternal feelings between the North and South.

In the month of April, the Virginia legislature made provision for the removal of the remains of Ex-President James Monroe from the city of New York to the capital of Virginia.

Mr. Monroe had been buried in New York with appropriate honors, interred in a private cemetery vault, pur-

chased by his daughters, and there his ashes " awaited
the call of his native State " for twenty-seven years. At
the time the Virginia legislature made that call, his only
surviving descendants were three children of Mrs. Gouverneur. The eldest, bearing his name, deeply afflicted
by Providence, and the second, a daughter, spoke through
their father, Samuel L. Gouverneur of Frederick County,
Maryland ; the third, Samuel L. Gouverneur, Jr., spoke
for himself. All assented to the removal.

The public announcement of the intention of his native
State to reclaim his ashes was the signal for a great out-
burst of patriotic fervor in Virginia and in New York.

Virginians residing in New York held meetings looking to the disinterment there with appropriate ceremonies ;
the city authorities at once passed the necessary resolutions. Committees of conference were sent from Virginia.
A steamship was chartered to convey the remains, and the
New York military vied with one another for the honor of
acting as military escort. So great was the enthusiasm
that it culminated in a tender, by the Seventh Regiment
of New York, of their escort of the remains at their own
expense, as a guard of honor from New York to Richmond. This being accepted, that splendid body of citizen
soldiery chartered the Ericcson steamer, and made ready
for their patriotic pilgrimage.

The Richmond military were all busy with preparations
to receive their guests. The public grounds, the Capitol,
all public places, were filled with workmen erecting arches,
painting patriotic emblems, hanging thousands of colored
lanterns, and draping the city in mourning. The Fourth
of July fell that year upon Sunday. Consequently, the
arrival of the remains and the military escort was timed
for Monday, July 5. At daybreak and at sunrise the
Fayette Artillery, a local volunteer organization, fired the

national salute in the Capitol Square. At six o'clock, the flags upon the public buildings, hotels, and shipping were placed at half mast. The citizens were still engaged draping their residences and places of business in the habiliments of mourning. The Henrico Light Dragoons, the Public Guard, the First Virginia Regiment, the Young Guard Battalion, and the Rocky Ridge Rifles from the neighboring town of Manchester formed line at seven o'clock and marched to Rocketts, the landing-place of the steamer Jamestown, bearing the remains of President Monroe. Upon the neighboring hillsides were gathered thousands of people, men and women, white and black, of every condition in life. Carriages, omnibuses, and baggage-wagons were drawn up in long lines near the wharf ; marshals and field-officers rode hither and thither giving orders, and scattering the crowds to right and left before them. Flaunting flags, and signals at half mast, were visible everywhere; civic organizations with bands and banners followed the military. The whole community was in a ferment of expectation.

" The day opened clear and beautiful, the intense heat relieved by a pleasant southerly breeze. The local troops stacked arms, and waited the arrival of the steamers.

" The Jamestown came in sight at ten minutes past eight o'clock, and slowly approached the wharf, with flags and signals at half halliards. As the ship came alongside her wharf, the committee and guests from New York stood on the upper deck, and regarded with much interest the exciting scene on shore.

" The remains of President Monroe having been re-moved from the forward saloon to the upper deck and placed under an awning, the governor and mayor pro-ceeded on board the Jamestown and received the guests, and an interchange of friendly greetings took place. The remains were attended by a detachment of the New York National Guard, but after their arrival, they were relieved by a platoon of the Richmond Grays, detailed for the purpose.

" The steamer Glen Cove, with the New York Seventh Regiment on board, came in sight at ten minutes past ten, and, despite the solemnity of the occasion, the younger portion of the assembled throng gave vent to their feelings in a cheer.   As the steamer approached the wharf, her appearance was really imposing.   The soldiers, with their glittering arms, were paraded ready for debarkation, while the splendid band of the Seventh, stationed on the forward deck, played a solemn dirge.

" The Virginia troops were drawn up in line, facing the river, ready to receive the visitors, and without unnecessary delay the Seventh left the boat, and passed on to the right of the line, the Virginia military presenting arms as they marched by.

" The hearse, drawn by six white horses, attended by six negro grooms dressed in white, now proceeded to the steamer, and, under the direction of the pall-bearers, received the remains.   The troops presented arms, flags were lowered, drums rolled, and trumpets sounded, after which the Armory Band played a dirge, while the hearse proceeded to its place in the line.   Minute-guns were fired and bells tolled, continuing during the progress of the procession to the cemetery.

" The procession moved at half past eleven o'clock.

" The route lay directly up Main Street to Second, down Second to Cary, and thence out to Hollywood.   All along the route of the procession, a distance of more than two miles, the sidewalks were lined with spectators ; every balcony, porch, and window overlooking the street, every available spot on the line, was crowded with ladies, chil-

dren, and men. The minute-guns continued firing ; the
bells in the vicinity of the route tolled, answered by peals
from others in the distance ; business was universally suspended ; and the attention of the entire community was
concentrated on the imposing pageant in honor of the
memory of the illustrious man whose bones were now on
the way to their earthly resting-place.

" The troops marched with reversed arms, and the
bands played music appropriate to the occasion.

" The grave of Monroe is located in the southwest corner of Hollywood, on an eminence commanding a magnificent view of the city, the river, and the environs.

" After the line was formed around the grave, the coffin
was removed from the hearse. When the remains were
lowered into the grave, the troops presented arms, the
Seventh Regiment rested on arms, and the band played a
dirge. This portion of the ceremony being over, the governor appeared on the front of the platform and spoke : —

" ' COUNTRYMEN AND FELLOW CITIZENS : The General
Assembly of the Commonwealth has ordered that the
remains of James Monroe, one of the most honored and
best beloved of her sons, shall, under the direction and at
the discretion of the governor, be removed from the public burying-ground in the city of New York to the cemetery at the city of Richmond. The remains are removed,
the cenotaph is open, and we are here assembled to inter
them in their last resting-place with becoming ceremonies.

.   .   .   .

" ' Venerable Patriot ! — he found his rest soon after
he retired. On the 4th of July, 1831, twenty-seven years
ago, he departed, like Jefferson and Adams, on the anniversary of the Independence. His spirit was caught up
to heaven, and his ashes were enshrined in the soil of his
adopted State, whose daughter he had married, — of that

grand and prosperous Commonwealth whose motto is " Excelsior," our sister New York, the Empire State of the United States of America.   Virginia was the natural mother of Monroe, and New York was his mother-in-law, — Virginia by birth and baptism, New York by marriage and burial.   This was well, for he gave to her invaders the glaived hand of " bloody welcome " at Trenton, and New York gave to him a " hospitable grave."   Virginia respectfully allowed his ashes to lie long enough to consecrate her sister's soil, and now has dutifully taken them to be " earth to her earth and ashes to her ashes," at home in the land of his cradle.   New York has graciously bowed to the family request, has disinterred the remains, has laid them out in state, and has sent the élite of her chivalry to escort them with banners and trumpets, in military and civic procession, to our cemetery.   Who knows this day, here around this grave, that New York is of the North, and that Virginia is of the South ?   " The North has given up," and " the South shall not hold back," and they are one, even as all the now proud and preëminent thirty-two are one.

" ' We affectionately, then, welcome New York, and cordially embrace her around the grave of him, Virginia's son, to whom she gave a resting-place in life and in death. And now I call the minister of God to pray for his blessing on this passing scene.   I ask the righteous man to pray fervently and effectually for the example of this patriot's life to be blessed to the youth of our country, — blessed to the people of this generation ; blessed to the public men of New York and Virginia and the United States; blessed to the cause of truth and justice and human freedom ; and blessed to the perpetual strength, peace, liberty, and union of this confederacy, " one and indivisible, now and forever ! "   May the good which this patriot did be revived by the disinterment of his bones, and may monuments of wisdom and virtue like his be so multiplied and raised around yonder Capitol of the Mother of States, that the very statues of her heroes and sages and patriots dead and departed shall be the moral guide-marks of her living and active servants, to preserve this Commonwealth, untorn in destiny and untarnished in glory, to "the last syllable of recorded time," when the tenants of Hollywood, this beautiful city of the dead, shall rise to immortal life!'"

Of these inspiring scenes I was a silent but interested witness. Every manifestation of patriotic and fraternal feeling thrilled me to my inmost soul. From time to time I had heard the mutterings of discontent and the prophesies of approaching conflict, but the scenes which I beheld, and the burning words and thundering shouts I heard that day, put at rest the last feeling of fear for the future of my country.

At the close of the ceremonies at the grave, the artillery, stationed outside the inclosure, fired three salvos.

Upon the day following, the delirious city was given a specimen of the drill and efficiency of the glorious Seventh Regiment. Its appearance and perfection in drill and discipline were beyond all expectations. After a review by the governor, Colonel Duryee drilled the regiment, without music, in various battalion movements.

I stood agape at every evolution. The Virginia troops, which I had theretofore regarded as perfection itself, seemed to me now a mere incongruous lot of painted toys, contrasted with this homogeneous mass of military, neat, brilliant in cleanliness, and absolutely without gaudiness. In the Richmond regiment no two companies were of the same size, and no two uniformed alike. The Grays were gray, the Blues were blue, the Montgomery Guard was green as the waters of Niagara, the Riflemen blue and green, the Young Guard blue and red. One company had waving plumes of white, another short pompons, a third red and white plumes. When they were drawn up in line, they looked deplorably irregular, contrasted with the absolute uniformity of the handsome Seventh.

It seemed incredible that I, a protégé, in fact a veteran, of the Richmond military, — I, who until now had looked upon the First Virginia Regiment as the finest body of troops on earth, — could come to regard it as almost contemptible in the short space of twenty-four hours.

Yet there were others like me.

Said one paper : —

" The recent visit of the Seventh Regiment of New York to our city, it is to be hoped, will have a good effect on our volunteer organization. We could but regard the simple uniform of the entire regiment, and the neat and unostentatious dress of its officers, as presenting a wide contrast with the parti-colored line of our volunteers, and the fine decorations and pompous display which meet the eye in surveying our regimental parades.

" We have not a doubt that the volunteer force of the city would be strengthened, would be increased in numbers and improved in discipline, if they would consolidate themselves into one regiment, abandon their uniforms, and adopt a new and plain dress for the whole body of soldiers."

Little did the writer know, and less did the Seventh Regiment suspect, that upon this visit they fixed, in the Southern mind, a type of uniform which, within three years, was substantially adopted by the Confederate States.

Three years after this date, the First Virginia Regiment had fought in the battle of Manassas ; and the Seventh was encamped at Arlington Heights, but fifteen miles' distant, being part of a hostile force moving against Mount Vernon and Richmond. Such was the rapid march of events.

After the scenes above described had closed, and the military had departed, the remainder of the year glided away uneventfully; but the glorious memories of July 5 lingered, and all Richmond was busy in the effort to have a real military force such as it had seen, and to abandon the past methods of its volunteer system. As for patriotic national feeling, it is safe to say that, when the year 1859 opened, in spite of Southern fire-eaters and Northern fanatics, there were not, in the whole State of Virginia, five thousand men who had any sort of sympathy with the idea of secession.

CHAPTER IX

THE declamation against disunion and the mutual pledges of fraternal love between North and South, which attended the banquet to the Seventh New York Regiment in Richmond, arose in great part from a knowledge of sectional feeling, threats of disunion, and of partisan recriminations between politicians, but too familiar to all who spoke. At the same time, an intense antagonism to slavery existed in sections of the North and West, accompanied by the determination to abolish it by any means in their power, lawful or unlawful.

Little effort has been made to record the fact, yet it is nevertheless true, that many Southern men were working earnestly and loyally towards the adoption of some plan of gradual emancipation which, while it would free the slave, would not destroy the labor system of the South or leave the slave-owner impoverished. The abolitionist did not believe this. He was uncharitable in his judgment of the humanity of the slave-owner; and his demand that a difficult problem, requiring time for its solution, should be disposed of at once and in his way — *per fas aut nefas* — was strongly provoking. The attitude of the people of the North generally concerning escaped slaves seemed to the Southerners inconsistent, and tended to increase the friction between the sections. The people of the North professed great reverence for their constitutional obligations, and constantly disclaimed a purpose to interfere with slavery where it existed. They insisted that they were only opposed to the spread of slavery into the free States or Territories, and would respect the rights of the slave-owner where slavery already existed. Yet, whenever a slave escaped, the Northern community in which he sought asylum was practically unanimous in thinking it a great outrage and hardship if he was pursued into their territory and taken back to his owner. It is often said that, before the war, only a small portion of the Northern people belonged to the abolition party. Whether that was true or not, it is certain that a vast majority of every Northern community was in sympathy with obstacles thrown in the way of recapturing escaped slaves. Everybody, North and South, was well aware that in many instances the slave was enticed from his home by abolition emissaries. Yet when he reached the North, thousands who would not have gone South to incite him to escape did all they could to make the work of the emissaries effectual.

In such a condition of affairs, the practical difference between the abolitionist and the sympathizer, to the man who lost his slave and could not recover it, was very nebulous. From certain descriptions of these times, one would think that all the threats and taunts were made, and all the provocations were given, by the Southerners. At this late day, such a contention is nonsense. No more defiant, vindictive, or aggressive speech was ever made than that of Charles Sumner, senator from Massachusetts, in the United States Senate in 1859, on the " Barbarism of Slavery." He had a personal grievance, it is true; he had been brutally assaulted in that chamber years before, and his speech bore every mark of being the result of

> " The patient watch and vigil long
> Of him who treasures up a wrong."

It is not justifying the assault made upon Mr. Sumner by Preston S. Brooks to say that no man ever did more to provoke an attack upon himself than did Mr. Sumner. His speech in 1856 was able, studied in its malignity, and all the more provoking from its strength. Nor was Sumner the only man of that class. We may search through the congressional debates in vain for more coarse and insulting language than that used by Senator Ben Wade, of Ohio, upon the floor of the Senate. Every opportunity was taken by him to lead the debates in the Senate into sectional channels.

Acquisition of Cuba is more advocated in the North to-day than in the South. In 1860, the project was branded by the Republicans in the Senate as a slaveholder's scheme for securing additional representation. The proposition then made by Senator Slidell, to purchase Cuba for thirty million dollars, was flouted by Wade and his party as a mere ruse for providing " niggers for the niggerless." Jealousy, antagonism, and hatred between the sections animated the representatives of both, and neither lost any opportunity to vituperate and recriminate.

While this was the condition of feeling among the politicians, it had not yet extended to the masses. For several years, the conflict had been in progress between the free-soilers and pro-slavery men in Kansas. The Virginians were conservative in their views about that struggle. They realized that the men engaged in it on both sides were a bloodthirsty and disreputable lot. Leading Virginians, supporters of Mr. Buchanan, warned him not to go too far in subserviency to the extreme pro-slavery men, or to force a pro-slavery constitution upon the State. Virginians, while they heard of the fanatical and bloody butcheries committed in Kansas by one " Old Brown," and men of his class, also heard of equally horrid crimes committed by the pro-slavery men. They held both in abhorrence, and indorsed neither.

It was not the Kansas trouble that occasioned them concern, or excited their apprehensions concerning the Union. It was the announcement by Abraham Lincoln, of Illinois, in his debate with Douglas in 1858, that the Union was a house divided against itself, and that slavery and union could not coexist. It was declarations like those of Senator Seward, of New York, that " an irrepressible conflict " existed between the North and South. It was speeches of men like Charles Sumner, breathing deep malice against the South, and denouncing it in polished oratory. These and a hundred others like them from men of the North, less prominent but not less representative, made Virginians realize that the times were perilous, and say to themselves : " If this temple of union is divided against itself and must fall, if slavery and union cannot coexist, if an irrepressible conflict is upon us, if Mr. Sumner expresses the state of Northern sentiment, it is manifest that the hour of disunion is here. The only thing remaining for us to do is to begin to consider which side of us the line of cleavage shall come, north or south. "

Virginians were no more angels or philanthropists than people to the north or to the south of them. They were moved by their affections, their interest, and their resentments, just as humanity is moved to-day. Their strongest social ties were with the Southern people. They had a great part of their wealth invested in slaves ; and, while far in advance of the States to the south of them in the desire for some plan of gradual emancipation, they were not willing to have their property unceremoniously jostled out of their hands without compensation, to gratify Mr. Lincoln, Mr. Seward, Mr. Sumner, Mr. Wade, or the

constituencies which they represented.   They thought the
conditions of future association announced by these men a
rather high and hasty price for the privilege.   And, lastly,
their very love of the Union inflamed them against men
who, as they viewed it, were making union impossible,
except on terms involving humiliating surrender to the
abolitionist.

It is often said by writers that Mr. Lincoln and Mr.
Seward, when they spoke of a divided house, the im-
possibility of the coexistence of union and slavery, and
the " irrepressible conflict," were simply stating abstract
propositions, and did not mean that they would counsel
a physical assault upon slavery or the enactment of
unconstitutional laws, and that their figures of speech
referred only to the logic of the political situation.   Their
language may have been intended as statements of
abstract principles ; but, assuredly, what they said was
susceptible of, and received, quite another construction.
By their followers and opponents they were understood as
declaring war on slavery, immediate and uncompromising.

As for Mr. Sumner and Mr. Wade, nobody pretended
that they meant anything else.   The Southerners may
have been more demonstrative and noisy in their quarrels ;
but they were not a whit more stubborn, aggressive,
defiant, or irritating than the men of the North.   The
Southern man scoffed the pretense that the Northern man
really desired union, when he refused to subordinate his
demands concerning slavery to any other consideration.
The Northern man denounced the Southern man as hating the Union, because he would not consent to remain
in it, even if he believed that the North, while professing
the purpose of respecting his right, at heart intended to
deprive him of his slave property on the first opportunity.

This political warfare was very intense in 1858-59.   The

debates between Lincoln and Douglas on the slavery
question, in the autumn of 1858, kindled the fires of
slavery and anti-slavery discussion on every hilltop. In
1859, the awful tragedy in which Senator Broderick was
killed by Judge Terry in California, in a duel growing
out of the slavery question, lent fuel to the flame.

Just at this crisis an event occurred, which was made a
test, in the mind of the average Virginian, of the real feeling of the North towards the South. After it happened, he
set himself to determining what was the real meaning,
the real tendency, and what was to be the outcome, of the
doctrines announced by Mr. Lincoln, Mr. Seward, Mr.
Sumner, and others during the years 1858 and 1859.
He believed that in the expressions of the North, concerning this event, he would find the best evidence of what
their real sentiments were towards the South.

The attack of John Brown upon Harper's Ferry came
upon Virginia like a clap of thunder out of a clear sky.

In the afternoon of October 17, 1859, I was passing
along Main Street in Richmond, when I observed a crowd
of people gathering about the bulletin board of a newspaper. In those days, news did not travel so rapidly as
now; besides which, the telegraph lines at the place from
which the news came were cut.

The first report read : —

" There is trouble of some sort at Harper's Ferry. A
party of workmen have seized the Government Armory."

Soon another message flashed : " The men at Harper's
Ferry are not workmen. They are Kansas border ruffians,
who have attacked and captured the place, fired upon and
killed several unarmed citizens, and captured Colonel
Washington and other prominent citizens of the neighborhood. We cannot understand their plans or ascertain
their numbers."

By this time an immense throng had assembled, agape with wonder.

Naturally reflecting that the particulars of an outbreak like this would first reach the governor, I darted homeward. I found my father in the library, roused from his afternoon siesta, in the act of reading the telegrams which he had just received. They were simply to the effect that the arsenal and government property at Harper's Ferry were in possession of a band of rioters, without describing their character. I promptly and breathlessly told what I had seen on the bulletin boards, and, while I was hurriedly delivering my news, other messengers arrived with telegrams to the same effect as those posted in the streets. The governor was by this time fully aroused. He was prompt in action. His first move was to seize the Virginia code, take a reference, and indite a telegram addressed to Colonel John Thomas Gibson, of Charlestown, commandant of the militia regiment within whose territory the invasion had occurred, directing him to order out, for the defense of the State, the militia under his command, and immediately report what he had done.

Within ten minutes after the receipt of the telegram, these instructions were on the way. Similar instructions were flashed to Colonel Robert W. Baylor, of the Third Regiment of Militia Cavalry.

The military system of the State was utterly inefficient, having nothing but skeleton organization. The telegrams continued to come rapidly, describing a condition of excitement amounting to a panic in the neighborhood of Harper's Ferry. The numbers of the attacking force were exaggerated, until some reports placed them as high as a thousand. The ramifications of the conspiracy were of course unknown.

I was promptly dispatched to summon the Secretary of

the Commonwealth, the Adjutant-General, and the colonel
and adjutant of the First Regiment. I found almost immediately all but the adjutant, for whom I searched long.
At last this young gentleman was discovered, all unconscious of impending trouble, playing dominoes in a German restaurant, and regaling himself with the then
comparatively new drink of " lager." Hurrying back
with my last capture, we found the others assembled, and
instantly the adjutant received instructions to order out
the First Virginia Regiment at eight o'clock P. M., armed
and equipped, and provided with three days' rations, at
the Washington depot.

In those days, the track ran down the centre of the
street, and the depot was in the most popular portion of
the city. News of the disturbance having gone abroad, it
was an easy task to assemble the regiment; and, by the
time appointed, all Richmond was on hand to learn the
true meaning of the outbreak, and witness the departure
of the troops. Company after company marched through
the streets to the rendezvous. The governor transferred
his headquarters to the depot, where he and his staff
awaited the last telegrams which might arrive before his
departure. Telegrams were sent to the President and to
the governor of Maryland for authority to pass through
the District of Columbia and Maryland with armed
troops, that route being the quickest to Harper's Ferry.
The dingy old depot, generally so dark and gloomy at
this hour of the night, was brilliantly illuminated. The
train of cars, which was to transfer the troops, stood
in the middle of the street. The regiment was formed
as the companies arrived, and was resting in the badly
lighted street, awaiting final orders.

The masses of the populace swarming about the soldiers presented every variety of excitement, interest, and
curiosity.

As for me, my " mannishness " (there is no other word expressive of it) was such that, forgetting what an insignificant chit I was, I actually attempted to accompany the troops.

Transported by enthusiasm, I rushed home, donned a little blue jacket with brass buttons and a navy cap, selected a Virginia rifle nearly half as tall again as myself, rigged myself with a powder-horn and bullets, and, availing myself of the darkness, crept into the line of K Company. The file-closers and officers knew me, and indulged me to the extent of not interfering with me, never doubting the matter would adjust itself. Other small boys, who got a sight of me standing there, were variously affected. Some were green with envy, while others ridiculed me with pleasant suggestions concerning what would happen when father caught me.

In time, the order to embark was received. I came to "attention" with the others, went through the orders, marched into the car, and took my seat. It really looked as if the plan was to succeed. Alas and alas for these hopes! One incautious utterance had thwarted all my plans. When I went home to caparison myself for war, the household had been too much occupied to observe my preparations. I succeeded in donning my improvised uniform, secured my arms, and had almost reached the outer door of the basement, when I encountered Lucy, one of the slave chambermaids.

" Hi! Mars' John. Whar is you gwine? " exclaimed Lucy, surprised.

" To Harper's Ferry," was the proud reply, and off I sped.

" I declar', I b'leeve that boy thinks hisself a man, sho' 'nuff," said Lucy, as she glided into the house. It was not long before she told Eliza, the housekeeper, who in

turn hurried to my invalid mother with the news. She
summoned Jim, the butler, and sent him to father with
the information.

Now Jim, the butler, was one of my natural enemies.
However the Southern man may have been master of the
negro, there were compensatory processes whereby certain
negroes were masters of their masters' children. Never
was autocracy more absolute than that of a Virginia butler. Jim may have been father's slave, but I was Jim's
minion, and felt it. There was no potentate I held in
greater reverence, no tyrant whose mandates I heard in
greater fear, no ogre whose grasp I should have felt with
greater terror. This statement may not be fully appreciated by others, but will touch a responsive chord in the
heart of every Southern-bred man who passed his youth in
a household where " Uncle Charles," or " Uncle Henry,"
or " Uncle Washington," or uncle somebody, wielded the
sceptre of authority as family butler. Bless their old souls,
dead and gone, what did they want with freedom ? They
owned and commanded everything and everybody that
came into their little world. Even their own masters and
mistresses were dependent upon them to an extent that
only increased their sense of their own importance. What
Southern boy will ever forget the terrors of that frown
which met him at the front door and scanned his muddy
foot-marks on the marble steps ? What roar was ever
more terrible — what grasp more icy or relentless — than
those of his father's butler surprising him in the cake-
box or the preserve-jar ? What criminal, dragged to justice, ever appeared before the court more thoroughly
cowed into subjection than the Southern boy led before
the head of the house in the strong grip of that domestic
despot ?

" What ! " exclaimed the governor, on hearing Jim's

report of my escapade, " is that young rascal really trying to go ? Hunt him up, Jim ! Capture him ! Take
away his arms, and march him home in front of
you ! " Laughing heartily, he resumed his work, well
knowing that Jim understood his orders and would execute them.

Think of such authority given to a negro, just when
John Brown was turning the heads of the slaves with
ideas of their own importance ! Is it not monstrous ? I
was sitting in a car, enjoying the sense of being my country's defender starting for the wars, when I recognized a
well-known voice in the adjoining car, inquiring, " Gentlemen, is any ov you seed anythin' ov de Gov'ner's little boy
about here ? I 'm a-lookin' fur him under orders to take
him home."

I shoved my long squirrel-rifle under the seats and followed it, amid the laughter of those about me. I heard
the dread footsteps approach, and the inquiry repeated.
No voice responded ; but, by the silence and the tittering,
I knew I was betrayed. A great, shiny black face, with
immense whites to the eyes, peeped almost into my own,
and, with a broad grin, said, " Well, I declar' ! Here
you is at las' ! Cum out, Mars' John." But John did
not come. Jim, after coaxing a little, seized a leg, and,
as he drew me forth, clinging to my long rifle, he exclaimed, " Well, 'fore de Lord ! how much gun has dat
boy got, anyhow ? " and the soldiers went wild with laughter.

In full possession of the gun, and pushing me before
him, Jim marched his prisoner home. Once or twice I
made a show of resistance, but it was in vain. " Here,
you boy ! You better mind how you cut yo' shines.
You must er lost yo' senses. Yo' father told me to take
you home. I gwine do it, too, you understand ? Ef

you don't mind, I 'll take you straight to him, and you
know and I know dat if I do, he 'll tare you up alive fur
botherin' him with yo' foolishiss, busy ez he is." I realized that it was even so, and, sadly crestfallen, was delivered into my mother's chamber, where, after a lecture
upon the folly of my course, I was kept until the Harper's
Ferry expedition was fairly on its way.

What I learned of events at Harper's Ferry was derived from the testimony of others. The First Virginia
Regiment reached Washington; but, on arrival there,
the Richmond troops returned, in consequence of the
news of the capture of all the insurgents at Harper's
Ferry by the United States Marines.

This mad effort, so quickly and so terribly ended, was
in itself utterly insignificant. John Brown, its leader,
was the character of murderous monomaniac found at
the head of every such desperate venture. He has often
been described as a Puritan in faith and in type. It is not
the province of this writer to inquire into the correctness
of this classification. He was an uncompromising, bloodthirsty fanatic. Born in the year 1800, he lived for fifty-
six years without any sort of prominence. He was never
successful in business ventures, had farmed, raised sheep,
experimented in grape culture, made wine, and engaged
in growing and buying wool. At one time in his life, and
up to a period not long before his death, he was regarded
as an infidel by his associates, although at the time of his
death he declared himself a true believer. In October,
1855, he appeared in Kansas, and at once became prominent as a leader of armed bands of free-soilers. On his
way to the defense of Lawrence, in 1856, he heard of the
destruction which had taken place there, and turned back.
He resolved to avenge the acts of the pro-slavery horde.
He reckoned up that five free-soil men had been killed,

and resolved that their blood should be expiated by an equal number of victims.

" Without the shedding of blood, there is no remission of sins," was a favorite text with Brown. He called for volunteers to go on a secret expedition, and held a sort of Druidical conclave before starting out. Four sons, a son-in-law, and two others accompanied him. He had a strange power of imbuing his dupes with his own fanaticism. When he avowed his purpose to massacre the pro-slavery men living on Pottawatomie Creek, one of his followers demurred. Brown said, " I have no choice. It has been decreed by Almighty God that I should make an example of these men."

On Saturday night, May 24, 1856, John Brown and his band visited house after house upon Pottawatomie Creek, and, calling man after man from his bed, murdered five in cold blood. They first visited the house of Doyle, and compelled a father and two sons to go with them. The next morning, the father and one son were found dead in the road about two hundred yards from the house. The father was " shot in the forehead and stabbed in the breast. The son's head was cut open, and there was a hole in his jaw as though made by a knife." The other son was found dead about a hundred and fifty yards away in the grass, " his fingers cut off and his arms cut off, his head cut open, and a hole in his breast."

Then they went to Wilkinson's, reaching there after midnight. They forced open the door and ordered him to go with them. His wife was sick and helpless, and begged them not to take him away. Her prayer was of no avail. The next day Wilkinson was found dead, " a gash in his head and side."

Their next victim was William Sherman. When found in the morning, his " skull was split open in two places,

and some brains were washed out. A large hole was cut
in his breast, and his left hand was cut off, except a little
piece of skin on one side." The execution was done with
short cutlasses brought from Ohio by Brown.

"It was said that on the next morning, when the old
man raised his hands to Heaven to ask a blessing, they
were still stained with the dry blood of his victims." [1] In
his life by Sanborn is a picture of him made about this
time. It represents him clean-shaven, and is, no doubt,
the best picture extant by which to study the physiog-
nomy of a man capable of these things.

The tidings of these executions caused a cry of horror
to go up, even in bloody Kansas. The squatters on
Pottawatomie Creek, without distinction of party, met
together and denounced the outrage and its perpetrators.
The free-state men everywhere disavowed such methods.
The governor sent a military force to the Pottawatomie
to discover the assassins. The border ruffians took the
field to avenge the massacre. One Pate, feeling sure
"Old Brown," as he was called, was the author of the
outrage, went in search of him. Brown met him, gave
battle, and captured Pate and his command.

Kansas was in a state of civil war; the governor ordered all armed companies to disperse; and Colonel Sumner, with fifty United States dragoons, forced Brown to
release his prisoners, but, although a United States
marshal was with him, made no arrests.

This gives an insight into the character of John
Brown, "the martyr." Drunk with blood, inflamed by
the death of one of his sons in these border feuds,
impelled to further deeds of violence, no doubt, by the
immunity secured from those committed in Kansas, John
Brown began, as early as the fall of 1857, in far-away

[1] See Rhodes's *History of the United States*, vol. ii. p. 162, etc.

Kansas, to formulate his plans for an outbreak in Virginia. His confederate Cook, in his confession, has left the whole story.

Inducing Cook and eight or ten others, over whom he seems to have possesed complete mastery, to join him, they started east to attend a military school, as it was said, in Ashtabula County, Ohio. The party united at Tabor, Iowa; there, in the autumn of 1857, he revealed to this choice band that his ultimate destination was the State of Virginia. His companions demurred at first, but his strong will prevailed. They shipped eastward two hundred Sharp's rifles that had been sent to Tabor for his Kansas enterprises the year previous. In May, 1858, Brown held a convention in Chatham, Canada, in a negro church, with a negro preacher for president, and adopted a constitution, which, without naming any territory to which it was to apply, said: "We, the citizens of the United States, and the oppressed people, who, etc., do ordain and establish for ourselves the following provisional constitution and ordinances." This constitution, drawn up by John Brown, and adopted by himself and half a dozen whites, and as many more negroes in Canada, provided for legislative, executive, and judicial branches of his government. It also provided for treaties of peace, for a commander-in-chief, for communism of property, for capturing and confiscating property, for the treatment of prisoners, and for many absurd things besides. After providing for the slaughter or the robbery of nearly everybody in the United States who did not join the organization, or voluntarily free their slaves and agree to keep the peace, it culminated in a declaration: —

"Art. 46. The foregoing articles shall not be construed so as in any way to encourage the overthrow of

any state government, or of the general government of
the United States, and look to no dissolution of the
Union, but simply to amendment and repeal, and our
flag shall be the same as our fathers fought under in the
Revolution."

No one can read the absurd jargon and believe that
it was the product of the same brain. Yet the last
declaration of the document is no more inconsistent with
the facts than were the repeated declarations of Brown,
after he had killed a number of people at Harper's
Ferry, that he proposed no violence. Nor was it a whit
more absurd than the pretended loyalty to State and
country of those who applauded his career of murder
and robbery, and treason both state and national.

From May, 1858, to October, 1859, Brown pursued his
plans. He rented a farm near Harper's Ferry, and there
collected his arms and ammunition, without exciting suspicion. Delays occurred from lack of funds, etc. An
anonymous letter was sent to the Secretary of War, in
the spring of 1859, revealing his plans and purposes, but
it seems to have made no impression, although the Secretary of War was a Southern man.

Shortly before Brown made his demonstration, his
cohorts, to the number of twenty, black and white,
assembled at his farmhouse, and Sunday night, October
16, 1859, they descended upon Harper's Ferry. About
10.30 P. M., they seized and captured the watchman upon
the railroad bridge across the Potomac, and proceeded
with him to the United States armory, of which they took
possession. Brown then sent forth a party, headed by his
lieutenant, Cook, to capture Colonel Lewis Washington
and Mr. Allstadt, leading citizens, who were to be held as
hostages. These gentlemen were compelled to leave their
beds, and accompany the invaders. Their slaves, to the

number of thirty, were also compelled, against their will, to join the party. Colonel Washington was a grand-nephew of George Washington, and a member of the staff of the governor of Virginia.

A sword of Frederick the Great, which had been presented to George Washington, was "appropriated" for use by John Brown. At this point we are introduced to the word selected by Brown as descriptive of his taking other people's property. He did not call it stealing, or robbery, or violent seizure. He invariably referred to it as "appropriating," and he pronounced the word in a peculiar way, — putting the whole emphasis upon the second syllable, as if it were a-*prop*-riating. It was a favorite and oft-repeated word with him. Here also we see, in his appropriating the sword of Frederick the Great to be worn by himself, that overshadowing egotism which was one of his most prominent characteristics, — the inordinate vanity of lunacy.

It was an ill omen for his venture that the first person killed by his band in the early morning was an inoffensive colored man, a porter at the railroad station, who, being ordered to stop and seeking to escape, was shot as he ran away. The next victim was a citizen killed standing in his own door. The next, a graduate of West Point, who, having heard of the trouble at the Ferry, was shot from the armory as he rode into town on horseback armed with a gun.

It is impossible to describe the consternation which these scenes produced among the citizens of Harper's Ferry.

When the marines had completed their lawful and proper work the following morning, John Brown lay on the grass desperately wounded. His entire party was killed, wounded, or captured, and the dead bodies of two of his sons were beside him. It was a ghastly ending of a horrid venture. As has been truly said of it by an eminent Northern historian : " In the light of common sense, the plan was folly ; from a military point of view, it was absurd." The first question which arises in the mind of every one is, Did John Brown know the nature of his own acts? As far as man may answer such a question, he answered it himself on many occasions.

While in the engine-house, receiving and returning the fire of the marines, one of his prisoners, Mr. Daingerfield, told him he was committing treason. One of his followers spoke up and said : " Captain Brown, are we guilty of treason in what we are doing? I did not so understand it."

" Certainly," said Brown, and coolly kept up his fire.

When examined after his surrender, and upon his trial, he said he fully understood the nature of his acts and the consequences, and peremptorily refused to permit any plea of lunacy to be interposed in his defense.

John Brown was tried for treason, murder, and inciting slaves to insurrection. His trial occupied six days. He was defended by able counsel, of his own selection, from Massachusetts and Ohio. Every witness he desired summoned appeared. The evidence of his guilt was overwhelming, and he was sentenced to death. Any other penalty would have been a travesty of justice, and a confession that the organized governments which he assailed were mockeries, affording no protection to their citizens against midnight murder and assassination. Did the Virginians exult over the wretched victim of his own lawlessness? NO!

The " New York Herald " published the account of how that verdict was received : " Not the slightest sound was heard in the vast crowd, as this verdict was returned

and read; not the slightest expression of elation or triumph was uttered from the hundreds present. . . . Nor
was this strange silence interrupted during the whole of
the time occupied by the forms of the court."

When Brown was asked if he had anything to say
why sentence should not be pronounced, he said among
other things: " I admire the truthfulness and candor of
the greater portion of the witnesses who have testified.
. . . I feel entirely satisfied with the treatment I have
received on my trial. Considering all the circumstances,
it has been more generous than I expected." He admitted a design to free the slaves, but denied all intention to commit treason, or murder, or violence in so doing,
and declared that in what he had done he felt fully justified before God and man.

There was nothing remarkable or unusual in talk like
this by a man like that. It has been the usual jabber
of desperate, unbalanced egotists and law-breakers since
vanity, ignorance, and fanaticism produced the first
assailant of organized government. It was heard again
when Wilkes Booth, assassinating Lincoln, exclaimed:
" 'Sic semper tyrannis!' " and again, when Guiteau slew
Garfield, claiming that he served his country in committing the base deed.

The Virginians took the life of John Brown to preserve
their own lives, and the lives of their wives and children,
from destruction. He had, indeed, " whetted knives of
butchery " for them, and had come a thousand miles to
kill people who had never heard his name.

Yet, when the majesty of the law was vindicated, they did
not gloat over his dead body or mutilate his corpse, as he
had done his Kansas victims. They did not boil his bones
and articulate them to be hung in a public museum. When
justice was satisfied, his body, unmutilated, was delivered

to his wife to bear back to his home, and she is a witness to the fact that she was shown all the sympathy, all the tenderness, all the consideration, of which the awful situation admitted.

When the Virginia people first came into possession of the facts of the John Brown fiasco, they did not believe the outrage had been promoted or would be justified by any considerable number of sane, law-abiding people anywhere. With an inborn love of courage, the bearing of John Brown was so fearless throughout that, even in their anger at his impotent violence, they admired his fortitude. Even the governor of the State testified to this. Describing his appearance as he lay wounded before him, he said he could liken his attitude to nothing but "a broken-winged hawk lying upon his back, with fearless eye, and talons set for further fight if need be," and such was undoubtedly the man; such have been many others like him. The quality of perfect courage, coupled with an unbalanced judgment, narrow-mindedness, and fanaticism, has produced a hundred characters in history like Brown. Pity, pity, pity it is to see that splendid quality perverted and destroyed by such fatal accompaniments. It was with a genuine sigh of admiration for this fortitude that, without one doubt about their duty, the Virginians imposed the penalty for his crime upon John Brown.

To one who knows the truth, the most tantalizing reflections upon the John Brown raid are these: The man who, as colonel in the army of the United States, captured Brown; the governor of Virginia, under whose administration he was justly hung; ay, a majority of the people of Virginia — were at heart opposed to slavery. Uninterrupted by madmen like Brown, they would have accomplished, in good time, the emancipation of the slave without the awful fratricidal scenes which he precipitated. Of course there are those who will still deny this, and conclusive proof is impossible. History took its course. Yet it is hard that one madman was able to warp that course, and it is wrong to glorify him as saint and martyr, while men infinitely his superiors in intellect, in broad philanthropy, in civilization, and his equals in moral and physical courage, were driven by his folly into apparent advocacy of slavery. Neither Colonel Lee nor the governor of Virginia were champions of slavery. Both rejoiced at its final overthrow, even at the great price in blood and treasure at which it was accomplished. The fanaticism which applauded Brown's acts made them feel that there was no possible peace or union with such people, and made them resolve that, sooner than submit to such savage fraternity, they would fight for freedom from its dictation, its taunts, and its interference.

When Virginia had performed her duty in executing Brown, her next step was to inquire what sympathy she received in the hour of her trial. She expected, as she had a right to expect, that the North, boasting of its superior civilization and its greater regard for the maintenance of the laws protecting person and property, would be practically unanimous in condemnation. Even the half-civilized free-soilers of Kansas had denounced Brown's barbarism.

When it was learned that, in many parts of the North, churches held services of humiliation and prayer; that bells were tolled; that minute-guns were fired; that Brown was glorified as a saint; that even in the legislature of Massachusetts, eight out of nineteen senators had voted to adjourn at the time of his execution; that Christian ministers had been parties to his schemes of assassination and robbery; that women had canonized the

bloodthirsty old lunatic as "St. John the Just;" that
philanthropists had pronounced him "most truly Christian;" that Northern poets like Whittier and Emerson
and Longfellow were writing panegyrics upon him; that
Wendell Phillips and William Lloyd Garrison approved
his life, and counted him a martyr, — then Virginians
began to feel that an "irrepressible conflict" was indeed
upon them. Still, they waited to ascertain how widespread this feeling was.

Horace Greeley, editor of the "New York Tribune,"
the leading Republican journal of the North, contented
himself with referring to Brown and his followers as
"mistaken men," but added that he would "not by one
reproachful word disturb the bloody shrouds wherein
John Brown and his compatriots are sleeping." John
A. Andrew, of Massachusetts, presided at a John Brown
meeting, proclaiming that whether the enterprise was
wise or foolish, John Brown himself was right. The
next year, Mr. Andrew was elected governor of Massachusetts. The Northern elections in the month succeeding
John Brown's raid showed gains to the Republicans in
the North. Lincoln spoke in February, 1860, at Cooper
Institute, New York. His comments on Brown were
looked for with anxiety. He said John Brown's effort
was "peculiar;" and while he characterized it as absurd,
he had no word of censure. Seward spoke soon afterwards in the Senate. He was a man of more refinement than Lincoln. He represented a constituency more
highly civilized, and one in which a greater regard for
law existed than in the West. He dared to say that
Brown "attempted to subvert slavery in Virginia by
conspiracy, ambush, invasion, and force," and to add that
"this attempt to execute an unlawful purpose in Virginia by invasion, involving servile war, was an act of

sedition and treason, and criminal in just the extent that it affected the public peace and was destructive of human happiness and life."

Seward's detestation of slavery was more widely known than Lincoln's. Up to that time, he had no formidable competitor for the Republican nomination for the presidency. It is not improbable that, in the then excited state of Northern feeling, the two candid admissions above quoted cost him the nomination for the presidency.

While these scenes were being enacted, a great change of feeling took place in Virginia towards the people of the North and towards the Union itself. Virginians began to look upon the people of the North as hating them, and willing to see them assassinated at midnight by their own slaves, led by Northern emissaries ; as flinging aside all pretense or regard for laws protecting the slave-owner ; as demanding of them the immediate freeing of their slaves ; or that they prepare against further attacks like Brown's, backed by the moral and pecuniary support of the North.

During the year 1860, the Virginians began to organize and arm themselves against such emergencies. They knew that, while James Buchanan was President, the power of the federal administration could be relied upon to suppress such violence ; but they also knew that his term of office was nearly at an end, and they had little hope of such protection if the federal administration fell into the hands of the Republicans. While the State was still unprepared to secede, her citizens were a unit in the resolve that Northern fanatics, who thenceforth appeared on Virginia soil upon any such mission as that of John Brown, should " be welcomed with bloody hands to hospitable graves."

When the troops came back from Harper's Ferry, they

were amply supplied with songs. The first and most
popular was one upon John Brown, sung to the tune
of "The Happy Land of Canaan." It had a number
of verses, only one of which I remember, running something after this fashion: —

> "In Harper's Ferry section, there was an insurrection,
> John Brown thought the niggers would sustain him,
> But old master Governor Wise
> Put his specs upon his eyes,
> And he landed in the happy land of Canaan.

> REFRAIN.
> "Oh me! Oh my! The Southern boys are a-trainin',
> We 'll take a piece of rope
> And march 'em up a slope,
> And land 'em in the happy land of Canaan."

It is surprising how popular this rigmarole became
through the South, and many a time during the war I
heard the regiments, as they marched, sing verses from it.
It is in contrast with the solemn swell of "John Brown's
Body," as rendered by the Union troops. The latter
is only an adaptation of a favorite camp-meeting hymn
which I often heard the negroes sing, as they worked in
the fields, long before the days of John Brown. The old
words were: —

> "My poor body lies a-mouldering in the clay,
> My poor body lies a-mouldering in the clay,
> My poor body lies a-mouldering in the clay,
> While my soul goes marching on.

> REFRAIN.
> "Glory, glory, hallelujah,
> Glory, glory, hallelujah,
> Glory, glory, hallelujah,
> As my soul goes marching on."

CHAPTER X

HOW THE " SLAVE-DRIVERS " LIVED

OUR life during the year 1860 was in strange contrast with the busy and exciting scenes of 1858 and 1859. Father's term of office expired January 1, 1860. He sold his plantation in Accomac, and bought another in the county of Princess Anne, near Norfolk. This change was due partly to domestic and partly to political considerations.

During a period of rebuilding at " Rolleston," our new home, I was sent, January 1, 1860, to live with a favorite sister, and attend a private school presided over by the parish minister, a Master of Arts of the University of Virginia. The location was in the county of Goochland, about twenty miles west of Richmond, in the beautiful valley of the upper James.

From Lynchburg, which is near the foot-hills of the Blue Ridge, the James River courses eastward to Richmond, a distance of about two hundred miles, through a valley of great fertility and beauty. The width of this valley seldom exceeds a mile, and at many points it is much narrower than that. The flat lands along the course of the stream are known as the " James River low grounds," an expression which conveys to the mind of the Virginian an idea of fatness and fecundity such as others conceive in reading of the valley of the Nile. About Lynchburg, high bluffs hang over the stream, and the flat lands are narrow and small in extent ; but from Howardsville, in Albemarle, to Richmond, a hundred miles below, the valley broadens, and the bluffs grow less beetling as the gently rolling lands of lower Piedmont are reached. In general characteristics, the section resembles the valleys of the Genesee and the Mohawk in New York, with a greater luxuriance of woodland and more extended vistas.

Upon the swelling hills overlooking the James were built, at the time of which I write, for a distance of a hundred miles or more, the homes of many of the wealthiest and most representative people of our State.

No railroad penetrated the valley. The only means provided for transporting products to market was the James River and Kanawha Canal, an enterprise projected by General Washington. It had been completed as far as Lexington, passing through the Blue Ridge Mountains at the point known as Balcony Falls, a spot suggestive of the Trosachs pass in Scotland.

For their own transportation up and down the valley, these prosperous folk had private equipages and servants. When the distance was greater than a day's journey, the home of some friend, generally a kinsman, stood wide open for their entertainment. The canal was available upon emergency as a means of travel, but as its speed was only about four miles an hour, few of the grandees resorted to it. A fine road ran along the foot-hills, parallel with the canal and river, from Richmond to Charlottesville, often keeping companionship for a mile or two with the route of the canal. The hills were of that stiff red clay celebrated afar for its adaptability to corn and tobacco; and the soil of the low grounds, often refreshed and rejuvenated by the overflow of the James, was a deep alluvial deposit of chocolate loam, inexhaustible in richness and fertility, and producing all the cereals in marvelous abundance.

Recalling a few of the princely dwellers in this favored section, one remembers the Cabells of Nelson; the Galts of Albemarle; the Cockes of Fluvanna; the Hubards of Buckingham; the Bollings of Bolling Island and Bolling Hall; the Harrisons of Ampthill, and Clifton, and Elk Hill; the Hobsons of "Howard's Neck," and "Snowden," and "Eastwood;" the Flemings of "West View;" the Rutherfords of "Rock Castle;" General Philip St. George Cocke of "Belle Mead;" the Skipwiths; the Logans of "Dungeness;" the Seldens of "Orapax" and of "Norwood;" the Warwicks; the Michaux of Michaux's Ferry; the Morsons of "Dover;" the Seddons of "Sabot Hill;" the Stanards of "Bendover;" the Allens of "Tuckahoe;" and many others: —

> " Their swords are rust,
> Their bodies dust;
> Their souls are with the saints, we trust."

Scattered along the valley, owning respectively from seven hundred to two or three thousand acres, with slaves enough to cultivate twice the lands they owned, they were the happiest and most prosperous community in all America; not rolling in wealth, like the sugar cane and cotton planters of the South, yet with a thousand advantages over them, in the variety of their productions, in the beauty of their lands, in the salubrity of their climate, in the society about them, and in their access to the outer world.

The home of my sister was on one of these fine James River estates, and her neighbors were of the most highly cultivated people of whom that region boasted. The plantation had been purchased from Colonel Trevillian, descendant of an old Huguenot family, and its name, "Eastwood," had been bestowed by its former owner, Peyton Harrison. My brother-in-law, after an education in Europe, had essayed business, but ill-health compelled him to adopt a country life. The house stood in a grove of oaks of original growth, in the midst of an extensive lawn carpeted with greensward. Behind it were the stables, the inclosures, and the household servants' quarters. In front, half a mile away, were the low grounds and river; and to the left again, half a mile distant, stood the overseer's house, the quarters of the farm hands, and the farm stables. Up and down the river were visible the handsome residences of the neighbors. On remote hillsides or in the wooded points, one saw, here and there, great barns of brick or wood for storing wheat or corn, and houses where tobacco was stripped and hung, and smoked and dried, and pressed into hogsheads. Interminable lines of stone or post and oak fences, without one missing panel, showed, as few other things in farming do show, the prosperity of the owners of these lands. Great fields — this one pale green with winter wheat, this sere and brown in pasture land, this red with newly ploughed clods, and this with a thousand hillocks whence the tobacco had been gleaned — were spread out to the vision, clean of weeds and undergrowth, and cultivated until they looked like veritable maps of agriculture.

Near at hand, or far away upon the hillsides, one beheld the working-bands of slaves, well clothed, well fed, and differing from other workmen, as we see them now, chiefly in their numbers and their cheerfulness and their comfortable clothing. Remarkable as the statement may seem, those slaves, over whose sad fate so many tears have been shed, went about their work more joyously than any laboring people I ever saw.

Our school was located a mile away, in rear of the river plantations, upon a road leading to what was known as "the back country." A little church, built from the pri-

vate contributions of the river planters, was used as the
schoolhouse. It was near the parsonage. That point was
selected, not only for its convenience to the teacher, but
also because of its accessibility to the children of the
smaller farmers in this " back country." It is often said
that antagonism existed between this humbler class of
whites and the wealthy nabobs living upon the river.
Perhaps there may have been something of the inevitable
envy which the less fortunate feel everywhere towards the
prosperous and great, but certain it is, there was little
manifestation of it there. The wealthy sought in every
way to be upon good terms with the poor; and one of the
best proofs that they succeeded is found in the fact that,
when war came, the two stood up together side by side,
and fought and slept and ate and died together, — never
thinking of which was rich or which was poor, until a time
when such as survived were all poor together, and those
who had always been poor were in their turn the more
fortunate of the two.

Our nearest neighbors were the Seddons, — one of the
loveliest families of people that ever lived. The head of
the house was a gentleman who, after a thorough education, had achieved distinction at the bar and in Congress,
but, owing to delicate health, had retired to his plantation. He entertained extreme views on the subjects of
slavery and the nullification doctrines of Calhoun; but
for years he had, owing to precarious health, taken no
active part in politics. Polished in manners, gentle in
his bearing, hospitable and considerate in all things, he
captivated visitors to his home as soon as they entered it.
And in whatever he failed, his wife more than atoned
for it by her graciousness. She was the accomplished
heiress, Sally Bruce. She and her sister Ellen, both
beautiful in person and in character, and thoroughly edu-

cated, took Richmond society by storm upon their first
appearance there in the 40's, and succumbed at last to
the blandishments of two young cousins, married them,
bought adjoining plantations in Goochland, and were
now rearing their children side by side. Such were the
families of Hon. James A. Seddon and James M. Morson,
Esq.

Some of the happiest days of my childhood, some
of the most elevating, purifying, and refining hours of
all my life, were passed in these two households. Both
Mr. and Mrs. Seddon were accomplished linguists, and
demanded that their children should be as well educated
as themselves. Their library was supplied with the best
thought of the world, and the course of literary culture
prescribed by them for their children was not only com-
prehensive, but was made attractive by the way in which
it was pursued. Often the evening gatherings of the
family were converted into reading classes, and, with the
charming voice of their mother added to the attraction of
the subject, the children became interested. That charming voice? Yes, one of the sweetest that ever sang. Not
only was she an admirable performer upon the piano, but
when she sang, accompanying herself upon the harp, she
was a very nightingale. Her tender Scotch ballads never
were surpassed upon the stage.

Love, intellectuality, refinement, hospitality, made that
home an abode fit for the most favored of mortals; and
her care for their welfare made " Mis' Sallie " the ideal,
in the minds of the servants, of what an angel would be
in the world to come. The children? They were numerous as the teeth in a comb. Three of the Seddon boys,
ranging from a year older to two years younger than myself, were my sworn allies. Morning, noon, and night, we
were together. Of course we all had horses, — everybody

had a horse. Often the three Seddon boys rode to school
upon the back of one filly, with a young darkey to fetch
her home. Their route brought them directly past the
Eastwood gate, and many a day in 1860 that blessed filly
took upon her back a fifth rider, as I slipped down from
the gatepost where I had awaited their coming. And
many a head-punching I received from the combined
forces of the Seddons because I tickled that filly in the
flank, and made her kick until she tumbled the entire
load, four white boys and a darkey, into the muddy road,
and then, kicking at us, scampered away, leaving us to
fish our Horaces and Livys and Virgils out of the mud,
and walk the remainder of the way to school.

The Morson children, first cousins of the Seddons, were
also numerous; and while their residence was at a little
distance from ours, the families were frequently together.
At school, during the week, plans were made for the
afternoons and Saturdays, and we ranged the whole
country-side, shooting, or riding, or visiting.

A favorite amusement was excursions up the canal in
our own boat, drawn by our own team, to a famous fishing-
place at " Maiden's Adventure " dam. Thither boys and
girls repaired together, making quite a boatload, taking
baskets of luncheon and spending the day.

The school-teacher, the Rev. Mr. Dudley, was an efficient man, who demanded that his pupils should study
hard, and was not at all squeamish about the proper use
of hickory. Notwithstanding this, he was popular, and
joined in the sports at recess with genuine zest. One of
our favorite games was called " Germany," or " Cher-
mony," in which a paddle, a certain number of holes in a
row, and a hard rubber ball were used. Under certain
regulations, each player claimed a hole in the ground, and,
when the ball went into it, was privileged to hit some

one else with the ball. Mr. Dudley was a large, fleshy man, and it was noticeable that, while the boys were always delighted to have him in the game, he was hit about twice as often as all the boys put together. However much he may have compelled them to rub themselves in school, the boot was very much on the other leg in these little outside pastimes; so much so, that Parson Dudley, after being "roasted" for a long time, appeared to lose his enthusiasm for the game.

It was during the recess hour, on a bright May day in 1860, that a boy rode by, returning perhaps from Richmond, and gave Mr. Dudley a copy of a newspaper. No sooner had he disposed himself comfortably to read the news, leaving us boys to our diversions, than with a loud exclamation he broke forth, "Ah! that settles it. I feared as much. Abe Lincoln is nominated for President. He will be elected, and that means war."

I, who was now in my fourteenth year, and deeply interested in political matters, was anxious to know why Mr. Lincoln's election portended war any more than that of any one else.

"Well," said Mr. Dudley, perfectly sincere in every word he spoke, "Mr. Seward was the logical candidate of the Republican party, entitled to the nomination by superior ability and by long service. He is a man of very pronounced anti-slavery views, but is a gentleman by birth and association, and if elected President, would respect his constitutional obligations and the rights of the Southern States. Everybody expected him to be the nominee; but his course and utterances of late, especially his utterances concerning old John Brown, are not radical enough to suit the Black Republicans. On the other hand, this man Lincoln has come to the front, venomous and vindictive enough to satisfy the most rabid abolitionist." He then proceeded to draw a picture of Lincoln horrible enough. He told how he was, in his origin, of that class of low whites who hate gentlemen because they are gentlemen; how, in personal appearance, he was more like a gorilla than a human being; how he possessed the arts and cunning of the demagogue to a degree sufficient to build himself up by appealing to the prejudices of his own class against gentlemen; and how, in his joint debates with Douglas, who had completely overmastered him, he had nevertheless brought himself into notice, and secured the nomination of his party, by going far beyond other leaders in advocacy of radical measures against slavery, and in abuse of the South.

That settled Abraham Lincoln with me. I was thoroughly satisfied that no such man ought to be President; but I could not yet conceive it possible that such a monster would be the choice of a majority of the people for President. Lincoln's nomination did not, however, interfere with my happiness or appetite. In fact, I had faith in the triumph of Mr. Lincoln's opponents.

A few days after this, I accompanied my sister and brother-in-law to a breakfast at the Stanards'.

In course of conversation at table, the nomination of Lincoln was discussed. That gave rise to the inquiry, on the part of our hostess, whether her guests had read the remarkable sermon recently delivered in the city of New Orleans by the Rev. Dr. Palmer, an eminent Presbyterian divine, upon "The Divine Origin of Slavery." As none of her guests had seen it, and all expressed the desire to do so, a servant was sent to the library for the newspaper, and one of the company proceeded to read aloud the salient points of Dr. Palmer's address. Undoubtedly, from his standpoint, the great minister put the case very strongly. His arguments were, however, chiefly based upon the

divine sanction of the patriarchal institutions of the Old
Testament. I was not a profound Biblical scholar, but a
number of very good women had spent a greal deal of
time, during the brief space of my life, hammering into
my head portions of the Old Testament. It so happened
also that during breakfast that morning the Mormon doctrines of Brigham Young had come up for discussion,
for Brigham was much in evidence then, and everybody,
especially the ladies, had joined in denouncing him as
monstrous.

The reading of Dr. Palmer's sermon occupied some
time. It bored me, but I found no opportunity to escape.
At its conclusion, the company agreed that it was an
able and conclusive argument. Mrs. Stanard, who was a
witty woman given to facetious remarks, declared a purpose to mail a copy of the sermon to Abe Lincoln. I,
who was inclined to be pert as well as facetious, proposed
to send another copy to Brigham Young. "For," said
I, "every argument of Dr. Palmer, based on the slavery
of the Old Testament, is equally available for Brigham
Young in support of polygamy; and I sympathize with
Brigham."

It is unnecessary to add that the assembled guests, in
their disgust at my "pertness," dropped the argument on
slavery.

Soon after this breakfast, I witnessed the first parade
of the Goochland Troop. The John Brown invasion had
given a pronounced impetus to the military spirit of Virginia. In almost every county, new military organizations
had sprung up. As the Goochland folk were rich, owners
of fine horseflesh, and every man of them a horseman
from his childhood, it was natural that they organized a
command of cavalry.

During the winter, the plan was conceived. The first

meeting looking to its consummation was held at February court. The preliminary drilling began in the early spring. And now in May, for the first time, the troop assembled in full uniform for drill and inspection. Julien Harrison, of Elk Hill was its commandant. Mr. Hobson, my brother-in-law, at whose house I lived, was the first lieutenant. The company was composed of the very flower of the aristocracy of the James River valley, and the capital invested in the arms, uniforms, and the horseflesh of the Goochland Troop would have equipped a regiment of regulars.

At their first parade and review, they were the guests of the master of Eastwood. Every man vied with every other in his mount. There were not ten horses in the company less than three quarters thoroughbred. It was indeed a gallant sight, — those spirited youngsters, men, and beasts. The uniforms of the privates were fine enough for major-generals. Their arms they bought themselves, — the carbines and pistols from Colt, the sabres from Horstmann. The shabrack of a Goochland trooper cost more money than the whole equipment of a Confederate cavalryman three years later. Little did they realize then that within a year they would be part of the best regiment in the brigade of the immortal Stuart, and that they would pass into history as the "Black Horse Cavalry," — a bugaboo scarcely less terrible to the imagination of their foe than "masked batteries." There was, in fact, but one company in the Confederacy called "Black Horse Troop," and that came from Fauquier County; but they were counted by thousands in the imagination of the Union soldiers.

Many years afterwards, in conversation with a Union veteran, something was said of handsome cavalry. He remarked that the most vivid picture of a perfect soldier retained by his mind was that of a Confederate cavalry officer named Captain Julien Harrison, of the Fourth Virginia Cavalry, who bore a flag of truce in 1861 into the Union lines at Manassas.

The thing which most impressed itself upon me, during my residence in Goochland in 1860, was the marked difference between slavery upon these extensive plantations and slavery as it existed in the smaller establishments which I had theretofore known. It could not be truly said of these people that they were cruel to their slaves, but it was certainly true that the relations between master and slave were nothing like so close or so tender as those with which I had been theretofore familiar. The size of the plantations and the number of slaves were such that it was necessary to employ farm managers or overseers, and to have separate establishments, removed from the mansion house, where the overseers resided, surrounded by the laborers on the plantation.

As a consequence, the master and his family saw little of this class of servants, and the servants saw and knew little of the master. There was lacking that intimate acquaintance and sympathy with each other which ameliorated the condition of the slaves where the farm was small, the servants few, and no overseer came between master and servant.

Wealthy men, too, like several of those in our neighborhood, had so many slaves that they were compelled to buy other plantations on which to employ them. For example, Mr. Morson owned nearly eight hundred negroes. In order to sustain them, he purchased large plantations in Mississippi. A portion of his time was passed there looking after his interests, and thither, from time to time, it was, in the nature of the case, necessary to transfer some of his Virginia slaves; for they increased rapidly, and the

Virginia plantation could furnish employment and sustenance for only a limited number.   Such transfers were
made as humanely as possible.   Families· were removed
together, in order to avoid harassing separations, and the
change bore as lightly as possible upon the blacks.   But,
after all, it was an unsympathetic proceeding; for the
negro race has the strongest of local attachments, and old
Virginia was, and still is, the dearest spot of earth to the
native darkey.

The weeping and wailing among those who were ordered
South was pitiful.   Although they were going to their
master's plantation, it was in a strange land and under
the government of unknown people, who felt none of the
softening influences of early associations.   Above all, it
was without regard to any consideration of their wishes or
their prejudices, and the expression of either would have
been vain.

The slaves upon our place presented another repulsive
feature of the institution.   The master and mistress were
both young persons of pure, elevated Christian lives, incapable of brutality, and most ambitious to deserve and to
possess the loyal love of their slaves.   They could have
had no country establishment without the possession of
slaves ; and, both being members of large families, they
could not hope to acquire by gift a sufficient number of
slaves to carry on their plantation.   As a consequence,
they were compelled to buy the essential quota.   These
purchases were made by families, as far as possible, but
the aggregate was made up of negroes who came from different places, and were strangers to each other.   Great cir-
cumspection was exercised in the effort to secure the proper
kind of servants, and large prices were paid in order to
secure such.   But everybody knows how little reliance is to
be placed in the advance characters given to servants, and

how often, when strange servants are brought together, unforeseen incompatibilities of temperament, or new conditions, affect them. Thus it was that the new establishment at " Eastwood," wealthy and luxurious as it seemed, had its troubles and its trials like all the rest of the world. The darkeys were jealous of each other. The ones represented as marvels of diligence and obedience turned out to be lazy and impertinent. And so it went. The most flagrant instance of this kind was a butler named Tom, a handsome fellow, quick, intelligent, and represented as a phenomenal servant. When Tom arrived, he was a joy and a comfort to master and mistress, and they felt that he was worth the $2500 they had paid for him. In a little while, Tom appeared, from time to time, in a condition of excitement or irritability or stupor, and his conduct was exceedingly perplexing. Suspecting liquor as the cause of his strange behavior, strict watch was kept upon the wine cellar and the sideboard, but no liquor was missed. At last, Tom developed a distinct case of *mania a potu*, and then it was discovered that he had been steadily imbibing from a large demijohn of alcohol to which he had access. As his distemper developed an inclination to knock the heads off his fellow servants, male and female, on the slightest provocation, his presence made matters very uncomfortable ; and while his first offense was overlooked and forgiven, under solemn promises of reform, he soon relapsed into bad habits, and became so violent that it was necessary to have him seized and bound by Alick the gardener and Ephraim the hostler, in order to prevent murder.

Now, what would our humane and philanthropic friend, Mrs. Harriet Beecher Stowe, think of a case like this? And how would the dear old lady have disposed of it? This was one of many of the perplexing situations of sla-

very.   There was nothing to do with Tom but to sell him
with all his infirmities on his head.   Of course the abolitionist will say it was awful ; but to have given him away
would have been imposing upon the friend to whom he
was presented, and to set him free was offering a premium
to drunkenness and faithlessness.   Tom shed tears of re-
pentance, and the family shed tears of regret and humiliation.   But as there were young children and women all
about him, — women and children of his own race as well
as the white race, — and as he was liable to get drunk
and violent, and to knock the heads off of any or all of
them at any moment, the question recurs on the original
proposition.   What was to be done with Tom ?

But enough of these instances.   This and many others
only confirmed me in the opinion, planted when I saw the
sale of Martha Ann, and growing steadily thereafter, that
slavery was an accursed business, and that the sooner my
people were relieved of it, the better.

June came, and with it the end of the school term and
my return to my father's home.   I had made decided ad-
vances in knowledge.   I had read the first six books of
Virgil; been drilled in Racine and Molière and Voltaire ;
finished Davies's Legendre ; and was fairly embarked in
algebra, besides a good grounding in ancient and modern
history and a smattering of natural philosophy.

So I boxed my books, packed my trunk, gathered together my effects, — including my gun, with which I had
become quite proficient, and a coop containing a game-
cock and pullets of the choicest James River stock, — and
hied myself homeward.

CHAPTER XI

THE proverb that a calm precedes a storm was never better illustrated than in the peaceful days of the summer and autumn of 1860, and the winter of 1860–61.

Our new home opened up a phase of existence entirely different from any I had theretofore known. Although it was within five miles of the city of Norfolk, which was easily reached either by land or by water, Rolleston, my father's new plantation, was as secluded a spot as if no city had been within a hundred miles. It was the ancient seat of the Moseley family, one of the oldest in the State. Located upon the eastern branch of the Elizabeth River, it embraced, besides a broad area of cultivation, a handsome body of timber of original growth, running from the water's edge back for a mile or more. The dwelling and curtilage were near the river, and the cultivated land, which was on its easternmost side, was bounded by a large millpond. Across the mouth of the pond a dam was erected, with floodgates admitting the tide and confining it at high water for the use of a gristmill.

Beside the gristmill, the new purchaser erected a sawmill on the woodland tract for his own use in erecting new buildings, and for the sale of lumber in the adjacent city. When I reached the place, a number of mechanics were remodeling the dwelling, and building new farmhouses and barns. Every boy who has lived on a farm knows the joys of the youthful heart at having access to a carpenter's bench, and to all the lumber and tools and nails he wants.

Besides myself, I had as companions and playmates my brother, a nephew near my own age, a white boy, — the son of the miller, — and my own slave, black John. From rosy morn till dewy eve, during all the vacation of 1860, this precious company was busy with new enterprises. The adjacent waters swarmed with fish and terrapin and crabs and oysters and clams, and every variety of sea food. The fields and forests and marshes abounded with game. The Elizabeth River was a beautiful sheet of water for sailing, and father had provided himself with the stanchest and fastest boats to be obtained.

The milldam and pond were our favorite rallying-point. There we anchored our craft, and fished and swam and sailed our miniature boats, and engaged in the many pastimes which make boyhood so happy a period. To-day, we were occupied, busy as bees, building hen-houses. To-morrow, the all-engrossing subject was a new boat, devised and constructed by ourselves. Another time, we might be seen, all hands, riding the high side of our fastest boat in a clipping sail to Norfolk, and, again, bending to the oars like tried seamen, rowing homeward in a calm. To-day would be devoted to fishing in deep water, to-morrow to crabbing on the shoals ; another time, to setting weir mats across the mouths of the little estuaries to catch " fatbacks " or jumping mullets when the tide went out; and another time, the whole company would be busy baiting and sinking terrapin traps. Sometimes we would drive away in the farm-carts to Lambert's or Garrison's Fishing Shores, ten miles away upon the Chesapeake Bay, to seine-hauling, from which we would return at evening, our carts loaded down with fish for salting and use during the winter season. On other days, we made up fishing

excursions in our sloop, the Know-Nothing, down to
the deep waters of Hampton Roads, for sea trout and
sheepshead. Every day had its new and busy occupation
and delight, and for several months we never put shoes
upon our feet, save when we were called upon to visit the
city. With great straw hats and brown-linen shirts, and
trousers rolled up above our knees, we were almost am-
phibians, and were sunburnt as brown as Indians.

It may not have been a period of great intellectual
growth, but it certainly was a time in which our physical
health was highly developed, and the qualities of enterprise and self-reliance were highly stimulated.

In the month of August, the Great Eastern, the largest
ship then afloat, came to Hampton Roads, which was the
signal for a general holiday, and everybody who was
anybody, far and near, went to visit her. We went
down the harbor with Captain Oliver upon our sloop,
the Know-Nothing, to inspect the English monster. From
the city to the Roads where the Great Eastern lay, ten
miles below, the waters of Norfolk harbor were alive with
river-craft, crowding all sails and decked in their best
bunting, firing small cannon and waving salutes. We
had bent the racing-sails of the Know-Nothing for the
occasion, and she showed her heels not only to the vessels
of her own class, but to many far larger than herself. I
was very proud of being one of the company of the smart-
est craft in Norfolk waters.

The Great Eastern, it will be remembered, was an immense ship, of a length and size never since equaled,
unless it be by the new steamer Oceanic, now under construction. She was 680 feet in length, with a width of
beam of over 80 feet, and a draft of 27 feet of water.
Her contrast with other ships of that time was, however,
much greater than it would be with the ships of to-day.

In general outline, she was, of course, very much like
other vessels of her kind. When she first came in view,
I felt disappointed ; for there were no other objects near
her with which to contrast her. But after a large steamer
of the Old Dominion line passed the Know-Nothing on the
way down the harbor, looming high above us, and rocking
us in her wake until our washboards were almost sub-
merged, and then passed on towards the Great Eastern,
where, by the side of the latter, she appeared to be no
larger than a tug, I began to realize the size of the magnificent newcomer. When the Know-Nothing sailed up
and around the visitor, her topmast not five feet above
the rail of the Great Eastern, the matter grew plainer ;
and when our party boarded the Great Eastern and
traversed the great spaces within, I found it difficult to
realize that she was the work of men, or that the colossal
whole moved and was directed in every motion by the
control of one human mind.

While the ship proved a failure, the ideas first advanced
in her were developed and applied to other ventures, in
such a manner that she produced a revolution in the construction of ships for merchant marine service, little less
marked than that in naval warfare resulting from the
conflict in Hampton Roads two years later.

The visit of the Prince of Wales to America occurred
about the same time as the arrival of the Great Eastern.

I was to remain at home during the next school year.
One of our neighbors, with a large family, had secured
the services of a young university graduate as private
tutor, and I was to attend his school, about two miles distant. Consequently, early in September, I went to Goochland to bring back some schoolbooks and other belong-
ings. It was on this visit that I happened to be in
Richmond at the time of the visit of the Prince of Wales,

and was in St. Paul's Church upon the Sunday when the prince attended divine worship there.

During our residence in Richmond, many eminent Englishmen had visited the city from time to time, and a mere English lord was no very great sight; but my interest was most decided in a British heir-apparent not much older than myself.

The young fellow was a typical Anglo-Saxon. His tawny hair, fair complexion, and blue eyes were exactly what one familiar with the type would have expected to see. At that time, he was rather slight in build, and did not display the best of physical development. His shoulders were drooping, and his hips rather broad; his movements were awkward, and his manner altogether boyish. I had no opportunity to converse with him, for, being a small boy, I secured no introduction; but I saw him several times, and wondered at the deference shown to him by the distinguished-looking old gentlemen who were his traveling companions, as well as by several of the leading citizens, friends of my father, by whom the prince was entertained.

One who saw him in 1860 would find it difficult to discover in the stout, bald, elderly, well-fed man of the world, still known as the Prince of Wales, whom I saw in London several years ago, any trace of the awkward boy who visited Richmond in 1860.

Never had boy more glorious liberty or greater variety of sport, and never did reckless youth pursue its bent more indifferent to the graver affairs going on about it. One day in October, I drove into Norfolk, and, seeing a great crowd assembled, paused and heard part of a speech by Stephen A. Douglas. I was greatly impressed by his tremendous voice, every tone of which reached me more than a block away, and I loudly applauded his Union sen-

timents. But having obtained the supply of powder and
shot I needed, I soon forgot Douglas. Not long afterwards, I heard, without its making a great impression
upon me, that on one of those gorgeous November days
Douglas had been defeated for President, and Abraham
Lincoln had been elected President of the United States.
More than once I heard, without believing it, that there
was serious and imminent danger of civil war as a result. " Let it come," was my only reflection ; " who 's
afraid ? "

Before the close of the year 1860, many men from
Southern States rode out to Rolleston from Norfolk to
visit and confer with father about the course Virginia
would pursue in view of that of South Carolina and
other States. Some of them remained to meals, and
some stayed overnight, and so I heard their conversa-
tions. Some of them had new and strange flags pinned
upon their lapels, or little palmetto rosettes, which they
gave me. When I visited the city, I heard new tunes
like " Dixie " and " The Bonnie Blue Flag ; " and men
said that Virginia would secede with other Southern
States. But father still declared that he was opposed to
secession, and believed that, if any fight was necessary,
the South should " fight in the Union." I did not know
what it all meant, and did not believe it could result in
actual war, and in fact had become so engrossed in the
pleasures of life at Rolleston that I gave little attention
to aught else but the pursuit of my boyish diversions.

I was a little over fourteen years of age when the civil
war began. No pair of eyes and ears in all America
were more alert than mine. Every event, as it wound off
the reel of time, excited my most intense interest, and
made its indelible impression.

As State after State passed ordinances of secession, the

disunion sentiment gained ground in Virginia. Father was hotly opposed to secession, but he always coupled that declaration with the further one that he was equally opposed to Northern coercion.

The Virginia legislature called a convention to consider what course the State should take in the impending crisis. The election for delegate from our county, Princess Anne, was exciting, and the result was in great doubt. Father was a candidate, opposed by Edgar Burroughs, Esq., a popular and outspoken Union man. Mr. Burroughs was a native of the county, had a large family connection, and was supported by a strong following, who wanted neither secession nor fighting. It required all the prestige of my father's name, and a careful declaration of his modified views upon secession, to elect him, and he was returned by a small majority.

Poor Burroughs, like many another who resisted secession to the last, went into the Confederate service, and sacrificed his life for his State.

The convention remained in session a long time before it took decisive action. When it assembled, it was composed of a safe majority of Union men, and a minority of secessionists. My father held unique views, and had a very small following. Opposing secession, he at the same time advocated preparations by the State for defense against what he considered the threatened aggression of the federal government. In his own book, " Seven Decades of the Union," he has fully set forth what he meant when he advocated "fighting in the Union." It is sufficient to say that, at the time, his views were regarded as impracticable, and that he failed to impress them upon the body, or to gain any considerable following.

The issue seemed likely to be decided in favor of the Union men, until the occurrence of two events which pre-

cipitated secession.   The first of these was the firing upon
Fort Sumter.   The second was the call issued by President Lincoln upon the States, Virginia included, for troops
to suppress the rebellion.

It has been said that the Southern leaders fired upon
Fort Sumter in order to force these issues, well knowing
that Virginia could not be relied upon to withdraw from
the Union in any other way.   Whether this be so or not,
this result was accomplished.

The Virginians realized that they had come to the parting of the roads.   The question presented was no longer,
Shall we fight?   War was flagrant.   The only question
to be decided was, On which side shall we fight?

Virginia was reduced to the alternative of furnishing
her quota of troops to the Union, or of refusing to do
so, which was the equivalent of secession.   It was a hard
situation, made doubly hard by the fact that, even at the
moment when these things happened, a peace conference,
presided over by her venerable ex-President John Tyler,
was in session at Washington, vainly endeavoring to bring
about a bloodless solution of the trouble.

Now, however, no time was to be lost in further negotiations.   Indecision in such a crisis would have been little
less than cowardice.

One by one, men who had steadily voted with the Union
men transferred their support to the secessionists.   Knowing that war was inevitable, they decided to fight for and
with their friends.   The ordinance of secession was passed
three days after Mr. Lincoln's call for troops; and while
the schedule provided for its indorsement by the people,
the march of events was so rapid that popular indorsement was not obtained until long after the State had
taken an unmistakable attitude in the conflict.

While these things were progressing, I visited Norfolk

daily to ascertain, and keep the family informed concerning, the progress of public affairs.

From the time Sumter was fired upon, and Mr. Lincoln's proclamation was made public, business was almost entirely suspended. The people assembled upon the streets, discussing the situation, breathlessly awaiting the decision of the convention at Richmond, and listening to popular harangues. The local military, anticipating the result, assembled, and paraded the streets with bands and Southern flags. When the telegraph flashed the announcement that the secession ordinance had been passed, it was greeted with great cheering, the firing of guns, and every demonstration of excited enthusiasm.

It is impossible to describe the feelings with which I saw the stars and stripes hauled down from the custom house, and the Virginia state flag run up in their place. I had become rampant for war, but never until then had I fully realized that this step involved making the old flag under which I was born in Brazil, and which, until now, had typified to me everything of national patriotism and national glory on land and sea, henceforth the flag of an enemy.

It was a beautiful spring morning. Across the harbor at the Gosport Navy Yard, the United States flag still floated from the garrison flagstaff, and from the ships, — the Pennsylvania, the Cumberland, the Merrimac, the Germantown, the Raritan, and others whose names were famous in our naval annals. Father had been chairman of the Naval Committee of the House of Representatives for many years, and had become, while minister to Brazil, personally acquainted with nearly all the prominent naval officers. Upon those ships, lying there, were many men who, but a short time before, were welcome visitors at our home. It was almost incredible that they were now, and were to be henceforth, enemies, or that they might at any time open fire upon the town which they had originally come to protect. A certain Confederate general was ridiculed for saying, after the war ended, that he had never seen the old flag, even in the battle-front, without tears in his eyes. That was doubtless a figure of speech. It was rather hyperbolical and beyond any feeling I had; but I can understand the emotion of every man who, having loved and honored the stars and stripes, could not bring himself, even while the war was going on, to hate them, or shut out from his remembrance what they had been to him.

The day after the State seceded, General Taliaferro, a militia general, arrived at Norfolk and assumed command. Troops from the South began to arrive. Among them I recall particularly the Third Alabama Regiment, one of the finest bodies of military I ever saw. It numbered full one thousand men, the best representatives of Montgomery, Selma, Mobile, and other places in Alabama. It was uniformed like the New York Seventh Regiment, and commanded by Colonel Lomax, a superb soldier. Those wealthy young fellows of the Third Alabama brought with them not less than one hundred servants, and their impediments were more than was carried by a division in Lee's army three years later.

All attention was concentrated now upon the navy yards and ships in possession of the United States. The advantage of securing the latter was fully understood. No less than six or seven vessels were sunk in the channel below the city, to prevent the ships from passing out. A demand for the evacuation of the navy yard and the surrender of the ships was, it was understood, made by General Taliaferro upon Commodore Paulding. Friday the 19th and Saturday the 20th were consumed in negotiations. Satur-

day, a party of Union officers landed at the Roanoke dock
with a flag of truce, and proceeded under escort to General Taliaferro's headquarters at the Atlantic Hotel.   A
long conference ensued, and then they returned to their
ships.   The fevered populace could gain no information
concerning the interview or its probable results.

Meanwhile, several companies of local military proceeded to old Fort Norfolk, which was on our side of the
river just below the town, and removed a large quantity
of ammunition stored there, unprotected by the Union
troops.   That ammunition was largely used in the first
battle of Manassas, which occurred three months later.

It was nearly dark, Saturday, April 20, when, despairing of getting further information, I secured my horse
and vehicle, bought all the thrilling newspaper bulletins I
could lay hands upon, and, tearing myself away from the
excitement of the town, started for home.   The erstwhile
silent woods skirting the homeward road were now trans-
formed into camps.   Places whose deep silence at night,
in time of peace, had been broken only by the uncanny
call of the whippoorwill, or the hooting of owls, were
lighted up with camp-fires, and resounded with the joyous
laughter of the soldiers, the calls of sentinels, the stroke
of the axe, or the singing of the cooks and servants.
Verily, this thing called war was a fascinating sport.
My heart sickened at the thought that it would probably
all be over before I was old enough to be a participant in
its glorious exhilaration.

At home, the family, impatient at my tardy return, de-
voured every item of news in the papers, and hung breath-
less upon every report of what was going forward in the
city.   Thoroughly fagged out by excitement, I went early
to bed, wondering " What next? "   Things happened so
fast in those days that, as soon as one thing occurred, we

began to expect something else, and in this case we were not disappointed. Some time after midnight, the household was aroused by a series of explosions in the direction of Norfolk, and on going out, we beheld a dense canopy of smoke hanging over the city, illuminated by fires, and flashing almost momentarily with the light of new explosions. It was easy to conjecture the meaning of this. The United States forces had abandoned and blown up the Gosport Navy Yard. I was keen to return at once to the city, but concluded to remain until daylight.

The next morning was Sunday, and bright and early I accompanied a party of our workmen in our sloop to the city. What a sight of devastation greeted us! The Pennsylvania and the Merrimac and other ships had been burned to the water's edge. Some of their guns had been loaded, and exploded as the heat of the fire reached them, but fortunately the ships had listed heavily before the discharge, and the shots had gone into the water or high over the town. The ship sheds were all destroyed. A futile effort had been made to blow up the dry dock. The barracks and officers' quarters and the machine shops had all been fired. Some of these fires had been extinguished, while others were still burning. The long rows of guns in the navy yard, fifteen hundred in all, had in many instances been spiked, or disabled by breaking their trunions with sledge-hammers. Old sails and clothing and masses of papers strewed the parade; and, altogether, it was marvelous to behold what destruction and disorder had been wrought within the space of a few hours where all had been construction and perfect order for many years.

As for the late occupants, the following were the facts: About nine o'clock Saturday night, the Pawnee had come up from Fortress Monroe, easily passing the obstructions. She doubtless brought the orders what to do. After knocking the navy yard into smithereens, and transferring all the valuable papers and the sailors to the Pawnee and Cumberland, and burning the Pennsylvania, Merrimac, and other ships, the Pawnee and Cumberland steamed down the harbor to Fortress Monroe. On their downward passage, the sailors manned the yardarms, and cheered the Union flag, as it was lit up by the blaze of the burning ships. The ease with which these vessels had passed the obstructions and escaped was a sore disappointment to the Confederates.[1]

We spent the greater portion of the day wandering about through the abandoned navy yard, and inspecting the first real devastation of war which we had yet beheld. Little did we realize that it was possible to rebuild the dry dock, or that in it, out of the charred remains of the Merrimac, would be constructed a ship which was destined to revolutionize naval warfare. Still less did we realize that this scene of destruction was, as contrasted with what we were yet to witness, as insignificant as the burning of a country smoke house beside the conflagration of Moscow.

Immediately after the evacuation of Norfolk by the Union forces, the fortification of the harbor began. Batteries were erected at Craney Island, Lambert's Point, Sewell's Point, and elsewhere. Obstructions were placed in the harbor to prevent the return of Union vessels. Long lines of intrenchments were erected in rear of the city, extending from the eastern branch of the Elizabeth River to Tanner's Creek. The military forces were distributed along what was known as the intrenched camp,

[1] For full and graphic description of this, see *Rebellion Records*, vol. i. Doc. p. 119.

and the fashionable amusement of the time was to visit
the various encampments, and witness the drills and
parades.

Our house, but a mile or two beyond the lines, was
constantly filled with visitors, and was gay beyond all
precedent.

Almost immediately after the passage of the secession
ordinance, father received a commission as brigadier-general in the Confederate service, with directions to repair to
West Virginia, recruit and organize a brigade, and protect that section of the State against any hostile advance.
His preparations for departure were immediately begun;
and I was desolate at learning that my brother Richard,
now seventeen, was recalled from William and Mary College to accompany him as aid-de-camp.

Just before their departure, the family was roused late
one night by a loud knocking upon the door, and the appearance of my brother Henry and two cousins who lived
upon the eastern shore peninsula. My brother was an
Episcopal minister, and had been up to this time in charge
of a church in West Philadelphia. He was exceedingly
popular with his congregation, and no man owed parish-
ioners more for love and kindness than he did. Hoping
against hope, he had clung to his charge, thinking that
possibly something might happen to avert hostilities.
Meanwhile, the feeling there had become intense.

One day, having occasion to visit the barber-shop of the
Girard House, the barber by some means discovered who
he was, and, seeking from him some assurances of loyalty
to the Union which he could not conscientiously give, the
barber threw down his razor, and refused to finish shav-
ing a rebel. Leaving the place, as a crowd was assembling, he hurried homeward, to find that his residence had
been protected from a mob through the prudent exhibi-

tion of a Union flag by a small boy whom he employed; and, under advice of friends, he left the city forthwith, and journeyed homeward via Wilmington, Del., down the eastern shore peninsula, to the home of two young cousins in Accomac. They joined him, and the three crossed the Chesapeake Bay in a small boat from Cape Charles, and reached our home as described.

My brother brought us the first tidings we had for a long time from our relatives in Philadelphia, and from his description they had become as intense partisans of the Union side as were we of the South. Poor fellow! he took the situation very much to heart. While loyal to kith and kin, he, even at that early day, declared that we did not know the power, the resources, or the numbers of our adversaries, and that the struggle of the South for independence was hopeless folly. We were all elated, and felt no doubts whatever. We were disposed to regard him as controlled in his feelings by his deep aversion to parting with a noble and devoted congregation.

A few days later, my eldest sister, wife of Dr. A. Y. P. Garnett, of Washington, D. C., arrived at our home with her family of children. They had abandoned their home, and reached Richmond on one of the last trains which came through. When they joined us at Rolleston, our family was a very large one. The teacher of my school volunteered, and the school closed. My father and young brother Richard departed for the war in West Virginia.

My oldest brother Jennings was about this time elected captain of the Richmond Light Infantry Blues, a volunteer organization founded in 1793. His company joined my father's forces, and became A Company, Forty-sixth Virginia Regiment, of Wise's brigade.

Bravely and gayly they all sallied forth to rendez-

vous at the famous White Sulphur Springs. Thence,
after organizing, they proceeded to Charleston Kanawha.
Every report from our own was watched for with intense
eagerness, of course, but the things occurring near at
hand were of the most exciting character.

After the evacuation of Norfolk by the Union forces,
the sound of cannon was almost hourly in our ears. In a
few days, Craney Island, Sewell's Point, Lambert's Point,
Pig Point, and other places commanding the entrance of
the Elizabeth and Nansemond rivers, were fully fortified
by the Confederates.

At these points, our own troops were constantly exercised in target practice ; and the Union forces at Fortress
Monroe and the Rip-Raps (then called Fort Calhoun,
now Fort Wool), and the Union ships in Hampton Roads
and the Chesapeake Bay, were engaged in similar drills.
At times, the reports, all of which we could hear, were
so loud and so frequent that we believed an engagement
was in progress.

Confederate cavalry patrolled the beach of the Chesapeake to guard against the landing of the enemy for an
attack upon Norfolk in rear. Major Edgar Burroughs,
my father's competitor for delegate to the Secession Convention, was in command of a squadron of this cavalry,
encamped near Lynnhaven Bay, to protect the seine-
haulers there who supplied Norfolk and the troops with
fish.

The camp was in a grove of live-oaks, behind the sand
dunes on the beach, but must have been visible with
glasses to those on the ships, and was easily in reach of
the guns of the Union cruisers constantly moving back
and forth along the coast between Fortress Monroe and
Cape Henry. Later in the war, that camp would have
been instantly bombarded ; but at this early stage, the

combatants were not altogether prepared to kill each other on sight.

The possibility of such an attack was, nevertheless, sufficient to make the place very attractive; and many a day, going down to the shore under pretext of securing fish from the seines, I remained in the cavalry camp all day, often watching the passing Union vessels through field-glasses, which made everything and everybody upon them plainly visible.

Then came the insignificant affair at Big Bethel. Exaggerated accounts of it frenzied us with joy. "The Happy Land of Canaan" was once more utilized for versification, and every little chap of my acquaintance went about singing : —

> " It was on the 10th of June that the Yankees came to Bethel,
> They thought they would give us a trainin',
> But we gave 'em such a beatin'
> That they never stopped retreatin'
> Till they landed in the Happy Land of Canaan."

My poor little mare Pocahontas paid heavily for all this war fervor. Not content with banging away half the day with the rifles at targets erected on land and water, I was ambitious also to become a cavalryman and a lancer. We had tournament every day; that is, riding at a run, trying to carry off suspended rings with a long pole. Then we would caparison ourselves with sabres and dash at dummy heads. In these exercises the riders changed; but the horse was the same, and no doubt Pocahontas felt deep regret at the condition of affairs which gave her such constant and violent exercise.

Then came the battle of Manassas. Until then, I had never conceived the intensity of feeling, the exaltation of exultation, to which men are aroused by the first deep draught of blood and victory. Fierceness, as we know it

in peace times, is, contrasted with human war-passion, as
the sweet south wind beside the desert simoom. Around
the telegraph offices in Norfolk, great throngs of citizens
and soldiers stood, roused to the highest pitch of excitement, as bulletin after bulletin was read aloud announcing a great Confederate triumph.

Men whose names had never been heard before leaped
at one bound into the front rank of the world's heroes,
in the minds of that delirious audience. Beauregard, Joe
Johnston, Stonewall Jackson, Bee, and Bartow were the
names on every tongue. The magnitude of the engagement was represented as equal to the greatest of ancient
or modern battles. The throngs gloated in the stories of
unprecedented carnage. One telegram announced a field
so covered with the dead bodies of gayly dressed Union
Zouaves that it resembled a French poppy farm. The
conduct of the Southern troops was represented as surpassingly brave and chivalric, while that of " the Yankees " was referred to as correspondingly base and cowardly. The boast that one Southerner could whip ten
Yankees seemed fully verified. The prediction followed
that within a month the Southern army would be encamped
about New York, and that it would dictate terms of peace
within sixty days.

It was many a year before I learned the historical fact
that the little battle of Manassas was one of the oddest
episodes in military history, in that it was fought at right
angles to the line of battle selected by both commanders,
and was virtually won by the Union forces when they be-
became panic-stricken and fled. It is almost incredible
now, remembering how it was represented at the time,
that only 750 men were killed in both armies, and less
than 2500 were wounded.[1]

[1] Official war records: Union, killed, 481; wounded, 1011; captured,
1460. Confederate, killed, 269; wounded, 1483; captured, none.

The war had begun successfully enough to the Confederates to fan and inflame into the most exaggerated proportions the vanity of a boy concerning Southern valor.

As the summer advanced, no other startling battles occurred.

Even at that early day, General Lee was the man to whom the Virginians looked with more confidence and more hope than towards any other Southern leader. His preëminence had been somewhat eclipsed by the brilliant success of Beauregard and Johnston at Manassas; but great things were expected of him in his campaign in West Virginia against McClellan. Lee's western campaign proved, as we all know, a failure. The mountainous character of the country was such as to preclude successful military operations.

My father, commanding to the south of General Lee, was forced, by the situation of the armies to the north of him, to retire from the Kanawha valley. Before doing so, he had made a successful foray upon the enemy at Ripley. The Blues, and some other troops under command of my brother, had surprised the enemy and captured a few men. It was a very insignificant affair, but we exaggerated it into a deed of great valor and importance. The Confederate forces retreated to the lines of the Gauley, Floyd won a handsome victory over the enemy at Carinfax Ferry, and my father's command took a strong position on Sewell's Mountain, awaiting attack and confident of victory.

Shortly after this, Floyd retreated with his command to a place called Meadow Bluff. He ranked my father, and ordered him to withdraw his forces to that place. This my father flatly refused to do, and his insubordination led to an angry controversy, necessitating the presence of General Lee. Upon General Lee's arrival, he fully sus-

tained the military views of General Wise ; but it was
evident that two civilians like Wise and Floyd could
not coöperate in harmony, and both were ordered elsewhere.

The exposures and excitements of the Virginia campaign resulted in a protracted illness of my father, and for
weeks he lay at the point of death in Richmond.   While
he was thus prostrated, campaigning in West Virginia
petered out, and both sides, Union and Confederate, realized that the fighting must be done elsewhere, and the
troops were withdrawn.   McClellan became commander
of the Army of the Potomac.

General Lee was ordered to Charleston to superin-
tend the fortifications there, followed by the sneer of the
cynical but brilliant editor of the " Examiner," John
M. Daniel, that it was hoped that he would do better
with the spade than he had done with the sword.   Floyd
dropped out of public view and died soon afterwards, and
my father's brigade was ordered to Richmond to reorgan-
ize and await a new assignment.

I shall never forget the impressions made by that brigade when it returned from the West Virginia campaign
in December of 1861.   They were the first troops I had
seen return from active campaigning.   During the very
rainy season in the mountains, all the gilt and newness
of their uniforms had disappeared.   The hair and beards
of the men had grown long, and added to their dirty appearance.   A famous charger, named " Legion," had been
presented to my father at Staunton as he went out in the
spring, and my brother had taken with him an exquisite
chestnut thoroughbred filly.   Exposure in bad weather
and bad feed had baked their coats and filled them with
mange, and had made these two, and all their companions, look like so many bags of bones.   When, spiritless,

dejected, and half starved, they were led from the box-cars
in which they arrived, I could not believe they were the
same horses I had known.

Altogether, a decided reaction had taken place since
the wonderful battle of Manassas. It had not been followed up by the extermination of "the Yankees," as I
expected it would be.

Although but two hundred and sixty-nine Confederate soldiers had been killed at Manassas, many of them
were our friends. But the deaths in battle were as nothing compared with other deaths. We were beginning
to dread measles and mumps and typhoid fever and dys-
entery in the camps. We were learning the ghastly truth
that, for every man who dies in actual battle, a dozen pass
away ingloriously by disease.

The skeleton had not yet clutched any of our family;
but, my! how many of our friends were already in mourning! And the war seemed no nearer to its end than
when it began.

Six months before that, the town would have turned out
to see the brigade pass through. To-day, under the command of the senior colonel, it marched through the city
quietly enough, and went into camp on the outskirts, without attracting great attention.

When father's health was partially restored, he returned
to our home near Norfolk to complete his recuperation.
One day we visited the Gosport Navy Yard, and saw
them building a great iron monster upon the original
framework of the Merrimac. My father felt great pride
and interest in this, for he it was who, before he had
departed for West Virginia, sent General Lee a description and model of a marine catapult, designed years before
by Captain Williamson; and he always insisted that

this was the first suggestion for the construction of the boat.

It was a very happy period, that time in the autumn of 1861, when my father and brother were at home with us. I was no longer anxious to see them in the field. I had heard too much of the exposures and dangers and deprivations of camp life. But in time the orders came. My father was assigned to the command of Roanoke Island. The brigade came down from Richmond. It was mightily spruced up and benefited by its sojourn in Richmond, and its soldierly appearance made a good impression as it passed through Norfolk.

At the head of his command in the 46th, my darling brother Jennings marched. When he saw me, he came out and patted and kissed me, and asked about everything at home. Before we parted, be sure he pressed into my hand a crisp new Confederate bill, for he and I were " partners."

The brigade was embarked on barges to pass down through the Albemarle Canal to Roanoke Island ; and the last I saw of them was as they floated away, towed by the tugs, singing " The Bonnie Blue Flag."

The thing which made me feel very proud was the news told me by quite a number of the officers that, in the reorganization near at hand, my brother was to be the colonel of the 46th. I asked him about it. He laughed and said it was all nonsense, and refused to discuss the subject. But I knew it was true, for everybody in the regiment turned towards him lovingly as the best and bravest and simplest and purest man among them.

I was lonesome enough January 3, 1862, when father and his staff rode off from Rolleston to join the brigade at its new station. They journeyed by land along the coast to Nag's Head, on the outer coast of North Carolina, whence they were to cross by ferry to Roanoke Island.

I felt a deep foreboding that trouble was in store for us from this new venture.

CHAPTER XII

THE ROANOKE ISLAND TRAGEDY

THERE are certain names whose mere mention produces feelings of horror, or pain, or sadness from association. To me, that of Roanoke Island is one of these.

The island commanded the passage by water through Hatteras Inlet and Pimlico Sound to Albemarle and Currituck sounds. It was a most important strategic point, for a force of Union troops passing it had at their mercy several towns upon the North Carolina coast, could cut off the supplies and railroad and canal communications of Norfolk, and were in position to attack that city in rear. About January 1, 1862, my father was assigned to the command and defense of Roanoke Island. Major-General Huger was the commander of the department embracing that position.

General Huger was one of those old West Point incompetents with whom the Confederacy was burdened. He was both by birth and personally a gentleman, and no doubt a brave man; but the only reason on earth for his being a major-general in command of an important department was that he was a graduate of West Point. The Confederacy felt this influence much more than the United States. Mr. Davis, our President, was a West Point graduate, as was everybody else connected with our military organization. General Bragg, his favorite military counselor, was the martinet of the old army; and Generals Hardee and Cooper, the leading advisers at headquarters, and Generals Lee and Johnston, the commanders in the field, were all West Point graduates.

I am not belittling the great advantages secured to the Confederacy by service of a number of very superior West Point officers, who joined their fortunes with hers; but with them came also a very inefficient and inferior lot, unfit for the high commands to which they were assigned, — men who stood in the way of better officers, and who were appointed and retained merely through favoritism. To this latter class belonged Major-General Benjamin Huger, the officer in command of Norfolk.

The Secretary of War at the time was Judah P. Benjamin, in many respects the most remarkable person in the Confederate States. The Confederate leaders were, as a rule, men of deep feelings and convictions, or men of intense or passionate natures. Not so with Benjamin: he had more brains and less heart than any other civic leader in the South. He was an English Jew, and a lawyer of the first rank. He entered upon employment as attorney for a client. For that client he worked with surprising acumen, with great learning, with boundless capacity for endurance, with unquestioned loyalty, and absolute fidelity. If his client was in any case hanged, it was only after Benjamin had done all in his power for him; but after Benjamin had exhausted the resources of defense, and come to the end of the business for which he was retained, he possessed the power of completely dismissing his client's affairs from his mind. Likely as not, he would be having a bottle of Madeira and a cigar at his club at the moment the hanging was taking place. His nature was such that he had no sentimental attachments, and seldom troubled himself about the troubles of others. His convictions were clear, vigorous, and strongly urged; but they were never passionate, or clouded by affection or

hate ; he was never harassed by reminiscences. When
a case was lost, he did not bemoan it ; he found another.
He played his part in the Confederacy as if he held a
hand in a game of whist ; a skilled professional, he lost
no trick that could be saved, and did everything possible
to win for himself and his partner. When he lost, he
indulged in no repinings ; he tore up the old pack, lighted
a fresh cigar, moved to another table, called for a fresh
pack, took a new partner, and played another game. His
last game proved to be much more successful than his
Confederate venture, for he moved to England, and
became justly eminent at the English bar. The Confederacy and its collapse were no more to Judah P. Benjamin than a last year's bird's-nest.

When my father was assigned to the command of
Roanoke Island, it was well known at the war department that General McClellan was fitting out an expedition to attack and capture the position.

The disastrous termination of the operations of 1861
in the mountains of West Virginia had not enhanced my
father's military reputation, or that of any other general
who was in the mountains. On the Union side, Mc-
Clellan had suffered, and even the prestige of Lee had
been damaged, in those impossible campaigns, so that he
had been assigned to the fortifications of Charleston,
followed by the jeering taunts of John M. Daniel, the
satirical editor of the " Richmond Examiner."

But while my father lacked the advantages of a military
education, he had a remarkably correct apprehension of
topography, and was quick to see the strategic value of
positions. As soon as he visited Roanoke Island, he
grasped its importance, and saw that it was not only
practically defenseless, but unsupplied with any adequate
means of erecting fortifications. He hurried back to the

headquarters of General Huger at Norfolk, and doubtless harassed that easy-going and high-living soldier with his importunities. Failing to obtain any assistance from General Huger, he repaired to Richmond, and endeavored to impress upon the Secretary of War the necessity for prompt action. Mr. Benjamin was an attorney, and not a soldier. He looked for instruction to his client, who in this case was General Huger. He doubtless thought that the West Pointer knew much more of such matters than the civilian, and regarded it as little less than insubordination for a brigadier-general to seek the department direct. Then, too, Mr. Benjamin was an easy-spoken, cool, suave Jew, quiet and diplomatic in speech, never excited. It disturbed his nerves to have General Wise in his department, — ardent, urgent, pressing, declaring that past neglect had been criminal and present delay was suicidal, and even guilty occasionally of some indignant swearing at the galling indifference shown to the urgent peril of the situation. The upshot of all this was a peremptory order from the war department to General Wise to return forthwith to Roanoke Island, and to do the best he could with what he had in hand.

After the inevitable disaster, the Confederate Congress declared that General Wise had done everything in his power, and that the blame for defeat lay entirely at the door of General Huger and the Secretary of War; but that never repaired the wreck, or gave us back our dead. [1]

[1] The report of the investigating committee, Confederate House of Representatives (Series I. vol. i. p. 190) : —

"The correspondence on file of General Wise with the Secretary of War, General Huger, his superior officer, the governor of North Carolina, and others, proves that he was fully alive to the importance of Roanoke Island, and has devoted his whole time and energies and means to the defense of that position, and that he is in no way responsible for the unfortunate disaster which befell our forces upon the island on February 7 and 8.

Our home was on the route between Norfolk and Roanoke Island. My father's haggard, perplexed appearance, as he passed back and forth on these fruitless trips, revealed only too plainly his knowledge that he had been placed in a death-trap. Indeed, we all knew, as well before as afterwards, what would be the result.

It was on the 8th of February, 1862 ; a cold, blustering northeast storm had prevailed for several days ; the leaden skies hung low; the rain, blown in sheets by the gusts, swept against the windows; all farm work had been suspended ; the tides were driven in high upon the marshes ; and the only time I left the house during the day was in an oiled sou'wester and gum boots, to look after the feeding of the cattle and the sheep, huddled in their sheds of myrtle-boughs, and to see that the stock was cared for in the evening. I was now the head of the plantation. A gloomy dusk was closing in; the cold

"But the committee cannot say the same in reference to the efforts of the Secretary of War and the commanding officer at Norfolk, General Huger. It is apparent that the island of Roanoke is important for the defense of Norfolk, and that General Huger had under his command at that point upward of 15,000 men, a large supply of armament and ammunition, and could have thrown in a few hours a large reinforcement upon Roanoke Island, and that himself and the Secretary of War had timely notice of the entire inadequacy of the defenses, the want of men and munitions of war, and the threatening attitude of the enemy ; but General Huger and the Secretary of War paid no practical attention to these urgent appeals of General Wise, sent forward none of his important requisitions, and permitted General Wise and his inconsiderable force to remain to meet at least 15,000 men, well armed and equipped. If the Secretary of War and the commanding general at Norfolk had not the means to reinforce General Wise, why was he not ordered to abandon his position and save his command ?

"But, on the contrary, he was required to remain and sacrifice his command, with no means, in his insulated position, to make his escape in case of defeat. . . . Whatever of blame and responsibility is justly attributable to any one for the defeat should attach to Major-General B. Huger and the late Secretary of War, J. P. Benjamin."

winds swept so keenly that they fretted the shallow pud-
dles collected in the yard.

With emptied feed-basket on my arm, I was returning
to the house, when I saw a horseman slowly approaching
by the farm road. He was so muffled as to be unrecog-
nizable, and even when he reached the yard gate, I did
not recognize the jaded beast that bore him as our pretty
little sorrel filly. It was my brother Richard, my father's
aid-de-camp, who for forty-eight hours had been riding
alone along the cheerless beach of the Atlantic to bring
the announcement to General Huger that the armada of
Burnside, consisting of about sixty vessels, had entered
Hatteras Inlet, passed up Pimlico Sound, and was in
sight of Roanoke Island when he left with his dispatches.
These he had delivered to the general at Norfolk, who,
as he reported, seemed almost indifferent to the announcement. Having performed his task, he had ridden back
to our home, seven miles upon the return journey, and now
reached it, himself and his steed half dead from exhaustion. There was little to lighten the gloom in the poor
fellow's appearance or conversation, for he reported our
father prostrated at Nag's Head from exposure in the
effort to prepare the island for the approaching assault.

A roaring wood-fire and a hearty supper somewhat
revived his spirits, and for a time we almost forgot war
troubles while he gave marvelous accounts of the great
flocks of sea-fowl through which he had ridden in the
storm. The strong winds and high tides had forced him
to ride, sometimes for miles, in water up to the knees
of his horse ; and the storm was so fierce that the geese
and brant and ducks, driven in-shore, were reluctant to
fly, and oftentimes barely moved out of the way of his
horse.

As we sat there, seeking such comfort as our home

and security from the storm outside gave us, and wondering what had happened below, we little realized that upon the day before, and on that very day, the battle of Roanoke Island had been fought and lost, and that our gallant brother, wounded to death, lay dying in the camp of his captors.

The battle of Roanoke Island, fought February 7 and 8, was the first of a series of disasters which befell the Confederates in the early part of 1862.

Roanoke Island is shaped something like an hourglass. Its northernmost half is higher ground than its southernmost, and the waters and wet marshes almost intersect it at its middle part. The engineers who planned its defenses placed all its fortifications upon the upper half, bearing upon the channel of Croatan Sound to westward. Not a work was erected to prevent a debarkation upon its lower portion. An attacking force landing there was absolutely safe from the water batteries, both while landing and afterwards. At the narrow neck of land which connected the upper and lower half of the island was a fortification, not one hundred feet in length and only four and a half feet high, mounting three field-pieces. This captured, every other artillery defense of the island was at the mercy of the enemy, who by that manœuvre were in their rear, — so emphatically in their rear that the vessels attacking the water batteries could not fire after the Union troops assaulted the redoubt, for their shot would have fallen into the ranks of their own troops.

The sea beach eastward of Roanoke Island, separated from it by shallow water, is known as Nag's Head. My father's headquarters were established at a seaside hotel on the outer beach. The announcement of the presence of Burnside's expedition found him prostrated with pneumonia, and the command of the troops devolved upon

Colonel Shaw, of North Carolina, although my father continued to give general directions from his sick-bed.

The entire available force of Colonel Shaw consisted of two regiments of North Carolina troops, numbering 1024 men, and a detachment of my father's brigade, numbering 410 men, under Lieutenant-Colonel Anderson, — total, 1434 men.

Upon the morning of February 7, the ships of General Burnside attacked what was known as the Pork Point battery, and a ridiculous little so-called fleet of Commander Lynch, consisting of seven tugs and river steamers. It was dubbed a " mosquito fleet," and such in truth it was. Although gallantly manœuvred, it was no more regarded by Commodore Goldsbrough than if the vessels had been so many tin pans armed with potato guns. Pork Point battery was bravely defended all day, but its guns could only be brought to bear upon objects within a limited segment.

The bombardment was kept up until night to cover the landing of the troops at a point known as Ashby's, just below the narrow part of the island. No serious damage was done to the battery, and but few men were killed.

Late in the afternoon, three Federal brigades were debarked. The first consisted of five full regiments under General Foster; the second, of four regiments under General Reno ; the third, of four regiments under General Parke, — thirteen full regiments in all, not to mention a detachment of New York Marine Artillery, with six Dahlgren guns, and Company B, New York 99th Regiment. The debarkation took place at Ashby's Landing.

Colonel Jordan, commanding the 31st North Carolina Regiment, was sent to this point with his command under

orders to resist the landing, but he retired without firing
a gun. He had but 450 men, and the overwhelming
number of the enemy, and the vast fleet covering their
landing and ready to open on him as soon as his firing
disclosed his position, perhaps justified Colonel Jordan in
returning. So the enemy, by night-time, in astonishing
force, was landed, and ready for next day's operations.

In his report, General Burnside gives a graphic description of the beautiful sight when one of his light-
draught steamers ran up, towing a hundred surf-boats
loaded down with men, and, " cutting loose " all at once,
the boats were beached side by side with such precision
that four thousand men were landed in twenty minutes;
and this was but one of his three brigades.

Fancy the feelings of that little band of raw North
Carolina troops under Colonel Jordan when, from the
adjacent woods, they witnessed these landings, and not
only knew they had but one thousand comrades to assist
them, but that, when the fight was lost, as lost it must be,
there was no hope of escape! Verily, the first colonists
were not more desperately situated. No one can blame
the poor fellows for quietly withdrawing up the dark
and narrow road to the earthworks at the causeway connecting the two sections of the island, a mile and a half
distant. There they found the Virginians and the 8th
North Carolina Regiment, numbering less than one thousand men in all. The earthwork facing south, and commanding the causeway by which the Union forces must
approach, was so insignificant in size that even the small
number of Confederates available more than filled it, and
a part of Jordan's regiment was placed in reserve in the
fight next day. The engineers who had erected this little
work had reported that the marshes to the right and left
were impassable. The same rainy, gusty night already

described settled down on our wretched soldiers, while, less than two miles away, between twelve and fifteen thousand of the enemy were building camp-fires, cooking their ample supplies of provisions, and preparing to advance upon the earthwork in the morning.

Anxious to obtain information, Colonel Anderson ordered Captain O. Jennings Wise, of Company A, 46th Virginia, with twenty of his Virginians, to reconnoitre the position of the enemy. In that wretched swamp, reconnoitring meant simply going down a narrow road until they struck the enemy. The road ran directly south, through the main embrasure of the earthwork, over the sunken causeway. In front of the work, for several hundred yards, the timber was cleared away. Beyond the clearing, the road entered the woods, and, turning to the right, ran down to Ashby's Landing where the enemy was bivouacked.

The task assigned to the brave fellows was simple enough. All they had to do was to walk right down through the silent pines until they came to the enemy's picket guard; when that happened, somebody was likely to be shot, and somebody likely to run away.

It all sounds very simple, does it not, dear reader? I am conjecturing, as I pen these lines, whether you ever had any such experience. If not, and if you really are anxious for a novel sensation, you can obtain it whenever you go on one of these little reconnoissances.

Cheerfully, and as uncomplainingly as if the allotted task was of their own choosing, the little party sallied forth. Across the opening they trudged in the gray darkness, and plunged into the silent woods beyond. In Indian file and in silence they pursued their route. Tramp, tramp, tramp, — on, on, on, every step bearing them, as all knew, nearer and nearer to the enemy they

were seeking. Now and again they paused and listened
for some sound ; then onward they pressed, the tension
constantly becoming greater. No picket fire warned
them.

Of a sudden, " Who goes there ? " came forth huskily
out of the darkness from a picket not twenty yards away.
Quick as a flash, they made a dash for him ; but he fired
and fled, followed by two or three companions, who, like
him, fired backwards as they ran, and our boys gave them
a volley, knocking one of them over. Pursuit was too
dangerous, for the sounds of the firing had aroused the
camp, and loud calls and hurrying voices, not far distant,
made it too plain that discretion was the better part of
valor. So, picking up the cap and gun of the man who
had been shot, the scouts started on a double-quick back
to the redoubt. What was learned was only that the
enemy had gone into camp near the spot where he landed.
Prepared for sleep by this little march and its excitements,
my brother and his men lay down on the wet ground behind the breastworks, and slept, some of them, their last
earthly sleep.

A heavy fog hung over Roanoke Island the morning
of February 8, so dense that the fleet opposite the Pork
Point battery was unable to open fire, except in a desul-
tory way. It was eight o'clock before the mists lifted
sufficiently for the attack, and then the gunboats fired
cautiously, lest their shells should fall among their
friends who were advancing towards our works.

General Foster's brigade, accompanied by the six Dahlgren guns, moved, about eight o'clock, up the narrow
roadway leading from Hammond's or Ashby's landings
to the redoubt. Their advance was completely concealed
from the Confederates, until a sudden turn to the left in
the road brought them to the clearing in front of our

earthworks. Then the Dahlgren guns, under Midship-
man Porter, went into position and opened fire, supported
by the 25th Massachusetts and 10th Connecticut regiments.

The disposition of the Confederate forces was as follows : three field-pieces, a 24-pounder, an 18-pounder,
and a 6-pounder, were mounted on the intrenchments.
For all three, they had nothing but 6-pounder ammunition. The 6-pounder was at the centre of the embrasure,
commanded by young William B. Selden, lieutenant of
engineers. The infantry supporting this artillery behind
the breastworks consisted of two companies of the 8th
North Carolina, two companies of the 31st North Carolina, and two companies of the 46th and 59th Virginia
regiments, in all about five hundred men. The Rangers
of the 59th Virginia under Captain Coles were deployed
as skirmishers to the right of the earthwork; and the
Blues of the 46th Virginia under Captain Wise were
deployed as skirmishers to the left, in order to guard
against any attempted flank movement. Every engineer
and every scouting party who had examined the ground
had pronounced the deep and heavily wooded marshes
to the right and left of the Confederate position to be
impassable.

General Foster, as soon as he engaged the fort with his
artillery and leading regiments, ordered the 23d and 27th
Massachusetts regiments of his brigade to pass into the
swamp on the right, with directions to spare no effort to
penetrate it, and, if possible, turn the Confederate left
flank. Moving rapidly along the edge of the clearing,
these two regiments with great pluck entered the bog and
undergrowth, and, toiling knee-deep in the muddy ooze,
soon hotly engaged the Blues in the effort to turn our
left flank. The fighting in front was stubborn, so stub-

born, indeed, that in three hours the 25th Massachusetts
exhausted its ammunition and was relieved by the 10th
Connecticut; and the artillery, having used all but a few
rounds of its ammunition, was ordered to suspend its fire.
Meanwhile, Reno's brigade, coming up, moved to the left
and penetrated the dense woods in the attempt to turn
our right flank. The assault of Reno's brigade was met
by the Ben McCulloch Rangers, alone. Poor Coles, their
commander, was killed. The onslaught of Reno was irresistible, and, as soon as his men could extricate themselves
from the morass and gain the higher ground where the
Rangers were posted, they drove the latter before them
like chaff before the wind.

Then came tremendous cheering from Reno's men, announcing their success in turning the right flank of the
fort. This so inspired the brigade of General Parke,
which had now come up and was deploying to the right
to aid the attack of Foster's flanking column, that the
last regiment of Parke (9th New York), while in the act
of passing the causeway, hearing the sound of Reno's
cheering and seeing a slackening of the fire from the
Confederate earthworks, changed direction and charged
the works in brilliant style. Whoever else may have
been appalled, young Selden still worked his gun, which
bore directly upon the advancing regiment. A discharge
passed over their heads. Deliberately lowering his piece
and reloading, he seized the lanyard in his own hand and
attempted to fire. The primer failed. Coolly securing
and adjusting a new primer, he once more sighted and
screwed down his gun so that it would rake mercilessly
through the ranks now close upon him. He straight-
ened himself from sighting, stepped back, and was actually making the motion to jerk the lanyard, when a
bullet from the rifle of a Union soldier not thirty yards

away pierced his brain, and he fell forward across his gun.

On the left, the Massachusetts men, inspired by the shouts from Reno's and Parke's commands, moved up and drove back the Blues. Captain Wise, scorning the protection of the trees behind which, by his command, his men were concealed, passed back and forth along his attenuated line, counseling the men to keep cool and fire close. In such a position, under the fire of two regiments concentrated upon a single company, his conduct was almost suicidal. It was not long before his sword arm fell helpless by his side, fractured near the wrist by a minie-ball. Untying a handkerchief about his neck, he bandaged the wounded limb, laughingly remarking that he was fortunate it was no worse; but he had scarcely resumed command of his men, when he fell mortally wounded.

His soldiers were passionately attached to him, and, although the fire was by this time becoming murderous, two of the Blues spread a blanket, lifted him gently upon it, and, bearing him between them, trotted off sullenly to the rear as the Union troops were climbing over the Confederate redoubt to their right.

All was over as far as the defense of Roanoke Island was concerned. Two small reinforcements landed on the north end of the island that morning, one under Colonel Green, another under Major Fry, but neither were in time to participate in the fight.

Our little band had done its best; two hundred and fifty-one killed and wounded in the Union ranks (more than half as many as our whole force engaged) testified to the honest fighting of our men.

The capture of the redoubt placed the Union forces directly in rear of the Confederate shore batteries; and, as no other positions on the island were defensible, Colonel Shaw surrendered his entire force.

My poor brother was borne by his men along an unfrequented path to the eastern side of the island. There they found a small boat, and, obedient to his earnest desire, were conveying him to my father's headquarters at Nag's Head, where he would have died. Unfortunately, a party of the 9th New York under Colonel Rush Hawkins pursued the same path as themselves, and, seeing the boat, opened fire upon it and ordered it to return. One of these shots gave my brother a third wound. A letter written thirty-two years afterwards by Colonel Hawkins, who in these days of restored amity I am proud to number among my friends, tells the sad, sad story of the death of that sweetest brother boy ever had.

A few days later, a flag-of-truce boat brought up the bodies of our dead. When, in the Capitol of Virginia at Richmond, I gazed for the last time in the cold, calm face ; when I saw the black pageant which testified to the general mourning as they bore him to his last resting-place in beautiful Hollywood, — I began to realize as never before that war is not all brilliant deeds and glory, but a gaunt, heartless wolf that comes boldly into the most sacred precincts, and snatches even the sucking babe from the mother's breast ; that the most cherished treasure is its favorite object of destruction ; that it ever plants its fangs in the bravest and tenderest hearts ; and that that which we prize the most is surest to be seized by its insatiate rapacity.

But, reader, the death of a dear one in war does not bring with it the chastened sorrow of a peaceful death. It inflames and infuriates the passion for blood; it intensifies the thirst for another opportunity to see it flow.

The feeling which possessed me then, I well remember.

It was, " How long, oh, how long, will it be, before I can bury these hands in the heart of some of those who wrought this deed ! "

In less than a month, the Confederate war-dogs tore, before my very eyes, their bleeding victims in a way that seemed an answer to my prayer for vengeance.

CHAPTER XIII

THE MERRIMAC AND THE MONITOR

THE building of the iron-clad afterwards famous all over the world as the Virginia, or the Merrimac, was a subject of daily conversation in our household from the time the Gosport Navy Yard was burned and abandoned by the Union troops in April, 1861.

My father, during his service in Congress, was for some years upon the Committee on Naval Affairs; his acquaintance with naval officers resulting from that fact, and from his long residence at Rio de Janeiro, was unusually widespread. Commodore James Barron was one of his constituents and warm friends. Commodore Barron was the gallant but unfortunate officer who killed Decatur in a duel, and was himself severely wounded. Besides other contributions of value to the navy, he conceived the idea of an impregnable steam propeller, armed with a pyramidal beak, and a terrapin-shaped back at an acute angle to the line of projectiles fired from its own level. He called it a marine catapulta, and had complete models, plans, and descriptions, which he exhibited to the naval committee, in the effort to have a ship constructed on these lines. He made little impression, however; for in those days steam navigation had attained no very great success,—much less the utilization of iron upon ships. He subsequently presented the model to my father, who had also a large number of models of other vessels.

In our rummaging about the place, we boys found these

models in some old boxes, and took them down to our millpond, where we anchored them as part of our miniature fleet. The Barron model, and one constructed by Lieutenant Williamson of the navy, were the most conspicuous, making quite a proud addition to our naval display. This was in 1860.

We also possessed a brass cannon about eighteen inches long, which had been cast for us by a convict in the Virginia Penitentiary. That cannon was stamped with the words "Union and Constitution," but its use by its possessors was most lawless. Modeling slugs for it by pouring melted lead into holes made by sticking our rammer in the sand, we were constantly firing these slugs, to the great peril of everybody in the vicinity.

One of our neighbors, a Captain Johnson, an old seaman, living about a mile down the creek, had a flock of geese; and from one of his voyages in Indian seas he had brought back six coolie boys, who were probably apprenticed to him. These coolies were passionately fond of the water, and were almost constantly in sight, bathing, or rowing, or sailing a felucca-rigged boat. After trying the range of our gun upon Captain Johnson's geese, we began to practice upon the coolies. On a certain evening, Captain Johnson appeared in full marine rig at our landing, rowed by his six coolies, and, announcing to our father the sport in which we had been engaged, gave notice that he had a gun of his own, with which, if we did not promptly cease our diversion, he would open a return fire.

My father, who was a friend of Captain Johnson, and indignant at our reckless misconduct, gave us all a bad half hour in consequence of this visit. We were summoned before him, and, after considerable discussion concerning the punishment we should receive, were marched in a body to the landing and made to apologize to the coolies, who grinned and showed their teeth. After that we were good friends of the coolies, and our future operations with the gun were confined to the millpond on the opposite side of the farm. In our new field, it promptly occurred to us, as it would to most boys, that the best targets for our cannon were the models of the iron-clads anchored out in the pond. Unfortunately, they had no iron upon them; and, such was the precision we had acquired in our practice upon Johnson's geese and coolies, that in a few days the models of Commodore Barron and Lieutenant Williamson were riddled, and ignominiously disappeared. They were resting in the mud at the bottom of our millpond when the war broke out.

The following spring, after visiting the navy yard and seeing the partially burned Merrimac, my father became enthusiastic upon the subject of raising her and building upon her frame an iron-clad ship on the lines of Commodore Barron's model. Imbued with this idea, he instituted rigorous inquiries for the model; but, for reasons which may well be understood, none of us boys aided him much in the search. Failing to find his model, he wrote to General Lee, who was then commander-in-chief of the Virginia forces, an elaborate description of Commodore Barron's invention, and made rough drawings, urging the use of the Merrimac for carrying out the design. He always believed and declared that this was the first suggestion which led to the building of the Virginia.

We all knew that an iron-clad ship was being built, and from time to time informed ourselves of the progress made; and great things were expected from her. So deep was my father's interest in her, that he several times visited the navy yard to inspect her. He repeatedly expressed the opinion that she was being built to draw too much water, and that her beak or ramming prow was improperly constructed in this, that it was horizontal at the top and sloped upward from the bottom, whereas it should have been horizontal on the bottom and made to slope downward to a point. When the ship was launched, he was indignant because the lower edge or eaves of her armor-clad covering stood several feet out of the water, and it was necessary to ballast her heavily to bring her sheathing below the water line. This increased her draught to eighteen feet, which was, as he declared, entirely unnecessary. He insisted that this condition was due to the failure of the naval architects (in calculating the water which she would draw when sheathed with iron) to deduct from the weight of her sheathing the weight of masts, spars, rigging, and sails, which were dispensed with.

Admiral Buchanan, Commodore Forrest, Captain Brooke, and all the prominent naval men connected with the Norfolk Navy Yard were personal and warm friends of my father. He did not hesitate to express his views concerning these things, but they, as professional men generally do, made light of the criticisms of a layman. Nevertheless, I think that many naval authorities are now disposed to admit that the chief reason why the Virginia did not triumph completely over the Monitor was her great draught of water, the loss of her prow, and the twisting of her stem in ramming the Cumberland.

After the disaster of Roanoke Island, my father returned to his home on sick leave, where for some time his life was in danger from pneumonia, aggravated by exposure on the retreat from Roanoke Island. Our house was visited almost daily during this period by distinguished military and naval officers from the city, who came to express their interest and sympathy.

It was before the day of steam launches, and the ap-

pearance of the distinguished officers and of the naval
boats which came up, manned by a dozen oarsmen, whose
stroke fell as that of one man, was very striking. During
these visits, they diverted my father with full descriptions
of the progress made in arming and equipping the Virginia, and we were advised that the time of her completion, and the attack upon the vessels in Hampton Roads,
was rapidly approaching.

There was dear old Commodore Forrest, tall, dignified,
and with a face as sweet as that of a woman, surmounted
by a great shock of white hair like the mane of some royal
beast ; and Captain Buchanan, far less striking in appearance, quiet, kindly, and as unpretentious as a country
farmer, but with an eye which age had not dimmed, and
which even then was filled with the light of battle. They
were both old men. Commodore Forrest was sixty-five,
and Captain Buchanan sixty-two. There was also Captain
Brooke, taciturn and dreamy ; and Lieutenant Catesby
Jones, a quiet man of forty ; and Lieutenant Minor, young,
quick, and fidgety as a wren ; and all the rest of them,
mingling with us simply and unostentatiously, as if unconscious that the issues of one of the greatest struggles
the world ever witnessed were committed to their keeping,
and that they were to emerge from it with names which
will be remembered as long as the records of naval warfare are preserved.

Almost daily we boys went to Norfolk for the mail,
or on some domestic mission. We preferred our boat,
and seldom failed, before we left Norfolk harbor, to
stand over toward the Gosport Navy Yard and sail around
and take a look at the Merrimac. Such we called her,
for we had never become accustomed to the new name,
Virginia. My father was now convalescent, and secured
the promise that he would be advised when the ship was

ready to sail for the attack. On March 7, he received a note from Commodore Forrest, or one of those who knew, advising him that the attack would be made upon the following day. He consented that my brother Richard and myself should accompany him, and the next morning the horses, which now had been well fed and rested for a month at home, were saddled and ready for us at the door.

When we reached the city, the Merrimac, accompanied by two little gunboats, the Beaufort and the Raleigh, had already passed out, and all three were below Fort Norfolk. The waterway is more circuitous than that by land, and we were sure we should reach Sewell's Point, the most favorable position for observing the conflict, before the slow-moving vessels ; in this we were correct. After a sharp gallop of eight miles, we rode out upon the sandy hills facing Hampton Roads at Sewell's Point.

The scene was truly inspiring. Hampton Roads is as beautiful a sheet of water as any on the face of the globe. It is formed by the confluence of the James, the Nansemond, and the Elizabeth rivers. The James enters it from the west, the Nansemond from the south, and the Elizabeth from the east. The tides in the Roads run north and south, and pass to and from the Chesapeake Bay through a narrow entrance at the north, between Old Point Comfort and Willoughby's Spit. Midway between these is the fort then known as Rip-Raps, the proper name of which was Fort Calhoun, now changed to Fort Wool. On the eastern side of the Roads the Confederates had fortified two points, — Sewell's Point, where we were, and Lambert's Point, at the mouth of the Elizabeth. On the southern side, between the mouths of the Elizabeth and Nansemond rivers, were the Confederate fortifications on Craney Island. On the western side, at the entrance to the Roads, is Fortress Monroe. From there the land runs westwardly to Hampton, thence southwardly to Newport News, which marks the entrance of the James River. The Roads are about four miles in width and seven in length. From where we stood, looking north, Fortress Monroe and the Rip-Raps were, perhaps, four miles away; looking westward across the Roads, Newport News was five miles away; and, looking south, Lambert's Point and Craney Island were plainly visible three miles off.

Upon the battlements of Fortress Monroe and the Rip-Raps great numbers of Union troops could be seen through field-glasses, and we could also make out the camps and fortifications of the enemy at Newport News, and between that point and Hampton, while our own people lined the shores and crowded the ramparts at Craney Island and Lambert's Point.

Anchored in the Roads were a great number of vessels of every description, steam and sail, from the smallest tugs and sloops to the largest transports and warships. Rumors of the attack had brought down to Sewell's Point a number of civilians, and the whole appearance of the scene was suggestive of the greatest performance ever given in the largest theatre ever seen. The Merrimac and her attendants had passed Craney Island, and were coming down the channel east of Craney Island light, when we arrived. As she passed our fortifications, she was saluted and cheered, and returned the salutes. From the way in which she was shaping her course when first seen, it looked to the uninitiated as if she proposed to sail directly upon the Rip-Raps. Such hurrying and scurrying was seen among the non-combatant craft in the Roads as was never witnessed before. From great three-masters and double-deck steamers to

little tugs and sailboats, all weighed or slipped anchor
and made sail or steam for Fortress Monroe, except three
dauntless war vessels, — two steamers, the Minnesota and
the Roanoke, and one sailing vessel, the St. Lawrence, —
whose duty called them in the opposite direction. A
long tongue of shoal, running out from Craney Island,
compelled the Merrimac to go below Sewell's Point
before she struck the main channel; then she swung
into it and pointed westward, showing her destination,
for she headed straight for Newport News, where the
masts and spars of the Congress and the Cumberland were
plainly visible.

It was now past midday. The Merrimac on her new
course was nearly stern to us, and grew smaller and
smaller as she followed the south channel to Newport
News. The three United States vessels — Minnesota,
Roanoke, and St. Lawrence — started after her by what
is known as the north channel. It was a bitter disappointment to us that the battle was to be waged so far
away, but the ships and their movements were still in
view. The sun was shining, and a fresh March breeze
would, we thought, blow away the smoke. It seemed an
eternity before the first gun was fired. The Merrimac,
Cumberland, and Congress were nearly ranged in our
line of vision. The Merrimac appeared to us as if she
was almost in contact with the nearest of the two vessels.
Captain Buchanan states in his report that he was within
less than a mile of the Cumberland when he commenced
the engagement by a shot at her from his bow gun. We
saw a great puff of smoke roll up and float off from the
Merrimac; a moment later, the flashes of broadsides
and tremendous rolls of smoke from the Congress, the
Cumberland, the batteries on shore, and the Union gunboats; and then came the thunderous sounds, follow-

ing each other in the same order in which we had seen
the smoke. The engagement had begun.

It was a time of supreme excitement and supreme
suspense ; for the details, we who had no glasses were
dependent upon those who had. " She has passed the
Congress ! " exclaimed an officer, who was straining forward, trying to descry the positions of the ships through
the smoke, which now enveloped the point of Newport
News and the water beyond. Bang — crash — roar —
went the guns, single shots and broadsides, making all
the noise that any boy could wish. " She is heading
direct for the Cumberland ! " shouted another between
the thunders of the broadsides. " She has rammed the
Cumberland ! " was announced fifteen minutes after the
first gun was heard, and our people gave three cheers.
Our teeth chattering with excitement, we awaited the
next announcement ; it soon came : " The Cumberland
is sinking ! " and again we cheered. Then came an
ominous lull, the meaning of which we did not know.
Those watching through the glasses notified us that three
steamers were in sight, standing down James River,
and we knew it was Commander Tucker with the Patrick Henry, Jamestown, and Teazer. Think of it ! The
Jamestown, which, but four years ago, had brought the remains of President Monroe to Richmond, with the New
York Seventh Regiment, on that visit of fraternity and
good-will. Here she was, armed as a war-vessel, fighting those very men !

Once more the cannon belched and thundered. This
time what we saw and heard was alarming: " The Merrimac is running up the river, away from the Congress and
other vessels ; she is fighting the shore batteries as she
goes." It looked indeed as if she was disabled in some
way ; again a lull and anxious waiting. " The Merrimac

is turning around and coming back!" Again the roar
of a hot engagement with the forts; another lull and
another heavy roll. "She is back pounding the Congress,
and raking her fore and aft. The Congress is aground."
Again our people went wild with enthusiasm. Poor fellows on the Congress! When the Merrimac withdrew
and passed upstream, it was only to gain deep water in
order to wind her, for where she had rammed the Cumberland, her keel was in the mud and she could not be
put about. The fearless sailors on the Congress, deluded
by the appearance of retreat, believed that she had hauled
off, and, leaving their guns, gave three cheers. Having
brought his ship around into position to attack the Congress, Captain Buchanan now came back at her, and, as
he approached, blew up a transport alongside the wharf,
sunk one schooner, captured another, and proceeded to
rake the Congress where she had run ashore in shoal
water.

Describing this stage of the fight, Captain Buchanan
says in his report: "The carnage, havoc, and dismay
caused by our fire compelled them to haul down their
colors and to hoist a white flag at their gaff and half mast,
and another at the main. The crew instantly took to
their boats and landed. Our fire immediately ceased, and
a signal was made for the Beaufort to come within hail.
He then ordered Lieutenant Commander Parker to take
possession of the Congress, secure the officers as prisoners, allow the crew to land, and burn the ship. This
Captain Parker did, receiving her flag and surrender
from Commander Smith and Lieutenant Pendergrast,
with the sidearms of those officers. They delivered themselves as prisoners of war on board the Beaufort, and
afterwards being permitted, at their own request, to
return to the ship to assist in removing the wounded,

never returned.   The Beaufort and Raleigh, while alongside the Congress after her surrender, and while she had
two white flags flying, were subjected to a heavy fire from
the shore and from the Congress, and withdrew without
setting her afire, after losing several valuable officers and
men.

Then Lieutenant Minor was sent to burn the ship,
when he was fired upon and severely wounded.   His boat
was recalled, and Captain Buchanan ordered the Congress
to be destroyed by hot shot and incendiary shell.

By this time the ships from Old Point opened fire upon
the Merrimac.   The Minnesota grounded in the North
channel; the shoalness of the water prevented the near
approach of the Merrimac.   The Roanoke and St. Lawrence, warned by the fate of the Cumberland and Congress, retired under the guns of Fortress Monroe.   The
Merrimac pounded away at the grounded Minnesota until
the pilots warned her commander that it was no longer
safe to remain in that position ; then, returning by the
south channel, she had an opportunity to open again upon
the Minnesota, although the shallow water was between
the two ; and afterwards upon the St. Lawrence, which
responded with several broadsides.   It was too tantalizing
to see these vessels, which in deep water would have been
completely at her mercy, protected from her assaults by
the shoals.   By this time it was dark, and the Merrimac
anchored off Sewell's Point.   The western sky was illuminated with the burning Congress, her loaded guns were
successively discharged as the flames reached them, until,
a few minutes past midnight, her magazine exploded
with a tremendous report.

Thus ended the first day's doings of the Merrimac.
Soon after she anchored, some of her officers came ashore,
and we, who had been waiting all day, and who had now

decided to remain all night in order to see the next day's operations, were gratified with a full and graphic description of the fighting. Captain Buchanan, Lieutenant Minor, and the other wounded were sent to Norfolk. Having been tendered the hospitality of Sewell's Point by some of the officers, our party remained, and were lulled to sleep by the firing of the guns of the burning Congress, and rudely aroused about midnight by the tremendous explosion of her magazine.

Up betimes in the morning, we saw the Minnesota still ashore. She was nearly in line with us, and about a mile nearer to us than Newport News. A tug was beside her, and a very odd-looking iron battery. We expected great things from this day's operations. About eight o'clock, the Merrimac ran down to engage them, firing at the Minnesota, and occasionally at the iron battery. She was now under command of Lieutenant Jones. We confidently expected her to be able to get very near to the Minnesota, but in this the pilots were mistaken. When about a mile from the frigate, she ran ashore, and was some time backing before she got afloat. Her great length and draught rendered it difficult to work her. Notwithstanding these delays, she succeeded in damaging the Minnesota seriously, and in blowing up the tug-boat Dragon lying alongside her.

While this was going on, the iron battery, which looked like a cheese-box floating on a shingle, moved out from behind the frigate and advanced to meet the Merrimac. The disparity in size between the two was remarkable; we could not doubt that the Merrimac would, either by shot or by ramming, make short work of the cheese-box; but as time wore on, we began to realize that the newcomer was a tough customer. Her turret resisted the shells of the Merrimac, and not only was she speedier,

but her draught was so much less than that of her antagonist that she could run off into shallow water and
prevent the Merrimac from ramming her.   There was no
lack of pluck shown by either vessel.   The little Monitor
came right up and laid herself alongside as if she had
been a giant.   She was quicker in every way than her
antagonist, and presented the appearance of a saucy
kingbird pecking at a very large and very black crow.

The first shot fired by the Merrimac missed the Monitor, which was a novel experience for the gunners who
had been riddling the hulls of frigates.   Then, again, when
the eleven-inch solid shot struck the casemates, knocking the men of the Merrimac down and leaving them
dazed and bleeding at the nose from the tremendous
impact, they realized that the cheese-box was loaded as
none of the other vessels had been.   Neither vessel could
penetrate the armor of the other ; both tried ramming
unsuccessfully : the Monitor had not mass sufficient to
injure the Merrimac ; the Merrimac only gave the Monitor a glancing ram, weakened by the Monitor's superior
speed ; and then the Monitor ran off into shallow water,
safe from pursuit.

Twice we thought the Merrimac had won the fight.
On the first occasion, the Monitor went out of action, it
seems, to replenish the ammunition in the turret, it being
impossible to use the scuttle by which ammunition was
passed unless the turret was stationary and in a certain
position.   The second occasion was about eleven o'clock,
when a shell from the Merrimac struck the Monitor's
pilot-house, and seemed to have penetrated the ship.
She drifted off aimlessly towards shoal water ; her guns
were silent, and the people on board the Minnesota gave
up hope and prepared to burn her.   This was when
Lieutenant Worden, commander of the Monitor, was

blinded and the steersman stunned. Their position was so isolated that no one knew their condition for some minutes; then Lieutenant Greene discovered it, took command, and brought the vessel back into action.

Shortly afterwards, Lieutenant Jones withdrew the Merrimac. In his report of the action, he said: "The pilots declaring that we could get no nearer the Minnesota, and believing her to be entirely disabled, and the Monitor having run into shoal water, which prevented our doing her any further injury, we ceased firing at twelve o'clock and proceeded to Norfolk. The stem is twisted and the ship leaks; we have lost the prow, starboard anchor, and all the boats. The armor is somewhat damaged, the steam-pipe and smoke-stack both riddled; the muzzles of two of the guns shot away."

When from the shore we saw the Merrimac haul off and head for Norfolk, we could not credit the evidence of our own senses. "Ah!" we thought, "dear old Buchanan would never have done it." Lieutenant Jones was afterwards fully justified by his superiors, but it did seem to us that he ought to have stayed there until he drove the Monitor away. Beside the reasons assigned above, Lieutenant Jones declared that it was necesary to leave when he did, in order to cross the Elizabeth River bar. The inconclusive result of that fight has left to endless discussion among naval men the question, "Which was the better ship of the two?" It is not within the scope of this volume to investigate that problem. It is certain that, up to the time the Monitor appeared, the Merrimac seemed irresistible, and that but for the presence of the Monitor, she would have made short work of the Minnesota. It is equally certain that the Monitor performed her task of defense. It is said she was anxious to renew the fight; but two weeks later, the

Merrimac went down into deep water, where the Monitor was lying under the guns of Fortress Monroe, and tried to coax her out, but she would not come, and even permitted the Jamestown and Beaufort to sail up to Hampton and capture two schooners laden with hay. The truth is that, if the Merrimac could have induced the Monitor to meet her in deep water, she would easily have rammed and sunk her.

On our ride back to the city, my father, while greatly elated at what had been done, continued to deplore the errors of construction in the Merrimac, which the two days' fighting had made all the more manifest; but we boys thought she had earned glory enough, and joined the others in the general jubilation.

Everybody in Norfolk knew the officers and men on board our ships; many of them were natives of the town. When they were granted shore leave, they were given a triumphal reception. Some time since, I read an account of the Dutch admiral, De Ruyter, who, the day after his four days' battle with the English fleet, was seen in his yard in his shirt-sleeves, with a basket on his arm, feeding his hens and sweeping out his cabin. It reminded me of the simple lives and unpretentious behavior of those splendid fellows who handled the Merrimac. Yesterday, they revolutionized the naval warfare of the world; to-day, they were walking about the streets of Norfolk, or sitting at their firesides, as if unaware that fame was trumpeting their names to the ends of the earth.

CHAPTER XIV

A REFUGEE

NOTWITHSTANDING our elation over the performances of the Merrimac, which every one in the Confederacy regarded as brilliant victories, the fact that Norfolk was in imminent peril became more and more apparent.

The lodgment gained by the Union forces at Roanoke, and their possession of the sounds and rivers on the North Carolina coast, had given them control of the canals tributary to the city, and their presence was a constant menace to the railroads, which were now the chief remaining means of supplies. Union troops could at any time be transported up the North Carolina rivers to within a few miles of the Seaboard and Petersburg lines.

If our army should at any time retreat from the lower peninsula between the York and the James, the Petersburg line would be further imperiled ; for in that event, it would be easy to throw a force of Union troops across the James to cut the railroad. The fifteen thousand Confederate troops in and about Norfolk would then be in a position of extreme danger.

These things were, of course, much more apparent to those in command than to us boys ; but throughout March and April we saw and heard enough to make us realize that there was a grave prospect that Norfolk might at any time be evacuated, and our home left within the Union lines.

My father became so thoroughly satisfied of the approaching evacuation of Norfolk that he suspended farming operations, directed the sale of surplus stock to the Confederate commissary, ordered that all the hogs should be killed and cured, and that all the corn upon the place should be ground and sold. Out of abundant precaution, the family was removed in the latter part of April to the vicinity of Richmond, and thither also were sent a number of the young, able-bodied slaves.

Meanwhile, his military duties called him to Richmond, where he was placed in command of the inner line of defenses at Chaffin's farm, on the James River.

Our home was thus left in the temporary custody of the miller, a white man, and a few of the old trusted slaves, my father having arranged with a friend in Norfolk, a man past the age of military service, that, in the event of the evacuation of the city, he would move out and take possession of Rolleston, occupy it, and as far as possible act as protector.

About May 1, satisfied that the crisis was near at hand, my father gave my brother Richard a leave of absence, and he and I, with an orderly, were sent to Rolleston to do what we could towards disposing of the remaining stock, and shipping our movables to a place of safety.

The plans of the military authorities were of course guarded with as much secrecy as possible, but upon our journey to Norfolk, the crowded condition of the railroads and the immense shipments of government stores and munitions not only confirmed us in the opinion that this was preparatory to evacuation, but satisfied us it was almost idle to hope to secure transportation for our private effects.

Still, we hustled around in a very lively way. We sold some horses and cattle to the government, and, with a little more time, would have succeeded fairly well in strip-

ping the old place "down to bare poles," as the sailors
say. It was a sad and lonely mission. The farm was
just beginning to assume an orderly and well-kept appearance. Two years of hard work, and the expenditure of a
large amount of money in new buildings and fences and
in painting, had brought it out wonderfully. New roads
had been built, trees had been planted, and ragged spots
had been cleaned up, until Rolleston, while nothing grand
or fine, was a sweet, home-like old farm, endeared to us
especially by the memory of the delightful days of boyhood which we had spent there. Now everything about
it was gloomy and sad enough. Not a human being was
in the house with us, except Skaggs, the white orderly,
who was sent to assist us, and old Aunt Mary Anne, the
cook, and Jim, the butler. Jim my father regarded as
his man Friday. Jim was to accompany us on our return
to Richmond. Nobody doubted that one so faithful and
so long trusted would prove true in this emergency.

We wandered back and forth through the old house,
looking over the deserted rooms to see what particular
articles, most prized, we might wrap in small packages
for removal, in case we could not arrange for the transportation of everything. It was a difficult problem to
solve. The house was filled with souvenirs from all parts
of Europe and North and South America. That was
before the days of bricabrac, but our house abounded in
the things now so called. Our drawing-room contained
several pictures of great value, and many valuable historical relics. Among the pictures were the original of Herring's Village Blacksmith ; a beautiful Bacchante, painted
in 1829 by Pauline Laurent, presented to my father by
Baron Lomonizoff ; and a set of exquisite Teniers (paintings of Dutch drinking-scenes), beside sundry works of
less note but great value. The cabinets were literally

loaded with pretty souvenirs of foreign travel, and articles
of historic interest.

We determined that these things should be first packed
and shipped, and had succeeded, on our visit to the city
the day before, in securing a promise from a friend in the
transportation department that, if we had them in Norfolk
the next day, he would send them through for us, even
if they went along with government goods. Accordingly,
we had ordered up the lumber for boxing them, and with
Skaggs and Jim were just preparing to pack, when, looking out of the window, we saw, rapidly approaching in a
buggy, the friend whom our father had engaged to occupy
the farm in case Norfolk was evacuated. As he drove up
to the yard gate, opened it hastily, and hurried to the
front steps, he exclaimed excitedly, even before alighting,
" The Yankees are coming! The Yankees are coming!
You had better get out of here quickly, if you don't want
them to catch you! " Then, in calmer tones, he told us
that the city was being evacuated ; that the garrison from
Sewell's Point and Lambert's Point had been withdrawn
during the night, and, together with the troops in the
intrenched camps between us and Norfolk, had all been
marched into the city, and transported quietly under
cover of darkness to the south side of the Elizabeth River ;
that the work of destroying the Gosport Navy Yard at
Portsmouth had begun ; that the Merrimac had sailed out
of the harbor to go up James River ; that the enemy at
Fortress Monroe were landing troops at Sewell's Point and
Willoughby's Spit; that they were rapidly approaching,
if they had not already reached, the city ; and that there
was not a Confederate soldier between us and them.

It took us about two minutes to decide upon our course
of action. By taking the Princess Anne County road
via Great Bridge, we could pass around the head of the

eastern branch of the Elizabeth River, and, going thence westwardly to Suffolk, get once more within the Confederate lines. We bore in mind that the Union troops in North Carolina were probably acting in concert with those at Fortress Monroe, and, marching up from the South, might intercept us. Skaggs hurried to the stable, harnessed four mules to a farm wagon, and went straight to the smoke house. We harnessed a pair of carriage horses to our best carriage, and proceeded to the house. The faithful Jim was on hand to aid in loading the carriage with such silverware and valuables as it would hold, and such of the farm hands as were left aided Skaggs in loading the wagon with meat.

Just before we were ready to start, Jim disappeared. In vain we called and searched for him. We never saw him again. The prospect of freedom overcame a lifetime of love and loyalty. There never was an hour of his life at which he could not have had his freedom for the asking. He had several times refused it. But now the opportunity was irresistible.

Skaggs with his wagon drove out ahead of us. My brother for the last time disappeared in the house. When he returned, he had in his hands a long roll of canvas. He had with his knife cut " The Village Blacksmith " out of its frame, and wrapped it upon a roller. We tied it firmly, and strapped it in the top of the carriage. After the war, we sold that picture for fifteen hundred dollars, and the money came at a very good time. During the present year (1897), the press has announced its sale in England at a very large sum. Some years afterwards, I found the Bacchante of Pauline Laurent in the parlor of a Union volunteer general in Washington, and have it now. He delivered it upon a very persuasive note from General Schofield, then Secretary of War. Our Teniers paintings, and several others of considerable value, have never been recovered. Soon after the war ended, General Brown, of the Freedmen's Bureau, returned to my father a valuable meerschaum pipe, the gift of the King of Holland to a friend; and when I was in Congress, General B. F. Butler presented me with a cup made from the original timber of the United States ship Constitution, received by my father from Captain Percival, of the navy. Thus, from time to time, a few of the things we left that day drifted back to us; but the great bulk of them were swept out by the tide, and lost upon the all-engulfing sea of war. My father's correspondence, which was very extensive, was left in his library. It was placed by the Union authorities in the hands of the late Ben: Perley Poore, of Boston, for examination. It was said that the chief purpose of such searches was to find, if possible, disloyal correspondence between Southern leaders and people in the North known as Southern sympathizers. Many years after the war, a box of unimportant letters was returned to me by one of the departments. The valuable portions of the correspondence were missing. When Mr. Poore died, a few years ago, his effects were advertised for sale, and among them were a great number of letters from my father's files.

We bade farewell to Rolleston with heavy hearts, and bent our cheerless way to Great Bridge. Even before we left, the explosions in Norfolk began, and we heard them as we drove along. We were very anxious lest the enemy, coming up from the South, should reach Great Bridge before we did, but we passed it safely, and late in the night reached Suffolk. It was a profound relief when we found ourselves once more safely within the Confederate lines. We saved our bacon in more senses than one; for a party of Union troops reached our place a few hours

after we left it, and the next day the Union forces occupied the route we had traveled to Suffolk. Not long
after our arrival there, we heard an unusually loud explosion, which, as we afterwards learned, was the blowing-up
of the magazine of the Merrimac, an event which depressed us greatly.

Reaching Richmond after several days' quiet driving,
we were directed to proceed to my sister's home in Goochland County, whither the women of our family had preceded us. There I remained until shortly after the seven
days' fighting about Richmond, when I was sent in charge
of some of our slaves to a temporary home secured by my
father in the mountains of southwest Virginia, at Rocky
Mount, in Franklin County. He correctly foresaw that,
whatever happened, no enemy would penetrate into that
remote region.

Before our departure for Franklin County, I made several visits to Richmond, which was now on all occasions
crowded to overflowing with troops. The most vivid impression of handsome soldiery made upon me during the
war was by the Third Alabama Regiment. In the two
months which had elapsed since the evacuation of Norfolk, I had not seen the regiment. Of its splendid conduct in the battle of Seven Pines, and in the other engagements, I had of course heard, and, knowing many of
its members, was naturally interested in everything concerning it. Passing along the streets of Richmond one
day, I saw three or four soldiers, looking as ragged and
dirty as the average, and I should have passed them by
without further attention but for hearing my name called.
Then it was I recognized a party of the dear old boys
whom I had known in the intrenched camp at Norfolk.
It is impossible to convey any idea of the change which
had been wrought in their appearance by two months of

hard campaigning on the Peninsula. Their uniforms, once so neat, were worn and torn and patched, marked with mud and clay, and scorched by camp-fires. Their bright buttons and trimmings had lost all lustre. Their hair was long, the freshness of their complexions gone, and their eyes seemed lustreless and bleared by camp-fire smoke. Even their voices were softened and subdued. Oh! nobody knows, until he has seen it, how marching and fighting by day, and sleeping under the stars or in the storm at night, can wear men out. The Third Alabama had had many a hard knock since we parted. In one of its earliest engagements, it had been subjected by the mistake of some commander to a murderous attack, in which it lost its noble colonel, Lomax, whose body was never found. I was shocked and surprised, upon inquiry for this or that light-hearted fellow whom I had known in the gay days of mandolin and guitar and moonlight sails, when they camped at Norfolk, to hear that he was killed at such a place, or wounded at such a place, or lay ill in such and such hospital, or was granted sick leave. Nothing I had ever seen or heard before so brought home to me the vivid realization that this war was becoming all-consuming and all-devouring.

"And where is the regiment now?" I asked. It was on the nine-mile road, facing the enemy, about seven miles from the city, near the Chickahominy bottoms, waiting to yield up yet other victims to the Confederate cause in the seven days' fighting about Richmond. That evening, I rode down to see them, but there was little to cheer one in the visit. There were no more tents, or cooks, or attendant servants, or bright uniforms, or bands, or dress parades. The camp was located in a copse of pines in rear of a line of breastworks from which the Union troops had been driven in the battle of Seven Pines, and

which were now made to face the enemy. The men slept
on the ground, without any covering. The few camp-fires
were built along the line, and the soldiers were cooking
their own rough fare. Out at the front, picket firing
resounded all along the line, and the men seemed to be
silently brooding upon the deadly storm then gathering.
The seven days' fighting, from Mechanicsville to Malvern
Hill, began a little later, and many another friend among
them yielded up his life in those sultry summer days of
1862.

As we were returning to Richmond that afternoon,
attracted by artillery firing upon the Mechanicsville pike,
we rode out to Strawberry Hill, a beautiful farm overlooking the Chickahominy valley, and witnessed an artillery duel between Captain Lindsay Walker's battery and
a Union battery stationed in a field just above Mechanicsville. The firing was across the Chickahominy valley.
Through field-glasses, large masses of the enemy were
plainly visible about Mechanicsville, and the spires of
Richmond were the background of the battery at which
the Union troops were firing. One of General McClellan's anchored balloons rode high in the heavens behind
Mechanicsville, and altogether the sight was exceedingly
inspiring. The distance between the combatants was not
more than two miles; but the damage done in these encounters, with the short-ranged artillery of that day, was
insignificant.

It was on this occasion that I first saw President Davis,
who had ridden out with several members of his staff to
inspect the lines. Mr. Davis was an excellent horseman,
and looked well on horseback. He had a passion for military life, and was a man of cool nerves under fire. His
presence was always greeted with considerable enthusiasm
by the troops, although he never had the hold upon their

hearts possessed by "Ole Joe," or "Mars' Robert," as
General Johnston and General Lee were called. I do not
recollect distinctly who accompanied him, but have an
impression that his young secretary, Burton Harrison,
was one of the party. It was a time of deep solicitude
for Mr. Davis, no doubt, as the army had just changed
commanders. General Johnston had been wounded at
Seven Pines, and General Lee had been relieved from
duty at Charleston and appointed to succeed him.

The war had by this time produced two comparatively
new industries. One was the issuing of "shinplaster"
currency, and the other was the manufacture of fruit
brandy.

The United States laws relating to currency and revenue no longer obtained, and the Confederate laws had
not been put into enforcement. The lack of small currency soon gave rise to the issue of one dollar and fifty-
cent and twenty-five-cent bills, by nearly all the towns
and counties of the State. Private bankers also issued
these bills, and even private individuals. I remember
particularly one Sylvester P. Cocke, an old fellow who
had formerly kept a country store at Dover Mills, in
Goochland County. In 1862, he had a little office upon
the bank of the "Basin" or terminus of the James River
and Kanawha Canal, in Richmond. The office was not
exceeding ten feet square, and stood in the corner of a
large vacant coal-yard. Mr. Cocke's banking facilities
consisted of a table, a small safe, a stack of sheets of bills,
and a stout pair of shears. He had his I. O. U.'s printed
on ordinary letter-paper. They had in one corner a picture of a mastiff lying in front of an iron safe, holding
its key between his paws, and, besides the date, declared,
"On demand I promise to pay to bearer" one dollar,
fifty cents, or twenty-five cents, or ten cents, and were

signed by Sylvester P. Cocke in a clerical hand. There
he sat signing, or clipping his promises apart with his
shears, and, although Mr. Cocke's means of redemption
were an unknown factor, his notes passed current with
people in Richmond, and all through the valley of the
James, as if they had been obligations of the Bank of
England.

Everybody in the country was engaged in converting
his fruit into brandy. Wherever there was a clear stream
and a neighboring orchard, there was sure to be a still.
Where all these stills and worms and kettles came from,
nobody could conjecture. It was a great fruit year, and
there were no markets, and it was apparent that liquor
would be scarce and high. In July, 1862, I drove our
horses and carriage from a point just above Richmond to
the abode of the family in Franklin County, a distance of
two hundred miles or more, and I feel confident that there
was not ten miles upon the route in which I did not pass
one or more fruit distilleries.

The passion for speculating in things which were likely
to become high-priced as the war progressed took possession of everybody about this time. Staple articles, like
sugar and coffee and flour, were growing scarce. Prudent housekeepers who had the means to procure these
things laid in large supplies. Speculators were buying
them up, and storing them for the rise which was sure to
come. About this time also, in view of the scarcity of
sugar and molasses, people began to cultivate sorghum,
which thrived in our climate, and yielded a reasonably
good substitute for cane molasses.

But the spirit of speculation was not confined to the
larger products; it extended to every variety of small
manufactured articles. On my drive to Rocky Mount, I
stopped one night in Buckingham County with an old fel-

low who had a wayside tavern and a country store. During the evening, conversation turned upon the increased price of everything, and the profits to be made by purchasing and holding articles which it would soon be difficult to procure. I became infected with the trading spirit, and on the following morning my host admitted me to his store to inspect his stock, and determine whether there was anything which I particularly desired.

War had made sad changes in the appearance of country stores. The shelves, once filled with bright prints and cloths and rolls of gleaming white goods, were now almost empty. Only here and there were a few bolts of common cloth, such as the Confederate mills could produce. The posts were no longer decorated with bright trace-chains and horse-collars and currycombs, but simply displayed a few rough shuck collars and improvised farming gear. The showcases had been utterly cleaned out of their stock of ribbons and laces, cakes and candies, and cotton and scissors and gilt things. Perfumed soaps and toilet articles, the glory of country stores in peace time, had disappeared. A few skeins of yarn for knitting socks, and cakes of home-made soap and moulds of beeswax, a few chunks of maple-sugar, all at very high prices, constituted about all the stock in trade that was left. I cast about in vain for rare articles in which to invest for a rise, until at last I spied, upon a dusty shelf, a box of watch-crystals ! Timidly I inquired the price, and it was not very high.

" Do you think they will increase in value ? " I asked hesitatingly.

" Increase ? " said the storekeeper ; " young man, you have a trader's instincts. Increase ? Why, in a year there will not be a watch-crystal in the Confederacy. You can name your own profit, and anybody will be glad to give it." So I bought the nest of watch-crystals, feeling sure I had a fortune in them. Perhaps I should have made a great profit. With this idea firmly in my mind, I nursed them carefully for several days, fully intending to put them aside until watch-crystals were at the top notch of Confederate prices, and then pocket a princely gain; but unfortunately, before I reached the end of that journey, I one day, in a fit of absent-mindedness, sat down upon the seat in the carriage beneath which my watch-crystals were stored, and thus ended my first and last Confederate speculation.

CHAPTER XV

AMONG THE MOUNTAINS

ROCKY MOUNT, our place of refuge, was a typical Virginia mountain village. Even at this present time, when it has its railroad and telegraph, one in search of seclusion from the outside world might safely select it for his purpose. Month after month, year after year, roll by without other things to vary its monotony than the horse-tradings, or public speakings, or private brawls of court days, or an occasional religious "revival."

But in the summer of 1862, the excitement of war, and the feverish anxiety to know of its progress, and the unusual activity in every sort of trading, pervaded even that secluded locality.

The nearest point to us reached by railroad or telegraph was a station named Big Lick, upon the Virginia and Tennessee Railroad, in the county of Roanoke. Round about Big Lick, whose population did not exceed thirty persons, the valley of the Roanoke River was, as it still is, a veritable land of Goshen. The adjacent farms, now covered by the populous city of Roanoke, were in a state of excellent cultivation, and counted among the most fertile in that beautiful valley. Hereabouts were the stately homes of the Tayloes, the Wattses, the Prestons, and many other representatives of the oldest and wealthiest families of southwestern Virginia.

When a visitor known to them arrived at Big Lick, it was useless, whithersoever he was bound or howsoever urgent his mission, to decline their generous hospitality. He was sure to encounter some of them at the station, and no protestation availed against first accompanying them to their homes, and then accepting their equipages in lieu of the public conveyance for the remainder of his journey.

My brother Henry, being a clergyman and non-combatant, was in charge of our family in Franklin. After driving our horses across country and conducting our slaves to their new abode, I again went East for some household effects, and he and I, returning together to Big Lick, were there seized upon by some friends, detained for several days, and finally dispatched to our journey's end in the private vehicle of a Mr. Tinsley. His home stood near the river bank, in a handsome inclosure, surrounded by fields of harvested wheat, where the very heart of the city of Roanoke is now located.

His adjoining neighbors, not far distant, were the Tayloes, whose mansion stood in a stately grove with well-kept lawns, at a spot where engine-shops and the houses of railroad men are built at present.

The thing which impressed me most, upon the visit to these good folk, was the absence of all the males of fighting age. The Tayloes of Roanoke were prominent people, and in all public affairs had figured conspicuously as representatives of their county and their section. The only members of the family at home to welcome the stranger within their gates were the aged, white-haired head of the house and four or five daughters and daughters-in-law, clad in mourning. We were received with faultless courtesy, and entertained with exquisite hospitality.

Tremulously and anxiously the fine old gentleman, with his female brood about him, asked for the latest news from the front. Eagerly they plied us with new questions concerning the progress and prospects of the struggle. Insatiable and unabated seemed their desire to talk on and on concerning that bloody phalanx aligned about Richmond, whence we came.

And well might their deepest interest be centred there, for every arms-bearing Tayloe — son, brother, husband — was in the forefront of the fight, save one. He had already fallen; his portrait hung in the spacious drawing-room beside the others. His name was spoken and spoken again with gentle tears, and with that reverence which the devout render to the Christian martyr.

In this spacious, peace-embowered home, nestled close to the river, under the looming Mill Mountain, whose afternoon shadows were already creeping across the lawn of oaks and elms, and maples and hickories, with the summer breezes stealing around its white pillars and through its wide hallways and swaying its muslin curtains, with naught but gently murmured conversation to break the delicious quietude, how far away seemed the war! how startling was the contrast with the seething cauldron of strife in which their strong men struggled about Richmond!

Yet which were suffering the most? Who shall measure the agony which racked those hearts, outwardly so placid, during the long years they waited while the strife went on?

Who can picture the desolating sorrow which engulfed them as, one by one, the strong arms on which that household depended fell helpless, and the news came home that the brave hearts for whose safety they prayed had ceased to beat! for it was so. The war filled grave after grave in the graveyard of the Tayloe family, until, when it ended, the male line was almost extinct.

Our visit to these good folk was charming, and from

time to time, when wearied of our mountain isolation, we would return to their lovely valley to mingle anew with such congenial friends.

To the east and south of them was the Blue Ridge, and beyond it our home. From the railroad station the stage road ran for a mile or two through the valley, then crossed the Roanoke River by a ford at the base of the mountains, then plunged into the rugged range. Winding up hill and down vale it went on, through pass and gorge and over tumbling mountain-stream, until it emerged into the rough foot-hill country east of the Blue Ridge, in which was our new home.

Twenty-eight miles of travel over such a route seems much more than the measured distance, and carried us indeed into a new class of population, as distinct from that which we left behind as if an ocean instead of a mountain range had separated the two communities. Soon the broad pastures and fields of grain had disappeared. In their place were rough, hillside lots, with patches of buckwheat or tobacco. Instead of the stately brick houses standing in groves on handsome knolls, all that we saw of human habitations were log-houses far apart upon the mountain sides, or in the hollows far below us. No longer were pastures visible, with well-bred cattle standing in pooly places, shaded by sugar maples, bathing their flanks at noontide. No more did we meet smart equipages drawn by blooded horses. No more the happy darkey greeted us with smiles.

Up, up, up, — until the mountain side fell far below our track; down, down, down, — until our wheels ground into, and our horses scattered about their feet, the broken slate of a roaring stream. Now, following the sycamores along its banks, with here a patch of arable land and its mountain cabin, whence a woman smoking a pipe, and

innumerable tow-headed children hanging about her
skirts, eyed us silently ; and there another roadside cabin,
with hollyhocks and sunflowers and bee-hives in the yard,
the sound of a spinning-wheel from within, a sleeping cat
in the window, and a cur dog on the doorstep ; here a
carry-log, with patient team drawn aside upon the narrow
road to let us pass, the strapping teamster in his shirt-
sleeves, with trousers stuck into his cowhide boots, leaning
against his load so intent in scrutiny of us that he barely
noticed our salutation ; here a bearded man, clad in homespun and a broad slouched hat, riding leisurely along on
his broad-backed, quiet horse, carrying the inevitable
saddle-bags of the mountaineer ; here a woman on horseback, with long sunbonnet, and coarse, cotton riding-skirt,
and bag slung at the saddle-bow, and small boy, with
dangling bare feet, riding behind her ; here a spout-spring
by the roadside, where the living water of the mountain
side leaped joyously from a hollow gum-tree log grown
green in service ; now mounting upward again until all
that is visible is the winding road, with the blue sky
above it, and the massed tree-tops below, and the curling
smoke of some mountain distillery, with nothing to break
the stillness but the heavy hammering of the log-cock
upon some dead limb, or the drumming of the ruffed
grouse far away. So, on and on we toiled, until we
reached the open country beyond the mountains, and late
in the evening our steaming horses drew up at our new
home, which was strange and different from any we had
ever had before.

Our house was large, among the newest and most
modern in the village, prettily located on the outskirts,
on the highest knoll in the place, and commanded a fine
view of the little valley and Bald Knob, and the mountains through which we came. The stage road, after

passing our house, entered the main street of the village, which was a rocky lane upon a sharp decline, with stores and houses scattered on either side, terminating at an inclosure where stood the court house, clerk's office, and county jail. Halfway down this street was the tavern, an antiquated structure, with a porch extending along its entire front, its brick pillars supporting a second story overhanging the porch. This porch, which was almost on a level with the street, was provided with an ample supply of benches and cane-bottom chairs. At one end of it, suspended in a frame, was the tavern bell, whose almost continual clang was signal for grooms to take or fetch horses, or summons to meals.

The tavern porch was the rallying-point of the town: hither all news came; here all news was discussed; hence all news was disseminated. From this spot the daily stage departed in the morning. Here villagers and country folk assembled in the day and waited in the evening; and to this spot came the stage in the evening, bearing the mail, the war news, and such citizens as had been absent, visitors who drifted in, or soldiers returning sick, wounded, or on furlough.

Supreme interest centred ever about the arrival or departure of the stage. In the foggy morning it appeared with its strong four-in-hand team, and took its place majestically in front of the old tavern. The porters rocked it as they dumped the baggage into the boot; the red-faced driver came forth from the breakfast-room with great self-importance. With his broad palm he wiped away the greasy remnants of his meal, lit his brier-root pipe, drew on his buckskin gloves, settled his slouched hat over his eyes, clambered to his seat upon the box, gathered his reins and whip, and cast a glance towards the post-office across the way; an aged man and a meek-

eyed woman in simple garb slipped quietly into the rear
seats, going perhaps on some sad mission under summons
to a far-off hospital at the front ; a dainty miss, with bonnet-box and bunch of flowers, kissed papa and mamma
and took her place within, full of joyous anticipation,
doubtless, for even in war times girls love to visit each
other ; a fat commissary, returning from his search in
the back country for supplies, came forth, reeking with
rum and tobacco, and swung up awkwardly to the seat
beside the driver. Tom, Dick, and Harry, the new
recruits bound for the front, proud in their new and
misfit uniforms, seized mother, wife, sister, or sweetheart
in their arms, kissed them, bade them have no fear, and
scrambled lightly to the top. The lame and tardy post-
master hobbled forth at last, and threw his mail-pouch up
to the dashboard. The coachman gave his warning cry
of " All aboard," the hostlers drew off the blankets, the
long whip cracked its merry signal; with discord in each
footfall at the start and concord as they caught the step,
the horses pulled away ; and the lumbering stage went
grinding up the stony street, its horn singing its morning
carol to those who were awake. As they disappeared
over the hill-top, a last merry cry of parting came back
from the bright boys on the stage-top, and the last they
saw of home was the waving tokens of love from those
they left behind.

As the day advanced, the tavern porch again took on
an air of life.

Everybody traveled upon horseback. By midday, the
country folk began to stream in. Up and down the street
a gradually increasing line of saddle-horses were "hitched."
Women, old and young, arrived, — all of conventional
dress, and with horses singularly alike. Their bonnets
were the long-slatted poke-bonnet ; their riding-skirts, of

coarse cotton. Alighting at the horse-blocks, they untied
and slipped off the skirts and tied them to their saddle-
bows, revealing their plain homespun dress. Their horses
were broad-backed, short on the leg, carried their heads
on a level with their shoulders, and moved with noses
advanced like camels. They had no gaits but a swift
walk, a gentle fox-trot, or a slow, ambling pace. When
they had " hitched the critturs," these women went pok-
ing about the stores, or the tavern kitchen, or the private
houses, with chickens or butter, or other farmyard produce, seldom speaking further than asking one to buy ;
and when their sales were effected and little purchases
made, they went away as silently as they had come.

The men came by themselves. Their principal occupation seemed to be horse-trading. At times, the neighboring stables, and even the street itself, were filled with men
leading their animals about, and engaged in the liveliest
of horse-trading. A considerable proportion of the population belonged to a religious sect known as Dunkards.
In appearance, they were solemn and ascetic. The men
wore long, flowing beards, and their homespun dress was
of formal cut. Their doctrinal tenets were opposed to
slavery and to war. Whenever political or military discussions arose, they promptly withdrew. They were very
strict temperance men, and decent, orderly, law-abiding
citizens, but horse-traders ! It must have been a part of
their religious faith. A Dunkard was never so happy as
when he was horse-trading.

There were others, too, to whom temperance was not
so sacred as to the Dunkards. By three or four o'clock,
the tavern bar was liberally patronized. The recruiting-
office had its full quota of young fellows inquiring about
the terms of enlistment. The tavern porch was filled
with people discussing war news, and the quartermaster

down the street had more horses offered to him than he
was authorized to buy.

At such times, a favorite entertainment was to draw
General Early out upon his views of men and events, for
the edification of the tavern-porch assemblage.

He was a resident of Franklin, and at that time sojourn-
ing at the tavern. He had been severely wounded in the
battle of Williamsburg in May, 1862, and was now quite
convalescent, but still on sick leave. He was a singular
being.

Franklin County had been strongly opposed to secession. Jubal A. Early was a pronounced Union man, and
was elected from his county as her representative to the
Secession Convention. In that body he had opposed and
denounced secession until the ordinance was passed. As
soon as the State seceded, he declared that his State was
entitled to his services, and tendered them. He was a
man of good family, a graduate of the West Point Military Academy, and possessed unsurpassed personal courage. In 1862, he was a brigadier-general, and had been
conspicuously brave in the battle in which he was wounded.
His subsequent career in higher commands was disastrous.
After the war, he became notorious as the most implaca-
ble and "unreconstructed" of all the Confederate generals. He was a man deeply attached to a small circle of
friends, but intensely vindictive and abusive of those he
disliked.

At the time of which I write, he was the hero of Franklin County, and, although he professed to despise popularity and to be defiant of public opinion, it was plain that
he enjoyed his military distinction. It had done much to
soften old-time asperities, and blot out from the memory
of his neighbors certain facts in his private life which had,
prior to the war, alienated from him many of his own

class. In fact, I doubt not he was a happier man then than he had been for many a year before, or was at a later period, when he became more or less a social and political Ishmaelite.

He was eccentric in many ways, — eccentric in appearance, in voice, in manner of speech. Although he was not an old man, his shoulders were so stooped and rounded that he brought his countenance to a vertical position with difficulty. He wore a long, thin, straggling beard. His eyes were very small, dark, deep-set, and glittering, and his nose aquiline. His step was slow, shuffling, and almost irresolute. I never saw a man who looked less like a soldier. His voice was a piping treble, and he talked with a long-drawn whine or drawl. His opinions were expressed unreservedly, and he was most emphatic and denunciatory, and startlingly profane.

His likes and dislikes he announced without hesitation, and, as he was filled with strong and bitter opinions, his conversation was always racy and pungent. His views were not always correct, or just, or broad; but his wit was quick, his satire biting, his expressions were vigorous, and he was interestingly lurid and picturesque.

With his admiring throng about him on the tavern porch, on summer evenings in 1862, General Early, in my opinion, said things about his superiors, the Confederate leaders, civic and military, and their conduct of affairs, sufficient to have convicted him a hundred times over before any court-martial. But his criticisms never extended to General Robert E. Lee. For Lee he seemed to have a regard and esteem and high opinion felt by him for no one else. Although General Lee had but recently been called to the command of the army, he predicted his great future with unerring judgment.

The arrival of the stage not infrequently interrupted

General Early's vigorous lectures. For half an hour or
more before the event, the expectant throng would increase, and, as those who "brace" themselves for the
crisis were there, as everywhere else, conversation grew
louder and agitation greater as the time approached.
Then the stage would heave in sight in the gloaming, and
come rattling down the rough street, the horseshoes knocking fire from the flints. Before the smoking and jaded
beasts had fairly stopped, loud inquiries would be made
on all hands, of driver and passengers, for war news.
Somebody would throw down the latest newspaper; somebody would mount a chair and read aloud; and, just as
the news was encouraging or depressing, there would be
cheering or silence. Then would come the rush for the
mail to the post-office across the way.

The passengers, also, were a source of engrossing interest. There was young So-and-so, with his empty sleeve.
A year ago he had left the place, and passed safely
through all the earlier battles; but at Malvern Hill a
grapeshot mutilated his left arm. Amputation followed,
and now, after a long time in hospital, here he was, home
again, pale and bleached, with an honorable discharge in
his pocket, and maimed for life. And there, collapsed
upon the rear seat, more dead than alive, too weak to
move save with the assistance of friends, was a poor, wan
fellow, whom nobody knew at first. How pitiful he
seemed, as they helped him forth, his eyes sunken yet
restless, his weak arms clinging about their necks, his
limbs scarce able to support his weight, his frame racked
by paroxysms of violent coughing! "Who is it?" passed
from mouth to mouth. "Good God!" exclaimed some
one at the whispered reply, "it can't be! That is not
Jimmie Thomson. What! Not old man Hugh Thomson's son, down on Pig River? Why, man alive, I knew

the boy well. He was one of the likeliest boys in this whole county. Surely, that ar skeleton can't be him!" But it was. The exposure of camp life had done for poor Jimmie what bullets had failed to do.

There, perched gayly in air, and tumbling down upon the heads of the bystanders with joyous greeting, was the sauciest, healthiest youngster in the village, come home on his first furlough in a twelvemonth, wearing on his collar the bars of a lieutenant (conferred for gallantry at Seven Pines), in place of the corporal's chevrons on his sleeve when he marched away. Camp life had made no inroads on his health. The sun and rain had only given him a healthy bronze. His digestion would have assimilated paving-stones. The bullets had gone wide of him. And his little world, the dearest on earth to him, — the little world which had laughed and cried over the stories of his capers and his courage in the field, — stood there surprised and delighted, with smiling faces and open arms, to welcome him home, their own village boy, their saucy, gallant fighting-chap, their hero, — home again, if only for a week!

Each day opened and passed and closed, with its excitements. It was all very narrow and primitive, the out-of-the-way world of the obscure village in an unknown region. Yet in it were the same old hopes and fears and joys and tears, hearteases and heartaches, loves and hates, and all the moods and tenses of human nature, to be found in the most populous and cosmopolitan hives of humanity.

I was now nearly sixteen. Many youths of my age were in the army. I had written more than once for my father's consent to enlist, but received stern denials. The war talk at the old tavern, the stories of camps and fights and military glory, the daily enlistments, the desire to appear a man in the eyes of certain girls, were all coöperating to inflame my desire to be a soldier. I was growing mannish and rebellious. My brother saw it all, and heard me threaten to run away, and wrote father seriously, advising him that I was getting beyond his control, and urging him to send me to the Virginia Military Institute, where I would be under restraint, and receive instruction, instead of growing up in ignorance and idleness.

It was soon settled. September 1, 1862, I left Rocky Mount, took the train at Big Lick, went to the neighboring station of Bonsacks, and there perched myself upon the stage-top, booked for Lexington. It was a long journey, occupying sixteen hours. We started at six P. M., and, riding continuously, reached Lexington at ten o'clock the following morning. It was a glorious ride in brilliant autumn weather, with moonlight. We passed through Fincastle and Buchanan, and over the Natural Bridge.

As we approached Lexington, and I caught sight of the Virginia Military Institute and its beautiful parade grounds, and professors' houses and other buildings, my mind was filled with thoughts of glorious military life, and the commission in the army which awaited me when I graduated, for I was now a cadet in the West Point of the Confederacy.

CHAPTER XVI

PRESBYTERIAN LEXINGTON

GREAT differences in soil, climate, and scenery exist between the grand divisions into which Virginia is cut up geographically. But they are not more striking than the diversity of the populations, one from the other, in these several sections, springing from differences in the time and the manner in which, and the people by whom, her several early settlements were made.

Two or three centuries of common government would ordinarily seem sufficient to produce a homogeneous population in a State. While this result has been attained in Virginia in essentials, it is nevertheless surprising to observe in each section local peculiarities, types, and characteristics plainly traceable to its earliest settlement.

We were first introduced to the lower Tidewater section, where the soil is sandy, the climate balmy, the landscape flat, viewless, save as it is redeemed from monotony by the boundless, ever-changing grandeur of old Ocean. The people, while of her oldest strains, are simple in their mode of living, and admit neither lineage nor wealth as basis for any caste or class distinction. Then we turned to the region of the upper and lower James, with Richmond as its centre, settled later than Tidewater by the so-called Cavalier immigration of 1649–60. There, of old, social relations were akin to those of Rome's patricians and plebeians, patrons and clients. Not alone was the haughty descendant of Charles I. owner of a plantation

and of slaves, — he was more: the poor whites and the
shopkeepers of country and town alike, consciously or
unconsciously, willingly or unwillingly, rendered him
homage as if he were their superior. And he, while often
proclaiming principles of social equality, seldom practiced them, and quietly accepted, as his legitimate due,
the preëminence granted him by his humbler neighbors.

Then, with a mere glimpse of the Roanoke region, we
passed into the rocky soil, the wild and mountainous
landscape, and the rough, new, and nondescript population which, from one direction and another, has collected
upon and taken possession of the eastern slope of the
Blue Ridge range. Here, again, we found a democracy
full of independence and courage, but in all things of
education and refinement, far inferior to that in Tidewater.

Now, at Lexington, we are in the heart of the valley
lying between the Blue Ridge and Alleghany ranges. It
is a region with a different soil, a different climate, different scenery, and a population more distinctly *sui generis*
than any yet described. The soil is based upon blue
limestone. It is where the grasses grow. The lands lie
tumbled into knobby hills and rolling fields, with here and
there narrow fertile valleys traversed by limpid streams,
whose banks are cedar-clad bluffs of limestone shale.
The great valley is more broken here, less pastoral, and
not so charming as in its lower section to the north, where
it widens, and is watered by the Shenandoah; but this is
the bolder landscape, with a rugged beauty peculiar to
itself. The mountain framing of the picture is the same;
but the land is higher, for, as the cloud-capped peaks of
the Blue Ridge and Alleghany ranges draw nearer to
each other, the vale between them is nearer to their own
altitude. We are in Rockbridge County, so called be-

cause within its limits is the superb natural arch of limestone known the world over as the Natural Bridge.

Lexington, the county seat of Rockbridge, is near the
summit of the transverse watershed of the great valley.
Within a few miles of the town, streams rise, some pouring their waters southward into the tributaries of the
James, and others coursing northward, tributary to the
Shenandoah, which enters the Potomac at Harper's Ferry.
The place itself is beautiful. Looking east and south,
the rolling country falls away to the base of the Blue
Ridge, where the South River and North River unite and
flow onward to join the James, where their united waters
turn eastward through the pass at Balcony Falls. The
magnificent Blue Ridge range bounds the eastern view,
and is last seen to southward, where the twin breasts of
the Peaks of Otter rear themselves against the distant
blue. Northward, beyond the wooded bluffs of the North
River, steep hills of farming lands are tilted towards us,
their sides dotted with cattle, their summits crowned with
forests. Beyond these, crest after crest of the smaller
foothills of the Alleghanies appear. To the northwest,
looming in isolated majesty, is the House Mountain, with
the peak of the Devil's Backbone behind it, marking the
route through historic Goshen Pass. North and south, as
far as the eye can reach, shading away in their tints from
deep emerald to dreamy blue as they become more and
more remote, are masses of hills. To the west and southwest, now strongly outlined, now melting into the last visible things of the distance, are the azure peaks of the
Alleghanies. Such is the country about Lexington, where
Virginia has her Military Institute. It is a spot almost
as beautiful as West Point, and the school is second only
to the Military Academy in thoroughness. It is an ideal
spot for healthfulness, and the isolation of youth from the

temptations and distracting influences of crowded communities.   The boy who finds allurement to idleness and
vice in that town would discover it anywhere.

It is a community of Scotch-Irish Presbyterians.   For
more than a hundred years after the settlement of Jamestown, and for over fifty years after Richmond was an
incorporated city, this valley remained unviewed by the
eye of any white man.

As early as 1608, Newport, on his second visit to the
Virginia colony, brought with him a boat built in sections, to be transported by him under orders to find the
South Sea beyond the mountains.   The extent to which
he performed that order was that he marched to the Monacon country, about twenty miles west of Richmond, and
his company returned footsore to Jamestown.

One hundred and two years later (1710), Governor
Spotswood wrote to the Council of Trade in London that a
party of adventurers had found the mountains "not above
a hundred miles from our upper settlements, and went up
to the top of the highest mountains with their horses,"
and looked over into the valley.   This is supposed to have
been near Balcony Falls.   It was not until 1716 that the
first passage of the Blue Ridge was effected.   Then Governor Spotswood and his "Knights of the Golden Horseshoe" entered the lower or Shenandoah valley by way of
Swift Run Gap, and took possession in the name of George
the First.   Governor Spotswood's expedition resulted in
nothing important.   The only diary of its performance
extant is principally devoted to description of the liquors
which the party carried with it, whereof eleven sorts are
enumerated.   A few adventurers may have straggled into
the valley after this, but it was not until 1732-36 that it
was settled by any considerable population.

Shortly prior to 1732, an immense number of Scotch-

Irish and Germans poured into Pennsylvania and the Jerseys. Within thirty years, the population of Pennsylvania increased from about thirty thousand to two hundred and fifty thousand. The Scotsmen, who, for religious liberty, had originally sought the north of Ireland, were the people who saved Ireland to William and Mary from Catholic James. Their loyalty was rewarded by new persecutions for non-conformity, until they resolved to seek asylum in America. So, also, about the same time came to America a great migration of German Lutherans, who were induced to settle in Pennsylvania. The Scotsmen occupied the regions about Princeton, New Jersey, Easton, Carlisle, and Washington. The Germans settled about York, Lancaster, Columbia, and Harrisburg. Governor Logan, himself a Scotch-Irishman, enforced some laws about 1730 which were so offensive to the Presbyterians and Lutherans that great numbers of them left the Pennsylvania colony, crossed the Potomac west of the Blue Ridge, in the vicinity of Harper's Ferry, entered Virginia, and settled the Blue Ridge valley.

As if by agreement, the two bands separated. The lethargic Germans, as soon as they escaped the Pennsylvania jurisdiction, occupied the lower valley from Harper's Ferry to Harrisonburg. The aggressive Scotch-Irish pressed on to the upper valley, then called West Augusta, now divided into the counties of Augusta, Rockbridge, Botetourt, Roanoke, and Montgomery. From then until now, the two races have retained possession of and dominated their respective settlements.

And a very striking race of men are these Scotch-Irish, so called, yet with nothing Irish about them save that for a little while they tarried in Ireland. Hated by the Irish because they were Protestants, persecuted by the English because they were Presbyterians, they in turn cordially detested both, and, in our Revolutionary struggles, were among the earliest and most intense rebels against the king. For liberty, as they conceived it, whether it was liberty of conscience or liberty of the person, the Scotch-Irishmen and their descendants have never hesitated to sacrifice comfort, fortune, or life. Their mountain origin has always manifested itself by the places they have chosen in their migrations. The few who went to the Puritan settlements of New England soon moved from among them and sought the inhospitable highlands of New Hampshire, where they bestowed on their new settlement the name of Londonderry. The little band who found asylum among the Dutch of New York pressed onward from uncongenial associates to the mountainous frontier, and named the county where they settled Ulster, in memory of their Irish home. Those who wearied of Pennsylvania and went to Virginia avoided the light society of the Cavaliers in Tidewater and Piedmont, preferring the mountain wilds of West Augusta.

Wherever they appeared, they seemed to be seeking for some secluded spot, where, undisturbed by any other sect, they might enjoy liberty unrestrained, and worship God after their own fashion.

And great have they been as pioneers. They populated western New England, northern New York, western Pennsylvania, and the Virginia valley. Then they pressed onward through western North Carolina, even to northern South Carolina. Then they spread westward through Cumberland Gap to the settlement of Kentucky. In later days, their Lewis and their Clarke were the explorers of the Northwest; another Lewis was the first to view Pike's Peak; and even the territory of Texas was in part reclaimed by Sam Houston, son of a Rock-

bridge County Presbyterian. The pioneer work of the
Scotch-Irish has been greater than that of all other races
in America combined.

Great also have they been as fighters. John Lewis,
their first leader in the Virginia valley, was the terror of
the frontier Indians from the day of his arrival. Never
after his coming did the Indians come east of the Blue
Ridge. Another Scotch-Irishman, Patrick Henry, uttered
the immortal sentence, " Give me liberty or give me
death."

General Henry Knox, of Revolutionary fame, the only
New England representative in Washington's cabinet,
was a Scotch-Irishman.

It was the Scotch-Irish of Mecklenburg, North Carolina, who framed the first resolutions embodying the principles of the Declaration of Independence. It was of the
Scotch-Irish and their valley home that Washington was
speaking when, in the darkest hours of the Revolution, he
declared that, if the worst came to the worst, he would
retire to the mountain fastnesses of West Augusta, and
there, with a few of his brave followers about him, defy
forever the power of Great Britain. It was from the
same spot that Stonewall Jackson, another of the stock,
went forth in our great civil war, followed by his brave
men of Scotch-Irish ancestry recruited here, to revive, by
his grim prowess and their unshaken valor, the memory of
Old Ironsides and his Presbyterians.

And great have they been as disseminators of learning.
They founded the ancient college of New Jersey now
known as Princeton University. To their efforts are we
indebted for the colleges of La Fayette at Easton and
Washington-Jefferson College at Washington in Pennsylvania ; and Liberty Hall Academy, now called Washington and Lee University, at Lexington, Virginia ; and
Chapel Hill in North Carolina.

And successful politicians and statesmen have they been; for Calhoun, Andrew Jackson, Franklin Pierce, James Buchanan, Ulysses S. Grant, Chester A. Arthur, Grover Cleveland, Benjamin Harrison, and William McKinley were all rich in this Scotch-Irish blood.

In his great work upon the Puritans, Douglass Campbell has admirably sketched the Scotch-Irish. Much has been written of them of late years by writers less distinguished; and just now Professor John Fiske, under the title of " Old Virginia and her Neighbors," has published a most interesting account of the great Scotch-Irish migration and its influences on our American civilization.

At Lexington, Virginia, these folk were and are, as their ancestors have been for centuries, men of earnest, thoughtful, and religious natures; simple in their lives to the point of severity, sometimes severe to the point of simplicity; intense in their religious fervor, yet strangely lacking, as it seems to us, in that quality of mercy which is the greatest attribute of religion; loving and possessing education, yet often narrow-minded, in spite of thorough training; almost ascetics in their wants, not bountifully hospitable, but reasonably courteous and considerate towards strangers, and methodically charitable; regarding revelry and dissipation of body or mind as worthy of supreme contempt; of dogged obstinacy, pertinacity, and courage ; dominant forces in all things wherein they take a part.

I had heard of their race, and heard them described, long before I went there ; and now I was among them, — those old McDowells, and McLaughlins, and McClungs, and Jacksons, and Paxtons, and Rosses, and Grahams, and Andersons, and Campbells, and Prestons, and Moores, and Houstons, and Barclays, and Comptons, and all the tribe of Presbyterians of the valley. All they possessed, and what they were, I curiously scrutinized as a type of humanity wholly new to me.

Their impress was upon everything in the place. The blue limestone streets looked hard. The red brick houses, with severe stone trimmings and plain white pillars and finishings, were stiff and formal. The grim portals of the Presbyterian church looked cold as a dog's nose. The cedar hedges in the yards, trimmed hard and close along straight brick pathways, were as unsentimental as mathematics. The dress of the citizens, male and female, was of single-breasted simplicity ; and the hair of those pretty Presbyterian girls was among the smoothest and the flattest things I ever saw.

Shall I describe their habitations ? Would it violate the laws of hospitality to do so ? I hope not. We have entered a hallway, tinted gray, furnished with an oaken hat-rack and straight oak chair of Gothic features, and passed into a parlor. Although it is autumn, the polished floors are uncovered save by strips of deep-red carpet, such as one sees in chapel aisles. There is a fireplace, but the fires are unlit. The furniture is straight up and down mahogany covered over with haircloth. I have often wondered what a Presbyterian would do if he could not secure mahogany haircloth furniture for his drawing-room. The room is dark ; the red curtains are half drawn. Upon the black marble mantelpiece, under a glass shade, are cold, white wax flowers. On the walls are solemn engravings of Oliver Cromwell, Stonewall Jackson, and The Rock of Ages. A melodeon, with church music, stands in the corner. If, perchance, it be a pianoforte, it seems like a profanation. There is also a Gothic table, on top of which is the family Bible, beside it a candle-stick, Jay's "Morning Exercises," and the "Life of Hannah More." Drawn near to these is a long-armed, low easy-chair. Facing the fireplace are two rocking-chairs, and six others, all in haircloth, stand stiff as horse-guards' sentries about the walls.

If your call is timed in the evening, you will learn the uses to which these articles are put, for, as nine o'clock approaches, the sweet little Presbyterian girl you are vis-iting will begin to fidget; and when the hour strikes, the family will file into the room with military silence and precision. Before you know it, the head of the house will occupy that chair by the table, and open that Bible, and give you the benefit of at least twenty minutes of Chris-tian comfort. Then, if you have not the good sense to leave, he will proceed to fasten the window-blinds.

If your visit is in the daytime, other things will sug-gest themselves to your mind. For example, you will wonder what is the family dinner-hour. If you are so fortunate as to receive a formal invitation in advance, you will not only learn, but you will have a bountiful and well-cooked meal, — not, perhaps, an Episcopalian epicurean feast, but bountiful and nutritious food. If, however, your notion was to drop in unexpectedly, and take an in-formal family dinner, let me beg you to give it up. You may go a hundred times, and the sleek-headed girl in pop-lin will give no sign, and the bell will never ring. She would starve before she would ask you out, but she would die before she would ask you in, for Presbyterians are not built that way. Her father would immolate her for tak-ing such a liberty. The best you can hope for, on an occa-sion like that, is a cold red pippin on a cold white plate, served where you sit shivering, in that vault-like parlor.

If you wish to be frisky with Miss Westminster, it is possible in but one way. Ask her to go to church. Sun-day morning church is the most tumultuous of her gaye-ties; Sunday night service is to her what an ordinary dancing party would be, as compared with a state ball, to Miss Litany; and Wednesday evening lectures are to her what excursions for ice-cream or soda-water are to "unregenerate" girls.

My! for wild hilarity commend me to a coterie of strictly reared young female Presbyterians. An evening spent among them is like sitting upon icebergs, cracking hailstones with one's teeth.

Yet, dear reader, believe me, after one has tried it awhile, surprising as the statement may seem, one comes to like it. Now and again, one of them says something, or does something, like ordinary mortals; and what she says or does is in such a fetching, fascinating, feminine way that it makes one want to go again, and makes one feel glad that such gentle, pure, refined, simple, and true people countenance an outside barbarian like one's self in their society.

There is, believe me, a lot of outcome in one of these little, demure Presbyterian lassies. Of course, if she has no better luck than to marry one of her own people, that settles it! She will go through life mooning and mincing about, like a turkey hen come off her nest. She will pass her life thinking that going to hear sermons and lectures is the chief end of man, and that pippins, spiced gingerbread, and cracked walnuts, served in a chilly parlor, are fit Christian entertainments.

She may even live and die thinking she is happy, not knowing any better.

But if, perchance, good fortune brings her a knight with a feather in his bonnet, and it catches her little meek eye, as it is mighty apt to do; if, after prayerful consideration, her strait-laced parents decide that it is best for her happiness to let her go, even at her soul's peril; if, all doubts and dangers past, she is borne triumphantly away, her bonnet-box stuffed with the Shorter Catechism and all orthodox kirk rudiments, — I assure you it is surprising how promptly the little bud expands, and how quickly she adapts herself to new surroundings.

I speak whereof I know.

How long we have been in Lexington without reporting for duty!

CHAPTER XVII

A NEW PHASE OF MILITARY LIFE

LOOKING eastward from the front of the tavern where the stage-coach deposited us, the barracks, mess-hall, professors' houses, parade ground, and limits of the Virginia Military Institute were in view upon a hill about half a mile distant.

My first care was to send a messenger with a note announcing my arrival to my cousin Louis, who had preceded me at the Institute by a year. When he came, he explained that his tardiness was due to the length of time it required for an application for permission to leave the limits of the Institute to pass through the necessary official channels.

His greeting was hearty and joyous; it had been a long time since he had seen any relative from the outside world, and this little release was quite a lark. How well and bright-eyed he looked in his tight-fitting shell jacket! When we parted at Norfolk a year before, he was an easy-going, slack-twisted little civilian, without particularly attractive dress or bearing. Now, he carried himself like a fighting-cock. Exercise had hardened him and developed his figure, his clothing fitted him like a glove, and there was an easy confidence in his manner. In a word, he had been licked into military shape.

We sallied forth together to report for duty at the office of the superintendent, General Francis H. Smith. His study was a very attractive place : it was a hexagonal room, well lit; bookcases stood about the walls, and it was ornamented with a number of striking military pictures, chiefly French; a bright wood-fire crackled in the open fireplace. In a former chapter I alluded to General Smith. He had, at the time about which I write, been superintendent twenty-three years, although he was then only about fifty.

Your elderly soldier is generally of one of two types: one is the rubicund, thunderous type; the other, the lean, pale, spectacled, quiet type. There are modifications and variations of these two generic classifications, of course: but under one or the other the great mass of elderly soldiers may be grouped.

To the latter belonged General Smith. He was tall, thin, agile; in youth he had been an extreme blonde; his lithe figure still bore a soldierly aspect. His face was that of a student, with that expression emphasized by the gold spectacles through which he looked keenly; those spectacles were so much a part of him that he was universally known as "Old Spex." As he sat in his office in his blue uniform, with one leg crossed over the other, many a cadet has no doubt wondered how thin those long legs really were, seeing how close they lay together. His life had been given up entirely to his work as superintendent; he had traveled abroad to study foreign schools and secure their best features; he was author of several mathematical treatises, as well as a most admirable teacher. A prominent churchman; a man of abstemious habits and boundless industry; one of the best politicians in the State, — he knew every man of importance in Virginia, and had the faculty of enlisting the interest of politicians of all parties in the success of the Virginia Military Institute. No matter what might be the acrimony of factions, or the stress of public necessities in other directions, his legislative appropriations never failed, and support of his school never flagged. His tact in management and insight into the character of cadets was marvelous. His acquaintance with the minutest details of every department in the school was perfect, and the personal interest which he manifested in every cadet intrusted to his care was at once a warning and a stimulus to the boy. He was in truth a very remarkable man; his peculiarities were as marked as his excellencies; and, while those peculiarities did not seriously detract from him, they gave him a distinct individuality. A monument to Colonel Thayer stands in front of the United States Military Academy, describing him as the father of the institution. One like it should be reared to General Smith at the Virginia Military Institute, for to it he was even more a father than was Thayer to West Point, or Arnold to Rugby.

Behind those gold spectacles, and with those long, thin legs lapped over each other, he sat at a table writing as we entered and stood near the door, caps in hand, at attention. He seemed engrossed; a moment later, he lifted his eyes; squinting a little and peering through his glasses, he caught sight of us and exclaimed, " Ah–h! who's this?" Louis explained. "Well, young man, how are you? Glad to see you. How is your father? What have you studied? How far have you been in mathematics? In French? In Latin?" And, going straight at the matter in hand, he plied me with queries until he knew all that was necessary; then " Fourth-class is best for him," he said.

Soon fixed up by the adjutant, we started for the commandant's office across the parade ground. The commandant of cadets, Major Scott Shipp, was a large man, with close-trimmed black hair and beard, a solemn bearing, and a deep voice. Although he was then but twenty-four years of age, I thought he was forty. He remained commandant for nearly thirty years after this, and is now superintendent. In its fifty-eight years of life, the school has had but two superintendents. Our business with the commandant consisted of securing an assignment to a room and to a company, and attending to some minor details. Then we reported to my first sergeant, who was no other than Benjamin Colonna, our room-mate.

Louis and I found my trunk at the sallyport, whither it had been sent from the hotel, and lugged it off to the arsenal, which stood in the quadrangle, for no trunks were allowed in rooms. Cadet clothing was kept in a large wardrobe, placed in each room, divided into compartments which were assigned to the respective occupants.

The cadet barracks was a handsome four-storied building, occupying three sides of a quadrangle, with towers at the corners and at a sallyport with central arch. On the inner side were three broad stoops running all around the building, reached by stairways upon the stoops. The cadet quarters opened upon these stoops. At the turrets, the rooms were double, occupied in most instances by tactical officers; elsewhere, the rooms were single. The ventilation, light, and heat of the quarters were excellent. The furniture of each room consisted of a gun-rack, washstand, wardrobe; large oak table in the centre of the room, under a gas-light; a chair for each cadet, a book rack and a blacking-stool, beds and bedsteads. Thirty minutes after reveille, the beds were required to be rolled up, strapped, and stood in the corner, flanked by the bedsteads folded. Beds could not be put down until after tattoo. The occupants of the room were alternately detailed as orderly for a week, and each was held responsible

for observance of regulations and for the police of the
room, which was inspected at least twice a day.

On arrival at our rooms, I had a bluff but pleasant
welcome from Colonna, who called me " Mr. Rat," and, as
it was a rule of the Institute that every plebe should be
" bucked," he and Louis proceeded to attend to my case.
A bed-strap was buckled about my wrists; I was ordered
up on the table and compelled to draw up my knees, over
which my bound arms were slipped; a ramrod was run
under my knees and over my arms, and then I was rolled
over on my side, and Louis and Colonna, with a bayonet
scabbard, spelled C O N S T A N T I N O P L E. The taps
given by these laughing friends were light, but sufficiently
stinging to make me appreciate what it might have been.

" Now, Rat, you have been bucked," laughed Colonna,
as they set me upright and loosened the cords. " If anybody asks you whether you have been ' bucked,' say,
' *Yes, sir ;* ' be sure to say *sir*, d' ye understand? Then,
if they ask you whose Rat you are, say, ' Mr. Colonna's
rat, *sir*.' Be sure to say *sir*, d' ye understand? And then
you take care to say as little more as you can, for it 's
these long-tongued Rats that get into trouble, d' ye understand?" Yes, I understood. I resolved to keep that
mouth, that has gotten me in trouble all my life, shut
tight.

Up to now, I had been agreeably surprised. I expected
that I should be seized upon as soon as I entered the
barracks, but so far I had seen very few cadets about.
I did not realize that it was study-hours, at which time
the cadets were in their class-rooms, or confined to
quarters, and were strictly forbidden to visit, or to loiter
on the stoops or about the archway.

" What is that?" I asked, as a drum was beaten in the
area, its sounds reverberating through the barracks.

"First drum for dinner," said Louis; "dinner roll-call in five minutes," and he, Colonna, and Phillips began polishing their shoes.

"Now, Mr. Rat, if you don't want to be bully-agged, you wait under the arch until I give the command, 'Fall in!' when the clock strikes, and then run to your place in ranks in front of barracks. My company is on the left; I'll wait, before giving the command 'Front,' until I see you are in ranks, so you will not be late."

This thoughtful advice from Colonna I obeyed strictly, so that nobody troubled me. I felt quite proud in ranks, and answered to my name clearly. The companies were side-stepped together, and then the first captain assumed charge, broke the battalion into columns of fours, and marched us off to the mess-hall. I had never seen a figure quite so trim, or heard a voice quite so clarion, as the first captain's. The crunching cadence of the step of three hundred boys upon the gravel walk would have made a muley cow keep step. Tramp, tramp, tramp we went up the broad stairway of the mess-hall, and, as we reached the hall, companies filed away to their respective seats at the eight long tables. When all were in place, the command "Seats" was given by the first captain, and in another instant, where all had been silent, it was a babel of voices. Colonna had his eye on me, and assigned me a seat; not up with him, of course, but down at the foot with some other plebes.

It was a good, hot, smoking meal, better than I expected, and every one of us had a good, hot, smoking appetite, as was evidenced by the quick disappearance of the food, and the cries from the heads of tables: "Beef here, waiter," "Bread here, waiter," "Potatoes here, waiter," which soon resounded through the hall.

Nobody but the non-commissioned officers, stationed at the head and foot of the table, could address the waiters. These later fairly ran in filling orders. I found a little fellow sitting next to me who had only been in a day or two, and we had some quiet, timid talk between ourselves.

"At-ten-*tion*!" rang through the hall after twenty-five minutes consumed in consuming. Dead silence reigned where everybody had been talking. "Rise up!" and we rose, re-formed in front of the mess-hall, were broken into columns of fours, marched back to barracks, and as the battalion reached its original position the command came, "Break ranks, march," which was the signal for a general mix-up, in a leisure period of thirty minutes which followed each meal, during which cadets were allowed to visit one another's rooms, and dispose of themselves as they saw fit, until "Study drum" beat. I thought trouble was in store for me then, for I discovered in the mess-hall not less than a dozen former acquaintances, most of whom were old cadets, and they discovered me. I apprehended that they would have something to say to me, and, knowing of my recent arrival, might amuse themselves at my expense; but it was not so bad as I expected. Such of them as I met after the corps was dismissed spoke to me with civility and passed on. It was, as I afterwards learned, etiquette in an old cadet acquaintance not to torture a plebe whom he had known elsewhere. Being old cadets, they would not associate with a plebe, but, unless he was "impudent," they so far recognized former acquaintanceship as to let him alone.

Before I reached the sallyport, however, several strange, saucy, and piratical-looking young Hessians had their eyes upon me, and my relief was very great when Louis, my guardian angel, came hurrying down from A

Company, and with an air of authority said, "Here,
Mr. Rat, you come with me." His whole manner changed
as soon as we were out of their presence, and he said,
"Those chaps would have drawn you into conversation in
another minute, and then they would have had a lot of
fun out of you."

The permit to go out of limits, which Louis had obtained in the morning, was good until dress parade, and
he proposed that we should go out and about. Before
we left, I learned the meaning of his talk about "buying
apples with my coat." During the half hour after dinner,
a number of mountain women, with bags and baskets of
apples, appeared in front of barracks, and the cadets carried on the liveliest imaginable trading with them, exchanging old clothes for apples.

At West Point, the cadet old clothes are religiously
preserved and sold, and their proceeds are applied to a
mess-fund. The interest on that fund is expended upon
the cadet mess, and the fund has already grown so large
that the character of cadet fare is much improved, and
the cost of the mess to cadets is materially reduced.
Think what might have been accomplished at the Virginia Military Institute if this same policy had been
pursued! Instead of that, for fifty-eight years the cadets
have been allowed to throw away their old clothes in the
most reckless fashion. I have seen many a cadet jacket
traded off for half a peck of apples ; and if a cadet were
really hungry, I think he would trade the coat on his
back for one apple-pie.

That afternoon our stroll took us down to the river,
where the terminus of the canal was located. There
were in those days no railroads running into Lexington.
The stage-coach and this primitive means of travel were
its only public means of communication with the outside

world. I soon learned where the laundries were, and where the boys skated in cold weather, and what were the different points of interest. Louis led me to the house of an old Irishman who sold cider and cakes to the cadets, and we regaled ourselves. Then we came back by the rear way up the stream called the Nile, which runs behind the Institute grounds, and clambered up the bluffs and stole around to the bakery where old Judge, the baker, gave us a hot loaf just drawn from the oven, it having been cooked for the cadets' supper. Louis explained that we were out of limits now, as cadets were forbidden to visit the bakery, and, if caught, received five demerits and an extra tour of guard duty. The sensation of disobeying orders was rather pleasant, I confess. Judge was a wonderful old negro; he had been there many years. In appearance, he was a black Sancho Panza, fat and puffing and jolly; he was a darkey of moods. Sometimes his mood was religious, sometimes it was profane; but, whether the one or the other, he was always amusing.

Out of that first introduction grew a long friendship with Judge, and when he confronted St. Peter, the pile of bread stacked up against him in Heaven must have been tremendous; for every cadet who was at Lexington in the thirty years of his stewardship received from him at least ten loaves stolen from the Commonwealth of Virginia. Bless his hot, jolly, fat, black, flour-smirched, roguish memory! His portrait, with his baker's cap jauntily tipped, now adorns the cadet mess-hall in the company of generals and other distinguished citizens departed.

Then we visited old Reilly, another famous character. Stone blind, the old fellow earned a good living making hair mattresses for the cadets. He measured, cut, sewed, trimmed, bound, filled, and knotted mattresses as well as any one could do with the finest eyesight. He was an ardent politician, and a devoted admirer of my father. The old man was always delighted to receive visitors, and was full of cadet knowledge and reminiscence as he sat there, blind as a bat, but working like a beaver.

Then we strolled to the regions in rear of the professors' houses, where Louis showed me, near the bluffs, in a wooded spot, a sort of natural amphitheatre, which he described as the "fighting-ground." Seated on the edge of this depression, he entered on a vivid and thrilling description of the last great battle here, which had taken place between the present first captain, in his third class year, and another cadet; it was very interesting.

"But," he said, "of course he would not fight any more. First and second class men are above fighting. They frown it down and punish it. Only yearlings like myself and plebes like you fight, you know."

"Yes," said I; but I did not know any such thing until he told it to me. Thus we went on, he teaching and I absorbing like a sponge, all the while having a suspicion that I might see the "fighting-ground" again some day. Just then we caught the sound of a drum: "Rap, rap, rap, — rap, rap, rap, — rap, rap, rap, — rap, rap, rap, rap, — rap, rap, rap."

Springing to his feet, he exclaimed: "Gracious! there is dress parade; we must run for it." So off we sped, running by the rear of the professors' houses and scrambling over the stile, reaching the barracks as the boys were streaming down the stairways, pulling on their gloves and arranging their accoutrements. Louis barely saved his distance, and came tearing through the arch just as the command, "Fall in!" was sung out by the four first sergeants. I went with a squad of plebes, who without arms were marched out after the companies and formed on the left of the battalion.

It was a brave sight when the drums and fifes struck up (we had no band in those days) ; the colors marched forth and gave the alignment; the companies followed and formed on the colors, and the officer in charge put the battalion through its drill. Then we marched back and were dismissed. Evening parade, supper, study hours, tattoo, taps, came in their regular order; and as I went to sleep, soon after taps inspection, it was with the thought that this had been one of the most eventful and delightful days I ever spent.

Reveille ! What part of cadet routine is so well remembered as that? Awakened at crack of dawn from dreamless sleep by the long-drawn notes of fife and drum, our first semi-conscious impulse was to slumber on, soothed by the drowsy tune. Not long such thoughts, however ; for, with a quick ruffle of the drums, the tune was changed. A gay and lilting quickstep took its place, crashing up and down and through the dormitories. Quick, responsive lights were twinkling in a hundred rooms, where but a few moments before all was silence. Three hundred youngsters were hurrying for the ranks. As if to mock their haste, the tune changed again, and the music went floating off once more into dreamland, while the cadets grew more impetuous in their preparations. Then the last tune came. This was no sluggard's lullaby. It was a ringing summons to the front, in which the drums seemed to be trying to drown the air the fifes were piping gayly. The latest plebe in barracks knew the words : —

> " Wake-up-rats-and-come-to Reveille
> If-you-want to get-your-corp-orality,
> Wake up rats ! Come to Reveille
> If you want to get YOUR corporalite-e-e-e-e ! "

Then, with three long rolls and two final thumps, the music ceased.

Towards the close of this matin concert, stoops, stairs, and archway swarmed with hundreds of cadets, half-awake, hurrying to their places in the forming ranks. As the last laggard whisked through the sallyport, struggling to avoid being late, the chill morning air resounded with the commands of the first sergeants: " Fall in A Compane-e-e-e ! Fall in B and C and D Compane-e-e-e!" Then, after a moment's pause, sergeant after sergeant gave the command, " Front ! " and away they went, rattling off the rolls with surprising noise and speed. Then came another pause, in which, as the boys stood shivering in the nipping daybreak, the first sergeants spotted absentees by repeating their names with marvelous and unerring accuracy.

Ranks broken, the cadets, with heads drawn in and hands stuck in their waistbands, went back to quarters in sullen silence, or with deep anathemas upon reveille.

Yet how beautiful it was ! On the eastern face of forest, peak, and barrack-tower the blush of morning shone, while all else was in shadow. Against the glowing east, the undulating sky-line of the distant Blue Ridge was cut clear and strong, with purple shadows filling in the space between us and them, save where the valley mists were tipped with morning light. Correggio could not paint nor Claud attain the limpid high-lights, the clear-obscure, the deep visible-invisible, of those exquisite autumn daybreaks in the mountains.

Old boys, wherever you may be, have you forgotten them ?

About them, even then, there was a sentiment, — a sentiment which deepens as the years roll by. We were looking upon the shining morning face not only of nature, but of life also. Yes, in memory the shining morning faces of those schoolboys still live, framed in a setting of mountain peaks and barrack towers, gilded by the first faint rays of sunrise.

Thirty minutes after reveille found the plebes assembled in squads of three or four, and marched away by old cadets for awkward-squad exercises upon the parade ground. Drill until the drum for breakfast dispensed with all need of appetizing tonics.

After breakfast, academic exercises not having been resumed as yet, the squad drills were continued, and far and wide on the parade the groups of plebes were to be seen, and the voice of the drill-master was heard.

So far, all had gone well with me. Beyond some little chaffing, no old cadet had troubled me, and the squad-marcher had complimented me on attention and promptness.

We were resting. A squad of plebes, moved at double time, were brought down to where we were standing and halted near us, by a stocky, aggressive-looking old cadet. Having ordered a rest, Sprague (that was his name) came over to speak to our drill-master. " I 'm giving those Rats thunder ! " said he, pointing to the panting plebes. And so he was. Instead of practicing his squad in setting-up exercises, he was prancing them all over the parade ground. " What sort of Rats have you got?" said he, looking us over in an insolent way. " Oh, a fair enough lot," said our squad-marcher, an easy-going but efficient man. Sprague looked at us keenly, and asked our names. Some look of mine, I presume, or the fact that I was nearest to him, made him continue his probing of me, and I was not very civil.

" Why, Mr. Rat, you are impudent," said he. Then, glancing around to see that the sub-professor in charge was not looking, he commanded me to "hold up." That meant that I was to hold up my hand and let him twist my arm. By this time I was piping hot, but had sense enough to keep silent.

"Hold up, sir!" said he peremptorily.

"Shut up, sir!" replied I; and there, all the wise counsel which Louis and Colonna had given me, and all the good resolves I had made, were vanished into thin air with those three words.

"Mr. Rat," said he, drawing close to me, and shaking his finger in my face as he hissed the words, "I will attend to you as soon as we get back to barracks. I'll take some of that rebellious spirit out of you. See if I don't." I was about to answer him with defiance, when our squad was called to attention and drill was resumed. It is not difficult to appreciate that the remainder of that drill was far from being a period of happiness. All the time, I was calculating how to receive the attack. Finally, I counted that if I could succeed in reaching our room, I might take a musket, and defend myself with a bayonet. Sprague looked like a game one, and I knew that he would have plenty of backers. When the recall beat, our squad was near barracks. We went in on double time, and when the squad was dismissed, I made a bold dash for the archway. I thought I was safe, for I had nearly reached the sallyport; but when almost in, I saw Sprague dismiss his squad and start after me, calling, "Catch that Rat!"

Through the arch we sped, and it seemed as if I would reach our room upon the second stoop, for I was nearly at the stairway. But! but! but! Just at that moment a tremendous fellow shot like a goshawk from the door I was about to pass, and, slipping his right arm about my waist, nearly lifted me from the ground and held me tight

as a vise, until Sprague and a dozen others came up. In-
furiated beyond all control, I struck out like a clever fellow,
but they bore me straight along, up the steps and into
the first room on the second stoop, and in a jiffy had me
bound and on a table. In another instant I should have
felt the brass ferrule of a bayonet-scabbard administered
without pity. The room was filled with cadets, all bent
on disciplining a rebellious Rat.

At the very crisis, the crowd near the doorway swayed
back and forth. Some one exclaimed, " Get out of the
way, or I 'll plunge this bayonet into you!" and Louis
bounded in, with gleaming eyes, his jaws set like a bull-
pup's. Rushing up to Sprague he said, " No, sir! You 'll
not buck that Rat!"

" Yes, I will," said Sprague.

" Not unless you can whip me!" was the game reply of
Louis, as he began to slip off his jacket. " I bucked him
yesterday, and I asked Boggess all about what happened
on the parade ground, and he says you provoked and
teased the Rat until you forced him to be impudent. You
shan't touch him." With that he sprang towards me to
unloose the fastenings. The crowd grew agitated. Sprague
made a motion to fight, and in another instant we should
have had a pretty mess, when —

" Rap, rap, rap! Rap, rap, rap!" came sharp and
loud upon the door. Everybody knew what it meant!
Somebody, quick as lightning, undid the straps, jerked me
off the table, and stood me on my feet; and Captain
Semmes, the officer in charge, walked into the room
serenely. With a dignified and inquiring look at the
cadets now crowded back against the walls, he said,
" Gentlemen, what 's all this disturbance? "

Louis was slipping on his cadet jacket, and, sidling up
to me, said, " Don't say a word. Whatever you do, don't
peach."

" What does this all mean, gentlemen ? " repeated the captain, in louder and more peremptory tones.

Sprague at last spoke up : " Oh, nothing ; I just had a little misunderstanding with that gentleman there," pointing to me.

I was so elated by the unexpected turn things had taken that my good-nature had returned, and when Captain Semmes turned to me and asked what it all meant, I said, " Oh, we were just trying to see who was strongest."

" Go to your rooms, gentlemen, all of you, at once ! " said Captain Semmes, waiting to see that his orders were carried out; and then he departed, without seeking too many explanations, for in his day he had been a terror to plebes.

" Well, Mr. Rat ! " said Louis, when we reached our rooms, and found fat Colonna sitting there, still wearing his sword and sash, laughing at our discomfiture, " you have put your foot in it, sure enough. You have not only made yourself a target, but I expect that round-shouldered, long-armed, bull-yearling of a Sprague will beat me to death about this business."

Then Colonna, who was above the dignity of such scrapes, but had witnessed my race and capture, nearly had fits describing how big Wood had seized me, and how they had turned me upside down going up the steps, and how I nearly kicked Billy Mason's eye out, and a lot of other things that did and did not happen ; for Colonna was a great tease.

Dinner drum was sounded, and I went down, reflecting that the first twenty-four hours of my military life were completed.

A day or two afterwards, academic studies were resumed. With mathematics, Latin, French, and drawing added to military duties, there was little time for play.

A half day's holiday on Saturday, during which we were permitted to leave the Institute limits, gave us but scant opportunity for diversion. Even the letters of introduction I had brought, to the families of some of the professors, remained undelivered for lack of time.

The winter of 1862–63 was cold enough. While the army of General Lee was encamped about Fredericksburg, after a gallant defense of the place, we, "the seed-corn of the Confederacy," as Mr. Davis called us, were very comfortably cared for in barracks, which were heated and lighted as well as if no war had been in progress.

There was no lack of news from the front. An older brother of Louis had been captured at Roanoke Island, and, while awaiting exchange, was acting as tactical officer of A Company, and sub-professor of mathematics. He was a sober-minded, earnest fellow, always watchful over us, and he occasionally sent for us to come to his quarters, that he might advise, or warn, or rebuke us in an affectionate and considerate way. We were devoted to him, and prized his good opinion more than that of anybody else. He bore my father's name, and counted me as much in his charge as his own brother. By our access to his quarters opportunity was given us from time to time to hear a great deal of news from the front, for never a great battle came off but numbers of Virginia Military Institute boys were in it, and they seemed to have a talent for getting killed or wounded. Those from far Southern States, instead of going to Alabama or Mississippi or Louisiana during their short leaves, would come to the Virginia Military Institute, room with some sub-professor of their own class, and assist in teaching, until sufficiently restored to return to duty.

Captain Henry A. Wise was a universal favorite with

the graduates, and his quarters were seldom without some
occupant of the class described above.   Everybody connected with the Institute had a nickname: General
Smith was "Old Spex," Colonel Preston was "Old
Bald," Stonewall Jackson was "Old Jack," General Colston "Old Polly," Colonel Williamson "Old Tom," Colonel Gilliam "Old Gill," and down to the youngest
"sub" all were nicknamed, and seldom referred to save
by their sobriquets.   For some reason, Captain Wise was
called "Chinook."   Nobody knew exactly why.   Among
the cadets, every man of prominence had a nickname:
there was "Dad" Wyatt, so called for age, and "Dad"
Nelson for extreme youth, and "Duck" Colonna for his
short legs, and "Bull" Temple for his strength, and
"Jane" Creighton for his gentleness, and so on, *ad in-
finitum*.   Louis and I escaped naming until a third cadet
of our name arrived.   He was an odd fish, a cousin of
both of us, who, while not very studious in things taught
there, had studied "The Adventures of Simon Suggs"
until he knew them by heart, and quoted them on all
occasions.   He soon became known as "Suggs," and the
cognomen spread until all three of us were called "Suggs
J.," "Suggs L.," and "Suggs W.," as if we never had
any other names.   One day the corporal of the guard
reported me for noise on the stoop, and inadvertently
entered me on the delinquent list as "Suggs J."   The
adjutant knew whom he meant, but reported him for
carelessness.

After the battle of Fredericksburg, we heard all about
it in the rooms of "Old Chinook," from men who had
participated in its glories.   I forget who they were, but
it was probably "Sheep" Floweree of Mississippi, or
"Bute" Henderson, or "Tige" Hardin, or "Marsh" Mc-
Donald, all of whom, at one time or another, turned up

there. To the outside world, they were colonels and majors, etc.: at the Virginia Military Institute, they were "Sheep" and "Bute" and "Tige." Many a day, out of study hours, from their lips we would drink in the story of the repulse of Meagher's Irish Brigade at Marye's Heights, or how Hayes made his stand at Hamilton Crossing, or Pender at the railroad, or how Stuart's Horse Artillery raked Franklin's Corps on the Rappahannock flats. Very few boys have had such practical lessons in the art of war.

Poor "Chinook," who longed for his exchange, and chafed at the delays which made him miss these battles, looked dreadfully depressed, and as for ourselves, Louis and I felt it was an outrage that we were penned up and kept away from these wondrous sights and scenes.

In February, we had a cold, hard freeze; all drills were suspended; the North River was hard-frozen. At evening parade on Friday, an order was published announcing that a supply of ice for the following summer was most desirable; that, owing to the number of laborers who had volunteered, the superintendent was unable to secure the necessary force to save the ice-crop; and that every cadet who would volunteer for Saturday to work at filling the ice-houses of the Institute should have three afternoons' leave, from dinner to dress-parade, the following week, for skating. At the call for volunteers the corps stepped to the front as one man. Of course they did; what better fun than that did anybody want?

The next morning, cadets were ordered to put on old clothes. The companies were divided into working squads, and marched to the river. We had all the saws, and axes, and ice-hooks, and slides, and horses we needed. The strongest men went out and cut the ice; the smaller

chaps were worked in teams, with ropes to secure it and
drag it to the wagons. Some of the country boys were
detailed as teamsters. Squads were stationed at the ice-
houses to receive and dump the loads. Fires were built
along the river banks. Those drowsy country horses
were never pushed so hard, or heard the whips crack so
loudly, as they did that day. We went to work in relays.
" Old Spex " had rations and hot coffee served upon the
river bank. And when the cold sun was sinking in a
red western sky, the corps, its work completely done,
filled with joyous anticipations for the coming week, was
trotting homeward across the bridge at a double-quick,
the happiest, jolliest set of youngsters in the Southern
Confederacy.

Then came the skating time. News of our holiday
spread over the town, and all the pretty girls in Lexington, and many of the citizens, were there to see the
sport.

There was no lack of skates ; the arsenal, long since
disappeared, stood in the barracks' quadrangle in those
days. It was the general depository of all the things left
by the cadets who marched to the war in 1861. I fear
little regard was paid to their vested rights. Nearly
every old trunk in that arsenal had by this time been
rifled. Many a cadet jacket and trousers, left there by
some old cadet with the purpose of returning for it some
day, had been " appropriated " long ago, worn out, and
traded off for apples. In cadet morals, this is not stealing. The conditions existing there at any time amount
almost to communism ; at the period referred to, the
seizure of everything required was justified under the
plea of military necessity. Fortunately, the arsenal was
burned by General Hunter in 1864, so that the absent
cadets who had been robbed of their skates doubtless

thought their goods were destroyed by fate of war, and never knew that they had been used by their own comrades ; else had there been, I fear, after the war, grave charges against all of us.

Among the débris piled helter-skelter in the arsenal, after the sundry pickings-over to which its contents had been subjected, somebody found an old drum-major's shako, relic of the pomp and panoply of peace times. The first appearance of this shako in public was on the head of a long-legged cadet, who wore it in a game of shinny at our ice carnival. It was not long before a bandy-stick knocked his shako in the air. That was suggestion enough. Soon another cadet took a crack at it, and its wearer, dodging and racing, went streaming away with fifty fellows following.

Out of this grew a famous game called " tapping the shako." Whoever was fast enough to catch the wearer, and tap his shako, became entitled to place it on his head, and wear it until a fleeter-footed skater won it from him. It was but a little while, of course, before it fell into the hands of the best skater and most adroit dodger in the corps ; and then the concentrated energies of a hundred men to overhaul its owner furnished marvelous excitement and noble sport. In one of these contests, the race was prolonged almost, if not quite, to Loch Laird, five miles down the river. The sport elicited wonderful displays of endurance, agility, and pluck.

On our last day, we gave an unexpected exhibition. The weather had moderated, but apparently not enough to make the ice dangerous. In fact, however, the freeze had been so sudden that the ice was filled with air-holes. Our great game had now been regulated, for in its earlier stages we found that certain cadets, like certain hounds, instead of running true to the line, would wait for the quarry to double and then take a short cross-cut upon him. So we staked the centre of the river, and forced every man to follow the course if he claimed a touch. This afternoon, a great crowd of spectators was assembled; we had had a glorious breakaway, and the old black shako, on the head of some fleet-footed fellow, went whirling down the river with the pack in full cry, the crowds on the banks delighted. For a little while the chase disappeared, and then came. back on the near side of the stream, but out towards the centre. The boys were well bunched; not less than six or eight were close upon the leader. The race grew intensely exciting; some men on horse-back were galloping along the bank. The women were waving their handkerchiefs and clapping their hands with delight.

The closest follower made a fine burst of speed, had raised his stick to tap the shako, when crash went the ice, and both men disappeared, the old black shako alone remaining in sight floating on the water. A wail and screams went up from the shore. One after another of those in hot pursuit plumped into the hole before they could check their headway, and in another moment six or eight of the best fellows in the corps were floundering in the deep water, the ice at the edges breaking under them at each attempt they made to scramble out. Then came an instance of the power of discipline.

A number of us smaller boys had not followed the chase; as soon as we saw the accident, we hurried towards the scene. No doubt further misfortune would have befallen us, but for the cool-headed behavior of Sam Shriver, a second-class man. Darting up like a general, his towering figure caught all eyes as he said, "Attention!" All was silence.

"Where are the safety ropes?" he demanded. We

had had them all the time until now; now, when we needed them *most*, they were gone, of course. He never paused a second.

Looking to the hole he cried, " Hold fast, boys. Don't exhaust yourselves. I 'll have you out in a moment."

They were making a fearful splutter in the hole, some calling for help, some swearing, some grunting, and one, as we afterwards heard, praying. What frightened Louis and myself most was that we saw dear old Colonna and Dad Nelson in there.

Turning to us, Shriver said, " Form a line — quick ! "

It was formed, consisting of about fifty men.

" Let the far end of the line get well ashore," said he, and it was there in a jiffy. " Small men in front," and small men came to the front. That put Louis and myself well to the front.

" Lock wrists," cried Sam, and each of us seized the wrist of the man in front of and behind us, and he ours ; we stretched out.

" Advance to hole," said he. " Ten front files lie down. Rear files shove away," said he, as soon as we were down.

" Louis, we 're in for it," said I.

" Yes, I know," he replied. " We 'll probably break in, but if we connect with them, the rear men will pull us all out together." So they shoved us over the ice on our stomachs until the front man reached the nearest fellow in the hole, and the man behind him fastened to him, and so on until all were firmly clutched together. When all those in the hole were fast to each other firmly, Sam gave command, " Haul away slowly ! "

As the rear men began to move backward, out came the first man from the hole, and the next and the next, and then their weight broke the ice and we all went down together, but were still moving shoreward, while Shriver called to us not to let our hold break. Thus dragged, we soon reached the sound ice, and man after man came up and out of the water until all were saved, by the promptness of gallant Sam Shriver, who became the lion of the hour. Men never hugged each other's wrists more tightly than did we that day, and the prints of fingers were so deep on my wrists I thought the blood would start from them.

Cold? It was fearful! "Old Spex" had witnessed it all. "Double-quick those men to barracks, Mr. Shriver," said he; "I'll ride forward to the hospital and have hot grog served to them when they are well rubbed down. You know I am a temperance advocate, but this is medicine. Look out there for little Nelson and Barton; they are nearly frozen." With that he managed to spur his fat sorrel to a clumsy trot, and we went jogging back to barracks, warm enough by the time we reached there, but not averse to the china mugs of steaming whiskey and ginger which were served from a tin bucket by the hospital steward. Nobody was the worse for it. Is it not surprising what youngsters of that age can stand?

The spring of 1863 opened, and with it began the hard work, first in company and then in battalion drill. Besides this, the period of examinations was approaching. I had been neither studious nor soldierly, and now, after the severe drills, it was difficult to bring one's self down to the hard study necessary to pass examinations. More than once during this springtime of 1863, the corps had lost valuable time from study in attending the burial of distinguished officers, — first, a Captain Davidson, who had fallen with great distinction; then General Paxton, a resident of Lexington; and lastly came an announcement which fell like a pall upon the school.

Stonewall Jackson was dead! Could it be possible? We had believed that he bore a charmed life. The Institute had sent a host of magnificent officers to the front. There were Rhodes, Mahone, Lindsay, Walker, the Patton brothers, Lane, Crutchfield, McCausland, Colston, and many others of lower rank; but "Old Jack" was, "from his shoulders and upwards, tallest among the people," in the estimation of the cadets. His career had not only been surpassingly brilliant, but it was altogether surprising.

Of the old Presbyterian stock of the valley, his people had not much social prominence, and he had gone to West Point without particular advantages. After faithful but not exceptional service in Mexico, he had resigned from the army and assumed a professorship here. His presence was not striking, his manners were not attractive, and his habits were so eccentric that he had not ranked high as a professor; even at the time of his most astonishing victories, and when any cadet there would have given all he possessed to be with him, the stories of "Old Jack's" eccentricities made daily sport for the cadets.

For example, it was a famous joke how, when he had been drilling the third class in light artillery, with the plebes as horses, the boys had drawn the linchpins from the cannon wheels, and, as the guns made the turn near the parapet, the wheels had come off and sent the pieces tumbling over the slope. When this would happen, as it often did, Major Jackson would gallop up, look ruefully down the slope, and remark, without the slightest suspicion: "There must be something defective in the construction of these linchpins; they seem inclined to fly out whenever the pieces in rapid motion change direction."

He was not very friendly with General Smith; it was

said that he would have nothing to do with him, except officially.   Professors were required to make their weekly report to the superintendent at four o'clock Friday afternoon.   It was told of " Old Jack " that Friday afternoon, within a few minutes of four o'clock, he would appear in front of the superintendent's office and walk up and down until the clock struck four.   It made no difference whether it was raining, hailing, snowing, or freezing, he would not enter until the clock struck ; then, with military precision, he would advance to the office of the superintendent, salute, lay his report upon the table, face about, and walk out.   It was also related that during the recitations he was frequently occupied in rubbing one side of himself, under the impression, confided to a select few, that one side of his body was not so well nourished as the other, and was gradually wasting away.

When the cadet corps, in the spring of 1861, was ordered to Camp Lee at Richmond, and its members were put to drilling recruits, it is safe to say that as little was expected of Colonel Jackson as of any member of the faculty.   Nobody suspected the great military genius, the untiring energy, the marvelous resourcefulness, the thirsting fury, which lurked beneath that impassive and eccentric exterior.

But when the story of Manassas came, and men learned that the day was saved by Jackson, standing like a stonewall ; when, in his independent command, he fought and won the battles of the valley campaign ; when, in the seven days' fighting at Richmond, he threw himself upon the flank of McClellan ; and as he went on and on, mounting ever upward, until he became Lee's right arm, — then the men who had known him only as an odd professor forgot his idiosyncrasies, and exulted that our school had furnished the paladin of the Confederacy.

It was a bitter, bitter day of mourning for all of us
when the corps was marched down to the canal terminus
to meet all that was mortal of Stonewall Jackson.   We
had heard the name of every officer who attended the
remains.

With reversed arms and muffled drums we bore him
back to the Institute, and placed him in the section-room
in which he had taught.   There the body lay in state
until the following day.   The lilacs and early spring
flowers were just blooming.   The number of people who
came to view him for the last time was immense : men
and women wept over his bier as if his death was a personal affliction ; then I saw that the Presbyterians could
weep like other folks.   The flowers piled about the coffin
hid it and its form from view.   I shall ever count it a
great privilege that I was one of the guard who, through
the silence of the night, and when the crowds had departed, stood watch and ward alone with the remains of
the great " Stonewall."

Next day, we buried him with pomp of woe, the cadets
his escort of honor : with minute-guns, and tolling bells,
and most impressive circumstance, we bore him to his
rest.   But those ceremonies were to me far less impressive
than walking post in that bare section-room, in the still
hours of night, reflecting that there lay all that was left
of one whose name still thrilled the world.

The burial of Stonewall Jackson made a deep impression upon the corps of cadets.   It had been our
custom, when things seemed to be going amiss in the
army, to say, " Wait until ' Old Jack ' gets there ; he
will straighten matters out."   We felt that the loss was
irreparable.   The cold face on which we had looked
taught us lessons which have been dropped from the
curriculum in these tame days of peace.

Many a cadet resolved that he would delay no longer
in offering his services to his country, and, although the
end of the session was near at hand, several refused to
remain longer, and resigned at once.

The session of 1862–63 was drawing rapidly to a close.
Louis and I both became alarmed about passing our
examinations, he to pass to the second class and I to the
third. I had nearly the limit of demerits, for besides
other weaknesses, I had developed a love affair uptown
with a pretty little Presbyterian, and, being caught out
of limits, had been confined to barracks, and assigned
to several extra tours of guard duty. At last the eventful 4th of July arrived, the day on which the graduating class receives its diplomas and class standings, and
cadet officers for the ensuing year are announced ; it is
also the day when the band plays " Auld Lang Syne," at
hearing which a rat becomes an old cadet.

When the announcements were read out, Louis and I
found that we had passed our classes fairly well, but
far from brilliantly ; when it came to publishing commissioned officers from the new first class, our old friend and
room-mate, Colonna, moved up to second captain. To
our agreeable surprise, Louis received a good sergeant's
appointment. I was left a private ; I deserved it. All
those most interested in me had warned me such would
be the result if I pursued my trifling, heedless course ;
and now I stood chagrined and crestfallen, while others
received the honors. Nevertheless, I acknowledged to
myself that it was just, and swallowed whatever disappointment I felt, inwardly resolving, however, that next
year should tell a different tale.

Those familiar with the history of that period will not
forget that on this 4th of July, 1863, when we were
engrossed with these petty concerns, the great battle of

Gettysburg was being fought, and the surrender of Vicksburg was taking place.

A few days before the final ceremonies, we had gone into camp for the summer in a grove in rear of the superintendent's house: there we remained for two months, chiefly engaged in drilling the new cadets. It was a stupid period for the graduates, and several of the sub-professors had departed for the war, and many of the second-class men had received furloughs. The monotony of camp life was broken in the latter part of August, when we were given an arduous march to Covington to meet a raiding party from West Virginia under General Averill; but the general had displayed great good sense, as we thought, by going elsewhere before our arrival.

The 1st of September, we broke camp, returned to barracks, and resumed academic duties with great earnestness.

I keenly realized the advantages lost by the trifling of my first year, and, in the long periods for reflection in camp, had fully determined to prove myself a better student and soldier than I had yet been. It is well enough to have people laugh at one's reckless escapades and foolish antics, but those things count against a fellow when it comes to choosing the boys who have the sterling stuff in them.

Our old and tried mentor Colonna, being now an officer, had gone to live with his own classmates in a tower room. Louis and I, in solemn conclave, selected as our room-mates "Squirrel" Overton, "Jack" Stanard, and a little rat named Harris, a cousin of Overton. In these we felt we had an earnest set of room-mates, and we resolved that there was to be no more skylarking, no more defiance of discipline, and a strictly moral and studious aggregation. Then came the sultry June days, when it was work, work, work at books preparing for examinations, and drill, drill, drill in the school of the battalion.

From reveille until four o'clock P. M., we were in the section-room reciting, or studying in our quarters on review. At four o'clock, the battalion was formed for drill, and exercised in the hot sun, until time for dress parade, in every intricate manœuvre. More than one little fellow fell exhausted from the intense strain, and every cadet in the corps was longing for the time when our arduous apprenticeship would end.

One hot, steaming evening, Charley Faulkner, Phillips, and I sat in an open window which overlooked the parade ground. It was during the half hour of leisure after dinner, — the only leisure time that was left to us. The parade ground shimmered with the noonday heat. Not a leaf of the guard-tree was shaken by the slightest breeze. We were commiserating each other at the sweltering prospect of two hours' drill in a tight-fitting uniform under the rays of such a sun.

" It 's brutal," exclaimed Faulkner. " It 's enough to kill a man." We all called each other " men."

" Yes," said Phillips, " somebody will be sunstruck. Poor little Jefferson fainted yesterday, and to-day is worse."

" Then why don't you faint, Reuben?" said I. " Charley and I will bring you off the field, and that will give us all a rest."

" I 'll ' cut ' with you two fellows which shall faint," said Reuben. All matters of lot were decided by opening a book, and the second letter, second line, left-hand page, decided the matter: " a " was best, and " z " was worst. Down came the book, and Reuben cut the lowest letter; so it fell to him to faint, and to us to bring him off the field. When the drill-drum beat that afternoon, we fell

in line with Reuben between us. As the company was
divided into platoons, we came near being separated, for
Faulkner was last man in our platoon. Breaking the
battalion into column of platoons, Shipp marched us to
the drill grounds. Oh, it was hot, — hot enough to dis-
arm suspicion at anybody's fainting.

Through all the evolutions we went, — "Right of company's rear into column;" "Close column by divisions
on second division, right in front;" "To the rear by the
right flank, pass the defile," and what not. The file-
closers were so near to us we could not talk. All we
could do was to nudge Reuben, and we began to think he
would never faint.

At last Shipp trotted his great gray horse to the flank
of the battalion, and gave the command, "Forward into
line, — forward double time, — march." The perspira-
tion was streaming from us.

"Now, if ever, Reuben," I whispered, as we started off;
and, sure enough, Reuben made a feint of stumbling, his
gun pitched forward from his shoulder, and he threw
himself forward in as beautiful a faint as ever was feinted.

"Help him there, Faulkner and Wise," said the left
guide, as the battalion swept on; and Charley and I bent
over him with infinite tenderness and concern. We were
about to pass some congratulations, when I looked up and
saw Shipp galloping, warning Phillips. That gave him
all the pallor he needed.

"Who is that man?" said the major.

"Phillips, sir," said Faulkner and myself, rising and
saluting.

"Is he seriously ill?"

"No, sir, hope not, — seems to be overcome by heat."

"Eh! take him to barracks and summon the surgeon,"
said he, and, roweling the old gray, he galloped back to

the command.   He did not order us to return, so Master
Faulkner and I remained in barracks to nurse the invalid,
after making a brave show of his helplessness as we
assisted him across the plain.   In barracks, we at once
began business.   Faulkner hurried to the hospital for a
bucket of ice for the invalid.   A happy thought struck
me.   I stole around behind Colonel Williamson's, and
milked his cow into our drinking-pail.   We three then
sat up in a quiet room, drinking iced milk, watching the
battalion drill.

It was all very well until next evening parade, when we
heard ourselves reported for not returning to ranks, and,
in spite of some very plausible excuses given to the commandant, five more demerits were added to our already
overflowing score.   The story of our ruse was all over barracks, and I have always thought it had reached Shipp's
ears.

Whether it did or not, I had by this time, and in many
ways, become known to the superintendent and commandant as mixed up in, and capable of, any sort of prank or
dereliction which took place, — a reputation by no means
enviable, let me assure you.

CHAPTER XVIII

A HUNT AND ALMOST A LICKING

THAT was a great flight of wild pigeons in the Brushy Hills in the autumn of 1863, and nobody ever before saw so many squirrels there. Louis and I had been behaving well. Our class standing was good, and our conduct exemplary.

We found it easy now to secure special permits, and for privileges were content to apply on Fridays for leave of absence from Saturday dinner roll-call. This gave us substantially all day for hunting. General Philip St. George Cocke, a wealthy patron of the school, had presented to it a stand of small smooth-bore muskets, which we found to be excellent fowling-pieces.

At this period of the war, no shot were purchasable in stores. The devices to which we resorted to provide shot may be interesting. Our lead we obtained from the roof of an unoccupied outhouse. In our earlier efforts, we beat the lead into thin sheets, then cut it into narrow strips, then cross-cut the strips into cubes. These we rolled between two drawing-boards until the pellets were approximately round. That method proving slow, we shifted to another. We obtained a piece of sheet tin, which we perforated with small nail-holes. To this sheet of tin we attached a long handle. Then we secured a brazier with some charcoal and a ladle. With this outfit we heated the lead on the brazier. When it was thoroughly melted, one man poured it slowly from the spoon upon the sheet of tin, while the other shook the tin gently over a bucket of water. The lead dropped into the water in little globules, through the perforations of the tin. When the operation was complete, we had shot shaped like exclamation-points. All that remained was to cut off their tails, and this we did with a patience and perseverance worthy of a more important cause. The shot were heavier than those we buy in stores, and very deadly in their effects.

One Friday night in October, 1863, we had obtained a permit to be absent next day from breakfast roll-call until dress parade. We had been so pressed with academic and military duties that we had not manufactured our supply of shot. Conic sections, Livy, and surveying had me in their grip, and Louis was wrestling with calculus and engineering. Something must be done, or our hunt, so cherished in anticipation, would fall to the ground. True, we were now good boys, but we had not been such so long that our old tricks were forgotten. In the busy days preparatory to examinations, a favorite method of studying out of hours had been to wait until after taps inspection, affix blankets around the sides of the square oaken table, and, crawling under the table with a candle, to study there for an hour or two. To-night we resolved to utilize that device.

It is providential that the fumes of the charcoal in the brazier did not smother us both. It was close quarters under there. With brazier, bucket, and lead spoon, little room was left for the workmen; but we made famous progress. Our legs stuck out under the blankets, and now and again we would pull out, or, so to speak, come to the surface, and have a breathing spell. Oblivious of all else, and unable to hear outside sounds, we had nearly finished our task, when " Rap, rap, rap ! " came the knock of an inspector upon our door. We blew out the light, and drew our legs inside, but the brazier sent forth a ruddy glow which betrayed us.

" Who is orderly here ? " asked the voice of a sub-professor. We crawled up, red and begrimed. " What does this all mean ? " said he.

We mumbled out some explanations. " The sentinel has been ordering lights out in this room for five minutes," said he sternly. I glanced at the confounded blankets, and saw that the corner of one of them had been sagged by our scrambling about, so that an aperture was left, through which a beam of light went straight out the glass doorway and shone upon a pillar of the stoop, making a flaring signal. Coming into barracks late, the officer had seen it, and this visit was the result of our calm disregard of repeated cries of " Lights out in 28," which cries we had not heard.

" Take that fire out and extinguish it. Open the windows, and let out these poisonous gases. It is a mercy you are not smothered to death, and that the barracks have not been set on fire," said the officer, as he departed.

On Monday morning, we answered to the following reports : " Lights up after taps ; repeated disobedience of orders in failing to extinguish lights ; introducing fire into barracks." We expected about ten demerits each, to say nothing of extra tours and confinement to limits. But my troubles were not ended with this episode. The quartermaster's store was only opened upon Saturday after breakfast. It was essential that both of us should have certain things from the store in the morning before starting on our hunt. With pass-books in hand, the cadets who sought supplies formed in line, and were admitted to the store in the order of their arrival. That we might leave as early as possible, Louis and I cast lots to decide which should remain from breakfast with the pass-books

and get near the store door.   The one who went to breakfast was to bring the other man's meal buttoned in the
breast of his jacket.   The lot to remain fell to me.   When
Louis came back from breakfast, he found a very dam-
aged-looking comrade in our room; and this is how it all
came about : —

The store was on the fourth stoop, in a large room over
the archway.   Only six or eight boys had remained from
breakfast.   I was fourth or fifth in line.   In front of me
were three plebes and an old cadet.   While waiting, a
quarrel arose between the old cadet and the plebes about
their respective places in line.   The old cadet insisted
that they should let him enter first, and they refused.   It
was a cold, gray morning, and none of us were in pleasant
humor at being kept standing there shivering during the
long delay.   The grumbling went on between them until
at last the old cadet punched the little fellow in front of
him in the ribs, and butted him with his knees, until he
began to cry.   The boy's name was Logan.   He was no
match for his antagonist.   It was a mean piece of bully-
ing, and such as no old cadet had the right to indulge in.
The old cadet had been there two years already, having
been found deficient the previous July; so that, while
we were both now third-class men, he had been an old
cadet when I was a plebe.   Our class relations had
been friendly enough, and at last I ventured to remon-
strate in a concilatory way with him about his cruelty to
Logan.

To my surprise, he wheeled about and said : " What
have you got to do with it ?   Maybe you want to take the
rat's part.   Ever since you came here, you have been that
way."   This was not true, for I had been a terror to
plebes in camp.

" No," I protested, still good-tempered.   " But you

have no right to take his place in line, and he is too small
to defend himself."

" You 're a liar ! " he blurted out.

" Don't say that," said I. " You and I are friends.
You don't mean it, and will be sorry when you are cool."

" Yes, I do mean it ! " shouted he. " You are a liar ;
and you sneaked out of the first row you got into when
you came here."

He proceeded no further in that story. I popped him
in the eye with the best left-hander I could plant; and at
it we went, like a pair of jack-snappers, the plebes dancing
about in wonder. He had a great reach. He fetched
me several very substantial cracks. Nevertheless, the
first blow I hit him gave me a decided advantage, and I
succeeded in closing with him and getting his head in
chancery. Thus holding him, I punched his nose and
eyes and mouth in fine form; but, in spite of all I could
do, I felt his long, sinewy arm steal up my back, and his
fingers close with a choking grip upon my collar. Hug !
I hugged his head with all my might and main, as he
tugged to extricate himself.

" Stop that noise on fourth stoop ! " shouted the sentry
in the area, time and time again ; but we were too busy
to pay attention to his commands. We were panting like
two young bucks with locked horns. Renewing the
whacking at his head under my arm, I asked, " Have you
got enough ? " I knew he did not have enough. Still I
thought it would do no harm to inquire.

" No ! " roared he ; " I 'll give *you* enough before this
thing is over." With that I slung him around and tried
to throw him ; but his bow-legs seemed set as firmly as
the towers of the arch. I not only found that he could
stand punishment, but that he had the advantage of me
in wind.

The sentinel shouted for the officer of the day, and the two commanded, "Stop that noise in barracks!" as if their throats would burst. At last, with a supreme effort, he dragged himself out from under my arm, whirled me about, seized me by the hair with both hands, dashed me down to my knees, bumped my head upon the frozen oak planks, and kicked me in the face. I saw a thousand stars. The poor little rats were almost frantic.

"Got enough, eh?" said he ironically, as, panting from his triumphant efforts, he planted me a savage uppercut under the arm with which I was trying to protect my face. "Maybe *you 've* got enough now?"

"Not much!" said I, trying to tear loose from his grip on my hair; but down I went again, for he overmatched me. Whack, thump, bang! he began afresh. I 'm glad I don't have to tell how that fight ended. Thank heaven, it did n't end. Just as matters seemed growing desperate, the officer of the day, with jangling sword, came bounding up the stairway three steps at a time, and, rushing to where we were clinched, he caught us in the collars and snatched us apart. Holding us at arm's length, and looking at us covered with blood, he commanded the peace, and ordered us to our rooms.

My adversary walked sulkily away. He was no beauty. He had a bulging eye like a crab, and some of his teeth were very loose. But I? My! oh, my! but I was a physical wreck. My jacket, where I held his head so long, was fairly soaked with gore. Two or three buttons were torn off, and my collar was under one ear. The toe of his shoe had raked off about an inch of skin from the ridge of my nose. A knot as large as a pigeon's egg was on my forehead, and the last I saw of him he was picking my hair off his fingers.

"Carried almost too many guns for you, did n't he?"

said Shafer, the officer of the day, as we descended together.

With a sickly grin, I answered, " I don't know. I was doing my best. But I'm mighty glad you came, Shafer."

Then the kind fellow, who evidently sympathized with my side of the story, went with me to the room and helped me wash up and preen my badly ruffled plumage. About this time, we heard the tramp of the corps returning; and Louis, who had heard some rumors at the archway, rushed up to know what it was all about.

" Here, take the pass-books. Hurry, and you'll get in line in time. I broke up the waiting line," said I.

" Are you able to go ? " asked he.

" Of course I am. I'll go to the hospital with the sick-list and get my nose patched by the time you finish at the store. Hurry ! " So off he darted, and I fell in at sick-call. Thirty minutes later, we were scampering across the hills with our guns, — I slightly disfigured by a long patch of adhesive plaster on my nose, and wearing my cap well back, to avoid contact with that pigeon egg on my forehead.

And a great day we had of it. As if to compensate us for our tribulations, we struck a flight of pigeons and found numbers of squirrels. In fact, we killed so many that we found it necessary to sling our game upon a pole, which we bore between us on our shoulders. When we appeared in barracks, in ample time for dress-parade, we were the envy of the corps. We sent a nice bunch of game to the superintendent's wife. Considering the great number of delinquencies for which we were to make answer Monday morning to the commandant, we seriously debated whether it would be counted as " boot-licking," if we sent some of our game to the officers' mess. " Boot-licking," or seeking favor with officers, was looked upon as a heinous crime in our code of deportment. However, as old Chinook belonged to the officers' mess, we concluded to let them have a few. Then we secured permit for private breakfast in the mess-hall Sunday morning, and to visit old Judge at the kitchens to deliver our game and make preliminary arrangements.

With invitations sent to a few to our choice symposium next morning, the day's work was complete. We made no effort that night, rest assured, to keep lights up after taps.

We came out of our troubles better than we expected. Shipp possessed excellent good sense in dealing with cadets. He rather sympathized with our venial struggles to provide ourselves with ammunition, and did not punish us severely, but warned us against fetching fire into barracks. Shafer, the cadet officer, who might have made it go hard with my foeman and myself, saw him, told him he was wrong, made him come and apologize to me, and after that he and I were good friends. And last, but not least, little Rat Logan, whose pretty sister I had visited in their home at " Dungenness " upon the James, memory of whose charms had probably made me take his part, came grinning around to our quarters to tell us he had a box from home. He said it was poor pay for the punishment I had got in his behalf. I suggested that he invite my antagonist also ; but he swore he should not have as much as a wishbone from his turkey. We made short shrift of Logan's box. With bayonets we ripped it open. Its stores of turkey, ham, biscuits, pickles, preserves, and what not were soon spread before us.

The best simile descriptive of cadets around a box from home is that of feeding a kennel of hounds. With undisguised impatience they watch the display of food.

With frank gluttony they fall upon it. With pop-eyed satiety they turn away only when all is consumed. And then they lie about in semi-comatose condition, refusing to attend meals until nature relieves itself of overloading.

Another piece of good luck was in store for me. I had kept the pledge about demerits, and stood well at the January intermediate examinations. One evening at dress parade, I had the unspeakable joy of hearing myself announced as a corporal, " vice Vaughan, resigned." Those chevrons were very stimulating. I even remembered that Napoleon had once been a corporal.

CHAPTER XIX

THE MOST GLORIOUS DAY OF MY LIFE

In the spring of 1864, I was still a cadet at the Virginia Military Institute. "Unrest" is the word to describe the feeling pervading the school.

Rosser's brigade had wintered in Rockbridge, but a few miles from the Institute. Lexington and the Institute were constantly visited by Rosser, his staff, and the officers of his brigade. They brought us in touch with the war, and the world beyond, more than anything else we had seen. They jangled their spurs through the archway, laughed loudly in the officers' quarters, and rode off as if they carried the world in a sling. In March, they broke camp, and came ambling, trotting, galloping, prancing past the Institute, their mounted band playing, their little guidons fluttering, bound once more to active duty in the lower valley. Before their departure, General Rosser presented a captured flag to the corps of cadets. His escort on the occasion was decked with leaves of mountain laurel, the evergreen badge which the brigade had adopted. We felt ashamed of having flags captured for us by others. When the Laurel Brigade took its departure, many a cadet followed it longingly with eyes and heart.

Then, too, we heard that Grant had been transferred to command in the East; and we all knew that there would be great fighting at the front. Many cadets resigned. Good boys became bad boys for the express purpose of getting "shipped," parents and guardians having refused to permit them to resign.

The stage-coaches for the railroad stations at Goshen and Staunton stopped at the sallyport on nearly every trip to take on cadets departing for the front.

Many a night, sauntering back and forth on the sentry-beat in front of barracks, catching the sounds of loud talk and laughter from the officers' quarters, or pondering upon the last joyous squad of cadets who had scrambled to the top of the departing stage, my heart longed for the camp, and I wondered if my time would ever come. I was now over seventeen, and it did seem to me that I was old enough.

The proverb saith, "All things come to him who waits."

It was the 10th of May.

Nature bedecked herself that springtime in her loveliest garb. Battalion drill had begun early, and the corps had never been more proficient at this season of the year.

The parade ground was firm and green. The trees were clothed in the full livery of fresh foliage. The sun shone on us through pellucid air, and the light breath of May kissed and fluttered our white colors, which were adorned with the face of Washington.

After going through the manœuvres of battalion drill, the corps was drawn up, near sundown, for dress parade. It was the time of year when townsfolk drove down, and ranged themselves upon the avenue to witness our brave display; and groups of girls in filmy garments set off with bits of color came tripping across the sod; and children and nurses sat about the benches at the guard-tree.

The battalion was put through the manual. The first sergeants reported. The adjutant read his orders. The fifes and drums played down the line in slow time, and came back with a jolly, rattling air. The officers advanced to music and saluted. The sun sunk beyond the House Mountain. The evening gun boomed forth. The garrison flag fell lazily from its peak on the barracks' tower. The four companies went springing homeward at double time to the gayest tune the fifes knew how to play. Never in all its history looked Lexington more beautiful.

Never did sense of secluded peacefulness rest more soothingly upon her population. In our leisure time after supper, the cadets strolled back and forth from barracks to the limits gate, and watched the full-orbed moon lift herself over the mountains. Perfume was in the air, silence in the shadows. Well might we quote : —

> " How beautiful this night!
> The balmiest sigh that vernal zephyrs breathe in evening's ear
> Were discord to the speaking quietude
> That wraps this moveless scene. Heaven's ebon vault,
> Bestudded with stars unutterably bright,
> Through which the moon's unclouded
> Splendor rolls, seems like a canopy which
> Love hath spread, to shelter its
> Sleeping world."

And so, tranquil, composed by the delightful scenes around us, three hundred of us closed our eyes and passed into the happy dreams of youth in springtime.

Hark ! the drums are beating. Their throbbing bounds through every corner of the barracks, saying to the sleepers, " Be up and doing." It is the long roll.

Long roll had been beaten several times of late, sometimes to catch absentees, and once for a fire in the town. Grumblingly the cadets hurried down to their places in the ranks, expecting to be soon dismissed and to return to their beds. A group of officers, intently scanning by the light of a lantern a paper held by the adjutant, stood near the statue of George Washington, opposite the arch. The companies were marched together. The adjutant commanded attention, and proceeded to read the orders in his hands.

They announced that the enemy in heavy force was advancing up the Shenandoah valley; that General Lee could not spare any forces to meet him; that General Breckinridge had been ordered to assemble troops from southwestern Virginia and elsewhere at Staunton; and that the cadets should join him there at the earliest practicable moment. The corps was ordered to march, with four companies of infantry and a section of artillery, by the Staunton pike, at break of day.

First sergeants were ordered to detail eight artillerists from each of the four companies, to report for duty immediately, and man a section of artillery.

As these orders were announced, not a sound was heard from the boys who stood there, with beating hearts, in the military posture of parade rest.

"Parade's dismissed," piped the adjutant. The sergeants side-stepped us to our respective company parades.

Methinks that even after thirty-three years I once more hear the gamecock voices of the sergeants detailing their artillery and ammunition squads, and ordering us to appear with canteens, haversacks, and blankets at four A. M. Still silence reigned. Then, as company after company broke ranks, the air was rent with wild cheering at the thought that our hour was come at last.

Elsewhere in the Confederacy, death, disaster, disappointment may have by this time chilled the ardor of our people, but here, in this little band of fledgelings, the hope of battle flamed as brightly as on the morning of Manassas.

We breakfasted by candle-light, and filled our haversacks from the mess-hall tables. In the gray of morning, we wound down the hill to the river, tramped heavily

across the bridge, ascended the pike beyond, cheered the
fading turrets of the school; and sunrise found us going
at a four-mile gait to Staunton, our gallant little battery
rumbling behind.

We were every way fitted for this kind of work by our
hard drilling, and marched into Staunton in the afternoon
of the second day, showing little ill effects of travel.

Staunton, small as it is, seemed large and cosmopolitan
after our long confinement. As we marched past a female
school, every window of which was filled with pretty girls,
the fifes were laboring away at " The Girl I Left Behind
Me." There was no need for the girls to cry, " Fie!
fie ! " at such a suggestion. Not one of us were thinking
of the girls we left behind us. The girls we saw before
us were altogether to our liking.

We found a pleasant camping ground on the outskirts
of the town, and thither the whole population flocked for
inspection of the corps, and to witness dress parade, for
our fame was widespread. The attention bestowed upon
the cadets was enough to turn the heads of much humbler
persons than ourselves. We were asked to visit nearly
every house in town.

Having an invitation to dine at the home of a friend,
Louis and I waded in a creek to wash the mud off our
shoes and trousers. With pocket-comb and glass we completed our toilet in a fence-corner. Then we walked about
until our garments were dry, and proceeded to meet our
engagement. Everything goes in war time.

At night, the town was hilarious. Several dances were
arranged, and, as dancing was a cadet accomplishment, we
were in our element.

The adoration bestowed upon us by young girls dis-
gusted the regular officers. Before our coming, they had
had things all their own way. Now, they found that fierce

mustaches and heavy cavalry boots must give place to the
downy cheeks and merry, twinkling feet we brought from
Lexington. A big blonde captain, who was wearing a
stunning bunch of gilt aiguillettes, looked as if he would
snap my head off when I trotted up and whisked his
partner away from him. They could not and would not
understand why girls preferred these little, untitled whip-
persnappers to officers of distinction. Veterans forgot
that youth loves youth.

Doubtless some feeling of this sort prompted the band
of a regiment of grimy veterans to strike up " Rock-a-bye,
Baby," when the cadets marched by them. Quick as soldiers' love of fun, the men took up the air, accompanying
it by rocking their guns in their arms as if putting them
to sleep. It produced a perfect roar of amusement with
everybody but ourselves. We were furious.

All this on the eve of a battle? Yes, of course. Why
not? To be sure, everybody knew there was going to be a
fight. That was what we came for. But nobody among
us knew or cared just when or where it was coming off.
Life is too full of trouble for petty officers or privates, or
young girls, to bother themselves hunting up such disagreeable details in advance. That was the business of
generals. They were to have all the glory; and so we
were willing they should have all the solicitude, anxiety,
and preoccupation.

At dress parade, May 12, orders were read for the movement of the army down the valley the following morning.
We always moved on time. Now, who would have believed that a number of girls were up to see us off, or that
two or three were crying? Yet it was so. And quick
work of the naked boy with the cross-bow I call that.

As we passed some slaughter-pens on the outskirts, an
old Irish butcher, in his shirt sleeves, hung over his gate,

pipe in mouth. With a twinkle in his eye he watched
the corps go by, at last exclaiming, " Begorra, an' it 's no
purtier dhrove av pigs hev passed this gate since this
hog-killing began."

We made a good day's march, and camped that night
near Harrisonburg. During the day, we met several
couriers bearing dispatches ; they reported the enemy
advancing in heavy force, and had left him near Stras-
burg and Woodstock.

Pressing on through Harrisonburg, which we reached
early in the morning, we camped the second night at
Lacy's Springs, in Shenandoah ; rain had set in, but the
boys stood up well to their work, and but few lame-ducks
had succumbed.

Evidences of the approach of the enemy multiplied
on the second day. We passed a great many vehicles
coming up the valley with people and farm products and
household effects, and a number of herds of cattle and
other livestock, all escaping from the Union troops ;
now and then a weary or wounded cavalryman came by.
Their reports were that Sigel's steady advance was only
delayed by a thin line of cavalry skirmishers, who had
been ordered to retard him as best they could until
Breckinridge could march his army down to meet him.

Towards evening, we came to a stone church and spring,
where a cavalry detail with a squad of Union prisoners
were resting ; the prisoners were a gross, surly-looking
lot of Germans, who could not speak English. They
evidently could not make us out ; they watched us with
manifest curiosity, and talked in unintelligible, guttural
sounds among themselves.

When we reached camp, the rain had stopped and the
clouds had lifted, but everything was wet and gummy.
To add to my disgust, I was detailed as corporal of the

guard, which meant loss of sleep at night, and a lonesome time next day with the wagons in rear of the corps.

Looking down the valley, as evening closed in, we could
see a line of bivouac fires, and were uncertain whether
they were lit by our own pickets or by the enemy. At
any rate, we were getting sufficiently near to the gentlemen for whom we were seeking to feel reasonably certain we should meet them.

Night closed in upon us ; for a little while the woodland resounded with the axe-stroke, or the cheery halloos
of the men from camp-fire to camp-fire ; for a while the
fire-lights danced, the air laden with the odor of cooking
food ; for a while the boys stood around the camp-fires
for warmth and to dry their wet clothing ; but soon all
had wrapped their blankets around them and laid down
in silence, unbroken save by the champing of the colonel's horse upon his provender, or the fall of a passing
shower.

I was on duty as corporal of the guard ; a sentry stood
post near the pike ; the remainder of the guard and the
musicians were stretched before the watch-fire asleep. It
was my part to remain awake, and a very lonesome, cheerless task it was, sitting there in the darkness, under the
dancing shadows of the wide-spreading trees, watching the
fagots flame up and die out, speculating upon the events
of the morrow.

An hour past midnight, the sound of hoofs upon the
pike caught my ear, and in a few moments the challenge
of the sentry summoned me. The newcomer was an
aid-de-camp, bearing orders for Colonel Shipp from the
commanding general. When I aroused the commandant,
he struggled up, rubbed his eyes, muttered something
about moving at once, and ordered me to arouse the
camp without having the drums beaten. Orders to fall

in were promptly given, rolls were rattled off, the battalion was formed, and we debouched upon the pike, heading in the darkness and mud for Newmarket.

Before the command to march was given, a thing occurred which made a deep impression upon us all, — a thing which even now may be a solace to those whose boys died so gloriously that day. In the gloom of the night, Captain Frank Preston, neither afraid nor ashamed to pray, sent up an appeal to God for his protection of our little band : it was a humble, earnest petition, that sunk into the heart of every hearer. Few were the dry eyes, little the frivolity, when he had ceased to speak of home, of father, of mother, of country, of victory and defeat, of life, of death, of eternity. Captain Preston had been an officer in Stonewall Jackson's command ; had lost an arm at Winchester ; was on the retired list ; and was sub-professor of Latin, and tactical officer of B Company : he was a typical Valley Presbyterian. Those who, a few hours later, saw him commanding his company in the thickest of the fight, his already empty sleeve attesting that he was no stranger to the perilous edge of battle, realized fully the beauty of the lines which tell that " the bravest are the tenderest, the loving are the daring."

Day broke gray and gloomy upon us toiling onward in the mud. The sober course of our reflections was relieved by the light-heartedness of the veterans. We overtook Wharton's Brigade, with smiling " Old Gabe," a Virginia Military Institute boy, at their head. They were squatting by the roadside, cooking breakfast, as we came up. With many good-natured gibes they restored our confidence ; they seemed as merry, nonchalant, and indifferent to the coming fight as if it were their daily occupation. A tall, round-shouldered fellow, whose legs seemed almost split up to his shoulder-blades, came among us with a pair of shears and a pack of playing cards, offering to take our names and cut off love-locks to be sent home after we were dead; another inquired if we wanted rosewood coffins, satin-lined, with name and age on the plate. In a word, they made us ashamed of the depressing solemnity of our last six miles of marching, and renewed within our breasts the true dare-devil spirit of soldiery.

Resuming the march, the mile-posts numbered four, three, two, one mile to Newmarket; then the mounted skirmishers hurried past us to their position at the front. We heard loud cheering at the rear, which was caught up by the troops along the line of march. We learned its import as General John C. Breckinridge and staff approached, and we joined heartily in the cheering as that soldierly man, mounted magnificently, galloped past, uncovered, bowing, and riding like a Cid. It is impossible to exaggerate the gallant appearance of General Breckinridge. In stature he was considerably over six feet high. He sat his blood-bay thoroughbred as if he had been born on horseback; his head was of noble mould, and a piercing eye and a long, dark, drooping mustache completed a faultless military presence.

Deployed along the crest of an elevation in our front, we could see our line of mounted pickets and the smouldering fires of their last night's bivouac. We halted at a point where passing a slight turn in the road would bring us in full view of the position of the enemy. Echols's and Wharton's brigades hurried past us; this time there was not much bantering between us. " Forward!" was the word once more, and, turning the point in the road, Newmarket was in full view, and the whole position was displayed.

At this point, a bold range of hills on the left parallel

with the mountains divided the Shenandoah valley into two smaller valleys; in the easternmost of these lies Newmarket. The valley pike on which we had advanced passes through the town parallel with the Massanunten Mountains on our right, and Smith's Creek, coursing along its base. The hills on our left, as they near the town, slope down to it from south and west, and swell beyond it to the west and north. Through this depression from the town to the Shenandoah River in the western valley runs a transverse road with heavy stone walls. Between the pike by which we were advancing and the creek at the base of the mountains lies a beautiful strip of meadowland, extending to and beyond the village of Newmarket; on these meadows, in the outskirts of the village, were orchards, where the enemy's skirmishers were posted, his left wing being concealed in the village. The right wing of the enemy was posted behind the heavy stone fence in the road running westward from the town, parallel with our line of battle. Behind the infantry, on the slope of the rising ground, the Union artillery was posted: the ground rose behind this position until a short distance beyond the town; to the left of the pike it spread out in an elevated plateau. The hillsides from this plateau to the pike were broken by several gullies, heavily wooded by scrub cedar.

It was Sunday morning at eleven o'clock. In a picturesque little Lutheran churchyard, under the very shadow of the village spire and among the white tombstones, a six-gun battery was posted in rear of the infantry lines of the enemy. Firing over the heads of their own troops, that battery opened upon us the moment we came in sight.

Away off to the right, in the Luray Gap, we could see our signal corps telegraphing the position and numbers of the enemy. Our cavalry was galloping to the cover of the creek to attempt to turn the enemy's left flank. Echols's brigade, moving from the pike at a double-quick by the right flank, went into line of battle across the meadow, its left resting on the pike. Simultaneously its skirmishers were thrown forward at a run and engaged the enemy. Out of the orchards and on the meadows, puff after puff of blue smoke rose as the sharpshooters advanced, the pop, pop, pop of their rifles ringing forth excitingly. Thundering down the pike came McLaughlin with his artillery. Wheeling out upon the meadows, he swung into battery, action left, and let fly with all his guns.

The cadet section of artillery pressed down the pike a little farther, turned to the left, toiled up the slope in front of us, and, going into position, delivered a plunging fire in reply to the Federal battery in the graveyard. We counted it a good omen when, at the first discharge of our little guns, a beautiful blue-white wreath of smoke shot upward and hovered over them. The town, which a moment before had seemed to sleep so peacefully upon that Sabbath morning, was now wrapped in battle smoke and swarming with troops hurrying to their position. We had their range beautifully. Every shell hit some obstruction, and exploded in the streets or on the hillsides. Every man in our army was in sight. Every position of the enemy was plainly visible. His numbers were uncomfortably large; for, notwithstanding his line of battle already formed seemed equal to our own, the pike beyond the town was still filled with his infantry.

Our left wing consisted of Wharton's brigade; our centre, of the 62d Virginia infantry and the cadet corps; our right, of Echols's brigade and the cavalry. Until now, as corporal of the guard, I had remained in charge of the baggage-wagon with a detail of three men, —

Redwood, Stanard, and Woodlief. My orders were to remain with the wagons at the bend in the pike unless we were driven back. In that case, we were to retire to a point of safety.

When it was clear that the battle was imminent, one thought took possession of me, and that was, if I sat on a baggage wagon while the corps of cadets was in its first, perhaps its only engagement, I should never be able to look my father in the face again. He was a grim old fighter, at that moment resisting the advance on Petersburg, and holding the enemy in check until Lee's army could come up. I had annoyed him with importunities for permission to leave the Institute and enter the army. If, now that I had the opportunity to fight, I should fail to do so, I knew what was in store for me, for he had a tongue of satire and ridicule like a lash of scorpions.

Napoleon in Egypt, pointing to the Pyramids, told his soldiers that from their heights forty centuries looked down upon them. The oration I delivered from the tail-board of a wagon was not so hyperbolical, but was equally emphatic. It ran about this wise : " Boys, the enemy is in our front. The corps is going into action. I like fighting no better than anybody else. But I have an enemy in my rear as dreadful as any before us. If I should return home and tell my father that I was on the baggage guard when the cadets were in battle, I know what my fate would be. He would kill me with ridicule, which is worse than bullets. I intend to join the command at once. Any of you who think your duty requires you to remain may do so."

All the guard followed. We left the wagon in charge of the black driver. Of the four who thus went, one was killed and two were wounded. We overtook the battalion as it deployed by the left flank from the pike. Moving at double-quick, we were in an instant in line of battle, our right resting near the turnpike. Rising ground in our immediate front concealed us from the enemy.

The command was given to strip for action. Knapsacks, blankets, — everything but guns, canteens, and cartridge-boxes, was thrown upon the ground. Our boys were silent then. Every lip was tightly drawn, every cheek was pale, but not with fear. With a peculiar, nervous jerk, we pulled our cartridge-boxes round to the front, laid back the flaps, and tightened belts. Whistling rifled shells screamed over us, as, tipping the hill-crest in our front, they bounded past. To our right, across the pike, Patton's brigade was lying down abreast of us.

" At-ten-*tion-n-n* ! Battalion forward ! Guide center-r-r ! " shouted Shipp, and up the slope we started. From the left of the line, Sergeant-Major Woodbridge ran out and posted himself forty paces in advance of the colors as directing guide, as if we had been upon the drill ground. That boy would have remained there, had not Shipp ordered him back to his post; for this was no dress parade. Brave Evans, standing six feet two, shook out the colors that for days had hung limp and bedraggled about the staff, and every cadet leaped forward, dressing to the ensign, elate and thrilling with the consciousness that this was war.

Moving up to the hill crest in our front, we were abreast of our smoking battery, and uncovered to the range of the enemy's guns. We were pressing towards him at " arms port," moving with the light tripping gate of the French infantry. The enemy's veteran artillery soon obtained our range, and began to drop his shells under our very noses along the slope. Echols's brigade rose up, and was charging on our right with the well-known rebel yell.

Down the green slope we went, answering the wild cry
of our comrades as their muskets rattled out in opening
volleys. " Double time ! " shouted Shipp, and we broke
into a long trot. In another moment, a pelting rain of
lead would fall upon us from the blue line in our front.

Then came a sound more stunning than thunder. It
burst directly in my face : lightnings leaped, fire flashed,
the earth rocked, the sky whirled round. I stumbled, my
gun pitched forward, and I fell upon my knees. Sergeant Cabell looked back at me pityingly and called out,
" Close up, men ! " as he passed on. I knew no more.

When consciousness returned, the rain was falling in
torrents. I was lying upon the ground, which all about
was torn and ploughed with shell, and they were still
screeching in the air and bounding on the earth. Poor
little Captain Hill, the tactical officer of C Company, was
lying near me bathed in blood, with a frightful gash over
the temple, and was gasping like a dying fish. Cadets
Reed, Merritt, and another, whose name I forget, were
near at hand, badly shot. The battalion was three hundred yards in advance of us, clouded in low-lying smoke
and hotly engaged. They had crossed the lane which the
enemy had held, and the Federal battery in the graveyard had fallen back to the high ground beyond. " How
came they there ? " I thought, " and why am I here ? "
Then I found I was bleeding from a long and ugly gash
in the head. That rifled shell, bursting in our faces,
had brought down five of us. " Hurrah ! " I thought,
" youth's dream is realized at last. I 've got a wound,
and am not dead yet."

Another moment found me on my feet, trudging along
to the hospital, almost whistling at thought that the next
mail would carry the news to the folks at home, with a
taunting suggestion that, after all the pains they had

taken, they had been unable to keep me out of my share in the fun. From this time forth, I may speak of the gallant behavior of the cadets without the imputation of vanity, for I was no longer a participant in their glory.

The fighting around the town was fierce and bloody on our left wing. On the right, the movements of Echols and Patton were very effective. They had pressed forward and gained the village, and our line was now concave, with its angle just beyond the town.

The Federal infantry had fallen back to the second line, and our left had now before it the task of ascending the slope to the crest of the hill where the enemy was posted. After pausing under the cover of the deep lane to breathe awhile and correct the alignment, our troops once more advanced, clambering up the bank and over the stone fence, at once delivering and receiving a withering fire.

At a point below the town where the turnpike makes a bend, the cavalry of the enemy was massed. A momentary confusion on our right, as our troops pressed through the streets of Newmarket, gave invitation for a charge of the Union cavalry. They did not see McLaughlin's battery, which had been moved up, unlimbered in the streets, and double-shotted with grape and canister. The enemy's cavalry dashed forward in column of platoons. Our infantry scrambled over the fences and gave the artillery a fair opportunity to rake them. They saw the trap too late ; they drew up and sought to wheel about.

Heavens! what a blizzard McLaughlin gave them! They staggered, wheeled, and fled. The road was filled with fallen men and horses. A few riderless steeds came galloping towards our lines, neighed, circled, and rejoined their comrades. One daring fellow, whose horse became unmanageable, rode straight at our battery at full speed,

passed beyond, behind, and around our line, and safely
rejoined his comrades, cheered for his courage by his enemies. This was the end of the cavalry in that fight.

Meanwhile, the troops upon our left performed their
allotted task. Up the slope, right up to the second line
of infantry, they went ; a second time the Federal troops
were forced to retire. Wharton's brigade secured two
guns of the battery, and the remaining four galloped back
to a new position in a farmyard on the plateau, at the
head of the cedar-skirted gully. Our boys had captured
over one hundred prisoners. Charlie Faulkner, now the
Senator from West Virginia, came back radiant in charge
of twenty-three Germans large enough to swallow him,
and insisted that he and Winder Garrett had captured
them unaided. Bloody work had been done. The space
between the enemy's old and new position was dotted with
dead and wounded, shot as they retired across the open
field ; but this same exposed ground now lay before, and
must be crossed by our own men, under a galling fire
from a strong and well-protected position. The distance
was not great, but the ground to be traversed was a level
green field of young wheat.

Again the advance was ordered. Our boys responded
with a cheer. Poor fellows ! They had already been put
upon their mettle in two assaults, exhausted, wet to the
skin, muddy to their eyebrows with the stiff clay ; some
of them actually shoeless after struggling across the
ploughed field : they, notwithstanding, advanced with tremendous earnestness, for the shout on our right advised
them that the victory was being won.

But the foe in our front was far from whipped. As
the cadets came on with a dash, he stood his ground most
courageously. The battery, now shotted with shrapnel
and canister, opened upon the cadets with a murderous

fire. The infantry, lying behind fence-rails piled upon the ground, poured in a steady, deadly volley. At one discharge, Cabell, first sergeant of D Company, by whose side I had marched for months, fell dead, and with him fell Crockett and Jones. A blanket would have covered the three. They were awfully mangled by the canister. A few steps further on, McDowell sank to his knees with a bullet through his heart. Atwill, Jefferson, and Wheelwright were shot at this point. Sam Shriver, cadet captain of C Company, had his sword arm broken by a minie ball. Thus C Company lost her cadet as well as her professor captain.

The men were falling right and left. The veterans on the right of the cadets seemed to waver. Colonel Shipp went down. For the first time, the cadets appeared irresolute. Some one cried out, " Lie down ! " and all obeyed, firing from the knee, — all but Evans, the ensign, who was standing bolt upright, shouting and waving the flag. Some one exclaimed, " Fall back and rally on Edgar's battalion ! " Several boys moved as if to obey. Pizzini, first sergeant of B Company, with his Corsican blood at the boiling point, cocked his rifle and proclaimed that he would shoot the first man who ran. Preston, brave and inspiring, in command of B Company, smilingly lay down upon his remaining arm with the remark that he would at least save that. Colonna, cadet captain of D, was speaking low to the men of his company with words of encouragement, and bidding them shoot close. The corps was being decimated.

Manifestly, they must charge or fall back. And charge it was ; for at that moment Henry Wise, " Old Chinook," beloved of every boy in the command, sprang to his feet, shouted out the command to rise up and charge, and, moving in advance of the line, led the cadet corps forward to the guns. The battery was being served superbly. The musketry fairly rolled, but the cadets never faltered. They reached the firm greensward of the farmyard in which the guns were planted. The Federal infantry began to break and run behind the buildings. Before the order to limber up could be obeyed by the artillerymen, the cadets disabled the teams, and were close upon the guns. The gunners dropped their sponges, and sought safety in flight. Lieutenant Hannah hammered a gunner over the head with his cadet sword. Winder Garret out-ran another and lunged his bayonet into him. The boys leaped upon the guns, and the battery was theirs. Evans, the color-sergeant, stood wildly waving the cadet colors from the top of a caisson.

A straggling fire of infantry was still kept up from the gully now on our right flank, notwithstanding the masses of blue retiring in confusion down the hill. The battal-ion was ordered to reform, mark time, and half wheel to the right ; then it advanced, firing into the cedars as it went, and did not pause again until it reached the pike, having driven the last of the enemy from the thicket. The broken columns of the enemy could be seen hurrying over the hills and down the pike towards Mount Jackson, hotly pressed by our infantry and cavalry. Our artillery galloped to Rude's Hill, whence it shelled the flying foe until they passed beyond the burning bridge that spanned the Shenandoah at Mount Jackson.

We had won a victory, — not a Manassas or an Appo-mattox, but, for all that, a right comforting bit of news went up the pike that night to General Lee, whose thoughts, doubtless, from where he lay locked in the death-grapple with Grant in the Wilderness, turned wea-rily and anxiously towards this attempted flank movement in the valley.

The pursuit down the pike was more like a foot-race
than a march; our fellows straggled badly; everybody
realized that the fight was over, and many were too exhausted to proceed farther.

As evening fell, the clouds passed away, the sun came
forth; and, when night closed in, no sound disturbed the
Sabbath calm save that of a solitary Napoleon gun
pounding away at the smouldering ruins of the bridge.
Our picket-fires were lit that night at beautiful Mount
Airy, while the main body of our troops bivouacked on
the pike, a mile below Newmarket. Out of a corps of
225 men, we had lost fifty-six, killed and wounded.
Strange to say, but one man of the artillery detail received a wound. Shortly before sundown, after having
my head sewed up and bandaged, and having rendered
such service as I could to wounded comrades, I sallied
forth to procure a blanket and see what was to be seen.
When we stripped for action, we left our traps unguarded;
nobody would consent to be detailed. As a result, the
camp-followers had made away with nearly all of our
blankets.

I entered the town, and found it filled with soldiers,
laughing and carousing as light-heartedly as if it was a
feast or a holiday. In a side street, a great throng of
Federal prisoners was corralled; they were nearly all
Germans. Every type of prisoner was there; some cheerful, some defiant, some careless, some calm and dejected.
One fellow in particular afforded great merriment by his
quaint recital of the manner of his capture. Said he,
"Dem leetle tevils mit der vite vlag vas doo mutch fur
us; dey shoost smash mine head ven I was cry zurrender
all de dime." A loud peal of laughter went up from the
bystanders, among whom I recognized several cadets.
His allusion to the white flag was to our colors. We

had a handsome corps flag, with a white and gold ground and a picture of Washington ; it disconcerted our adversaries not a little. Several, whom I have met since then, tell me that they could not make us out at all, as our strange colors, diminutive size, and unusual precision of movement made them think we must be some foreign mercenary regulars.

While standing there, my old partner Louis came running up, exclaiming, " Holloa !   Golly, I am glad it is no worse ; they said your head was knocked off." Then he held up his bandaged forearm, in which he had a pretty little wound. "Say, are you hungry ? There is an old lady round here on the back street just shoveling out pies and things to the soldiers."

Louis and I were both good foragers, so away we scampered, and relieved the dear old soul of a few more of her apparently inexhaustible supply. Then we started off to hunt up Henry. We had a good joke on him, but were afraid to tell it to him. Several of the cadets declared that, notwithstanding his piety, he had at the pinch in the wheatfield, when he ordered the charge, so far forgotten himself that he used some very plain old English expletives, as in days of yore. When we ventured to suggest it, he grew indignant, and he was such a serious fellow that we were afraid to press him about it ; when we found him, he gave us lots of sport. He was very tall and very thin. He had gone into action wearing the long-tailed coat of a Confederate captain. In the last charge, an unexploded canister had literally carried away his hind coat-tails and the pipe and tobacco in the pockets, without touching him. Probably he was so close to the guns that the bands of the canister had not burst when it passed him. However this may have been, when we found him, his coat-tails were hanging in short shreds behind, while in front they were intact. He was involuntarily feeling behind him, bemoaning the loss of his pipe and tobacco, and looked like a Shanghai rooster with his tail-feathers pulled out.

The jeers and banterings of the veterans had now ceased; we had fairly won our spurs. We could mingle with them fraternally and discuss the battle on equal terms : glorious fellows those veterans were. To them was due ninety-nine one-hundredths of the glory of the victory, yet they seemed to delight in giving all praise to "dem leetle tevils mit der vite vlag." The ladies of the place also overwhelmed us with tenderness, and as for ourselves, we drank in greedily the praise which made us the lions of the hour.

Leaving the village, we sought the plateau where most of our losses had occurred. A little above the town, in the fatal wheatfield, we came upon the dead bodies of three cadets; one wearing the chevrons of a first sergeant lay upon his face, stiff and stark, with outstretched arms. His hands had clutched and torn up great tufts of soil and grass. His lips were retracted; his teeth tightly locked; his face as hard as flint, with staring, glassy eyes. It was difficult indeed to recognize that this was all that remained of Cabell, who a few hours before had stood first in his class, second as a soldier, and the peer of any boy in the command in every trait of physical and moral manliness. A short distance removed from the spot where Cabell fell, and nearer to the position of the enemy, lay McDowell. It was a sight to rend one's heart! That little fellow was lying there asleep, more fit indeed for a cradle than a grave; he was about my own age, not large, and by no means robust. He was a North Carolinian; he had torn open his jacket and shirt, and even in death, lay clutching them back, exposing a

fair, white breast with its red wound. We had come too
late: Stanard had breathed his last but a few moments
before we reached the old farmhouse where the battery
had stood, now used as a hospital. His body was still
warm, and his last messages had been words of love to his
room-mates. Poor Jack, — playmate, room-mate, friend,
— farewell! Standing there, my mind sped back to the
old scenes at Lexington when we were shooting together
in the brushy hills; to our games and sports; to the
night we had gone to see him kneel at the chancel for
confirmation; to the previous night at the guard-fire,
when he confessed to a presentiment that he would be
killed; to his wistful, earnest farewell when we parted at
the baggage-wagon that morning; and my heart half
reproached me for my part in drawing him into the fight.
The warm tears of youthful friendship came welling up
to the eyes of both of us for one we had learned to love
as a brother; and now, thirty-four years later, I thank
God life's buffetings and the cold-heartedness of later
struggles have not yet diminished the pure evidence of
boyhood's friendship. A truer-hearted, braver, better fellow never lived than Jacquelin B. Stanard.

A few of us brought up a limber chest, threw our dead
across it, and bore their remains to a deserted storehouse
in the village. The next day, we buried them with the
honors of war, bowed down with grief at a victory so
dearly bought.

The day following that, we started on our return march
up the valley, crestfallen and dejected. The joy of victory was forgotten in distress for the friends and comrades dead and maimed. We were still young in the
ghastly game, but we proved apt scholars.

On our march up the valley, we were not hailed as sor-
rowing friends, but greeted as heroes and victors. At

Harrisonburg, Staunton, Charlottesville, — everywhere, an ovation awaited us such as we had not dreamed of, and such as has seldom greeted any troops. The dead and the poor fellows still tossing on cots of fever and delirium were almost forgotten by the selfish comrades whose fame their blood had bought. We were ordered to Richmond : all our sadness disappeared. What mattered it to us that we were packed into freight-cars ? it was great sport riding on the tops of the cars. We were side-tracked at Ashland, and there, lying on the ground by the side of us, was Stonewall Jackson's division. We had heard of them, and looked upon them as the greatest soldiers that ever went into battle. What flattered us most was that they had heard of us.

While waiting at Ashland, a very distinguished-looking surgeon entered the car, inquiring for some cadet. He was just returning from the battlefield of Spotsylvania. I heard with absorbed interest his account of the terrible carnage there ; and when he said he had seen a small tree within the " bloody angle " cut down by bullets, I turned to Louis and said, " I think that old fellow is drawing a longbow." The person speaking was Dr. Charles McGill. I afterwards learned that what he said was literally true.

At the very time when we were lying there at Ashland, the armies of Grant and Lee, moving by the flank, were passing the one all about us, the other within a few miles of us, from the battlefields of Spotsylvania Court House and Milford Station to their ghastly field of second Cold Harbor. We could distinctly hear the firing in our front. We reached Richmond that afternoon, and were quartered in one of the buildings of the Fair Grounds, known as Camp Lee. It is impossible to describe the enthusiasm with which we were received.

A week after the battle of Newmarket, the cadet corps, garlanded, cheered by ten thousand throats, intoxicated with praise unstinted, wheeled proudly around the Washington monument at Richmond, to pass in review before the President of the Confederate States, to hear a speech of commendation from his lips, and to receive a stand of colors from the Governor of Virginia.

No wonder that our band, as we marched back to our quarters, played lustily : —

> "There 's not a trade that 's going
> Worth showing or knowing,
> Like that from glory growing
> For the bowld soldier boy.
> For to right or left you go,
> Sure you know, friend or foe,
> He is bound to be a beau,
> Your bowld soldier boy."

CHAPTER XX

THE GRUB BECOMES A BUTTERFLY

AFTER a few days in Richmond, the cadets were ordered back to Lexington. We resumed academic duties promptly, and were just beginning to settle down to hard work, when General Hunter advanced up the valley of the Shenandoah, unopposed save by a small cavalry force under General McCausland.

McCausland was another Virginia Military Institute graduate. "Well," said we, when we heard the news, "we'll have to whip 'em again." But this time the story was to be very different from the last. Following almost immediately upon the heels of the first announcement came the alarming statement that Hunter had reached Staunton, but thirty-six miles to the north of us; and the next day we were advised that he had not paused in Staunton, but pressed on, and that his advance was skirmishing with McCausland at Midway, but twelve miles from Lexington.

Resistance to a force like Hunter's being out of the question, we were ordered to prepare for the evacuation of Lexington. A detail of sappers was sent forthwith to the bridge across the North River, with directions to load it with bales of hay saturated with turpentine, leaving space just sufficient for the passage of McCausland's retreating forces. We were kept under arms all night. Before sunrise, the main body of our troops came streaming down the hills across the river; and, half a mile behind them, their rear guard emerged from the woods along the hill-tops, skirmishing with, and hotly pressed by, the enemy. At the river, after crossing the bridge, McCausland deployed a force upon the bluffs above and below the bridge, to cover the crossing of his rear guard.

The rear guard, called in, rallied at a run to the bridge; and the Union skirmishers, emboldened by their quick movements, dashed after them down the hills. Coming too near to the force behind the bluffs, they were compelled to retreat under a heavy fire upon Hunter's advance guard, which was now coming up. A battery of Union artillery, under Captain Henry Du Pont, galloped out upon the hills overlooking Lexington from the north side of the river, and opened fire upon the Institute. A section of McCausland's artillery came up, after crossing the bridge, and took position at the northeast corner of the parade ground to respond to Du Pont. As soon as our troops were across the bridge, it was fired, and a fine column of black smoke rolled heavenward. Our sappers, their task performed, hurried back at double time to rejoin their respective companies. Along the pike in the valley in front of the Institute, the cavalry, weary and depressed, was retiring to the town.

The whole panorama, front and rear, was visible from the Institute grounds, and made a very pretty war scene.

When the Union battery opened, the corps was drawn up in front of barracks awaiting orders. It was, of course, invisible to the enemy from his position directly in rear of barracks. If his guns had been aimed at the centre of the building, his shells would have exploded in our midst. But the massive parts were at the corners, where the towers were grouped, and thither the fire was directed. The first shell that struck crashed in the hall of the Society of Cadets, sending down showers of brickbats and plaster when it exploded. Thereupon we were ordered to pass over the parapet in front of barracks, and thence were marched westward until clear of the building, so as to avoid the splinters and débris. It was very well, for while several of his guns turned their attention to our section of artillery on the parade ground, Captain Harry filled the air with fragments as he pounded away at our quarters.

In our new position under the parapet, about opposite the guard-tree, although fully protected, we were nearly in the line of fire of the shots directed at our battery. A number of shells struck the parade ground, some exploding there, and others ricocheting over our heads.

Soon after this we marched away. As we were leaving, the artillery was limbering up, and the only force opposing the entrance of the enemy was the thin line of skirmishers on the river bluffs.

With heavy hearts we passed through the town, bidding adieu to such of its residents as we had known in happier days. Our route was southward to Balcony Falls, which we reached late that evening. At a high point, probably five miles south of Lexington, we came in full sight of our old home. The day was bright and clear, and we saw the towers and turrets of the barracks, mess-hall, and professors' houses in full blaze, sending up great masses of flame and smoke. The only building on the entire reservation not destroyed by fire was the residence of General Smith. His daughter was very ill, and as the physicians declared it would cost her life to remove her, the house was spared through the intercession of Colonel Du Pont.

No words could describe our feelings as we rested on the roadside, and watched the conflagration. The place was endeared by a thousand memories, but above all other thoughts, it galled and mortified us that we had been compelled to abandon it without firing a shot.

Thinking that the enemy might follow us and attempt to reach Lynchburg through the pass at Balcony Falls, our commandant determined, if that should prove to be the purpose of General Hunter, to offer resistance there, for it was a very defensible position. Accordingly, upon reaching Balcony Falls, pickets were posted, the corps was deployed along the mountain side, and we were held ready for a fight all that night and until late in the following day. Then we ascertained that General Hunter had passed on up the valley to the approaches of Lynchburg by way of the Peaks of Otter. We impressed a canal-boat, and resumed our journey to Lynchburg, reaching there some hours in advance of the enemy. On our arrival, Early's division was pouring into the town, having just arrived by rail from Petersburg. It was hurried forward to the fortifications in the outskirts.

We remained in the streets of the town several hours, awaiting orders, and were finally sent to the front in reserve.

Our position was in a graveyard. The afternoon we spent there, sitting upon graves and among tombstones in a cold, drizzling rain, was anything but cheerful.

The enemy, unaware of the presence of Early's division, advanced to a brisk attack with infantry and artillery. Although he was roughly handled, the assault continued until dark, and he had pressed up very close to a salient in our front, at a point near the present residence of Mr. John Langhorne. A renewal of the attack on the following morning was confidently expected. About ten o'clock that night, orders came for the cadets to move to the front to relieve the troops in the salient, who had been fighting since midday.

When the corps was formed in line, Colonel Shipp, in low tones, explained the nature of the service, and the importance of silence. We were warned not to speak, and, as the night was very black, each man was instructed to place his left hand upon the cartridge-box of the man in front of him, so as to keep distance and alignment. Thus formed, we proceeded to the bastion, and entered it in gloomy silence. The troops occupying it were drawn up as we entered, and glided out after we were in, like the shadows of darkness.

The place was horrible. The fort was new, and constructed of stiff red clay. The rain had wet the soil, and the feet of the men who had been there had kneaded the mud into dough. There was no place to lie down. All that a man could do was to sit plump down in the mud, upon the low banquette, with his gun across his lap. I could not resist peeping over the parapet, and there, but a short distance from us, in a little valley, were the smouldering camp-fires of the enemy. Wrapping my blanket about me, its ends tucked under me, so as to keep out the moisture from the red clay as much as possible, I fell asleep, hugging my rifle, never doubting that there would be work for both of us at daybreak.

I must have slept soundly, for when I awoke it was broad daylight. The men were beginning to talk aloud, and several were exposing themselves freely. No enemy appeared in our front. He was gone. Hunter, discovering that he was overmatched, had retired during the night, and was now in full retreat.

Lexington was now accessible to us once more, and thither we proceeded in a day or two.

On our return to Lexington, we temporarily quartered in Washington College. Nothing worth having was left of the Virginia Military Institute. The scene was one of such complete desolation, and so depressing, that I avoided it as much as possible.

We were furloughed until September 1, and ordered to report at that time at the almshouse in Richmond.

This apparently absurd announcement was another illustration of the resourcefulness of General Smith. The city of Richmond had a very fine almshouse, but at this period of the war all our people were paupers, and the city could not maintain the almshouse. Knowing this, General Smith had opened telegraphic correspondence from Lynchburg with the Richmond authorities, and secured the place free of rent.

For myself, I now saw a chance of entering the service, and had no idea of going to live in an almshouse. My objective point was Petersburg, where my father's brigade was stationed. He was in command of the city, having been engaged with the enemy almost daily since his arrival from South Carolina in May. Against overwhelming odds, Beauregard had held the place until the arrival of General Lee.

It was about sundown on the 22d of June, 1864, that our train from Richmond stopped in a deep cut about a mile from Petersburg. We could not safely approach nearer to the city. When General "Baldy" Smith, with 22,000 men, attacked my father with 2200 men on the 15th of June, he captured several redoubts, numbered from 5 to 9, near the Appomattox River, just below Petersburg. From these, with his siege-guns, he could shell the town, and particularly the railroad depot and the Pocahontas Bridge near by across the Appomattox. As a consequence, the trains stopped at a point of safety, whence passengers could take a back route to the town, or go by way of the railroad without attracting attention. The disagreeable persons at the captured batteries soon ascertained the rail-

road schedules, and shelled the vicinity of the depot about
train time.

Soldiers had become accustomed to shells, and did not
fear them much ; so our party, consisting of several members of my father's brigade, followed the short route, notwithstanding quite a lively artillery fire. We crossed the
bridge at Pocahontas without incident. The firing seemed
directed higher up town. Passing on to Bolingbroke
Street, we saw evidences of recent damage in a great hole
made by a shell in the Bolingbroke Hotel, but a few
moments before, and a dead man was lying on the curb-
stone near where the shell had exploded. Turning into
Bolingbroke Street, which ran nearly parallel with the line
of fire from Battery 5, two heavy shells went screaming
over our heads, and burst near where Bolingbroke Street
terminates in Sycamore Street. It was a decided relief
when we reached the latter, and struck off at right angles
from the range of those guns. The official headquarters
were in the court house, which, while it was in the line of
fire, was protected by heavy masses of intervening buildings. Thither we repaired, but found they were closed
for the day.

The appearance of the town was exceedingly depressing. The streets were almost deserted, and the destructive
work of the shells was visible on every hand. Here a
chimney was knocked off ; here a handsome residence was
deserted, with great rents in its walls, and the windows
shattered by explosion ; here stood a church tower mutilated, the churchyard filled with new-made graves. As
we moved onward, one of our party pointed to where
Colonel Page of our brigade was buried. He had been
killed but a week before, and was buried near the front
door of a church, within three feet of the sidewalk. On
the court-house steps a group of dirty soldiers were gath-

ered about a poor little half-starved white girl, who sat singing. She had an attractive face, with large, wistful eyes, and a sweet child-voice. When she sang, her whole soul was in her song, which seemed to be highly appreciated by the soldiers. They joined in the chorus after each verse. I remember the name of the song, the first verse, and the chorus, although I never heard them before or since. It was called "Loula," and ran as follows: —

> "With a heart forsaken I wander
> In silence, in grief, and alone;
> On a form departed I ponder,
> For Loula, sweet Loula, is gone.

> CHORUS.
> "Gone where the roses have faded,
> Gone where the meadows are bare,
> To a land by orange-blossoms shaded,
> Where summer ever lingers in the air."

The soldiers seemed deeply touched by the plaintive melody, and joined with genuine feeling in the mournful chorus. Its sadness was in accord with their own desperate situation. They made her repeat it several times, and, when it was over, paid her in food, or such little trifles or trinkets as they possessed, — not in money, for they had none.

About the song, the singer, the soldiers, the scene, and its surroundings there was something intensely pathetic and depressing, and I turned away with a heartsick feeling, not relieved by the silence and desolation along the route to my father's quarters at the residence of a Mr. Dunlop in the western part of the town. I found him in the act of going to tea with his staff, if a meal at which there was neither tea nor coffee may be so designated.

Our meeting after two years' separation — years in which so much had happened to both of us — was inexpressibly delightful. In my father's greeting was blended love for his "little Benjamin," pride in recent events, and solicitude concerning my fate in the dangerous present-future.

The two years of war since we parted showed their effects upon him. He had aged decidedly. But his eye was as bright and his spirit as unconquered as at the outset.

We hugged and kissed each other as if I had been a boy of ten, and then, turning to his staff and a visitor, he introduced me as his boy, whose "head was so hard he had burst a bombshell against it."

The evening being very warm, the tea-table was spread under the trees in the Dunlop yard. Among those present were: Colonel Roman, of Beauregard's staff, young Fred Fleet, adjutant-general, my brother Richard, and Barksdale Warwick, the two aids-de-camp. The conversation was jolly, and the meal surprisingly inviting, for Lieutenant Warwick had returned that day from a short leave of absence, bringing a number of good things. My father occupied some outbuildings, where his generous host, Mr. Dunlop, had supplied him with knives, forks, plates, and table outfit, giving our tea-table under the trees quite a luxurious appearance. And there were my old companions, Joshua and Smith, two of my father's young slaves, who performed all the offices of grooms, butlers, and dining-room servants for the staff. Lieutenant Warwick's Jim was the cook. As Joshua and Smith appeared with plates and hot biscuits and a smoking pot of parched-corn coffee, they broke into broad grins at sight of me. Putting down their things unceremoniously, they rushed up, exclaiming, "How you do, Mars' John? Gord Amighty! how you is grow'd! Dey did n't hurt you much when dey shot you, did dey?" When my father repeated his joke about bursting a bombshell with my head, they guffawed and said, "Spec' it's so, fur he certainly always did have a pow'ful hard head." And then they hurried off about their duties, reserving more confidential chats about old times for later occasions when we should meet at the stables or the kitchen.

Although our beds were on the floor, the quarters were very comfortable, with some features of decent living, such as tables, chairs, and a few books. As we sat there, the picket-firing along the lines from the Appomattox on the east to the Jerusalem plank road to the south of the city was unusually brisk, making one think of corn rapidly popping. These sounds were interspersed with exploding shells at intervals of less than a minute, often as frequent as every few seconds. By stepping out beyond the cover of the trees, we could see the trajectory of the mortar-shells sent up from both sides. The burning fuses gave us the line through the darkness. The firing generally became more active in the evening. Our brigade was already in the trenches, but my father, being still in command of the city, had not yet joined his own command.

"There has been heavy firing on the right this afternoon, general," said Colonel Roman.

"Yes," replied my father, "Grant is evidently trying to extend his left as far as the Weldon Railroad. I met Mahone to-day, who said that he and Wilcox were moving out to intercept him. Whenever Mahone moves out, somebody is apt to be hurt."

"Mahone is a Virginia Military Institute graduate," said I, with undisguised pride.

"There he goes again," said my father, smiling; "up to this time we have had West Point, West Point, West Point. Now we shall have Virginia Military Institute, Virginia Military Institute, Virginia Military Institute, I presume. But seriously speaking, colonel, since the death of Stonewall Jackson, the two men who seem to me to be the most gallant, enterprising, and 'coming' soldiers of Lee's army are this little fellow Mahone and young Gordon, of Georgia." He then proceeded to give a sketch of Mahone, whom he knew well. Mahone was born in Southampton County, at Jerusalem, the county seat. It was only about fifty or sixty miles east of Petersburg. His father was known to everybody in the county as Major Mahone, and kept the tavern at Jerusalem. Keeping tavern did not imply that he was not as good as anybody else in the community, and in fact he was, although he may not have been of such patrician extraction as some of the other people thereabouts. He associated with the best of them, and they with him, and he was respected as a man of many sterling good qualities, possessed of strong individuality. Of Irish extraction, he inherited the most prominent characteristics of his race; was brave, open-hearted, free-spoken, a free liver, and not over-prosperous.

His son "Billy," as everybody called him, grew up in the atmosphere of a country tavern. He did not hesitate in his youth to hold a horse for one of his father's guests, and take a tip for the service. He saw a great deal of liquor drunk at his father's bar, and a great deal of card-playing in his father's tavern. He was not, in his day, above taking in a tray of toddies to the people in a private room playing draw poker, or brag, or lou. He heard a great deal of hard swearing, and had acquired that accomplishment himself. His youth was in the days of cock-fighting; and betting upon the result was by no means deemed disreputable. He not only witnessed cocking-mains between the Virginia birds and those from Weldon and vicinity in the adjoining counties of North Carolina, but soon had birds of his own, and scrupled not to fight them with all comers, or to back them with all the means he could command. It was the days of horse-racing also, and young " Billy " owned a crack quarter-nag, which he would race with anybody for all he had, at any time and in any place. He generally rode himself, for he was of very diminutive stature. And he usually won, for he was a youngster of precocious judgment, boundless enterprise, great ambition to win at any game he played, and indomitable grit. He also had the faculty of making friends, and interesting people in his success. Everybody in Southampton County knew him, and recognized in him elements of unusual power.

His father was perhaps too much interested in his business or his own diversions to concern himself overmuch about Billy's education, but the subject did not escape a neighbor, who had brought his influence to bear in favor of young Mahone. He was a state senator, with the right to appoint a state cadet to the Virginia Military Institute. This meant that the cadet so appointed received board and tuition free. Interested in Billy, he persuaded his father and himself that he ought not to waste his youth in dissipation and grow up in ignorance, but should accept this appointment. Mahone was prompt to do so. He entered the Institute, and graduated with distinction at the age of twenty-one in the class of 1847. He conscientiously performed the obligation which a state cadet assumes, to teach school for three years after graduation ; and meanwhile made other powerful friends, who advanced him in his subsequent career.

At the Virginia Military Institute, he developed a decided talent for engineering. Having completed his term as school-teacher, he secured a position as surveyor of a railroad running from Alexandria, Va., to Orange Court House. His talents were recognized ; he was promoted ; and finally, through the influence mainly of

Colonel Francis Mallory, of Norfolk, he was made engineer of a line from Norfolk to Petersburg. Here he was confronted by the problem of securing a roadbed through the oozy morasses of the Dismal Swamp. He solved the problem, built the road, and made it straight as an arrow for sixty miles, regardless of obstructions. His engineering methods to obtain a solid roadbed on marshy ground, then pronounced as impracticable, have now come to be accepted by the profession as the best yet invented. He rose from position to position, until, at the outbreak of the war, when but thirty-five years old, he was president of the Norfolk and Petersburg Railroad.

He promptly formed, and was elected colonel of, the Sixth Virginia Regiment, composed of the élite of Norfolk and Petersburg, and, when that regiment was brigaded, was made brigadier. Thenceforth, in every engagement in which it took part, his command was conspicuous. In the peninsular and Rappahannock campaigns, at second Manassas, in front of Petersburg, his course was like the eagle's, "upward and onward and true to the line," and, after all his fighting and losses, when Lee's army stacked arms at Appomattox, Mahone's division had maintained its organization better, and laid down more arms, than any in the Army of Northern Virginia. The facts of his youth and the brilliancy of his career up to date were that night the subject of conversation until the visitors departed.

We lay awake talking for some time after we retired. My father recounted his hard fighting from June 15 to June 19 inclusive, in the effort to hold the city until General Lee's arrival, and never seemed to tire of asking about the behavior of the cadets, seeking ever to conceal his pride in our achievements by denouncing the crime of putting such babies into battle. In his own command, the losses had been terrific. Many a fine fellow whom I knew well had been killed or maimed in the hard fighting of the previous week. Then we counted up the casualties in our own immediate family. Since 1861, he, three sons, and nine nephews had gone into the Confederate service. Thus far, two had been killed and six wounded.

"You must go down the first thing in the morning to the hospital, and see your cousin Douglas. It may be the last opportunity," said he, his voice softening as he spoke.

"Why, he is not much hurt, is he?" said I, for he had been reported only slightly wounded. We were talking of his brigade-inspector, a member of his staff, a favorite nephew, who had always been more like a son than a nephew.

"Yes, very seriously," he said; "at first we thought it a mere scalp wound like yours, but his brain is affected now, and I apprehend the most serious result."

I soon discovered that my own future was causing him great anxiety, and that before my coming, notwithstanding all the cares and anxieties surrounding him, he had been thinking and planning about me. He had not, perhaps, even confessed it to himself, but his plans involved putting me in a place of safety. He told me that General Kemper, of Gettysburg fame, now permanently disabled by the wounds received there, was organizing the Virginia reserve forces, that is, men over forty-five years old and boys under eighteen; that, in doing so, the services of a large number of drill-masters would be required; that they would have the rank of second lieutenants, and be assigned to staff duty in active service as soon as their work as drill-masters was completed; and, finally, that he had already been in correspondence with General Kemper, who was an old friend, and had secured the promise of one of these appointments for me.

It was all put very attractively and very seductively, but I saw the motive very clearly. I felt rebellious about it, but could not but love the dear old fellow all the more, and did not blame him, so fearless himself, for loving me to the point of pardonable cowardice concerning myself. Knowing his sacrifices and sufferings, I felt that I had no right to be refractory just then ; and the idea of being a lieutenant, with bars on my collar, tickled my vanity not a little.

I was awakened in the morning by our servant Smith exclaiming, as he awoke father, "I declar', Marster, it looks like Gin'l Mahone dun caught de whole Yankee army."

"What's that?" exclaimed father, springing out of bed.

Then Smith informed us that during the night a great number of prisoners, captured the preceding evening by General Mahone, had been brought into Petersburg, and were at that moment confined under guard on a piece of meadow in rear of our stable, near what were known as the Ettrick Mills. Dressing quickly, we walked down to where the prisoners were, and there we found over seventeen hundred Union soldiers, captured the preceding day from the divisions of Generals Mott and Gibbons by General Mahone.

We ascertained in a general way what had occurred. My father inquired for General Mahone, and was told he would be down a little later ; he left a message requesting General Mahone to call by his headquarters. They had been warm friends, personal and political, for years ; my father had faith in his ability, and had helped him materially in his early struggles, and he in turn thought the "Old General," as he always called him, one of the greatest of men. We had just finished breakfast when, trotting up through the yard, followed by a soldier on a

sway-backed, flea-bitten gray, came little General Mahone.

He was the sauciest-looking little manikin imaginable;
he rode a diminutive blood-like bay mare, fat, sleek, and
well-groomed, as if no war were going on; she was quick
and nervous, and tossed her head, and champed at her bit,
and sidled about like a real live horse, instead of being
poor, jaded, and half asleep, as were many others; her
trappings, too, were expensive, new, and stylish. The
little general looked like a perfect tin soldier. He threw
his reins to the orderly and dismounted. His person and
attire were simply unique: he was not over five feet
seven inches tall, and was as attenuated as an Italian
greyhound; his head was finely shaped; his eye, deep-set
beneath a heavy brow, was very bright and restless; his
hair was worn long; his nose was straight, prominent,
and aggressive; his face was covered with a drooping
mustache and full beard of rich chestnut color and exceeding fine texture; he wore a large sombrero hat, without plume, cocked on one side, and decorated with a
division badge; he had a hunting-shirt of gray, with
rolling collar, plaited about the waist, and tucked into
his trousers, which were also plaited about the waist-
band, swelled at the hips, and tapering to the ankle;
while he wore boots, his trousers covered them; those
boots were as small as a woman's, and exquisitely made;
his linen was of the very finest and softest, — nobody could
guess how he procured it; and when he ungloved one
little hand, it was almost as diminutive and frail as the
foot of a song-bird; he had no sword, but wore a sword-
belt with the straps linked together, and in his hand he
carried a slender wand of a stick. Altogether, he was the
oddest and daintiest little specimen of humanity I had
ever seen. His voice was almost a falsetto tenor.

"Ah! my dear general," he exclaimed, advancing cheerily, and extending his hand; "I received your message and was delighted, for I can never pass you by." Refusing to have breakfast replaced, he said, "No, no, no, you know I am tortured with my old enemy, dyspepsia. I can take nothing but milk; and I suffer so without that that I have brought my Alderney cow along with me in all our campaigns."

Most of the staff he knew; as he looked inquiringly at me, my father presented me. A bright, affectionate smile spread over his face.

"Good boy!" said he; "I knew the old Virginia Military Institute would show folks what fighting is, if she ever had a chance." Then he turned to my father and said, "General, give him to me; I 'll have plenty for him to do." That remark cost the old gentleman many an anxious hour.

Then the party sat down, and Mahone with his little stick, and in his peculiar graphic way, drew in the sand the diagram of yesterday's operations, and explained how he and his gallant division had "doubled 'em up," as he loved to call it. And this is how it was: —

Grant's left and our right were south of Petersburg, near the Jerusalem plank road. Grant had a way of putting one line immediately opposite us to occupy us, and then forming a second line a mile or so in rear, which he would extend beyond the first, and then throw it forward. By this process he sought to envelop our right flank. Learning that the Union troops on our right were in this position, General Lee sent out General Cadmus Wilcox, with a division of A. P. Hill's corps, to take position in rear of the enemy's rear line, and General Mahone, with his division, to interpose between the enemy's two lines and attack the line nearest to us. When Wilcox heard Mahone's attack upon the first line, he was to attack the rear of the second line.

Mahone went in, took his position, attacked, " doubled up " Grant's left, ran the Union soldiers out of their own lines into ours, and captured 1742 prisoners, four light guns, and eight standards, and Wilcox spent the day fumbling and fiddling about and doing nothing. From then until now he has been explaining, sometimes saying A. P. Hill never fully informed him of what he was expected to do, sometimes claiming that Mahone acted without coöperating with him, and always disposed to grumble and try to put the blame upon Mahone for achieving a success so much more brilliant than his own.

Be that as it may, " Little Billy Mahone," that sunlit June morning, was one of the brightest, merriest little soldiers in the Confederacy, and never imagined, as he told us how it was done and chuckled over the surprise of the enemy, that any one would afterwards blame him for what he had done. Even then he had, by his brilliant work, gained such lodgment in General Lee's regard that he was rapidly taking rank in his confidence alongside of Longstreet and A. P. Hill.

As he mounted his little thoroughbred, clapped his spurs to her, touched his hat, and galloped away, I felt as if I would give anything in this world if my father would consent to his proposition, — " Give him to me."

A little later, we walked down to the hospital, and found my poor cousin delirious; in a day or two he was dead, and our family contributed one more victim to the Juggernaut of war.

CHAPTER XXI

LIFE AT PETERSBURG

FOLLOWING close upon Mahone's successful manœuvre came the raid of General Wilson around our right flank, whereby he attempted to destroy General Lee's line of supply, — the Southside Railroad. He was promptly and hotly attacked and driven off near Black's and White's Station by General W. H. F. Lee; then, pursuing the line of the Danville Railroad, he was repulsed at Staunton River bridge by local militia; turning back from that point to rejoin the Union army, Hampton, Fitz Lee, Heth, and Mahone attacked him near Reams's Station, and handled him so roughly that he became the laughing-stock of Lee's army. We at Petersburg saw nothing of these operations, but the incidents of Wilson's discomfiture and final rout furnished merriment for the camps during the ensuing period of comparative inactivity.

About the middle of July, I visited Richmond to inquire about my appointment as drill-master. General Kemper's reception was pompous; he was a striking-looking man, notwithstanding a waxen pallor proceeding from the severe wounds he had received at Gettysburg; he apparently suffered great pain; hobbling back and forth upon his crutches, he descanted, with loud voice and consequential manner, upon the noble work of preparing raw troops for service in the field. He also indulged in sentimental flights upon military glory, not failing to refer to the fact that he was the only survivor of Pickett's three brigadiers who entered the fight at Gettysburg. General Kemper had a good record as a soldier, both in Mexico and in our own service; otherwise, judging by manner and conversation alone, he would have been classed as a Bombastes Furioso.

The upshot of our interview was the promise of a commission, coupled with the information that my duties under it would not begin before October 1, as his department was not yet fully organized; that was delightful, for Petersburg had fascinated me, and I hurried back there. My father was not overpleased at my reappearance. He had depended upon his friend Kemper to put me away in some safe place; I, on the other hand, still cherished the hope that he might yet listen to Mahone's request that he should give me to him.

If a boy just closing the Iliad, the Odyssey, or the Æneid, should be permitted to behold their heroes in the flesh, and performing the valorous deeds which immortalize them, fancy what would be his ecstasy! Yet, for three years past, modern heroes had come upon the stage who were, in my enthusiastic estimate of their powers, second to no half-clothed ancient whose deeds are celebrated by Homer or Virgil.

Until now, I had lived in torturing apprehension lest a perverse fate should deny me opportunity to see them, and to follow, however humbly, leaders who had been the subject of my thoughts by day and dreams by night since the great struggle began. Here they were all about me; a house, or a tent by the roadside, decorated with a headquarters flag, guarded by a few couriers, was all that stood between their greatness and the humblest private in the army. They were riding back and forth, and going out and coming in at all hours, so that everybody saw them.

Two of the immortals of that army had been snatched away before my day, — Stonewall Jackson of the infantry, and Jeb Stuart of the cavalry. But the presence of a glorious company still gave romantic interest to the deeds of the Army of Northern Virginia. Robert E. Lee, Beauregard, A. P. Hill, Ewell, Anderson, Hampton, Pickett, Mahone, W. H. F. Lee ("Rooney"), Gordon, Fitz Lee, Fields, Heth, Hoke, and a host of lesser lights were still actors in its heroic struggles. The first shall be last in the description of these men as I saw them almost daily. Of Anderson, Fields, and Hoke I remember very little, and Longstreet was absent.

Next to General Lee in point of rank and fame was General Beauregard. He had been hurried up with his command in May from Charleston to defend Petersburg until Lee's army would reach the scene. Under him, my father's command had borne the brunt of the first assaults upon Petersburg. He was attached to General Wise, and as he frequently visited our quarters, I saw him often. Beauregard was a soldier of decided ability, and deserves great credit for the early defense of Petersburg. He was heavily handicapped throughout the war by the dislike of Mr. Davis. If he had been given more favorable opportunities, General Beauregard would occupy a more prominent place in the history of the civil war. In appearance, he was a petite Frenchman. His uniform fitted to perfection, he was always punctiliously neat, his manners were faultless and deferential. His voice was pleasant and insinuating, with a perceptible foreign accent. His apprehension was quick, his observation and judgment alert, his expressions terse and vigorous. Like many of our other distinguished soldiers, especially of his race, he was fond of the society of the gentler sex, and at his best when in their company.

General A. P. Hill was the opposite of General Beauregard in appearance and in manner. He was of the old-fashioned American type of handsome men. He was what men call a "men's man." He had a high brow, a large nose and mouth, and his face was covered with a full, dark beard. He dressed plainly, not to say roughly. He wore a woolen shirt, and frequently appeared, especially in action, attired in a shell jacket. About his uniform he had little or no ornamentation, hardly more, in fact, than the insignia of rank upon his collar. Beauregard, like a true Frenchman, was often accompanied by a full staff. Hill, on the other hand, appeared to care little for a staff. When he was killed, at the time our lines were broken and Petersburg evacuated, although he was a lieutenant-general, he was in advance of his line, accompanied by a single courier. General Hill gave the impression of being reticent, or, at any rate, uncommunicative. Neither in aspect nor manner of speech did he appear to measure up to his great fighting record. Yet great it was, for he enjoys the unique distinction of having been named by both Lee and Jackson during the delirium of their last moments.

When Stonewall was unconscious and dying, " A. P. Hill, prepare for action," was one of the last things he said. When, long after the war had ended, General Lee lay unconscious, breathing his last, in quiet Lexington, he exclaimed, " A. P. Hill must move up." A. P. Hill would seem to have been the one to whom both these great leaders turned in a great crisis, as if feeling that, if he could not save the situation, nothing could. What nobler tribute from his commanders could a soldier wish? Yet, illustrious as were the services of General Hill, I do not recall ever hearing anybody speak of a close intimacy with him, or of his being deeply attached to any individual. He appeared to have no interest in the fair sex. His soul seemed concentrated and absorbed in fighting. What success he might have had in independent command, no one can conjecture. His fame rests in his intelligent, tireless, and courageous execution of the commands of Lee and Jackson.

Dear old General Ewell! No Southern soldier can recall his name without a flush of pride. Posterity will class him, under Lee and Jackson, with men like Picton under Wellington. When I first saw him, old " Fighting Dick," as he was called, had lost a leg; but he was still in the business enthusiastically, as if he possessed as many legs as a centipede. He was attached to my father. Our families were intimate. He would ride up to our quarters, and, seated on horseback, talk by the hour over the military and political outlook. He said his wooden leg made it too much trouble to dismount and remount. Removing his hat to catch the summer breezes, he displayed a dome-like head, bald at the top, the side-locks brushed straight forward; his fierce, grizzled mustaches sticking up and sticking out like those about the muzzle of a terrier. Fighting was beyond question the ruling passion of his life. His eye had the expression we see in hawks and gamecocks. Yet the man's nature, in every domestic and social relation, was the gentlest, the simplest, the most credulous and affectionate imaginable. He was small of stature, and his clothes, about which he was indifferent, looked as if made for a larger man. Up to the time he lost his leg, he was regarded as the toughest and most enduring man in the army. Not by any means an ascetic, he could, upon occasion, march as long, sleep and eat as little, and work as hard, as the great Stonewall himself.

The commander of Lee's cavalry at this time was General Wade Hampton, of South Carolina. My ideas of cavalrymen had been derived to a large extent from Lever's troopers in "Charles O'Malley," one of the most fascinating books ever placed in the hands of boys with military inclinations. Jeb Stuart's leadership of the Confederate cavalry had elevated that ideal somewhat, without detracting from the gallant, devil-may-care recklessness pervading the story of the Irish dragoon. The fighting morale of Stuart's cavalry was nowise impaired under the dashing leadership of Hampton. He was as dauntless as Stuart, and, if anything, a more distinguished-looking man. Thoroughly inured to fatigue by a lifetime spent in the saddle or in the field, his reputation as a sportsman was second only to his fame as a cavalryman. A born aristocrat, his breeding showed itself in every feature, word, and look. Yet his manners and bearing with the troops were so thoroughly democratic, and his fearlessness in action so conspicuous, that no man ever excited more enthusiasm. He rode like a centaur, and possessed a form and face so noble that men vied with women in admiration of General Hampton.

His two most prominent lieutenants were William Henry Fitzhugh Lee and Fitzhugh Lee; the former a son, the latter a nephew, of the commander of the army. These cousins were strikingly unlike.

General William H. F. Lee, familiarly called "Rooney," had lost much time from active service. He was captured early in 1863, and detained in prison until about May, 1864. Upon his return to active service, he quickly reëstablished himself by energetic work; and the manner in which he attacked and followed up General Wilson fixed upon him anew the affections of the army. He was an immense man, probably six feet three or four inches tall; and, while not very fleshy, I remember that I wondered, when I first saw him, how he could find a horse powerful enough to bear him upon a long ride! In youth, he had figured as stroke-oar at Harvard. Although of abstemious habits, his complexion was florid. His hands and feet were immense, and in company he appeared to be ill at ease. His bearing was, however, excellent, and his voice, manner, and everything about him bespoke the gentleman. Speaking of cavalry, a horse simile is admissible. "Rooney" Lee, contrasted with Hampton, suggested a Norman Percheron beside a thoroughbred; General Fitzhugh Lee, a pony-built hunter. I have known all the Lees of my day and generation, — the great general, his brothers, his sons, nephews, and grandsons, — and General "Rooney" Lee I regarded and esteemed more highly than any of the name, except his father. Yet he was the least showy of that distinguished family. This gentleman — a gentleman always and everywhere — would have made a more conspicuous reputation in the cavalry, if the war had not ended so soon after his return from his long imprisonment. He had not much humor in his composition, although keenly appreciative of it in others. He was a widower in 1864, and nothing of a society man, although a gallant admirer of women. After the war, he married a beautiful descendant of Pocahontas, Miss Tabb Bolling, of Petersburg. He had none of the tricks which gain popularity, but somehow he grappled to him the men of his command with hooks of steel, and is remembered by his veterans with as much affection as any officer in Lee's army.

His opposite in everything but courage was his cousin, Fitzhugh Lee, called "Fitz" by everybody. Fitz Lee combined in himself not only the blood of the Lees, but of George Mason, one of the greatest of our Revolutionary leaders. The strain of jollity pervading him probably came from the Masons; for while "Light Horse Harry" was in his day a rattling blade, the Lees were, as a rule, quiet folk. His father, Commodore Smith Lee, was all gentleness and urbanity. On the other hand, the Masons, from the first George Mason, of Stafford, who sympa- thized with Bacon in his rebellion, down to the grand- father of Fitz Lee, convey the impression of a decided fondness for " fighting, fiddling, and fun." Fitz gradu- ated at West Point in 1856, more distinguished for horse- manship than anything else. Doubtless he might have done better if he had tried. He had hosts of friends, and no end of enjoyment, and took to the cavalry as a duck does to water. In his service upon the plains prior to the war, an Indian found his short, stout thigh a good pincushion for a feathered arrow, and after his conva- lescence, he was assigned to duty as cavalry instructor at the United States Military Academy. From that position he resigned at the outbreak of the war. He was now, at the age of twenty-nine, a brigadier-general, a bachelor, and gay cavalier of ladies.

The first time I ever saw him was in June, 1864, in Richmond. In those days Third Street, leading out to the pretty heights of Gamble's Hill, was the favorite even- ing promenade. The people of Richmond, save such as visited friends in the country, remained in town through- out the summer, for no places of public resort were open, and nobody had the means to go, if they had been open. On summer nights the better classes, maid and matron, old men, high officers, soldiers, boys and girls, strolled back and forth on Third Street to catch the southern breeze upon the hill, cooled by its passage across the falls of the James ; to watch the belching furnaces of the Tredegar cannon foundry on the river banks below ; and to listen to the band which sometimes played upon the hill. While thus diverting myself one

evening with a party of young friends, we saw a string
of cavalry horses held in front of the residence of a prominent citizen, and, as we approached, heard the sound
of a piano, accompanied by a male and a female voice,
singing " The Gypsy Countess." The curtains of the
parlor were drawn back to relieve the intense sultriness,
and the party was visible from the street. A strong, deep
voice sang the familiar part of the duet, — " Come, fly
with me now." The sweet answer was returned in female
notes, " Can I trust to thy vow ? " Then the two warbled
the refrain together, and the performance finally concluded amid merry laughter and vigorous applause.

The performance was varied by the appearance of a
cavalryman with his banjo. He gave them some jingling
music, which sent everybody's blood bounding. Knowing
the host, we felt no hesitation about joining the party
of onlookers upon the portico, and there we beheld Fitz
Lee with his staff, making a jolly night of it as they
passed through Richmond on their way to Petersburg.
The house was the home of one of his favorite young
staff officers, whose sister was Fitz Lee's partner in the
duet. In appearance, General Lee was short, thickset,
already inclined to stoutness; with a square head and
short neck upon broad shoulders, a merry eye, and a joyous voice of great power; ruddy, full-bearded, and overflowing with animal spirits. At last the banjo struck up
his favorite air : —

> " If you want to have a good time,
> Jine the cavalry,
> Jine the cavalry,
> Jine the cavalry."

Fitz and staff joined in the refrain with mighty zest,
making the house ring with their hilarity.

This over, they announced their departure for Peters-

burg, and a mighty hubbub they made. The ladies of
the house and the young girls brought food and dainties
for their haversacks, and wearing apparel for use in
camp: the packing of these stores took place in the hallway, and then followed the farewells. It was "Good-by,
Lucy," "Good-by, Mary," "Good-by, Jennie," and Fitz
Lee must have been kin to a great many of those
pretty girls. His young staff officer kissed his mother
and sister farewell; Fitz Lee, true to his cavalry instincts,
began kissing also; this doubtless inspired his young
captain to extend like courtesies to visitors as well as
the family, and wherever he led, Fitz followed. By the
time their plunder had been placed upon their steeds, and
they, with jangling spurs, had scrambled to their saddles,
Fitz Lee and staff had taken "cavalry toll" from every
pretty girl in sight. Finally, with many fond adieus and
waving plumes, they rode away down Cary Street, their
mounted banjoist playing the air, and they singing in
chorus, — "If you want to have a good time, jine the
cavalry."

They passed over the bridge across the James, their
route to Petersburg illuminated by the harvest moon, and
a day or two afterwards were making it very uncomfortable for General Wilson at Reams's Station. In later
days, General Fitz and I were political opponents, but
that fact never obliterated my affectionate remembrance
of his merry, gallant cavalry leadership, or of the debt
I owe him for the noble tribute he has placed upon
record to my father's unflinching courage upon the retreat, and until the last gun was fired at Appomattox.

Less conspicuous than Hampton and the Lees was the
cavalry brigadier-general, Deering. "Jim" Deering, as
everybody called him, was a very young man; if I mistake not, he was a second-class man at West Point when

the war broke out; yet, when killed upon the retreat from Petersburg, he had risen to the command of a brigade. He was a man of remarkable health and strength and courage, with a multitude of friends. Pursuing the horse simile, under which the three others have been grouped, he may be likened to a promising colt of faultless breeding, with a brilliant record in his first year's performance. Deering was too young when killed to be classed among the great leaders, but was a youngster of unusual military instinct.

Returning to the infantry, there was Pickett, whose name is linked forever with that of Gettysburg. Pickett was a striking figure: he was a tawny man, of medium height and of stout build; his long yellow hair was thick, hanging about his ears and shoulders, suggestive of a lion's mane. He was blue-eyed, with white eyelashes, florid complexion, and reddish mustache and imperial emphasizing his blonde appearance; he was of the Saxon type. Pickett was a gentleman by birth. He had a great number of relatives and friends in Richmond and in the James River section; they were justly proud of his military career. He was a high and a free liver, and often declared that, to fight like a gentleman, a man must eat and drink like a gentleman. General Lee was a very prudent and abstemious man himself, but never censorious touching the mode of life of his inferiors when they discharged the duties assigned to them. In this respect he was different from Stonewall Jackson, who rather expected those under his command to conform to his simple mode of life. Pickett was a trained soldier and loved fighting. Fitz Lee tells a characteristic anecdote of him: As he rode into the fight at Gettysburg, in passing General Lee he cried out, pointing to the front, "Come on, Fitz, and go with us; we shall have lots of

fun there presently." It was an odd sort of fun he had
that day; but I have no doubt it was the life in which he
was happiest.

I have already described Mahone, and now come to
John B. Gordon, of Georgia, a division commander under
General Lee, who had attained marked distinction in
spite of the fact that he was not a West Pointer. Gordon is still alive, and not appreciably changed from what
he was in '64; he was then a tall, spare-built young
fellow, of very military bearing, his handsome face
adorned by a deep gash received in one of the battles of
the valley. The military genius of General Gordon was
never tested in any independent command, but his fearlessness and eagerness to assail the enemy, whenever and
wherever he was ordered to do so, made him one of the
most conspicuous and popular commanders under General
Lee. Wherever he appeared, the soldiers flocked about
him and cheered him ; wherever he commanded, they felt
confident of hot work ; and wherever he led (he never
followed), the soldiers were willing to go, because they
had sublime faith in his fidelity and courage. We often
saw General Gordon, who was a warm admirer of my
father ; and to this day I delight to honor him as one of
the truest and bravest of Lee's lieutenants.

It has always seemed to me that sufficient recognition
is not given to the great service rendered by the artillery.
This is probably due to the fact that it is under the
command and direction of some general officer, who receives credit for success. Then, too, the numbers of the
artillery are not sufficient to attract attention, as in the
case of cavalry or infantry, when, in large bodies, they
are conspicuously courageous. General Lee's chief of
artillery, General Long, is seldom heard of in the accounts
of the fighting about Petersburg, and although artillery

played a prominent part in every engagement, the commanders are seldom spoken of, while infantry and cavalry officers are noticed conspicuously. No general ever commanded a finer body of young artillery officers than General Lee. Alexander, Pegram, Haskell, Carter, Braxton, Parker, Sturtevant, Breathitt, and a number of others I might name, were counted as the very flower of the army. Yet they are gradually disappearing from view in the prominence given to the officers in higher command.

Colonel William J. Pegram was the most picturesque figure among these many distinguished artillerists. Without early military training, save in our little boy-soldier company in Richmond, he entered the service as a private, and by his pronounced courage and military talents became a colonel at the age of twenty-one, and was killed at the age of twenty-three years, when his promotion to brigadier-general had been ordered. Pegram was a boyish-looking fellow, very near-sighted, and, with his gold spectacles and clean-shaven face, looked more like a student of divinity than a soldier. He was reticent, modest, but of boundless ambition. He had indulged in none of the dissipations of youth, and was extremely pious. He loved fighting, feared nothing, and was an exacting disciplinarian. General Lee, while undemonstrative in most things, regarded " Willie " Pegram, as everybody called him, with undisguised affection and pride.

John Haskell, of South Carolina, was another of his artillery paladins, who was never so happy as when standing amid the smoke of his own batteries. To him primarily was due in a great measure the saving of Lee's army at the crater fight. But I must pass from the description of these lesser lights to one who, like Saul, towered, from his shoulders and upward, tallest among all the people.

It is impossible to speak of General Lee without seem-

ing to deal in hyperbole. He had assumed command of
the Virginia army under peculiar circumstances. It had
been organized at Manassas in '61 under Beauregard and
Joseph E. Johnston. In the winter of '61 and '62, it had
been transferred to the peninsula between the York and
the James, still under the command of General Johnston.
Under him it retreated towards Richmond, and he remained in command until wounded in the battle of Seven
Pines. General Johnston had inspired the army with
great confidence in his ability, and undoubtedly possessed
the quality of securing the deep and abiding faith and
affection of his troops. During the period above described, General Lee had not gained ground in public
esteem. In '61, he had been assigned to the command
and direction of those impossible campaigns in West Virginia from which he had emerged with a loss of prestige.
They failed, as any campaign must have done in such
a country. Whether or not due allowance was made for
conditions, in judging of Lee's ability, need not be discussed. Suffice it to say, that after the termination of
the West Virginia campaign, General Lee was sent to
Charleston, where he was engaged in strengthening the
fortifications until May, 1862, and that in June accident
called him to the command of the army about Richmond.

It is no disparagement of General Lee to say that there
were many who, at the time, regarded the wounding of
General Johnston as a profound misfortune. But it was
not long before Lee established himself in the affection
and confidence of that army, and took a place never occupied by any one else. Before the last gun fired at Malvern Hill, at the close of the seven days' fighting, the
army had become known as Lee's army. It never had
another name, and as such it will go down to history.

I have seen many pictures of General Lee, but never

one that conveyed a correct impression of his appearance. Above the ordinary size, his proportions were perfect. His form had fullness, without any appearance of superfluous flesh, and was as erect as that of a cadet, without the slightest apparent constraint. His features are too well known to need description, but no representation of General Lee which I have ever seen properly conveys the light and softness of his eye, the tenderness and intellectuality of his mouth, or the indescribable refinement of his face. One picture gives him a meatiness about the nose; another, hard or coarse lines about the mouth; another, heaviness about the chin. None of them give the effect of his hair and beard. I have seen all the great men of our times, except Mr. Lincoln, and have no hesitation in saying that Robert E. Lee was incomparably the greatest-looking man I ever saw. I say the greatest-looking. By this I do not mean to provoke discussion whether he was, in fact, the greatest man of his age. One thing is, however, certain. Every man in that army believed that Robert E. Lee was the greatest man alive, and their faith in him alone kept that army together during the last six months of its existence.

There was nothing of the pomp or panoply of war about the headquarters, or the military government, or the bearing, of General Lee. The place selected as his headquarters was unpretentious. The officers of his staff had none of the insolence of martinets. Oddly enough, the three most prominent members of his staff — Colonel Venable, Colonel Marshall, and Colonel Walter Taylor — were not even West Pointers. Persons having business with his headquarters were treated like human beings, and courtesy, considerateness, and even deference were shown to the humblest. He had no gilded retinue, but a devoted band of simple scouts and couriers, who, in their quietness

and simplicity, modeled themselves after him. General
Lee as often rode out to consult with his subordinates as
he sent for them to come to him. The sight of him upon
the roadside, or in the trenches, was as common as that
of any subordinate in the army. When he approached or
disappeared, it was with no blare of trumpets or clank
of equipments. Mounted upon his historic war-horse
"Traveler," he ambled quietly about, keeping his eye
upon everything pertaining to the care and defense of
his army. "Traveler" was no pedigreed, wide-nostriled,
gazelle-eyed thoroughbred. He was a close-coupled,
round-barreled, healthy, comfortable, gentleman's saddle-
horse. Gray, with black points, he was sound in eye,
wind, and limb, without strain, sprain, spavin, or secretion
of any sort; ready to go, and able to stay; and yet without a single fancy trick, or the pretentious bearing of
the typical charger. He was a horse bought by General
Lee during his West Virginia campaign.

When General Lee rode up to our headquarters, or
elsewhere, he came as unostentatiously as if he had been
the head of a plantation, riding over his fields to inquire
and give directions about ploughing or seeding. He appeared to have no mighty secrets concealed from his subordinates. He assumed no airs of superior authority. He
repelled no kindly inquiries, and was capable of jocular
remarks. He did not hold himself aloof in solitary grandeur. His bearing was that of a friend having a common
interest in a common venture with the person addressed,
and as if he assumed that his subordinate was as deeply
concerned as himself in its success. Whatever greatness
was accorded to him was not of his own seeking. He was
less of an actor than any man I ever saw. But the impression which that man made by his presence, and by his
leadership, upon all who came in contact with him, can be

described by no other term than that of grandeur. When I have stood at evening, and watched the great clouds banked in the west, and tinged by evening sunlight; when, on the Western plains, I have looked at the peaks of the Rocky Mountains outlined against the sky; when, in mid-ocean, I have seen the limitless waters encircling us, unbounded save by the infinite horizon, — the grandeur, the vastness of these have invariably suggested thoughts of General Robert E. Lee. Certain it is that the Confederacy contained no other man like him. When its brief career was ended, in him was centred, as in no other man, the trust, the love, almost the worship, of those who remained steadfast to the end. When he said that the career of the Confederacy was ended; that the hope of an independent government must be abandoned; that all had been done which mortals could accomplish against the power of overwhelming numbers and resources; and that the duty of the future was to abandon the dream of a confederacy, and to render a new and cheerful allegiance to a reunited government, — his utterances were accepted as true as Holy Writ. No other human being upon earth, no other earthly power, could have produced such acquiescence, or could have compelled such prompt acceptance of that final and irreversible judgment.

Of General Lee's military greatness, absolute or relative, I shall not speak; of his moral greatness I need not. The former, in view of the conditions with which he was hampered, must leave a great deal to speculation and conjecture; the latter is acknowledged by all the world. The man who could so stamp his impress upon his nation, rendering all others insignificant beside him, and yet die without an enemy; the soldier who could make love for his person a substitute for pay and clothing and food, and could, by the constraint of that love, hold together a naked, starving band, and transform it into a fighting army; the heart which, after the failure of its great endeavor, could break in silence, and die without the utterance of one word of bitterness, — such a man, such a soldier, such a heart, must have been great indeed, — great beyond the power of eulogy.

Not in five hundred years does the opportunity come to any boy, I care not who he may be, to witness scenes like these, or live in daily contact with men whose names will endure as long as man loves military glory.

CHAPTER XXII

THE BATTLE OF THE CRATER

MUCH of the month of July we passed in the trenches. Father was in command of Petersburg, and Colonel J. Thomas Goode commanded the brigade, but we visited it almost daily. It was assigned to Bushrod Johnson's division, and our position was next to the South Carolinians under Elliott. Our left was about a hundred yards south of a bastion known as Elliott's salient.

Life in the trenches was indescribably monotonous and uncomfortable. In time of sunshine, the reflected heat from the new red-clay embankments was intense, and unrelieved by shade or breeze; and in wet weather one was ankle-deep in tough, clinging mud. The incessant shelling and picket-firing made extreme caution necessary in moving about; and each day, almost each hour, added to the list of casualties. The opposing lines were not over two hundred yards apart, and the distance between the rifle-pits was about one hundred yards. Both sides had attained accurate marksmanship, which they practiced with merciless activity in picking off men. One may fancy the state of mind of soldiers thus confined, who knew that even the act of going to a spring for water involved risk of life or limb.

The men resorted to many expedients to secure some degree of comfort and protection. They learned to burrow like conies. Into the sides of the trenches and traverses they went with bayonet and tin cups to secure shade

or protection from rain. Soon, such was their proficiency
that, at sultry midday or during a rainfall, one might look
up or down the trenches without seeing anybody but the
sentinel. At sound of the drum, the heads of the soldiers
would pop up and out of the earth, as if they had been
prairie-dogs or gophers. Still, many lives were lost by
the indifference to danger which is begotten by living
constantly in its presence.

To appreciate fully the truth that men are but children
of a larger growth, one must have commanded soldiers.
Without constant guidance and government and punishment, they become careless about clothes, food, ammunition, cleanliness, and even personal safety. They will at
once eat or throw away the rations furnished for several
days, never considering the morrow. They will cast aside
or give away their clothing because to-day is warm, never
calculating that to-morrow they may be suffering for the
lack of it. They will open their cartridge-boxes and dump
their cartridges on the roadside to lighten their load,
although a few hours later their lives may depend upon
having a full supply. When they draw their pay, their
first object is to find some way to get rid of it as quickly
as possible. An officer, to be really efficient, must add
to the qualities of courage and firmness those of nurse,
monitor, and purveyor for grown-up children, in whom the
bumps of improvidence and destructiveness are abnormally
developed.

Thus, in spite of warnings and threat of punishment
for failure to approach and depart from the lines by the
protected covered ways, it was impossible to make the
men observe these reasonable precautions. For a long
time they had been shot at, night and day. A man, because he had not been hit, would soon come to regard
himself as invulnerable. The fact that his comrades had

been killed or wounded appeared to make little impression upon him. Past immunity made him so confident that he would walk coolly over the same exposed ground where somebody else had been shot the day before. The "spat," "whiz," "zip" of hostile bullets would not even make him quicken his pace. Mayhap he would take his short pipe out of his mouth and yell defiantly, "Ah-h — Yank — yer — kain't — shoot," and go on his way tempting fate, until a bullet struck him and he was dead, or maimed for life. At times I questioned whether these soldiers were not really seeking relief by death or wounds from the torture of such intolerable life. It was enough to make men mad and reckless.

Occasionally we had suspension of firing. At such times even ladies visited the trenches. I recall particularly one party of pretty girls who came over from Richmond, rode out on horseback to a point in rear of our position, and, dismounting, advanced boldly across the exposed ground, and stood for some time on our parapets watching the Union lines. The intrenchments of the enemy were lined with soldiers sunning themselves, or engaged in a favorite occupation familiar to all old soldiers, but not to be described in polite literature. "Hello, Johnnie! it's ladies' day, ain't it?" called out a fellow from a rifle-pit, when he saw the riding-habits outlined against the sky.

We often talked to each other. Sometimes our conversation was civil and kindly enough. Sometimes it was facetious. At others it was of the grossest and most unmentionable character. On an occasion like this, the presence of ladies was greeted as a high compliment by our men, and accepted by the enemy as gratifying evidence of our confidence in their good faith. By both sides the fair visitors were treated with the utmost deference.

A truce like that described would be terminated by some one calling out from the rifle-pits that orders had come to reopen fire at a designated time, sufficiently remote to allow everybody to seek cover. When the hour arrived, at it again they would go, as fiercely as ever. The following incident will convey some idea of the precision of marksmanship attained by constant practice. It was told me repeatedly by Isaac Newman, one of the most fearless and truthful men I ever knew. He was the survivor of the episode. Newman and a comrade, whose name was Blake, I think, were detailed as sharpshooters in one of the rifle-pits in our front. Sharpshooters were posted and relieved at night, and but once in twenty-four hours. The attempt to reach or return from a rifle-pit in the daytime would have been followed by certain death. The pit was a hole in the ground large enough to contain two men. A curtain of earth was thrown up in front, with a narrow embrasure through which to fire. On the inside was a small banquette in front, upon which the men could sit or kneel when firing. Newman and Blake were reckless and resourceful chaps. They hit upon the device of taking a small looking-glass into the pit with them. This they hung opposite the embrasure.

By this arrangement they could sit on the banquette, with their backs to the enemy, and see in the looking-glass all that was going on in front, without exposing their heads. They were inveterate card-players. Neither had any money, but for stakes they used square bits of tobacco cut the size of a "chaw." This was high stakes for Confederate soldiers. With a greasy, well-thumbed pack of playing-cards, they indulged in the excitement of seven-up for several hours. The stakes were placed, and the cards thrown down upon the part of the banquette which lay between them under the embrasure. As the game proceeded, both congratulated themselves that they had discovered a device and diversion which made life in a rifle-pit comparatively safe and endurable. Instead of craning and peeping on the lookout, all that was necessary was to cast a glance now and then at the looking-glass. Occasionally, one or the other would stick his cap on the end of a gun, and put it up above the breastwork, and some watchful sharpshooter would bang away at it. After a while, Newman, who had lost all his tobacco, seeing his last chew was to be won by Blake, snatched the stakes, and stuck a chew into his mouth. This was followed by some friendly scuffling and horse-play, in the course of which Blake's head was incautiously exposed for an instant at the embrasure. It was for but a moment, but that moment was fatal. Zip! spat! came a bullet, quick as a flash. It crashed through poor Blake's temples and broke the looking-glass. Newman was left in the pit with the dead body of Blake until midnight. When relieved, he returned to the lines bearing the remains of his friend upon his shoulders.

In telling this story, Newman always followed it by adding that he believed the man who killed Blake had a personal grudge against him, because the next morning he made a pot of coffee, the last he had, and set it on the parapet to cool ; and just as he reached up for it, a shot, fired from the same rifle-pit whence Blake had been killed, struck the coffee-pot, and emptied its scalding contents down his jacket sleeve.

When our troops first manned the lines, the things most dreaded were the great mortar-shells. They were particularly terrible at night. Their parabolas through the air were watched with intense apprehension, and their explosion seemed to threaten annihilation. Within a week, they had ceased to occasion any other feeling among the

men than a desire to secure their fragments. They had
learned to fear more danger from minie balls than from
mortar-shells. There was little chance of a shell's falling
upon the men, for they could see it and get out of the
way. Unless it did actually strike some one in its descent,
the earth was so tunneled and pitted that it was apt to fall
into some depression, where its fragments would be stopped
and rendered harmless by the surrounding walls of dirt.
Iron was becoming scarce. As inducement to collecting
scrap-iron for our cannon foundries, furloughs were
offered, a day for so many pounds collected. Thus, gathering fragments of shell became an active industry among
the troops. So keen was their quest that sometimes they
would start towards the point where a mortar-shell fell,
even before it exploded.

Such was life in the trenches before Petersburg. Looking back at it now, one wonders that everybody was not
killed, or did not die from exposure. But, at the time, no
man there personally expected to be killed, and there was
something — nobody can define what it was — which made
the experience by no means so horrible as it now seems.
I doubt if all these little things made such deep impressions upon older men. I was very young, very much interested, and, being without defined duties or command,
could come and go as I saw fit; and so, I fancy, it was
not so irksome to me as it must have been to those more
restrained.

All during the month of July, the fact that the enemy
was mining in our front was discussed and accepted by
the troops. How soldiers get their information is one of
the mysteries of the service, yet they are often in possession of more accurate knowledge than those high in authority. For some time the reports about the mine were
exceedingly vague. More than one Union picket had

hinted at a purpose to "send you to Heaven soon," or threatened that they were "going to blow you up next week." For some time, no less than three salients were discussed as the possible points. Our engineers had some sort of information, for countermining was begun at all these salients; but, for some unknown reason, it was abandoned. Their information must, however, have been more or less definite concerning the Elliott salient, for, while they abandoned countermining, they did erect a gorge line, or retrenched cavalier, at this point, and planted batteries of eight and ten inch Coehorn mortars bearing upon the spot. The gorge line was a curved line of parapet in rear of the salient, connecting with the main line of our breastworks; so that, if the salient should be blown up, our troops could occupy the gorge line in rear, and resist an assault at the breach. Placing the Coehorn mortars so as to command the salient showed that the explosion was apprehended. And these evidences of knowledge made it all the more surprising that the men and guns in this salient were not removed back to the gorge line in time to save them. Whatever doubts the engineers may have felt, the privates knew where the works were being mined. Elliott's men told the fellows on the left of our brigade all about it long before the explosion. Our men would go down there, and, lying on the ground with Elliott's men, would listen to the work going on below, and come back and tell all about it.

About daybreak, July 30, the mine was exploded. We were so accustomed to extraordinary explosions that nothing short of an earthquake would have occasioned surprise. At our quarters, the sound was not extraordinary, although we were only about two miles distant; and I have frequently heard General Mahone, whose headquarters were along the lines about the same distance from the

mine as our own, say the same thing. It was fully half
past six o'clock when a messenger from our own brigade
arrived announcing the explosion, the breach in the line
to the left of my father's brigade, and the very perilous
situation of our army.

This was the outcome of a long and patient series of
operations on the part of the Union forces. When Petersburg was first attacked, our army had been driven from
certain positions on an outer or more extended line of
defenses. About one hundred yards in front of Elliott's
salient, the second division of Burnside's corps (Ninth)
occupied a heavy line of rifle-pits, from which we had
retired. Behind these rifle-pits, which originally faced to
the east, the ground dipped, so that operations at that
point were fairly well concealed. The troops located there
were the 48th Pennsylvania Regiment, recruited in the
Schuylkill mining districts, and commanded by Lieutenant-Colonel Henry Pleasants, a mining engineer. He it
was who conceived the idea of sinking the mine.

While he secured official sanction of his plan, he
seems never to have had official support. General Meade
and his chief of engineers spoke of it contemptuously ;
and Pleasants, in his testimony before the Committee on
the Conduct of the War, complained bitterly of lack of
assistance. Notwithstanding all obstacles, the mine was
complete by July 23. It consisted of a shaft 510 feet
long, with lateral galleries under our works 38 and 37
feet long respectively ; in these, 320 kegs of powder, containing 25 pounds each, — in all 8000 pounds, — were
placed, and preliminary to the explosion, 81 heavy guns
and mortars and over 80 light guns of the Union army
were brought to bear on the position to be mined and
attacked.

General Grant was by this time fully aroused to the

dignity of the assault, and, in order to divert General
Lee, made a demonstration in force on the north side
of the James. General Sheridan with the cavalry and
General Hancock with a corps of infantry were sent
across the James, necessitating the withdrawal by General
Lee from in front of Petersburg of all his forces,
except the divisions of Bushrod Johnson and Hoke, and
two brigades of Mahone's division. General Lee, in fact,
had left to defend Petersburg, on the morning of the
mine explosion, but 13,000 men. It is proper I should
state that, in the many accounts from which I compiled
this narrative, none is so terse, and none so fortified by
historic data, as that of Captain Gordon McCabe, of
Petersburg; and, while I have not that paper before me,
I am following it so closely that I should be liable to the
accusation of plagiarism if I did not make this acknowledgment.

Grant quietly recalled Hancock the night of July 29,
and had him in supporting distance of Burnside when
the mine was fired. The plan of attack was for Burnside
to assault; Ord on his right and Warren on his left
were to close in and sustain him. The preparations were
elaborate. The assaulting column numbered 15,000 men,
and the supports brought the aggregate Union forces employed
up to 65,000 men. Burnside's negro division was
at first considered for leading, but the final determination
was to let the white troops take the advance, and the
choice fell by lot to the division of Major-General Ledlie,
who has been so severely denounced by his own commander
and comrades that I will not discuss his merits
or demerits. The columns were massed for the attack
overnight, and the fuse of the mine was lighted about
3.30 A. M.

The ragged remnant of the Confederate army still left

before Petersburg enjoyed unusual repose that night, for the firing along the lines had almost ceased. A long delay ensued. After waiting more than an hour for the explosion, two Union soldiers, at the risk of their lives, crawled into the gallery of the mine and found that the fuse had failed; they relit it and returned. Colonel Pleasants and his friends stood watching with intense solicitude the culmination of their five weeks' labors; fifteen thousand Union troops stood in hushed expectancy behind the Union parapets, under orders that the moment after the explosion they should leap the breastworks and advance across ground upon which, for weeks, certain death had awaited any man who trod it, and mount into those lines whence their oft-tried foe had so long hurled defiance. While this was the condition of the Union troops, the Confederate infantrymen and cannoneers at the doomed salient slept on, as the fuse sparkled and sputtered inch by inch towards the four tons of gunpowder which were to rend with the violence of an earthquake the spot on which they were resting.

"There she goes!" exclaimed one of the watchers. The ground trembled for an instant; an immense mass of earth, cannon, timbers, human beings, and smoke shot skyward, paused for an instant in mid-air, illumined by the flash of the explosion; and, bursting asunder, fell back into and around the smoking pit. The dense cloud of smoke drifted off, tinged by the first faint rays of sunrise; a silence like that of death succeeded the tremendous report. Nearly three hundred Confederates were buried in the débris of the crater; their comrades on either side adjacent to the fatal spot fled from a sight so much resembling the day of judgment. To the south of the crater, our lines were unmanned even as far as our brigade, and a similar condition existed on its northern

side ; at least three hundred yards of our lines were deserted by their defenders, and left at the mercy of the
assaulting columns. Beyond that breach not a Confederate infantryman stood to dispute their passage into the
heart of Petersburg. A prompt advance in force, a
gallant dash, not into the crater, but around it and
three hundred yards beyond it, would have crowned the
great explosion with a victory worthy of its grandeur.
From the eminence where Blandford church and cemetery
stood, in rear of the mine, Grant's forces might, within
ten minutes after the mine was sprung, have looked
backward upon the Confederates, stunned, paralyzed,
and separated ; and, looking forward, they might have
seen the coveted city undefended and at their mercy.

The imbecility which marked the commencement of
the assault, the folly which crowned its conduct, cannot
be explained save by the incompetency of General Burnside. What occurred led to a bitter controversy between himself and General Meade ; and General Grant
is upon record as declaring that General Ledlie, who
commanded the leading division, was unfit for the task
assigned to him. Certain it is that General Meade,
the commander of the army ; ought not to have taken
personal charge of the advance ; and equally certain it
is that General Burnside, intrusted with the conduct
of a movement of such moment, ought to have superintended and led it in person. A soldier like Picton,
or Ney, or Stonewall Jackson, or Phil Sheridan, would
never have frittered away an opportunity so glorious
by directing subordinates from a distant position of
safety. One can picture to himself the way in which
any one of a hundred great military lieutenants would
have seen and availed himself of this rare chance for
immortal fame. The very silence of the Confederates

after the explosion was in itself the loud-mouthed voice of opportunity, calling in tones which military genius would not have failed to recognize.   One can almost see the quick rush of the assaulting columns through the uncleared smoke of the crater, as they would have come under a real leader; and can almost hear their cheering as they mounted the abandoned trenches, paying no attention to the pit of their own making, but pressing on beyond it without pause until in full possession of the position in our rear.   The commanding generals knew the importance of such a course.   General Burnside had explicit instructions to pursue it.   If he had once shown himself at the head of his command, whether it was organized or disorganized, it might, could, and would have followed him to his objective point, and could and would have carried his advantage to its legitimate results. Yet, in the whole history of war, no enterprise so auspiciously begun ever resulted in a conclusion more lame and impotent.

The Union troops designated for the assault, instead of drawing inspiration from the sight of the breach they had effected, actually appeared to recoil from the havoc. For some time no demonstration followed the explosion; when they finally advanced, it was not with the eagerness of grenadiers or guardsmen, but with rushes and pauses of uncertainty; and when they reached our lines, instead of treating the opening as a mere passageway to their objective point beyond, they halted, peeped, and gaped into the pit, and then, with the stupidity of sheep, *followed their bell-wethers into the crater itself*, where, huddled together, all semblance of organization vanished, and company, regimental, and brigade commanders lost all power to recognize, much less control, their respective troops.   Meade, from his position a mile away, was demanding of Burnside why he did not advance beyond the crater to the Blandford cemetery. Burnside, safely in the Union lines, and separated from his assaulting columns, was replying that difficulties existed, — difficulties which he could not specify, for the double reason that he did not know what they were, and that they did not in fact exist.

If he, the well-known corps commander, had but shown himself and placed himself at the head of his troops, there was no obstacle in the way of that advance for fully three hours after his troops were in full possession of our works. True, he might have been killed; the chance was, however, remote under the circumstances, but that was a legitimate contingency connected with the business he had undertaken. Whether killed or not, his presence would have put his column in motion and accomplished the object, instead of leaving his command to headless and huddled disaster. Many a soldier would have deemed it a privilege to risk his life in averting the slaughter of that day, and in converting a threatened rout into a brilliant victory.

But, if Burnside was deficient on the aggressive, the Confederate officer in command of the division defending the position was a Roland for his Oliver.

Bushrod Johnson held the rank of major-general. How he gained it, or why he retained it, — whether by accident or favoritism, — is unimportant; he had under him as gallant troops as ever fought. Elliott's South Carolinians, Gracie's Alabamians, our own beloved brigade, were ready to do and die whenever called upon, and to follow wherever dauntless leadership directed; but to their division commander they were almost strangers. He selected headquarters at a house in rear of the lines. It was tucked under the hill by the roadside, just north of the Blandford cemetery, and there he had remained, vegetating, without any friendly intercourse with his command, or communicating with it save through official channels. Seldom, if ever, was the man seen in the trenches; he was barely known by sight to his men; toward him they felt no affection, of his prowess they had no evidence, and in his ability they felt no confidence. So slight was the dependence of his brigadiers upon him, so little their habit of communication, so indifferent his own conduct, that when General Lee, some hours after the mine had been exploded, reached General Johnson's headquarters, Johnson knew no details of the disaster, or of the dispositions made to repair it, although it was his own division that was involved, and the enemy over the hill was not four hundred yards distant. If the enemy had pressed forward at any time within two hours after the explosion, they would in all probability have found General Bushrod Johnson in bed. When General Lee arrived about eight o'clock, he found him actually ignorant of the peril.

But the merciful Gods of War, if they permit such people as Burnside and Johnson to masquerade as military men, atone for it by furnishing others whose brilliant deeds divert us from pity for incompetents.

General Elliott promptly disposed the portion of his brigade left to him in the traverses commanding the crater; Colonel Goode, commanding our brigade, concentrated on his left flank, and with the fragment of Elliott's brigade, which was driven into ours by the explosion, opened a brisk fire upon the assailants. From our ten-inch and eight-inch mortars in the rear of the line, a most accurate fire was opened upon the troops in the breach; and our batteries to north and south began to pour a deadly storm of shell and canister upon their crowded masses. The situation looked desperate for us, nevertheless, for it was all our infantry could do to hold their lines, and not a man could be spared to meet an advance upon Blandford cemetery heights, which lay before the Union troops. At this juncture, heroic John Haskell, of South Carolina, came dashing up the plank road with two light batteries, and from a position near the cemetery began the most effective work of the day.

Exposed to the batteries and sharpshooters of the enemy, he and his men gave little heed to danger. Haskell, in his impetuous and ubiquitous gallantry, dashed and flashed about: first here, next there, like Ariel on the sinking ship. Now he darted into the covered way to seek Elliott, and implore an infantry support for his exposed guns; Elliott, responding to his appeal, was severely wounded as he attempted with a brave handful of his Carolinians to cover Haskell's position; now Haskell cheered Lampkin, who had already opened with his eight-inch mortars; now he hurried back to Flanner, where he had left him, and found him under a fire so hot that in mercy he resolved to retire all his guns but six, and call for volunteers to man them, but that was not the temper of Lee's army: every gun detachment volunteered to remain. Hurrying to the right again, he found but one group of cowards in his whole command, and these he replaced by Hampton Gibbs, and Captain Sam Preston of our brigade, whose conspicuous bravery more than atoned for the first defection; both fell desperately wounded, and were replaced by peerless Hampden Chamberlayne, who left the hospital to hurry to the fight, and won promotion by the brilliancy of his behavior; again, like Ariel, Haskell, almost superhuman in the energy of his defense, " flamed amazement" upon the foe, and staggered him with " the fire and crack of sulphurous roaring" until help came. To whomsoever else honor

may be due for that day's work, the name of Haskell
should never be dissociated from it, for he was a born
and a resourceful artilleryman, and knew no such thing
as fear.

Where were the Confederate commanders during all
this time? Bushrod Johnson was near by, but nobody
considered him; Generals Lee and Beauregard had their
headquarters on the north side of the Appomattox. It
was fully six o'clock before General Lee heard the news,
from Colonel Paul, of Beauregard's staff! Colonel Paul
lived in Petersburg, and, being at home that night and
learning of the disaster, galloped out and informed General Lee as he was sitting down to his breakfast. Before
Lee even knew of the occurrence, General Meade had had
time to converse with prisoners captured at the crater,
and to advise Burnside that Blandford cemetery was
unprotected; that none of our troops had returned from
the James ; that his chance was *now ;* and to implore him
to move forward at all hazards, lose no time in making
formations, and rush for the crest.

General Lee immediately sent Colonel Venable, of his
staff, direct to Mahone, with instructions to come with
two brigades of his division to Blandford cemetery to
support the artillery. The urgency was so great that he
did not transmit the order through General Hill, the
corps commander. Mounting his horse, General Lee
proceeded to Bushrod Johnson's headquarters, which he
reached about seven A. M., but the information obtained
from him was valueless: he knew nothing of the extent
of the disaster, and had not even been to the front, — he
probably learned more from General Lee than he knew
himself. Then General Lee was joined by General Hill,
and they passed into the lines at a traverse near the
Rives salient, where Colonel Venable found them sitting.

Meanwhile, Venable had communicated with Mahone, and Mahone, always cunning, had retired his two brigades from the lines so quietly that General Warren, opposite to him, reported that no troops had been withdrawn from his front. The Virginia and Georgia brigades of Mahone's division were the troops selected. The message to Mahone was to send them, but he insisted that he should go with them. They passed rapidly by way of a ravine from Mahone's position on the lines covering the Jerusalem plank road to a point in rear of the crater. The Virginia brigade, commanded by Weisiger, led. It was now eight o'clock. One cannot but think of what might have happened during all this time, if Burnside had acted upon Meade's urgent appeals.

The appearance of this infantry was balm and solace to the artillery blazing away upon the crest just above them. For hours they had been fighting there, almost decimated by the artillery concentrated upon them, and the distant firing of sharpshooters. They could not have withstood even a feeble assault of infantry, and had expected it during every minute they had been engaged : the coming of Mahone was their deliverance. With but an instant's pause in the ravine to strip for battle, Mahone's division, headed by their gallant little general, clambered up the slope, crossed the Jerusalem road, and passed in single file at double-quick into a covered way. There was no cheering, and no gaudy flaunting of uniforms or standards ; with them, war's work had become too grim and too real for all that. In weather-worn and ragged clothes, with hats whose brims could shade their eyes for deadly aim, with bodies hardened down by march and exposure to race-horse lines, they came, not with the look or feelings of mercenaries, but like anxious, earnest men whose souls were in their work, who knew what the

crisis was, and who were anxious to perform the task
which that crisis demanded. Agile as cats, they sprang
across the road and entered the covered way; as they
skipped by, many a fellow kissed his hand to the artillerymen to right and left, or strained on tiptoe to catch
sight of the ground in front, before entering the sheltered
passage. For the first time during the day, a line of
infantry was between our guns and the enemy; and the
boys at the guns, knowing what reliance could be placed
upon Mahone's veterans, took new heart and new courage, and pounded away with redoubled energy.

Venable parted with Mahone at the mouth of the covered way, and, seeking General Lee, informed him that
Mahone was up, and proposed to lead his two brigades
in person. The general expressed his gratification, and
gave a sigh of relief. Soon leaving the Rives salient,
General Lee rode to the point in the covered way at
which Mahone had entered, and, dismounting, proceeded
on foot to a house at Lampkin's mortar battery, about
two hundred and fifty yards from the crater. The house
was riddled by shot and shell; from a window in its basement Generals Lee and Beauregard observed the fight.
The ground from the crater sloped to the north and west
into a little ravine, into which the covered way, by which
Mahone had entered, debouched; in this hollow Mahone
formed his troops for battle, the Virginia brigade on the
left.

Springing quickly from the covered way, the eight hundred Virginians lay flat upon the ground. The Georgians were forming on their right. Before the Georgians
could come into position, the enemy, occupying our gorge
line, succeeded in forming an attacking column, and
advanced to the assault. Weisiger, commanding the Virginians, was a grim, determined man. Our boys were

lying down within one hundred and sixty yards of the works, and saw within them a vast throng of Union troops, and counted eleven Union flags. A gallant Union officer, seizing a stand of Union colors, leaped upon their breast-works and called upon his men to charge. Fully realizing the paucity of his own numbers, and the danger of being overwhelmed by the mass of the enemy if they poured down upon him, Weisiger determined to anticipate the threatened movement by charging. Cautioning his men to reserve their fire, he ordered them forward. Those who saw this assault pronounce it to have been, in many respects, the most remarkable which they ever witnessed. At the command " Forward! " the men sprang to their feet; advanced at a run in perfect alignment; absolutely refrained from firing until within a few feet of the enemy; then, with their guns almost upon the bodies of their foes, delivered a deadly fire, and, rushing upon them with bayonets and clubbed muskets, drove them pell-mell back into the intrenchments which they had just left.

General Lee, when advised of this brilliant assault, remarked, " That must have been Mahone's old bri-gade." When news came confirming it, he again said, " I thought so."

My heart beat high when all the army rang with the praises of " Mahone's old brigade." Part of them were " our boys " from Norfolk, — many of them little older than myself; companions, playmates, friends. At the outbreak of the war, they called them " tender-feet " and " dandies." Their uniforms were very smart, and their feet were very tender. From one of their earlier marches they came back limping, with their feet bleeding and their shoes upon their bayonets; the boys named them in derision the " Bloody Sixth." But their hearts were true, and soon their feet grew tough enough. They were the sons of the best of the old Tidewater Virginians of English descent, and, by the time second Manassas and Crampton's Gap were fought, the "Bloody Sixth," of "Mahone's old brigade," had earned its title by blood from the heart as well as from the feet. To-day it crowned its record, for old F Company of Norfolk, now known as K Company, Sixth Virginia Regiment, a company modeled in happier days after the aristocratic company of the New York Seventh, took sixteen men into action and lost every man but one, — eight killed outright and seven wounded.

In the position gained by Mahone's old brigade, nothing intervened between them and the enemy but the pile of breastworks, — they on the outside, the enemy within the crater and gorge line. The fighting by which they established themselves was desperate and hand-to-hand.

Superb Haskell once more came to their rescue : he moved up his little Eprouvette mortars almost to our lines, and, cutting down his charge of powder to an ounce and a half, so that his shell scarcely mounted fifty feet, threw a continuous hail of small shell into the pit, over the heads of our men. Our fellows seized the muskets abandoned by the retreating enemy, and threw them like pitchforks into the huddled troops over the ramparts. Screams, groans, and explosions throwing up human limbs made it a scene of awful carnage. Yet the artillery of the enemy searched every spot, and they still had a formidable force of fighting men.

The Georgia brigade, charging a little after Weisiger's, was decimated and repulsed. Our own brigade, which was engaged from first to last and never yielded a foot of ground, lost heavily, and Mahone's brigade, the "immortals" of that day, was almost annihilated. About one o'clock, the Alabama brigade of Mahone's division, under Saunders, arrived upon the scene, formed and charged, and the white flag went up from the crater. Out of it into our lines filed as prisoners eleven hundred and one Union troops, including two brigade commanders, and we captured twenty-one standards and several thousand of small arms. Over a thousand of the enemy's dead were in and about the breach, and his losses exceeded five thousand effective troops, while our lines were reëstablished just where they were when the battle began.

The crater fight was not only one of the bloodiest, but one of the most brutal of the war. It was the first time Lee's army had encountered negroes, and their presence excited in the troops indignant malice such as had characterized no former conflict. To the credit of the blacks be it said that they advanced in better order and pushed forward farther than the whites, on that day so unfortunate for the Union cause; but when our men, in frenzy, rushed upon and drove the cold steel into them, they did not show the stubborn power of endurance for which the Anglo-Saxon is preëminent, nor do I believe they ever will on any field. On the other hand, our men, inflamed to relentless vengeance by their presence, disregarded the rules of warfare which restrained them in battle with their own race, and brained and butchered the blacks until the slaughter was sickening.

At the first report of the battle, my father promptly repaired to the lines. His interest in and affection for his brigade was like that of a father for his children; although not in actual command, the duties of his temporary position were such that he might with propriety go forth and reassure his own troops by his presence. Moving out rapidly to the opening of the covered way leading to our brigade, we left our horses and hurried forward to the lines. We came upon the outer works about midway of the brigade, and found the troops manning them at intervals of fully ten feet apart, for the brigade was massed upon the left in the traverses and covered ways, firing steadily and rapidly upon the crater. A tremendous artillery fire from both sides raked the vicinity of the crater, and the danger to our troops from several of our light batteries to the north was almost as great as that from the Union guns. Every shot which missed the crater came bounding down our lines. Exchanging a few words with the fearless Goode, who had his troops well in hand, my father at once proceeded to report the condition of affairs to General Lee, whom we had seen as we entered the works, and to order up reinforcements from the teamsters and cooks at our wagon camp.

One of the first wounded men we saw was my cousin, "Old Suggs," whose eternal talk about the "Adventures of Simon Suggs" had named the family at the Virginia Military Institute. Now he was sergeant-major of our left regiment, and a glancing ball had struck him on an eye tooth and knocked it out. I presume he had his mouth open, possibly talking about Simon Suggs. His wound proved insignificant, but when we met him, he was as bloody as a butcher's cleaver.

Hurrying back through the covered way, we overtook two stretcher-bearers with what seemed to be the dead body of an officer.

"Who is it?" exclaimed my father.

"Captain Preston, of the 34th," was the reply.

Removing the handkerchief across his face, we saw that a minie ball had pierced him over the eye. "Poor fellow," almost sobbed my father, as he bent over him, "gallant and true to the last." For in the lines we had heard how a craven in one of our salients near the Baxter road had deserted his guns, and Preston had called for volunteers, manned them, and worked them until he was thus shot down. He was a handsome fellow as he lay there, apparently dead: thank Heaven he was not dead, but lived to hear the army resounding with praise of his courage. The minie which pierced him was in sight, and the surgeons extracted it. He recovered, and for years after peace returned was clerk of a court in Lynchburg, where one might see him writing and the deep scar over his eye, his handsomest dimple, throbbing with his thoughts as he wrote them down.

While we were back in the town, hurrying every available teamster and clerk and cook and man of any kind to the front, the famous charge of Mahone took place, and others were reaping the glory of that day. By the time our work was done, the Alabamians arrived, the surrender occurred, the firing slacked, and the prisoners came running into our lines from the ravine. It was a motley gathering, composed of troops, white and black, from every command and every branch of service in Burnside's corps. There they were, from the refined and distinguished-looking General Bartlett, who bore his misfortune like the Christian gentleman he was, down to the wildest-looking darkey, who expected every moment that he would be massacred.

The prisoners were corralled at Poplar Lawn, in Petersburg. It was soon discovered that nearly all the negroes were from eastern Virginia, many of them owned by the men they were fighting. A notice was posted permitting owners to reclaim their property, and the negroes were delighted at the prospect of being treated as slaves, instead of being put to death or sent to a Confederate military prison. Some of the reclamations made were dra-

matic, some pathetic, and some highly amusing. This last
expression seems out of place in connection with this
awful tragedy, but it is true, nevertheless. The negroes
had witnessed such fierce butchery of their companions up
to the time they had raised the white flag, that they were
frantic with fear, and saw no hope of escape. As they
came running into our lines through the dangers of the
firing from their own friends, they landed among our
men, falling on their knees, their eyes rolling in terror,
exclaiming, " Fur God sake, Marster, doan' kill me. Spar'
me, Marster, and I 'll wuk fur you as long as I lib."
" Marster " never fell from their poor lips so glibly or
so often in all their lives; and even after they had been
with us long enough to know it was not our purpose to
put them to death, when one of them discovered his
real " Marster," he greeted him as if he beheld an angel
of deliverance. According to the story of every mother's
son of them, he was not a volunteer, but had been forced
into the Union service against his will. Of course we
knew just how much of these tales to believe; but it is
safe to say that every master who reclaimed a slave from
the Federal prisoners captured at the crater felt reasonably certain his man would never again volunteer upon
either side in any war.

It seems fitting to close this ghastly narrative with one
ludicrous incident, which shows that no situation is so
bloody or so tragic that it has not some episode to relieve
its horrors. In our brigade was a young fellow who,
while fighting gallantly at the traverse near the crater, received a bullet in the forearm. His wound was dressed,
and he was given a ten days' furlough. He was from
eastern Virginia, and his home was in the Union lines.
He had no friends, no money, and nowhere to go. In
this condition, he was wandering about the streets of

Petersburg the day after the crater fight, when his eye fell upon the notice to owners that they might reclaim their slaves from the prisoners. Thinking that possibly he might find one of his father's slaves among them, he wandered down to Poplar Lawn. In vain he sought for a familiar face, and was turning away, when an attractive, smiling young darkey caught his eye and said, " Boss, fur God sake, claim me fur yo' nigger."

" What do you mean, you rascal? I never saw you before," was the reply.

" I knows it, sah," said the darkey; " but ef I says I belongs to you, who gwine to dispute it, if you don't? "

" If I had you, I'd sell you to-morrow," was the quick reply of the young fellow, whose eye brightened with a happy thought.

" I doan' keer ef you does sell me, sah," said the darkey. " Dat's a heap better dan goin' to a Confederick prison pen."

" Done! " said the soldier; " when I come back here, you speak to me and call me ' Mars' Ben,' and I 'll attend to the rest."

So out he went, and soon came back ; and, as he went searching for his slaves, accompanied by an officer in charge, the darkey greeted him with " How you do, Mars' Ben? " Then Ben swore at him, and denounced him for his ingratitude and desire to kill his master and benefactor, and they carried it off so well that no one suspected the ruse, and the darkey was delivered to " Mars' Ben " as his owner, and " Mars' Ben " took him to Richmond and sold him for $5000 in Confederate money. " Mars' Ben " had a great furlough with that $5000. At the end of ten days, he returned to duty with a new suit of clothes and fed like a fighting-cock, but without a dollar in his pocket. The darkey went to some plantation and never saw a prison pen, and a year afterwards was a free citizen of the United States, and probably wound up his career in some scalawag legislature, or even as a member of Congress, — who knows? Such things were possible in those days.

A short while ago, I met Ben. He is gray-headed now. I asked him where he was going. He said to a protracted meeting. He told me he had become religious, and said he wished I would reform.

"Is it an experience meeting, Ben?" said I.

"Yes," said he.

"Have you ever told them about that darkey you sold after the crater fight?" said I.

"Now, look here, old fellow," said he, growing confidential, and with a genuine touch of pitiful pleading in his voice, "I wish you would not give me away about that thing. I have prayed for forgiveness for that many a night. But I don't believe the Lord wants me to expose myself before my neighbors, and I hope you will not." I agreed to spare him, and so I will; but, if necessity should demand it, I can put my hand upon him now, within eight hours' ride from the spot on which I write.

CHAPTER XXIII

THE CONFEDERATE RESERVES

In September, 1864, the commission as drill-master, with rank and pay of second lieutenant, arrived, accompanied by orders to report for duty October 1 to Colonel Robert Preston, commanding a newly organized regiment of reserve forces at Dublin Depot, in southwestern Virginia. The red seal and signature of the Secretary of War, and the idea of being addressed as lieutenant, made their distinct impressions, but did not overcome the desire to remain with the army at the front.

Vain, however, were all pleadings ; and even Mahone, when appealed to to intercede for my services, seemed indifferent, and dwelt upon the honor to be gained by faithful work in preparing raw troops for actual service, and the duty of deferring to the judgment and wishes of a parent. It was easy to see that he and " the old general " had been talking together since that first meeting.

When, September 30, I boarded a west-bound train at Petersburg to join my command, the new, bright bar upon my collar and gilt scrolls upon my sleeves gave little satisfaction. I felt as if I had been treated like a baby, tucked away in a place of safety, and was consenting to turn my back upon the enemy just when every man was most needed in Lee's army. And was I not a man ? Of course I was. I was nearly eighteen ! When my father parted with me, after much good advice and an affectionate farewell, I know it was with the solacing reflection that I, at least, was out of harm's way. If such were his feelings and his purpose, great must have been his astonishment on opening his first letter from me.

When the train reached Dublin Depot next morning, I inquired of a soldier standing on the platform for Colonel Preston's headquarters. " He was camped on yonder hill," said the person addressed; " but him and his regiment left here last night for Saltville. The Yankees is comin' over the mountain from Kentucky to the salt-works."

Trains did not move, in those times, upon precise schedules. Ours had not yet pulled out of the depot. It was in a leisurely way taking on wood and water, and receiving or discharging army stores. Without another word, I resumed my place in the car, resolved to follow and join the regiment. On and on we went, until we came to Glade Spring Junction, near Abingdon and the Tennessee line. There, to my great delight, I found Colonel Preston, with his regiment of nondescripts, waiting for an improvised train of flat cars, which was to bear them to Saltville, eight or ten miles distant. Swinging off the car almost before it stopped, I hurried up to the colonel. I told him who I was. He gave me a merry and characteristic greeting.

From the number of Prestons so far mentioned, one might think this a history of the Preston family. It is, in truth, a large family, but, so far as I know, none of those referred to were kin to, or even connected with, each other. This dear old man, known to everybody in the army and in his section of the State as " Colonel Bob," was one of the most lovable and unique characters it was ever my good fortune to be thrown with. He was short, thick-set, and had an immense snow-white beard, extending nearly to his sword-belt. He often buttoned it into and beneath his coat or waistcoat. When, as on this occasion, it was unconfined, his appearance, figure, beard, merry twinkling eye, and ruddy face instantly suggested Santa Claus.

At the outbreak of the war, he commanded a regiment in the Manassas campaign; brave as a lion, he was utterly ignorant of military tactics; and it was told of him that on one occasion, when his regiment was attacked in flank while marching in column of companies, he, after vainly endeavoring to think of the command by which to wheel by companies into line and charge the enemy, burst into an explosion of oaths and said, " Twenty-eighth! swing around in companies, like gates, and sick 'em ! " On another occasion, reaching a fence and not knowing how to defile his troops through an opening, he gave the following startling order, " Battalion! Oh, battalion! bust up! climb fence, and line up again on t' other side ! " These were but samples of the many tales concerning him as a tactician; notwithstanding these slight defects, Colonel Bob was honored, respected, and counted one of the gamest fighters in the army ; and nothing but the infirmities of age had reconciled his beloved " 28th " to parting with him.

When the growing necessities of the war forced upon the authorities at Richmond the formation of these reserve regiments, composed of old men and little boys, Colonel Bob was among the first appealed to for aid in the undertaking, for no man was more beloved or exercised a stronger influence in his section.

The day I joined him, he had a veritable Falstaffian army: his regiment of eight companies presented every stage of manhood, from immature boyhood to decrepit old age. One of his companies drawn up in line looked as irregular as a pile of barrel-hoops. There was no pretense of uniform ; they wore everything, from straw hats to coon-skin caps. A vision of Colonel Bob's regiment must have presented itself to the mind of General Grant when he informed the country that the Confederacy was, like Micawber, "robbing the cradle and the grave."

One thing uniform they had, — every man had a Belgian rifle, and a cartridge-box filled with pretty fair ammunition. To my surprise, they handled these weapons effectively and most courageously the following day.

Nobody realized the ludicrous appearance of his soldiers, or enjoyed it more thoroughly, than did Colonel Bob. He would have had a laugh at his own funeral, if opportunity had occurred. "Look at that!" said he, stroking his beard and chuckling a comfortable, inside-shaking laugh; "look at that! Your cadets couldn't beat it." He was pointing to his command, scrambling pell-mell, helter-skelter, upon the dirty flats which now had been backed up. Two strapping young fellows were tugging at an old one, who looked as if he would come to pieces, pulling him up on the car, while a third was pushing him from behind.

"Henry!" shouted Colonel Bob, "you must ride Robin and lead Bob down to the salt-works. Take your time, Henry; you'll get there as soon as we do, I think. I must stay with my ragamuffins, Henry; do you understand?"

Henry was his smiling, handsome, and deferential mulatto body-servant, who looked after his comfort as if the colonel were a baby. Bob was his strong, blood-bay, half-bred charger. The way he uttered the word Henry, and the tone in which he spoke of Bob, showed how he loved them, and how dependent he was upon them. Both Henry and Bob were very proud of their master. Henry bowed and smiled, assured him all would be as he wished,

and, before departing, whispered to him that he had placed
some food for him in the locker of the caboose car which
we were to occupy.

"Did you put my bottle of brandy there, Henry?"
said the colonel.

"Yes, sir," said Henry, grinning and looking around
suspiciously.

"Well, don't do it," said the old man, raising his
voice; "these —— —— *soldiers* are honest enough
about other things, but the last —— one of them will
steal whiskey, Henry, and you ought to know that by this
time. Fetch it right here and put it in my haversack;
even then it won't be safe." The old fellow chuckled
and Henry grinned as he tucked the flask snugly away
in the corner of his bag. He was not a hard drinker, or
at all dissipated, but was at his age somewhat dependent
upon a regular stimulant.

"Boy," said he, turning to me, for by this time he had
begun to be familiar, — "boy, I hope you're not a little
drunkard; it's the meanest, lowest, dirtiest passion in
the world. When a man gets to loving whiskey, he'll
steal it from his best friend." Then, lowering his voice,
he told me it was not the *soldiers* he feared, but one of
his officers, who never left him a drop whenever he could
lay hands upon his "poor little flask."

By this time our troops were mounted on the train,
and, with a snort and a jerk and a bump and a thousand
thumps, we began the trip to Saltville. After a most
uncomfortable ride, we reached the place. Darkness was
upon us. Like other localities where salt is found, it was
a galled, cheerless spot, without verdure in the vicinity of
the wells and troughs and boilers. The adjacent country
was, however, pretty enough, and we soon found a camp
in a neighboring wood. The hills about Saltville were

almost as regular as hemispheres; some were prettily wooded and others were pasture lands to their summits. A mile below the town flowed the Holston River, which on our side had high, bluffy banks. The only crossing was at a ford, which was very defensible. The Union general, Burbridge, with a force organized in eastern Kentucky, was advancing to destroy these salt-works, which were important to the Confederacy. We were not well informed concerning the strength of the expedition, the direction of his advance, or the troops opposing him. The orders received by Colonel Preston had simply directed him to report with the regiment at Saltville as quickly as possible. Now we were to ascertain the situation.

By the time we had located our camp, Henry arrived with the horses. Our headquarters were established under a wide-spreading sugar-maple, where he proceeded to build a roaring fire, and spread our blankets upon the first incline of a hill. After unbuckling his sword and standing it against a tree, the colonel, seated upon a camp-stool, produced a comb, with which he caressed his long beard, and proceeded to swear, in livid and picturesque fluency, about everybody and everything he knew, without any ill temper or malice whatsoever. Henry busied himself brewing a pot of tea and preparing a really dainty meal. He always had a mysterious store of good things supplied by "Ole Missis," who warned him to hide them from "Ole Marster" until used, because she knew he would surely give them away to some poor soldier, if they came into his possession. Whenever provisions ran low, Henry disappeared for a day or two, and when he returned he came "bearing sheaves." The colonel's home in Montgomery County was not so far away that it was out of striking distance

of the faithful slave, and there he found " Ole Missis,"
one of God's noblest and best creatures, praying for
" Ole Marster " and preparing comforts for him.   Mrs.
Preston was known far and wide as the most devout
woman in all the countryside.   She often wept at the
unregenerate profanity of her husband, whose only fault
was that inveterate habit.

Once I asked Henry if the colonel swore at home.

" Yes, *sir*, he do ! " said Henry emphatically.   " Ole
Marster will cuss anywhar; nothin' kain't stop him.
But, Lord, lieutenant, he doan' mean nothin' by it.   Outside of cussin' he's des as good and des as 'ligious as
Ole Missis; and bofe of 'em gwine to be saved, as sho'
as you born, fur Ole Missis prays enough to wipe out Ole
Marster's swearin', an' neither doan' do no harm in de
world, and I know Gord ain't gwine to separate no such
pa'r of people ez dey is, in Heaven."

We sat in the cheery light of our camp-fire and refreshed ourselves with an excellent cup of tea.   The
autumn air was nipping, and the newly risen moon struggled through the mists which rose from the valley around
the salt-wells.

" How are the horses feeling, Henry ? " inquired the
colonel.

" Fuss rate, sir.   We tuk it easy comin' down, and
they is fresh as kittens."

" Can you ride, young 'un ? " said the colonel, turning
to me, as he dropped a coal from his hand into his long
pipe and puffed away contentedly.   Assured that I could,
he directed Henry to saddle Bob and Robin, and said, " I
want to ride out somewhere and find out something.   I
don't know what we came here for, or who is coming, or
who is going to do the fighting."

We rode out together to the depot.   Ascertaining there

that General Jackson, of Tennessee, called "Mudwall," was the commanding officer, we repaired to his headquarters. From him we soon ascertained what troops were on hand, and the location of the enemy. During the day, General Jackson's forces north of the Holston had been skirmishing with Burbridge's advance, and retiring before him. To-night, Burbridge was camped a short distance across the river, and our picket lines were only about three miles from town. Our main body of cavalry was camped near the ford, and there it was proposed to give the enemy battle on the morrow.

Old "Mudwall" was a common-looking man, with a drawl in his voice, and appeared to be taking things very easy. Still, he showed courage and intelligence in his dispositions. He told us he was expecting to be reinforced by Robertson's cavalry, which was coming up from east Tennessee. He hoped they would arrive before morning, but intended to fight whether they reached him in time or not.

"Kernel," said he, "my men tell me the Yanks have got a lot of nigger soldiers along. Do you think your reserves will fight niggers?"

"Fight 'em?" said the old colonel, bristling up; "by ——, sir, *they 'll eat 'em up!* No! not eat 'em up! That's too much! By ——, sir, we 'll cut 'em up!'"

General Jackson explained the plan of battle to Colonel Preston; showed him how his line of battle would be formed upon the river, above and below the ford; explained what troops he proposed to place in front; and then pointed out to us a little valley on the left of, and at right angles to, the road to the ford. In that valley we were to take our position in reserve as soon as the enemy appeared and firing began. It was but a short distance from our camp. As we rode homeward, the colonel visited the ground we were to occupy. It was now bright moonlight. After going a short distance down the depression he said, " This place is as snug and safe as a dovecote. We can sleep here to-morrow until we are ordered in."

He was jolly at the prospect of a fight. I told him what a good joke on my father I considered it that, sending me down here to get me out of harm's way, I had come straight to a battle. He and my father were old and devoted friends. When he heard that, instead of joining in my laughter, he grew silent, and at last, with an effort at badinage, he said, " I don't care a —— whether *you* get shot or not, but, *boy*, I would not be compelled to tell the general about it, if you are hurt, for all the wealth of the Indies." The idea seemed to prey upon him. In the few short hours we had been together, he had evidently begun to look upon me as his pet. He had few congenial companions among his rough command, and he preferred always the society of young people. When we reached camp, he stood warming himself by the fire, musing, as he held out his hands to the glare.

" Fetch my woolen nightcap, Henry," said he, at last; and, as he fitted it over his white locks, he gave a sigh, saying, " what the devil did they send you here for anyhow? There's nothing for you to do." Changing his mood as he turned towards his pallet, his face broke into a broad grin, and he exclaimed, " Oh, I know! They sent you to keep my back warm. I told Kemper I had the rheumatics, and he sent you to snuggle up to me o' nights. Come on to bed."

So, doing as I was bid, I crawled up close to Colonel Bob, and, for many and many a night thereafter, that was the way we always fell asleep together. God bless him! I know he is in heaven. A heart more tender, a soul more generous, a courage more dauntless, no man ever possessed ; and in battle, in bivouac, or under his own roof-tree, he was the sweetest old man that ever granted to a young one the privilege of his instruction and confidence, — barring one fault, that he " swore like our army in Flanders."

Up betimes in the morning, we found the road to the ford filled with cavalrymen. Some had fallen back before the advance of the enemy ; some had arrived from Abingdon during the night. All were dismounting to fight on foot. Horse details were leading the beasts back to positions of safety.

We moved our command out promptly, and defiled to our assigned position on the left. The hill in our front, on which our advance line was posted, concealed us completely from the enemy. Behind us, another hill of unusual height, cleared on its summit, gave a battery planted there the range of the ford and of the ground beyond. Our front lines had not completed their formations on the river bluffs when we heard first a volley, and afterwards a dropping fire of musketry. Our pickets beyond the river were engaged, and falling back before the advancing enemy. Climbing the hill behind us, the view was excellent.

Soon our videttes were all safely across the ford and within our lines, and the next move in the game was to be made by the enemy. Out he came in due time, in battle array, — infantry, cavalry, and artillery, — showing himself along the edge of the woods which crowned the slopes of pasture land beyond the ford.

"Bang!" went the guns of the battery on the hill behind us, and a flock of little six-pound shells flew singing over our heads towards some cavalry debouching from the woods a mile away. The artillery of the enemy promptly

took position and delivered a return fire, but was unable
to secure an elevation sufficient to reach our battery.

Out of sight, fully protected, our regiment lay there
between those dueling batteries. It was very noisy, for
the shells of the enemy exploded in the woods on the hillside in our rear. Curious to know how our raw recruits
would behave under fire, I returned to where they were,
and was much gratified at the spirit of the men, especially
the youngsters. It was with difficulty that the colonel
kept them from scrambling up to the top of the hill in our
front to watch the fight. The men were conducting themselves like veterans. Many of the boys were sighting
their guns, and showing how they would "shoot a nigger,"
if they had a chance.

"Where are your field officers, colonel?" said I, observing that he was the only one upon the ground. "The
lieutenant-colonel is on furlough, and the major cut his
foot with an axe last week, and is in the hospital at
Dublin," said he, apparently unconscious that their absence made any difference, or should be supplied. "Say,
young 'un, you'll have to give orders to the left side.
I'll attend to the right." By the left side he meant the
left flank of the regiment. He proposed that he should
act as colonel and lieutenant-colonel, and was unconsciously promoting me to be major.

"But, colonel," I protested, "will not your senior captains take offense that you do not assign them to the positions to which their rank entitles them?"

"Shut up!" said he fiercely; "I'm running this regiment. They don't know, and don't care a —— ——
about that! I know what I want. If you put such
notions in their heads, there'll be no end of trouble here.
You go and do what I tell you! Do you hear?" So off
I went, and perched myself opposite the left battalion. I

did not know a man in the regiment, or half a dozen officers. It would not have surprised me to hear them tell me to go to the devil when I undertook to give them commands. It seems, however, that they considered me as a *member of the colonel's staff*, and nobody raised any question of precedence.

The battle of Saltville was a very pretty affair. The enemy advanced with great spirit to the attack, but our troops on our first line had little difficulty in repulsing him. Only once were we brought under fire. Near midday, some colored troops of the enemy found a rather open place on the left of our line, near where the streamlet, coursing through the depression we occupied, entered the river, at a point where it was shallow and rocky. They pushed up dangerously near to this possible crossing, and their bullets began to search our valley. The officer commanding the line in our front ran down to where we were asking for reinforcements. Colonel Bob, without a moment's hesitation, moved our left battalion down the valley and up the hill.

There the men laid down on the bluffs, and were hotly engaged for fifteen minutes, driving the enemy back with a loss of but one or two of our men. Then we were ordered to withdraw and resume our place in reserve, and took no further part in the action.

The Confederate losses were quite heavy, especially upon the hill in our immediate front. There Colonel Trimble, in command, was killed in sight of, and but a hundred yards in front of, our men. His death was remarkable. He was standing still, directing the firing of his troops. Of a sudden he sprang high in the air, with arms and legs extended at full length. He leaped at least five feet, and fell to the ground collapsed and stone-dead. We afterwards learned that he was shot through the heart, and were told that this spasmodic action is not at all unusual in such instances.

Our forces captured about two hundred prisoners, mostly wounded. By three o'clock, Burbridge was in full retreat, pursued by our cavalry. All danger being past, we were directed the next day to repair to Wytheville and go into camp. While our reserve regiment had not been seriously engaged, another regiment of reserves, commanded by Colonel Tom Preston, was in the front line, acquired a great reputation for its gallantry in the action, and sustained severe losses.

"Not much of a fight for us," said Colonel Bob contemptuously, that night. He seemed graveled at the better luck of his cousin Tom. His impatience to have a hand in the sport had given me some very unpleasant moments. All during the day he would beckon to me to leave my post as major, and, converting me into a courier for a while, he would send me to the general with requests for leave to "move up." The general was on the other side of the road leading to the ford. The bullets were singing up that road like bumble-bees, and every time I crossed it, my heart was in my mouth. My sudden transitions from major to courier and back again were most amusing.

"Well, the Yankees did n't kill papa's little bouncing boy after all," said he contentedly, as we hugged up together under the blankets that night. "I 'm glad of it, for you 're warm as a toast, and my back is better already." I knew how much stronger his feeling was than he expressed it.

At Wytheville, the regiment was ordered to drill, and an additional drill-master arrived. We two toiled away at our hopeless task of making men sixty years old stand straight and keep step with sixteen-year-old boys. One day I suggested to Colonel Bob that, if he would let me make up a company of boys by selections from several companies, I would give him a really efficient company. He liked the idea, and before long we had a real slashing company of soldiers, worthy of any regiment.

About November 1, we were ordered to move to Christiansburg, and march thence into Floyd County, deserter-hunting. The mountainous regions of southwest Virginia, western North Carolina, and east Tennessee were the places of rendezvous for runaway Confederate soldiers. So numerous and so bold had they become in Floyd County, Virginia, that they not only defied arrest, but often formed bands, seized Confederate supplies, and threatened the property and even the lives of Confederate soldiers and sympathizers. Our command was ordered there to break up some of these organizations, and to capture the ringleaders. It was a thankless task, but one requiring some ability, and not unattended with danger.

Marching out from Christiansburg to a point in the mountains of Floyd, we went into camp in the very heart of what was known as Sisson's Kingdom. That was the name of a large family residing there. Many of them had volunteered, and then deserted; and now they and their friends held sway, defied the law, invited other runaways to join them, and resisted all control of Confederate authority.

When this state of affairs, extending over a wide stretch of country, became known to me in the autumn of 1864, it caused my first misgivings concerning our ultimate success; it was so widespread, and so strangely in contrast with the loyalty of the mountaineers in the Revolution, when Washington proclaimed that to them he looked as his last reliance in extremity.

Colonel Preston, notwithstanding his genial nature, was a man of resources and firmness. If he hated one mean thing worse than another, it was a sneak. He counted these deserters among the most contemptible of the human race; and, while he was incapable of brutality towards any living creature, he knew when to be severe, and believed it was his duty to deal with them summarily, and break them up.

His first advices upon our arrival were to the effect that our presence had caused the deserters to abscond. He did not believe a word of this, but pretended that he did. With great cunning, he acted as if he proposed making no efforts to secure them. At the same time, through a well-planned system of spies, he was ascertaining accurately their whereabouts and habits. More than once, he sent me many miles away to receive reports from his spies, so as to avoid having them seen about our own camp.

In due time, he was ready to act. The deserters, who had in fact left their homes when we appeared, began to make their presence felt. Lured by our apparent indifference, they became incautious. The old fellow knew the location of the house of every deserter, and which were ringleaders, and which of them were at home. He had also located several deserter camps in the mountains. Now came the part of his plan most difficult of execution. Awaiting the time when the moon rose late, he divided several companies of our regiment into small parties under command of intelligent officers. The men were not told of the nature of the expedition. Only the officers intrusted with the work were thoroughly instructed in the locations to be sought, and the duties to be performed.

Upon the night selected, we started forth. Those having the greatest distances to travel left earliest. The man whom I was assigned to capture was a notorious fellow, living about six miles away in a sequestered gorge of the mountains, quite remote from any road. I had a party of ten men. A guide conducted us, and the way in which he threaded his course in the darkness through a trackless forest was truly marvelous. Towards midnight he whispered that we were nearing the deserter's cabin.

Leaving the men behind us, we approached and walked around the premises to get the correct location. Returning, I brought the men up and instructed them in their duties. They were deployed in a circle around the premises, and advanced by signals given from man to man. It was a business calculated to make a man's blood run very chilly. A dog barked! He came bounding out. One of the men plunged a bayonet into his breast, between his forelegs, so true that he never yelped or whined.

"Who's there?" called a sharp, nasal, female voice from within. No one answered. The words were repeated. I was to do the talking.

"Is that Mrs. ——?" I asked, as soon as I could control my voice.

"Yes. Who are you? what do you want?" came back quickly and excitedly. I dropped to the ground, placed my ear to it, and was sure I heard shuffling about within the house, and a sound like that of a closing door.

When she had repeated her questions, I said quietly, "We have come to arrest your husband. He need not attempt to resist or escape. The house is surrounded."

Betraying her excitement by her strident answer, she exclaimed: "William ean't here, thank God, and ean't bin here for more 'n a month. I hope by this he has reached the Yankee lines. Thar's whar he started fur, and whar I told him to go ef he did n't want to be killed."

"You must permit us to search the house, madam," said I, as kindly as I could.

"Cert'nly. You kin search the house," said she; but she delayed some time before unbolting the door.

While waiting for admission, I took four men and posted them opposite the ends and sides of the house, telling them to watch beneath it, and not to move or utter a word. One of them sat down on what seemed to be a goods box, about twenty feet from the gable end of the cabin. Then I detailed two other men to build a fire in the yard. With the four other men, I entered the cabin. It was a pathetic sight, and my heart chided me for the part I bore in it. The woman's teeth were chattering with excitement and fright. Three children sat up in a trundle-bed. The poor woman had tried to beat up a feather-bed, and had drawn the covering over it on one side, so as to give it the appearance of having had but one occupant; but when I threw the sheets back, there were the prints of two bodies, and it was warm on both sides. The babies began to cry. One pleaded, "Where's my papa?" The mother hushed its mouth with her hand.

There was no doubt about his being there. The only question was, where was he? Vain was the search in the closets, under the bed, in the half room under the roof, and up the chimney. At last we examined the floor, and found a broad, loose plank. But the ground underneath the plank was unbroken, and our men could, by the light of the newly-lit fire, see under the whole structure. In one corner beneath the house we noticed a pile of loose dirt, but it made no impression at the time. We had almost abandoned the search, when, of a sudden, a tremendous hubbub in the yard sent all of us running there. It was on the dark side of the house. We heard a stifled cry of "Help! Here he is! Help!" and, as we came up, we saw two men, half buried in the earth, grappled and struggling for the possession of a gun.

The deserter, escaping, had run into the arms of my sentinel. Sitting there on the goods box, watching intently, the sentinel heard a sound below him. He was an intelligent, strapping youngster of about eighteen. Remembering my caution to be quiet, he stepped aside and listened. A moment later the box tilted towards him, and he squatted behind it so that it concealed him. He saw the man's head and shoulders emerge from a hole in the ground. The deserter passed up his gun, and was scrambling out of the hole, when the sentinel sprang upon him, and the struggle in which we found them engaged began. The deserter was the stronger of the two, and had nearly dragged the young fellow back into the hole with him when we came up. The other men promptly lent a helping hand, and we soon had our prisoner secured.

He had dug a tunnel under his house, so that when danger threatened he could drop through the floor, crawl to the opening of his secret passageway, and, passing through it, come out beyond the cordon of sentinels and escape. No one would have suspected that the box in the yard, with its dirty flooring of planks and grass, was the outlet of his subterranean gallery. On several previous occasions, he had eluded arrest in this way. Catching him now was simply accidental good luck. The fellow yielded without many words. He was a superb specimen of manhood, and not bad-looking. When we started away, he said, "Good-by, Sal. See you ag'in soon, I reckin," and then he looked at me and laughed, kissed the children, and said, "Wall, I guess I'm ready." The woman had become defiant and abusive, and refused some money which I offered her.

The reticence and secretiveness of these people was surprising. They were fearless, and hated inveterately. They declined favors of any kind. Before we had gone a quarter of a mile, we heard a cow's horn winded from the cabin. It was the signal of the woman to her friends. It was almost day when we reached the camp. Several other parties had returned before us. By eight o'clock, all our raiders were back. A few had made failures. One party had a sharp fusilade with the deserters, and had a man wounded. Most of us were successful, and our expeditions brought an aggregate of between fifteen and twenty deserters into camp. They were placed in charge of a strong guard, and sent back to Christiansburg. Having secured the most notorious of their leaders, we flattered ourselves that we had broken the back of their rebellion ; but in this we deluded ourselves.

Within a week, the surgeon of the regiment rode out with me to a farm where we heard we could procure good butter. As we were returning through a narrow pass, talking unconcernedly, and with no thought of danger, we saw two puffs of smoke away up among the rhododendrons on the mountain-side, and almost at the same moment that we heard the reports my horse gave a snort and plunge, and the doctor exclaimed, " I am shot ! " I saw him seize his bridle with his right arm. We put spurs to our horses, and galloped out of that pass in a lively way.

" Hurt much, doctor ? " said I.

" No ; but my bridle arm is disabled," he replied.

Just as we cleared the pass, my horse, which had been behaving singularly, stumbled and fell, and I found he was shot through the body, back of the saddle-skirts. A trail of blood marked our course along the road. By good luck the beast belonged to the Confederate States. The doctor and I lost no time riding home together on his horse. His arm, although broken, soon healed ; but we hunted for no more butter on that trip to Floyd.

Winter was coming on. We were ordered to return to Dublin Depot, and to build cabins or shelters for winter quarters. Soon snow fell, and we entered on a period of dreary inactivity. As Christmas approached, I obtained a short furlough, glad enough to return from the mountains to friends and relatives near Richmond. Two or three days after my departure, the regiment was again suddenly ordered to Saltville, which Burbridge captured December 20, with part of our command; but I did not hear of it until a week after the occurrence.

CHAPTER XXIV

THE BEGINNING OF THE END

HINTS from home indicated that by this time visitors to the Confederate capital were most welcome when they brought their rations.

I had been living in a land of milk and honey. In the rich pasture lands of the southwest, people were still blessed with comparative plenty. Their herds of cattle were unexhausted, and supplied them with abundance of dairy products. Before starting on furlough, I gathered together quite a supply of butter, eggs, maple sugar, honey, and other household comforts. We had no express service, and, to guard against the plunder of my treasures, I rode with them in a baggage-car. Butter cost only $8 a pound and eggs were but $3 a dozen, in southwest Virginia, whereas the prices in Richmond were $25 a pound and $6 a dozen.

On arriving in Richmond, I was hailed as a shrewd trader and rare purveyor. The city, in its chill winter garb, showed signs of desperate depletion. The problem of sustenance had become serious, even with the rich.

The clothing of the most prosperous was simple, domestic, even rough. The poorer classes were scantily clad in every kind of makeshift garment, ofttimes in rags. People without overcoats met one another upon the streets, and talked over the prospects of peace, with their teeth chattering, their thin garments buttoned over their chests, their shoulders drawn up, their gloveless hands sunk deep into their pockets for warmth. At meals, the dishes were few and simple, procured at prices which sound fabulous. Many a family existed upon little else than bacon and cornfield peas. General Lee, who had a keen sense of humor, and who, under less trying conditions, would have allowed his wit to play freely, was once asked by some idle chatterer who, in his opinion, was the best friend of the Confederacy. Answering a fool according to his folly, he replied, with a twinkle of his eye, "The only unfailing friend the Confederacy ever had was cornfield peas."

Many States have chosen flowers as their emblem. Some, if not all, of the members of the Confederate sisterhood ought, in gratitude, to select the blossom of the cornfield pea. Time was when it was their "friend in need and friend indeed." Nobody knows how many people in the Confederacy it kept from actual starvation. I never see a bag of cornfield peas without feeling like taking off my hat and saying, "Here is to you and the rest of your family. May you live long and prosper."

Even the banked and economically screened coals in the grates showed the pinch of hard times. When gas was produced at all, it was of the most inferior quality, and at such exorbitant prices that most people were reduced to the use of tallow candles.

Hospitable friends, with ample means, were ashamed to invite visitors to share their humble fare. Long lines of stores were closed : there was nothing to sell. Cigars of ordinary quality were $10 each, and whiskey was $5 a drink. I needed a uniform coat. After diligent bargaining, I engaged one at $2000, payable on delivery. My pay was $120 a month, but I borrowed the money, ordered the coat, and had to wait a month for it. A man who brought articles through the Union lines, by making trips in a canoe across the Chesapeake Bay, procured a black felt hat for me. I considered it a bargain when he delivered it for $100. I bought some leather from a tan-vat while in southwest Virginia, and the making of the boots with my own leather cost me $150.

The town was filled with hospitals. Several of them took their names from the people whose houses had been devoted to these uses. Many ladies had volunteered as matrons, and even as attendants. It was part of the daily life of Richmond for women to save something from their scant sustenance, and take or send it to the sick and wounded. One devoted woman so distinguished and endeared herself to everybody by her self-sacrifice that the name of Sally Tompkins is known to the Confederates as well as Florence Nightingale to the British, or Clara Barton to Americans. She was commissioned a captain, and the boys all call her, even now, "Captain Sally." God will make her an officer of higher grade.

My father had long since rejoined his brigade. They were now transferred to the right of our army at Hatcher's Run. The privations and sufferings which officers and men were undergoing were very fearful. They were huddled in snow and mud, without adequate supplies of food or fuel or clothing. I went out to the camp, but had not heart to remain long. The struggle was no longer a test of valor in excitement: it had become one of inactive endurance.

The Confederate authorities had adopted the policy of enlisting negro troops. One sunny afternoon, I visited the Capitol Square, and witnessed the parade and drill of a battalion of Confederate darkeys. The sight was in strange contrast with other parades I had witnessed there, — that, for example, of the New York Seventh in 1858, or of the cadets, even, in the preceding May.

" Ah!" I thought, " this is but the beginning of the end."

Yet were there thousands — many of them old, many of them actually pale from insufficient nutriment, many of them without money or employment to provide for present or future — who still believed that the Confederacy would achieve its independence.

The Confederate Congress passed resolutions of hope, and sent orators to the trenches and camps to tell the soldiers that " the darkest hour was just before day." One of these blatant fellows I recall particularly. He had been a fire-eater, a nullifier, a secessionist, a blood-and-thunder orator, foremost in urging that we " fight for our rights in the Territories." He was a young man, an able-bodied man, and a man of decided ability. But never for one moment was his precious carcass exposed to danger. There was something inexpressibly repulsive to me, and irritating beyond expression, when I saw men like this, from their safe places, in a lull in hostilities, ride down to the Confederate lines during that awful winter, and counsel our poor soldiers to fight on. Even if it was right to fight on, they had no right to advise it. Old Jubal Early had opposed the war until it actually came upon him, but when it was inevitable, he fought. Things were turning out just as he had predicted they would. When these people, whose extravagant oratory had done so much to bring on the fight, and who had then contributed nothing of personal service to sustain it, came among his starving men to urge them to sacrifices which they themselves had never made, he treated them with undisguised scorn. He refused to attend their meeting. From the door of his hut he blistered them with his biting satire : —

" Well — well — ——!" he shouted; " still sicking them on, are ye?" " Before you leave, tell them what you think of your rights in the Territories now." "One day out here with a musket would help the cause more than all your talk." "Don't talk the men to death. You can't talk the Yankees to death. Fighting is the only thing that talks now."

"Old Jubal" had his faults, but skulking in bomb-proofs was not one of them. The men had implicit faith in his unflinching courage. He punctured and embalmed the lip-service of these "last ditchers," as he called them; and his soldiers, taking the cue from him, hooted and derided them, and long resented their unwelcome intrusion.

Yet have I lived to see fellows of that very class and coterie successfully pose as surviving representatives of the Confederate cause, and avail themselves of the false assumption to belittle the loyalty and service of real Confederate soldiers, because, forsooth, those true and tried men, long after the Confederate cause was dead and buried, dared to differ from them on current policies.

Let us turn to the more interesting description of social conditions at Richmond during the last days of the Confederacy.

It is a merciful provision of Providence which supplies diversion to mankind in the most desperate of situations. In the beleaguered capital, even amid the darkest hours of our fortunes, there were hearts throbbing with old emotions which banish thoughts of grief; and places where people met, clothed in the impenetrable armor of youth and joy, to dance and laugh adversity to scorn. War, pestilence, and famine are impotent to slay, infect, or starve the little naked archer.

Richmond was filled with young girls betrothed to young officers in the trenches about that city and Petersburg. It was not susprising, for never did a city of its population contain more beautiful and brilliant women than did Richmond at that time.

The wedding bells chimed merrily in the wintry air for the coming nuptials of Colonel William B. Tabb, 59th Virginia Infantry, Wise's Brigade, and Miss Emily Rutherford.

The Tabbs were among the oldest people of Tidewater, and the Rutherfords were of the best of Richmond's earliest business men. Colonel Tabb was a tall, brown-eyed, winsome youth of twenty-eight, whose gallantry on many a field gave him more than ordinary title to his stars, and whose modesty and gentleness had brought him troops of friends.

Emily Rutherford, with her peach-bloom cheeks and great, wondering, fawn-like eyes, was "queen of the rosebud garden of girls" of her own circle ; and Mr. and Mrs. Rutherford presided over a home proverbial for its hospitality, even at a time when the hunger and thirst of Richmond society was abnormal.

Thus, from every point of view, whether of pride in Tabb, or love for Emily, or the hungry hopes and trust of society in the gastronomic abilities of the old folks, all things conspired to make the approaching wedding the social event of the season.

The scene at the church was far more brilliant than one would fancy it could be after the descriptions given. Few girls with any social pretensions in Richmond had failed to wheedle or cajole some admiring blockade-running magnate into fetching them a silk or ribbon or feather from the outside world for this occasion. These blockade-runners were the only nabobs in the place : carrying their fortunes, their liberty, and sometimes their lives in their hands, they alone seemed possessors of the secret wherewith, even amidst poverty and want, to conjure up wealth and luxury. They still wore broadcloth and fine linen, drank French brandy, and smoked black

cigars. To them, and them alone, could bride and brides-
maids, matron and maid, look for the brave toggery so
essential upon occasions like this; and the sea-dogs had
not failed their fair dependents.

To me, the Tabb-Rutherford nuptials was an event of
a lifetime; it had been years since I had seen such a
gorgeous function. Nothing like it had been possible in
Presbyterian Lexington, or the Petersburg front, or in
the western Virginia mountains. Not only was it to
seal the happiness of two dear friends, not only were the
brave and young to be there, but it was to be a notable
assembling of the great! What was I to wear?

I had a pair of "captured" trousers, originally destined
for a private in the Union army, now converted into a
Confederate officer's best attire. Pretty fair trousers they
were, worn with a long-tailed coat, but unfit for use with
a jacket. My boots, which cost me so much in the making, were finished, but of fair leather; that was a small
matter: lamp-black and oil were still plentiful, and, after
half an hour of hard work, they shone black and resplendent. But my $2000 coat: it was only in embryo.
There was no hope of its being finished in time. What
was to be done? Coats were coats in those days, and not
to be found hanging on every bush. Vainly, here and
there, I sought for the wedding garment. Every one
whose coat might fit me was as intent as myself upon
attending that entertainment.

We were talking it over at the mess, when, to my great
relief, Barksdale Warwick, one of my father's aids,
took me aside and whispered to me that he would be on
duty the day of the wedding, and, if I could use it, I
might wear his new coat. Now "Barkey" was a first
lieutenant in the "Canaries," as we called the staff, while
I was only a subaltern in the "Blues," as they dubbed

the infantry: arrayed in his coat with buff trimmings, with infantry stripes on my trousers, my attire would indeed be somewhat incongruous. President Davis, or the Secretary of War, if there, might, on close scrutiny, wonder what branch of service I represented. But these were minor considerations, for I was going to that ball, and this was my last chance.

The real question was not one of style, but one of fit. Ay, there was the rub! for Barksdale Warwick was fully six feet high, and thin as a riding-whip, while I was short, and plump as a partridge. But I gratefully accepted a note to his mother, and, on the day of the wedding, marched proudly to my lodgings with the coveted article under my arm.

It was not without grave misgivings that I stepped forth attired for the wedding. The length of Barksdale's waist was such that the bottom buttons of that coat somewhat constrained the movement of my hips; the coat-tails nearly reached my ankles; as for the sleeves, I was fortunate to get occasional glances at my finger-tips. The whole effect was to give me the appearance of a giant in body, a dwarf in legs, and an unfortunate who had lost both hands. As I came downstairs, drawing on a pair of new white thread-gloves, a married sister nearly paralyzed me by a well-intended compliment upon my "nice new overcoat," and my witty wag of a sister, whose escort I was, shrieked with merriment at my remarkable attire.

But what cared I? I would have gone in a meal-sack. The larger the coat, the better; it gave more commodious opportunity to fill it with Mr. Rutherford's good cheer. At church, the judicious handling of a military cape veiled somewhat this extraordinary outfit; but when the house was reached, no subterfuges longer availed. We

stood revealed and undisguised, such as we were. If my
appearance was extraordinary, in the vernacular of to-
day, " there were others." The men had misfits of many
makes ; some even displayed patches. As for the costumes of the ladies, they were wonderful to behold.
They seemed to have ransacked every old trunk in the
garrets of Richmond, and some had actually utilized the
lace and damask window-curtains of peace times. But a
jollier and happier seeming throng was never assembled.

Tent-flies inclosed the large rear veranda, where a military band was stationed ; holly and all kinds of evergreen
had been used for decoration. The bride and groom received under an immense wedding bell of evergreens, a
token of love for their colonel, made with their own
hands, from the bushes growing about them, by the men
of Tabb's regiment. Who were there ? Everybody that
was anybody.

There was Mr. President Davis : he was assuredly a
very clean-looking man ; his manners were those of a dignified, gracious gentleman accustomed to good society.
He claimed his tribute kiss from the bride, and well he
might, for seldom had he culled one more sweet or pure.
From the blushing girl he turned with a gracious compliment to her husband : " For a bribe like that, colonel,
you may demand a week's extension of your leave."
Tabb, with his hazel eyes, his red-brown hair and beard,
and two brilliant hectic spots glowing upon his cheeks,
towered above him, smiling, bowing, and supremely
happy. Mr. Davis looked thin and careworn. Naturally refined in his appearance, his hair and beard were
bleaching rapidly ; and his bloodless cheeks and slender
nose, with its clear-cut, flat nostril, gave him almost the
appearance of emaciation. Yet his eye was bright, his
smile was winning, and manner most attractive. When

he chose to be deferential and kindly, no man could excel
him. When strongly moved, few men of his day surpassed him in eloquence. On occasion, he could touch
the popular heart with a master hand. On his arm was
Mrs. Davis, his very opposite in physique, looking as if,
to use an old expression, " the gray mare was the better
horse." Physically, she was large and looked well fed.
Among us " irreverents," it was believed that Mrs. Davis
possessed great influence over her husband, even to the
point that she could secure promotion for us, if she liked.
She was intensely loyal to him, took no pains to conceal
her pride in him, and was, perhaps, a trifle quick to
show resentment towards those not as enthusiastic as she
thought they should be in their estimate of his abilities.
She had, among those who knew her best, warm, enthusiastic friends.

Close upon these came young Burton Harrison, the
President's private secretary, looking like a fashion-plate
in his perfect outfit. Harrison was popular, and everybody had some cordial inquiry as to how he maintained
such an immaculate wardrobe, when all the world besides
was in rags. Speaking a gracious word here and there
as he passed on, he soon joined willowy Connie Cary for
a waltz.

When Breckinridge, Secretary of War, strode up, he
brought the perfume of Kentucky Bourbon with him. As
he and Tabb stood side by side, one thought of the wide-
spreading forest oak topping up beside the slender pine.
There was the frankness of the soldier, the breadth of
the statesman, the heartiness and courtesy to woman, of
the Southern man of the world, in his every look and
word.

The oleaginous Benjamin, Secretary of State, next
glided in, his keg-like form and over-deferential manner

suggestive of a prosperous shopkeeper. But his eye
redeemed him, and his speech was elegantly polished,
even if his nose was hooked and his thick lips shone red
amidst the curly black of his Semitic beard. Tabb,
looking down upon him, suggested a high-bred greyhound condescending towards a very clever pug.

Then bluff old Secretary Mallory of the Navy came, —
with no studied speech, but manly, frank, and kind, — one
of the most popular members of the Confederate Cabinet.
After him, Postmaster-General Regan, of Texas, a large,
plain-looking citizen, of more than ordinary common
sense, but ill at ease in gatherings like this, and looking
as if he might have left his carry-log and yoke of oxen at
the door.

And so it went. There was Olivero Andrews, the most
insinuating beau of the capital ; and Cooper de Leon, the
poet, wit, and wag ; and John M. Daniel, the vitriolic
editor of the " Examiner," whose mission seemed to be
to torture the administration with the criticism of his
scathing pen ; and Willie Myers, soldier, dandy, dilet-
tante artist, and exquisite ; and the pompous fellow, blazing with gilt, and bearded like a pard, derisively called
" the Count,' who was best known for his constant absence from the front without leave when his command was
engaged ; and Baron Heros von Boerck, a giant German,
who had come to fight as a volunteer upon Jeb Stuart's
staff. O Vanity Fair of the dead Confederacy! How
your actors troop before me once again !

" Who is the red-headed fellow with the voice like a
foghorn ? " I asked of a companion, as I pointed to a
young subaltern standing in a group of men and women,
who were convulsed at some extravagant story he was
telling.

" Tom Ochiltree, of course," said she. " He is the

young Texan who distinguished himself at the battle of Valverde, and afterwards as volunteer aid to Longstreet in the seven days' fighting. He is the most unique character in Richmond, and is counted one of the bravest fellows and truest friends, and at the same time one of the drollest raconteurs, in all the world." A fresh peal of merriment from the throng about him almost drowned her last words.

"And who is the classic-looking young fellow near him, with the scars upon his face?" I asked.

"That is Clarence Prentice," she said ; "the oddest fish in all the Confederacy. The scars you see are souvenirs of Heidelberg, not wounds received in battle, although he has been in many fights. He looks like a poet or musician, but that man is everything : he plays divinely, speaks many tongues, is an exquisite dancer, sings like an angel, gets drunk, kills men, gambles, and is altogether startling. According to the mood in which you find him, he is a gentleman or ruffian, athlete, all-round sportsman, exquisite, desperado, or eccentric."

"And who are the ladies of the coterie?"

"Oh," she said, "that is what we call the White House set. The two large girls in white are the Misses Howell, sisters of Mrs. Davis. The handsome blonde is the daughter of Senator Wigfall, of Texas ; the striking girl in pink is Miss Campbell, daughter of the Confederate Chief Justice, Judge Campbell, of New Orleans."

"And who is this Burmese elephant?" I asked, as men and women fell back before a great waddling mass of obesity, who, in gray clothes and not over-neat linen, came elbowing his way into the room, puffing like a porpoise.

"That," said she, "is General Humphrey Marshall, of Kentucky. They say he was a brave general, and is a shrewd and brilliant politician ; in fact, almost a statesman.

He is at present in the Confederate Congress. His chief prominence now is as the most inveterate gambler and *bon-vivant* in Richmond. He is the man who stakes thousands on the turn of a card, and, while waiting, lights his $10 cigars with $5 Confederate bills."

In this grand rush of humanity there was more than life enough, and enough that was startling; but how in contrast with the gentle, elevating refinement of bygone days! The grosser breath of war had penetrated even to the innermost circle of society, and given it a heat and noise and indiscriminateness which, to speak mildly, was new, and by no means an improvement upon old manners and old customs.

As I saw them, it seemed to me that the men intrusted with the civic administration of the Confederate government were not of as fine clay as her immortal soldiers, nor was it, I believe, a mere boyish fancy. Time has deepened the impression.

The crush was becoming less dense. The older folk remained but a little while. The numbers of the guests necessitated providing refreshments for the most distinguished and the elderly people first, and for the young folk a little later.

The President and his cabinet had disappeared. The stars of the generals went one by one into eclipse behind the doors of the banquet-halls. Even colonels were rare. Majors, captains, and lieutenants were of the grades whence drafts were made for dancers, and here and there might even be seen a saucy private; for, in our army, many a private soldier was socially the peer of anybody.

A band of musicians with stringed instruments filed into the drawing-rooms when they were sufficiently cleared of the crowd to admit of dancing. Taking their position in a corner, the tuning and preliminary flourishes began, and people sought their partners for the cotillion.

Until now, I had felt abashed by the presence of distinguished people and superior officers ; but when it came to dancing, I considered that I was in my proper element. Recollections of cadet triumphs were still fresh. So forth I sallied for a partner. Meanwhile, a dreamy waltz floated through the rooms, and the " White House set " led off. Most striking among them was that Porthos Von Boerck dancing with one of the lovely Carys. But more striking still were the remarkable sounds which he emitted when the dance was finished. Von Boerck, while riding with Stuart, had been shot through the windpipe. The injury caused him, when breathing hard, to utter a sound like that made by a "roaring horse." After the violent exercise of waltzing, in defiance of instructions from his surgeon, the great rosy fellow stood leaning against a pillar, fanning his flushed face, and emitting this remarkable noise. His fair companion was at first alarmed. When assured that it was not dangerous, and would cease in a few moments, her sense of the ludicrous overcame both her fear and her sympathy, and she called to her companions to "come and hear Von Boerck whistle." Poor Von Boerck ! That most amiable and brave fellow — a universal favorite for both qualities among the girls — was nearly overcome by this ridiculous exposure. As the laughing maidens congregated about him, he grew red, and protested, in his awkward German way : " Oh-h ! Whew-w! — I beg you—whew-w!—spare me—whew-w!" But they did not spare him, and clapped their little hands with merriment. At last, roaring, and enjoying his own discomfiture as much as anybody, he burst through their ranks, and fled to the cool veranda to recover his composure and allow his whistle to subside.

My efforts to secure a partner were futile in several directions. Nearly all the girls had escorts. Several looked askance and declined, in a way which made me doubt whether my costume was altogether a success. Just as I was growing despondent, our gracious hostess approached and said, "Come with me. I have a charming partner for you." Then, threading our way to a corner, I was presented. Charming the young lady was, beyond question; and desirable, no doubt, in many ways; but candor compels the admission that she was older than myself, and not beautiful. And her dress? Oh, that costume! Shall I ever forget it?

Experience had not taught me then how dangerous a thing it is to permit a hostess, when the music has struck up and the sets are actually forming, to seize one and drag him to a "charming" girl. A year in society, nay, a month, teaches us that "charming" girls of that description have some inherent disqualification; for the young and pretty never have to invoke the aid of the hostess at so late an hour.

There she was, however, and it was too late to recede, even if I had wished to do so. I did not wish to recede. Why should I? She was gracious, refined, and not a whit more anxious for a partner than I was myself. Oh, yes, our families were intimate. Yes, I was aware that she knew my sisters. I did not mention that I knew she was schoolmate of an elder sister, now married. We were out for pleasant, not for unpleasant, speeches. Thus we chatted as we stood waiting in our places in the quadrille.

I could not help observing her costume. Indeed, she herself told me that the dress was her grandmother's, worn when La Fayette came to Richmond in 1824. She had discovered it in an old trunk. I think I never saw anything, either before or afterwards, exactly like it. I cannot, for lack of technical knowledge, correctly describe female attire, but from such vague efforts as I make, those versed in costuming may gain some idea concerning it.

First of all, the lady, viewed laterally, was the flattest lady I ever beheld. Viewed from front or rear, she was unusually wide. The laced bodice was cut with becoming modesty about the neck, but that same bodice ran downward to a point, until I thought it would never stop. I think that, in the vernacular of the times of its construction, it was called a stomacher. Viewed from rear, never another back was so long, unless it was my own in Barksdale Warwick's coat. At the hips, the dress rose up in fluffs. In coloring and texture, it resembled certain flowered goods I have since seen used in upholstering parlor furniture. The head-gear accompanying it was indescribable. Maybe it was Pompadour. There were ostrich-feathers with it. I think she said she wore prunella slippers. Possibly it was some other kind. All this I saw and learned as we were waiting for the music to strike up. More I saw, and I heartily wish I had not, for it cost me a newly formed and valued friendship. As we stood there waiting, two mischievous girls — one a blonde, the other a brunette, the brightest pair of wags and wits in Richmond — were leaning over a large sofa at the further end of the room. They had preferred not to dance. There they stood watching, laughing, giggling, observing everything that was grotesque, and making comments which were simply convulsing to all hearers. They were my choicest intimates. At an unlucky moment, I caught their wicked eyes. They were carefully dissecting the appearance of my partner and myself. Knowing what was coming, with a pleasant reprobatory smile I pleaded

with my eyes that they should not laugh at us, as if to
say, " I don't mind it for myself, but the lady is a comparative stranger, and you must not embarrass her."

I might as well have tried to check the incoming tide.
They had seen us. They were watching us, wild with
merriment. They were pointing at us. They were attracting the attention of others to us. I saw it. I knew
intuitively the inimitably funny things they were saying.
Their mirth was infectious, and I was scarce able to give
heed to the polite speeches my companion was making, or
to suppress the rebellious twitchings of my mouth. But
I did not quite realize how absurd our appearance really
was. Thus charged with merriment, I bowed, as the
music sounded for the dance.

A scream behind us nearly threw me off my balance.
My partner, all unconscious of the by-play, was serene
and gracious. On the opposite wall hung an old-fashioned
mirror, slightly convex, ornamented with a spread-eagle
over its top. It shone like burnished steel, but it was so
tilted against the wall that one could only see one's self
when near the middle of the room. " Balance to the
centre." We were doing famously. Holding her tiny
hand, we balanced forth. She was speaking low, and was
saying something very captivating. I had regained control of my risibles. Oh ! why did I look up ? Why did
I catch, in that old mirror, the full reflections of ourselves ? The effect was irresistible. I gave one fatal
snort, — that snort which is so deadly to all check of
mirth when we are striving hardest to control ourselves.
I was hopelessly gone. I clapped both hands to my face,
and laughed and laughed until the tears ran down my
cheeks.

Wonder, perplexity, wrath, in turn came over the face
of my partner. She could not understand. I could not

explain. We finished the figure in silence. At its conclusion, she asked that I take her to some friends. She
bowed frigidly to me, as if to say, " Go ! " and go I went.
She never again so much as nodded her head to me. I
rushed back to my tormentors to reproach them. They
called me " Wheelbench," and laughed anew. It was the
name of a certain breed of little vagabond dogs noted for
their long bodies and short legs. My rage only added
fuel to the flames of their ridicule. Never did such an
attired pair dance together, I ween. Never were there
such hilarious spectators.

A Cruikshank, a Nast, a Davenport might have supplied himself for life with caricatures at that memorable
gathering. For myself, I danced no more that night.

About midnight, a new and distinct coterie of guests
arrived.

They were a party of *bon-vivant* friends of the host.
By one means or another, this band secured the best to
be had. To this feast of their companion, each and all
had made their contribution. And now they had come to
join him in celebrating the happy event of his daughter's
marriage, and to partake of his good cheer.

There was big John Carvell, the Canadian blockade-
runner, who had sent a few bottles of champagne, — a
luxury then almost beyond price ; and Major Robert Ould,
the Confederate Commissioner of Exchange of Prisoners,
who never failed to secure for himself, on his trip down
the river to meet the Union Commissioners of Exchange,
an ample supply of the best food and drink ; and Major
" Buck " Allen, of Claremont, whose cellars were still
unexhausted ; and young Hatch, of Missouri, Assistant
Commissioner of Exchange ; and Major Legh Page, and
Major Isaac Carrington, of the Subsistence Department.

There was an air of business about these men. They

had come for good cheer. What of creature comforts they did not secure was simply not to be had. What this party enjoyed in their private room, what cigars they smoked, what games they played with their host, how long they stayed, is beyond my ken. All that we lesser lights knew was that they had the reputation of being the only habitually well-fed and luxurious citizens of Richmond.

Supper for the general public was announced in due time, and, doubt it as you may, it was a sumptuous repast.

There were no sweets and ices, such as are seen in piping times of peace. But there was ornamentation! The pyramids, built of little balls of butter, were really pretty. They towered like the spun sugar, and nougat, or divided oranges, we see to-day. And great piles of rosy apples gave color to the feast. Terrapin, canvas-back ducks, patés, and the like were missing. Our friends, the enemy, had even cut us off from oysters. But there were turkeys and hams and delicious breads, and most beautifully stuffed eggs, and great piles of smoking sausages, and dishes of unsurpassed domestic pickles. There were no oils for salads, no sugar for preserves. Some one had given the bride a wedding present of coffee, and the rooms were filled with its delightful aroma. This we drank sugarless, with great gusto. Great bowls of apple toddy, hot and cold, filled with roasted pippins, stood on the tables, and furnished all needful warmth and cheerfulness for any wedding feast.

So you see, dear readers, that, even to the last, there were times and places in the Confederacy where we got together and did like other and more prosperous folk, — " Eat, drink, and be merry, for to-morrow you die."

In the gray of a winter morning, the cold bright stars

twinkling above us, we men and women sought our homes afoot. Vehicles and horses were not to be had for love or money. Gathering their dainty skirts about them, matron and maid, who in other days had never walked three blocks away from home, picked their way through the deserted streets, laughing over the delightful scenes they had left behind. They laid their heads upon their pillows that night, happy, not discontented, because of the sacrifices they had made for a cause we all loved.

" Eat, drink, and be merry, for to-morrow ye die." Let us not inquire how many of the gallant souls who laughed and danced and ate and drank that night fulfilled the whole prophecy in the whirlwind of war which swept from Richmond to Petersburg, from Petersburg to Appomattox, in the next three months. The story is sad enough without such details.

" Eat, drink, and be merry, for to-morrow ye die." Within five years from that joyous night, the blooming bride was laid to rest in her Confederate wedding-gown. Within a decade, her parents, host and hostess of that night, slept side by side in the cemetery at Hollywood ; and the soldier-groom, spared by the bolts of war, but undermined in health by the exposure of the camp, lost a sweet life for a cause which was already lost.

The places which knew them know them no more. Their names are almost forgotten now, under the rule of another king that knew not Joseph.

So wags the world away.

CHAPTER XXV

THE END IN SIGHT

At the time of the evacuation of Richmond, in 1865, I had been in the Confederate army for about ten months, had reached the mature age of eighteen, and had attained the rank of lieutenant. I was for the time at Clover Station, on the Richmond and Danville Railroad, south of the fallen capital. A light glimmered in headquarters and at the telegraph station. Suspecting that news of importance had been received, and knowing the telegraph operator well, I repaired to his office. He was sitting at his instrument, closely attentive to its busy clicking.

"Any news, Tom?" inquired I.

Holding up his hand he said, "Yes! hush!" and continued to listen. Then, seizing his pad and pencil, he wrote rapidly. Again the clicking of the instrument began, and he resumed his attitude of intent listening. He was catching messages passing over the lines to Danville. During a lull, he informed me that heavy fighting on the right of the army at Five Forks had been going on all day, in which the slaughter on both sides had been very great, and that there were reports of the evacuation of Petersburg. Repairing to the quarters of General Walker, I found that he had substantially the same advices. Vainly and despondently we waited until late at night for more particulars.

Sunday morning broke clear and calm. It was one of the first of those heavenly spring days which to me seem brighter in Virginia than elsewhere. Sitting in a sunny spot near the telegraph station, a party of staff officers waited for telegrams until nearly eleven o'clock. Then a storm of news broke upon us, every word of which was freighted with deep import to our cause.

Click — click — click. "Our lines in front of Petersburg were broken this morning. General Lee is retiring from the city."

Click — click — click. "General A. P. Hill was killed."

Click — click — click. "Colonel William Pegram of the artillery also killed."

Click — click — click. "In the battle of Five Forks, which continued until long after dark last night, Pickett was overwhelmed by Sheridan with a greatly superior force of cavalry and infantry, and the enemy is now endeavoring to turn our right, which is retiring toward the Appomattox, to make a stand there."

Click — click — click. "Petersburg is evacuated. Our army in full retreat toward Burkeville."

Click — click — click. "General Lee has notified the President that he can no longer hold Richmond, and orders have been issued for the immediate evacuation of the city. The town is the scene of the utmost turmoil and confusion."

General Walker issued the necessary commands to place our own house in order. There was not much to be done. Such government stores and provisions as were at our post were promptly put on freight cars, and every preparation was made for an orderly departure, if necessary. We expected that Lee would make a stand at or near Burkeville, forty miles distant, and that, if he must, he would retreat along the line of the Richmond and Danville Railroad. From the accounts of the fighting, I felt

sure that my father's command was in the thick of it; and
this fear gave an added trouble to the gloomy reflections
of those sad hours.

When we recall the way in which the most startling
events in our lives have happened, we note how differently
they unfolded themselves from our previous thought of
them. Nay, more : we all recall that when great events,
which we had anticipated as possible or probable, have
actually begun to occur, we have failed to recognize them.
So it was now with me. That the war might end dis-
astrously to the Confederacy, I had long regarded as a
possibility; that our army was sadly depleted and in
great want, I knew; but that it was literally worn out
and killed out and starved out, I did not realize. The
idea that within a week it would stack arms at Appomattox, surrender, and be disbanded did not enter into my
mind even then. I still thought that it would retreat,
and, abandoning Richmond, fall back to some new position, where it would fight many other battles before the
issue was decided.

A few hours later, train after train, all loaded to their
utmost capacity with whatever could be transported from
the doomed capital, came puffing past Clover Station on
the way southward. These trains bore many men who, in
the excitement, were unwilling to admit that all was lost.
They frankly deplored the necessity of giving up the Confederate capital, but insisted that the army was not beaten
or demoralized, and was retreating in good order. They
argued that Lee, relieved of the burden of defending his
long lines from Richmond to Petersburg, and of the hard
task of maintaining his communications, would draw Grant
away from his base of supplies, and might now, with that
generalship of which we all knew him to be master, be
free to administer a stunning if not a crushing blow to

Grant in the open, where strategy might overcome force. These arguments cheered and revived me. I hoped it might so turn out. I dared not ask myself if I believed that it would.

Monday morning, April 3, a train passed Clover bearing the President, his Cabinet and chief advisers, to Danville. They had left Richmond after the midnight of that last Sunday when Mr. Davis was notified, while attending St. Paul's Church, that the immediate evacuation of the city was unavoidable. Mr. Davis sat at a car window. The crowd at the station cheered. He smiled and acknowledged their compliment, but his expression showed physical and mental exhaustion. Near him sat General Bragg, whose shaggy eyebrows and piercing eyes made him look like a much greater man than he ever proved himself to be. In this car was my brother-in-law, Dr. Garnett, family physician to Mr. Davis. I entered, and sat with him a few minutes, to learn what I could about the home folk. His own family had been left at his Richmond residence, to the mercy of the conqueror. The presidential train was followed by many others. One bore the archives and employees of the Treasury Department, another those of the Post Office Department, another those of the War Department. I knew many in all these departments, and they told me the startling incidents of their sudden flight.

I saw a government on wheels. It was the marvelous and incongruous débris of the wreck of the Confederate capital. There were very few women on these trains, but among the last in the long procession were trains bearing indiscriminate cargoes of men and things. In one car was a cage with an African parrot, and a box of tame squirrels, and a hunchback! Everybody, not excepting the parrot, was wrought up to a pitch of intense excitement. The last arrivals brought the sad news that Richmond was in flames. Our departing troops had set fire to the tobacco warehouses. The heat, as it reached the hogsheads, caused the tobacco leaves to expand and burst their fastenings, and the wind, catching up the burning tobacco, spread it in a shower of fire upon the doomed city. It was after dark on Monday when the last train from Richmond passed Clover Station bound southward. We were now the northern outpost of the Confederacy. Nothing was between us and the enemy except Lee's army, which was retreating toward us, — if indeed it were coming in this direction. All day Tuesday, and until midday Wednesday, we waited, expecting to hear of the arrival of our army at Burkeville, or some tidings of its whereabouts. But the railroad stretching northward was as silent as the grave. The cessation of all traffic gave our place a Sabbath stillness. Until now, there had been the constant rumble of trains on this main line of supplies to the army. After the intense excitement of Monday, when the whole Confederate government came rushing past at intervals of a few minutes, the unbroken silence reminded one of death after violent convulsions.

We still maintained telegraphic communication with Burkeville, but we could get no definite information concerning the whereabouts of Lee. Telegrams received Tuesday informed us he was near Amelia Court House. Wednesday morning we tried in vain to call up Amelia Court House. A little later, Burkeville reported the wires cut at Jetersville, ten miles to the north, between Burkeville and Amelia Court House. When General Walker heard this, he quietly remarked, "They are pressing him off the line of this road, and forcing him to retreat by the Southside Road to Lynchburg." I knew the topography of the country well enough to realize that if the army passed Burkeville Junction, moving westward, our posi-

tion would be on the left flank and rear of the Union
army, and that we must retire or be captured. Many
messages came from Mr. Davis at Danville, inquiring for
news from General Lee. Shortly after General Walker
reported that the wires were cut at Jetersville, another
message came from Mr. Davis. He asked if General
Walker had a trusted man or officer who, if supplied with
an engine, would venture down the road toward Burkeville, endeavor to communicate with General Lee, ascertain from him his situation and future plans, and report
to the President. I was present when this telegram
arrived. By good luck, other and older officers were absent. The suspense and inactivity of the past three days
had been unendurable; and I volunteered gladly for the
service. At first, General Walker said that I was too
young; but after considering the matter, he ordered me
to hold myself in readiness, and notified Mr. Davis that
he had the man he wanted, and requested him to send
the engine. The engine, with tender and a baggage car,
arrived about eight P. M.

General Walker summoned me to headquarters, and
gave me my final instructions. Taking the map, he
showed me that in all probability the enemy had forced
General Lee westward from Burkeville, and that there
was danger of finding the Union troops already there. I
was to proceed very slowly and cautiously. If the enemy
was not in Burkeville, I must use my judgment whether
to switch my train on the Southside Road and run westward, or to leave the car and take a horse. If the enemy
had reached Burkeville, as he feared, I was to run back
to a station called Meherrin, return the engine, secure a
horse, and endeavor to reach General Lee. "The reason
that I suspect the presence of the enemy at Burkeville,"
said he, " is that this evening, after a long silence, we have

received several telegrams purporting to come from General Lee, urging the forwarding of stores to that point. From the language used, I am satisfied that it is a trick to capture the trains. But I may be mistaken. You must be careful to ascertain the facts before you get too close to the place. Do not allow yourself to be captured."

The general was not a demonstrative man. He gave me an order which Mr. Davis had signed in blank, in which my name was inserted by General Walker, setting forth that, as special messenger of the President, I was authorized to impress all necessary men, horses, and provisions to carry out my instructions. He accompanied me to the train, and remarked that he had determined to try me, as I seemed so anxious to go ; that it was a delicate and dangerous mission, and that its success depended upon my quickness, ability to judge of situations as they arose, and powers of endurance. He ordered the engineer, a young, strong fellow, to place himself implicitly under my command. I threw a pair of blankets into the car, shook hands cordially with the general, buttoned my papers in my breast pocket, and told the engineer to start. I did not see General Walker again for more than twenty years.

I carried no arms except a navy revolver at my hip, with some loose cartridges in my haversack. The night was chilly, still, and overcast. The moon struggled out now and then from watery clouds. We had no headlight, nor any light in the car. It seemed to me that our train was the noisiest I had ever heard. The track was badly worn and very rough. In many places it had been bolstered up with beams of wood faced with strap iron, and we were compelled to move slowly. The stations were deserted. We had to put on our own wood and water. I lay down to rest, but nervousness banished sleep. The solitude of the car became unbearable. When we stopped at a water-tank, I swung down from the car and clambered up to the engine. Knowing that we might have to reverse it suddenly, I ordered the engineer to cut loose the baggage car and leave it behind. This proved to be a wise precaution.

About two o'clock, we reached Meherrin Station, twelve miles south of Burkeville. It was dark, and the station was deserted. I succeeded in getting an answer from an old man in a house near by, after hammering a long time upon the door. He had heard us, but he was afraid to reply.

"Have you heard anything from Lee's army?" I asked.

"Naw, nothin' at all. I heerd he was at Amelia Cote House yisterday."

"Have you heard of or seen any Yankees hereabouts?"

"None here yit. I heerd there was some at Green Bay yisterday, but they had done gone back."

"Back where?"

"I dunno. Back to Grant's army, I reckin."

"Where is Grant's army?"

"Gord knows. It 'pears to me like it 's everywhar."

"Are there any Yankees at Burkeville?"

"I dunno. I see a man come by here late last evenin', and he said he come from Burkeville; so I reckin there were n't none thar when he lef', but whether they is come sence, I can't say."

I determined to push on. When we reached Green Bay, eight miles from Burkeville, the place was dark and deserted. There was nobody from whom we could get information. A whippoorwill in the swamp added to the oppressive silence all about. Moving onward, we discovered, as we cautiously approached a turn in the road near Burkeville, the reflection of lights against the low-hanging clouds. Evidently, somebody was ahead, and somebody was building fires. Were these reflections from the camp-fires of Lee's or of Grant's army, or of any army at all? On our right, concealing us from the village and the village from us, was a body of pine woods. Not until we turned the angle of these woods could we see anything. I was standing by the engineer. We were both uncertain what to do. At first, I thought I would get down and investigate; but I reflected that I should lose much time in getting back to the engine, whereas, if I pushed boldly forward until we were discovered, I should be safe if those who saw us were friends, and able to retreat rapidly if they were enemies.

"Go ahead!" I said to the engineer.

"What, lieutenant? Ain't you afraid they are Yankees? If they are, we 're goners," said he hesitatingly.

"Go ahead!" I repeated; and in two minutes more we were at the curve, with the strong glare of many fires lighting up our engine. What a sight! Lines of men were heaving at the rails by the light of fires built for working. The fires and working parties crossed our route to westward, showing that the latter were devoting their attention to the Southside Road. In the excitement of the moment, I thought they were destroying the track. In fact, as I afterward learned, they were merely changing the gauge of the rails. Grant, with that wonderful power he possessed of doing everything at once, was already altering the railroad gauge so as to fetch provisions up to his army. The enemy was not only in Burkeville, but he had been there all day, and was thus following up his occupation of the place. Lee must be to the north or to the west of him, pushed away from Danville Road, and either upon or trying to reach the Southside Railroad, which led to Lynchburg. All these things I thought out a little later, but not just at that moment. A blazing meteor would not have astonished our foes more than the sight of our locomotive. They had not heard our approach, amid the noise and confusion of their own work. They had no picket out in our direction, for this was their rear. In an instant, a number of troopers rushed for their horses and came galloping down upon us. They were but two or three hundred yards away.

"Reverse the engine!" I said to the engineer. He seemed paralyzed. I drew my pistol.

"It's no use, lieutenant. They'll kill us before we get under away," and he fumbled with his lever.

"Reverse, or you're a dead man!" I shouted, clapping the muzzle of my pistol behind his ear. He heaved at the lever; the engine began to move, but how slowly! The troopers were coming on. We heard them cry, "Surrender!" The engine was quickening her beats. They saw that we were running, and they opened fire on us. We lay down flat, and let the locomotive go. The fireman on the tender was in an exposed position, and seemed to be endeavoring to burrow in the coal. A shot broke a window above us. Presently the firing ceased. Two or three of the foremost of the cavalrymen had tumbled into a cattle-guard, in their reckless pursuit. We were safe now, except that the engine and tender were in momentary danger of jumping the rotten track.

When we were well out of harm's way, the engineer, with whom I had been on very friendly terms till this last episode, turned to me and asked, with a grieved look, "Lieutenant, would you have blowed my brains out sure 'nuff, if I hadn't done what you tole me?"

"I would that," I replied, not much disposed to talk; for I was thinking, and thinking hard, what next to do.

"Well," said he, with a sigh, as with a greasy rag he

gave a fresh rub to a piece of machinery, " all I 've got to say is, I don't want to travel with you no mo'.''

" You 'll not have to travel far," I rejoined. " I 'll get off at Meherrin, and you can go back."

" What! " exclaimed he. " You goin' to get off there in the dark by yourself, with no hoss, and right in the middle of the Yankees? Durn my skin if I 'd do it for Jeff Davis hisself ! "

Upon our arrival at Meherrin, I wrote a few lines to General Walker, describing the position of the enemy, and telling him that I hoped to reach General Lee near High Bridge by traveling across the base of a triangle formed by the two railroads from Burkeville and my route, and that I would communicate with him further when I could.

It was a lonesome feeling that came over me when the engine went southward, leaving me alone and in the dark at Meherrin. The chill of daybreak was coming on, when I stepped out briskly upon a road leading northward. I knew that every minute counted, and that there was no hope of securing a horse in that vicinity. I think that I walked three or four miles. Day broke and the sun rose before I came to an opening. A kind Providence must have guided my steps, for at the very first house I reached, a pretty mare stood at the horse-rack saddled and bridled, as if waiting for me. The house was in a grove by the roadside. I found a hospitable reception, and was invited to breakfast. My night's work had made me ravenous. My host was past military age, but he seemed dazed at the prospect of falling into the hands of the enemy. I learned from him that Sheridan's cavalry had advanced nearly to his place the day before. We ate breakfast almost in silence. At the table I found Sergeant Wilkins, of the Black Walnut Troop, from Halifax County.

He had been on " horse furlough." Confederate cavalrymen supplied their own horses, and his horse furlough
meant that his horse had broken down, that he had been
home to replace it, and that he was now returning to duty
with another beast. His mare was beautiful and fresh, —
the very animal that I needed. When I told him that I
must take his horse, he laughed, as if I were joking; then
he positively refused; but finally, when I showed the
sign manual of Jefferson Davis, he yielded, very reluctantly. It was perhaps fortunate for Sergeant Wilkins
that he was obliged to go home again, for his cavalry
command was engaged heavily that day, and every day
thereafter, until the surrender at Appomattox.

On the morning of April 6, mounted upon as fine
a mare as there was in the Confederacy, I sallied forth
in search of General Lee. I started northward for the
Southside Railroad. It was not long before I heard cannon to the northeast. Thinking that the sounds came
from the enemy in the rear of Lee, I endeavored to bear
sufficiently westward to avoid the Union forces. Seeing
no sign of either army, I was going along leisurely, when
a noise behind me attracted my attention. Turning in
my saddle, I saw at a distance of several hundred yards
the head of a cavalry command coming from the east, and
turning out of a cross-road that I had passed into the
road that I was traveling. They saw me, and pretended
to give chase; but their horses were jaded, and my mare
was fresh and swift. The few shots they fired went wide
of us, and I galloped out of range quickly and safely.
My filly, after her spin, was mettlesome, and as I held
her in hand, I chuckled to think how easy it was to keep
out of harm's way on such a beast.

But this was not to be my easy day. I was rapidly
approaching another road, which came into my road from

the east. I saw another column of Union cavalry filing
into my road, and going in the same direction that I
was going. Here was a pretty pickle! We were in
the woods. Did they see me? To be sure they did. Of
course they knew of the parallel column of their own
troops which I had passed, and I think they first mistook
me for a friend. But I could not ride forward: I should
have come upon the rear of their column. I could not
turn back: the cavalry force behind was not a quarter of
a mile away. I stopped, thus disclosing who I was. Several of them made a dart for me; several more took shots
with their carbines; and once more the little mare and I
were dashing off, this time through the woods to the west.

What a bird she was, that little mare! At a low fence
in the woods she did not make a pause or blunder, but
cleared it without turning a hair. I resolved now to get
out of the way, for it was very evident that I was trying
to reach General Lee by riding across the advance columns of Sheridan, who was on Lee's flank. Going at a
merry pace, just when my heart was ceasing to jump and
I was congratulating myself upon a lucky escape, I was
" struck flat aback," as sailors say. From behind a large
oak a keen, racy-looking fellow stepped forth, and, level-
ing his cavalry carbine, called " Halt! " He was not ten
feet away.

Halt I did. It is all over now, thought I, for I did not
doubt that he was a Jesse scout. (That was the name
applied by us to Union scouts who disguised themselves
in our uniform.) He looked too neat and clean for one
of our men. The words " I surrender " were on my lips,
when he asked, " Who are you? " I had half a mind to
lie about it, but I gave my true name and rank. " What
the devil are you doing here, then? " he exclaimed, his
whole manner changing. I told him. " If that is so,"

said he, lowering his gun, to my great relief, " I must help to get you out. The Yankees are all around us. Come on." He led the way rapidly to where his own horse was tied behind some cedar bushes, and, mounting, bade me follow him. He knew the woods well. As we rode along, I ventured to inquire who he was. " Curtis," said he, — " one of General Rooney Lee's scouts. I have been hanging on the flank of this cavalry for several days. They are evidently pushing for the High Bridge, to cut the army off from crossing there."

After telling him of my adventure, I added : " You gave me a great fright. I thought you were a Yankee, sure, and came near telling you that I was one."

" It is well you did not. I am taking no prisoners on this trip," he rejoined, tapping the butt of his carbine significantly.

" There they go," said he, as we came to an opening and saw the Union cavalry winding down a red-clay road to the north of us, traveling parallel with our own route. " We must hurry, or they 'll reach the Flat Creek ford ahead of us. Fitz Lee is somewhere near here, and there 'll be fun when he sees them. There are not many of them, and they are pressing too far ahead of their main column."

After a sharp ride through the forest, we came to a wooded hill overlooking the ford of Flat Creek, a stream which runs northward, entering the Appomattox near High Bridge.

" Wait here a moment," said Curtis. " Let me ride out and see if we are safe." Going on to a point where he could reconnoitre, he turned back, rose in his stirrups, waved his hand, and crying, " Come on, quick ! " galloped down the hill to the ford.

I followed ; but he had not accurately calculated the

distance. The head of the column of Union cavalry was in sight when he beckoned to me and made his dash. They saw him and started toward him. As I was considerably behind him, they were much nearer to me than to him. He crossed safely; but the stream was deep, and by the time I was in the middle, my little mare doing her best with the water up to her chest, the Yankees were in easy range, making it uncomfortable for me. The bullets were splashing in the water all around me. I threw myself off the saddle, and, nestling close under the mare's shoulder, I reached the other side unharmed. Curtis and a number of pickets stationed at the ford stood by me manfully. The road beyond the ford ran into a deep gully and made a turn. Behind the protection of this turn, Curtis and the pickets opened fire upon the advancing cavalry, and held them in check until I was safely over. When my horse trotted up with me, wet as a drowned rat, it was time for us all to move on rapidly. In the afternoon, I heard Fitz Lee pouring hot shot into that venturesome body of cavalry, and I was delighted to learn afterward that he had given them severe punishment.

Curtis advised me to go to Farmville, where I would be beyond the chance of encountering more Union cavalry, and then to work eastward toward General Lee. I had been upset by the morning's adventures, and I was somewhat demoralized. About a mile from Farmville, I found myself to the west of a line of battle of infantry, formed on a line running north and south, moving toward the town. Not doubting they were Union troops, I galloped off again, and when I entered Farmville I did not hesitate to inform the commandant that the Yankees were approaching. The news created quite a panic. Artillery was put in position and preparations were made to resist, when it was discovered that the troops I had seen were a reserve regiment of our own, falling back in line of battle to a position near the town. I kept very quiet when I heard men all about me swearing that any cowardly, panic-stricken fool who would set such a report afloat ought to be lynched.

I had now very nearly joined our army, which was coming directly toward me. Early in the afternoon, the advance of our troops appeared. How they straggled, and how demoralized they seemed! Eastward, not far from the Flat Creek ford, a heavy fire opened, and continued for an hour or more. As I afterward learned, Fitz Lee had collided with my cavalry friends of the morning, and, seeing his advantage, had availed himself of it by attacking them fiercely. To the north, about four o'clock, a tremendous fire of artillery and musketry began, and continued until dark. I was riding towards this firing, with my back to Farmville. Very heavy detonations of artillery were followed time and again by crashes of musketry. It was the battle of Sailors' Creek, the most important of those last struggles of which Grant said, "There was as much gallantry displayed by some of the Confederates in these little engagements as was displayed at any time during the war, notwithstanding the sad defeats of the past weeks." My father's command was doing the best fighting of that day. When Ewell and Custis Lee had been captured, when Pickett's division broke and fled, when Bushrod Johnson, his division commander, left the field ingloriously, my fearless father, bareheaded and desperate, led his brigade into action at Sailors' Creek, and, though completely surrounded, cut his way out, and reached Farmville at daylight with the fragments of his command.

It was long after nightfall when the firing ceased. We

had not then learned the particulars, but it was easy to see that the contest had gone against us. The enemy had, in fact, at Sailors' Creek, stampeded the remnant of Pickett's division, broken our lines, captured six general officers, including Generals Ewell and Custis Lee, and burned a large part of our wagon trains. As evening came on, the road was filled with wagons, artillery, and bodies of men, hurrying without organization and in a state of panic toward Farmville. I met two general officers, of high rank and great distinction, who seemed utterly demoralized, and they declared that all was lost. That portion of the army which was still unconquered was falling back with its face to the foe, and bivouacked with its right and left flanks resting upon the Appomattox to cover the crossings to the north side, near Farmville. Upon reaching our lines, I found the divisions of Field and Malone presenting an unbroken and defiant front. Passing from camp to camp in search of General Lee, I encountered General Mahone, who told me where to find General Lee. He said that the enemy had "knocked hell out of Pickett." "But," he added savagely, "my fellows are all right. We are just waiting for 'em." And so they were. When the army surrendered, three days later, Mahone's division was in better fighting trim and surrendered more muskets than any other division of Lee's army.

It was past midnight when I found General Lee. He was in an open field north of Rice's Station and east of the High Bridge. A camp-fire of fence-rails was burning low. Colonel Charles Marshall sat in an ambulance, with a lantern and a lap-desk. He was preparing orders at the dictation of General Lee, who stood near, with one hand resting on a wheel and one foot upon the end of a log, watching intently the dying embers as he spoke in a low tone to his amanuensis.

Touching my cap as I rode up, I inquired, "General Lee?"

"Yes," he replied quietly, and I dismounted and explained my mission. He examined my autograph order from Mr. Davis, and questioned me closely concerning the route by which I had come. He seemed especially interested in my report of the position of the enemy at Burkeville and westward, to the south of his army. Then, with a long sigh, he said: "I hardly think it is necessary to prepare written dispatches in reply. They may be captured. The enemy's cavalry is already flanking us to the south and west. You seem capable of bearing a verbal response. You may say to Mr. Davis that, as he knows, my original purpose was to adhere to the line of the Danville Road. I have been unable to do so, and am now endeavoring to hold the Southside Road as I retire in the direction of Lynchburg."

"Have you any objective point, general, — any place where you contemplate making a stand?" I ventured timidly.

"No," said he slowly and sadly, "no; I shall have to be governed by each day's developments." Then, with a touch of resentment, and raising his voice, he added, "A few more Sailors' Creeks and it will all be over — ended — just as I have expected it would end from the first."

I was astonished at the frankness of this avowal to one so insignificant as I. It made a deep and lasting impression on me. It gave me an insight into the character of General Lee which all the books ever written about him could never give. It elevated him in my opinion more than anything else he ever said or did. It revealed him as a man who had sacrificed everything to perform a conscientious duty against his judgment. He had loved the Union. He had believed secession was unnecessary; he had looked upon it as hopeless folly. Yet at the call of his State he had laid his life and fame and fortune at her feet, and served her faithfully to the last.

After another pause, during which, although he spoke not a word and gave not a sign, I could discern a great struggle within him, he turned to me and said: "You must be very tired, my son. You have had an exciting day. Go rest yourself, and report to me at Farmville at sunrise. I may determine to send a written dispatch." The way in which he called me " my son " made me feel as if I would die for him.

Hesitating a moment, I inquired, "General, can you give me any tidings of my father?"

" Your father?" he asked. " Who is your father?"

" General Wise."

"Ah!" said he, with another pause. "No, no. At nightfall, his command was fighting obstinately at Sailors' Creek, surrounded by the enemy. I have heard nothing from them since. I fear they were captured, or — or — worse." To these words, spoken with genuine sympathy, he added: "Your father's command has borne itself nobly throughout this retreat. You may well feel proud of him and of it."

My father was not dead. At the very moment when we were talking, he and the remnant of his brigade were tramping across the High Bridge, feeling like victors, and he, bareheaded and with an old blanket pinned around him, was chewing tobacco and cursing Bushrod Johnson for running off and leaving him to fight his own way out.

I found a little pile of leaves in a pine thicket, and lay down in the rear of Field's division for a nap. Fearing that somebody would steal my horse, I looped the reins around my wrist, and the mare stood by my side.

We were already good friends. Just before daylight, she gave a snort and a jerk which nearly dislocated my arm, and I awoke to find her alarmed at Field's division, which was withdrawing silently and had come suddenly upon her. Warned by this incident, I mounted, and proceeded toward Farmville, to report, as directed, to General Lee for further orders. North of the stream at Farmville, in the forks of the road, was the house then occupied by General Lee. On the hill behind the house, to the left of the road, was a grove. Seeing troops in this grove, I rode in, inquiring for General Lee's head-quarters. The troops were lying there more like dead men than live ones. They did not move, and they had no sentries out. The sun was shining upon them as they slept. I did not recognize them. Dismounting, and shaking an officer, I awoke him with difficulty. He rolled over, sat up, and began rubbing his eyes, which were bloodshot and showed great fatigue.

" Hello, John ! " said he. " In the name of all that is wonderful, where did you come from ? " It was Lieutenant Edmund R. Bagwell, of the 46th. The men, a few hundred in all, were the pitiful remnant of my father's brigade.

" Have you seen the old general ? " asked Ned. " He 's over there. Oh, we have had a week of it ! Yes, this is all that is left of us. John, the old man will give you thunder when he sees you. When we were coming on last night in the dark, he said, ' Thank God, John is out of this ! ' Dick ? Why, Dick was captured yesterday at Sailors' Creek. He was riding the general's old mare, Maggie, and she squatted like a rabbit with him when the shells began to fly. She always had that trick. He could not make her go forward or backward. You ought to have seen Dick belaboring her with his sword. But the

Yanks got him!" and Ned burst into a laugh as he led me where my father was. Nearly sixty years old, he lay, like a common soldier, sleeping on the ground among his men.

We aroused him, and when he saw me, he exclaimed: "Well, by great Jehoshaphat, what are you doing here? I thought you, at least, were safe." I hugged him, and almost laughed and cried at the sight of him safe and sound, for General Lee had made me very uneasy. I told him why I was there.

"Where is General Lee?" he asked earnestly, springing to his feet. "I want to see him again. I saw him this morning about daybreak. I had washed my face in a mud-puddle, and the red mud was all over. it and in the roots of my hair. I looked like a Comanche Indian; and when I was telling him how we cut our way out last night, he broke into a smile and said, 'General, go wash your face!'" The incident pleased him immensely, for at the same time General Lee made him a division commander, — a promotion he had long deserved for gallantry, if not for military knowledge.

"No, Dick is not captured. He got out, I'm sure," said he, as we walked down the hill together. "He was separated from me when the enemy broke our line. He was not riding Maggie. I lent her to Frank Johnson. He was wounded, and, remembering his kindness to your brother Jennings the day he was killed, I tried to save the poor fellow, and told him to ride Maggie to the rear. Dick was riding his black horse. I know it. When the Yankees advanced, a flock of wild turkeys flushed before them and came sailing into our lines. I saw Dick gallop after a gobbler and shoot him and tie him to his saddlebow. He was coming back toward us when the line broke, and, mounted as he was, he has no doubt escaped, but is cut off from us by the enemy.

"Yes, the Yanks got the bay horse, and my servants Joshua and Smith, and all my baggage, overcoats, and plunder. A private soldier pinned this blanket around me last night, and I found this hat when I was coming off the field."

He laughed heartily at his own plight. I have never since seen a catch-pin half so large as that with which his blanket was gathered at the throat. As we passed down the road to General Lee's headquarters, the roads and the fields were filled with stragglers. They moved looking behind them, as if they expected to be attacked and harried by a pursuing foe. Demoralization, panic, abandonment of all hope, appeared on every hand. Wagons were rolling along without any order or system. Caissons and limber-chests, without commanding officers, seemed to be floating aimlessly upon a tide of disorganization. Rising to his full height, casting a glance around him like that of an eagle, and sweeping the horizon with his long arm and bony forefinger, my father exclaimed, " This is the end! " It is impossible to convey an idea of the agony and the bitterness of his words and gestures.

We found General Lee on the rear portico of the house that I have mentioned. He had washed his face in a tin basin, and stood drying his beard with a coarse towel as we approached. " General Lee," exclaimed my father, " my poor, brave men are lying on yonder hill more dead than alive. For more than a week they have been fighting day and night, without food, and, by God, sir, they shall not move another step until *somebody* gives them something to eat! "

" Come in, general," said General Lee soothingly. " They deserve something to eat, and shall have it; and meanwhile you shall share my breakfast." He disarmed everything like defiance by his kindness.

It was but a few moments, however, before my father launched forth in a fresh denunciation of the conduct of General Bushrod Johnson in the engagement of the 6th. I am satisfied that General Lee felt as he did ; but, assuming an air of mock severity, he said, " General, are you aware that you are liable to court-martial and execution for insubordination and disrespect toward your commanding officer ? "

My father looked at him with lifted eyebrows and flashing eyes, and exclaimed : " Shot ! You can't afford to shoot the men who fight for cursing those who run away. Shot ! I wish you would shoot me. If you don't, some Yankee probably will within the next twenty-four hours."

Growing more serious, General Lee inquired what he thought of the situation.

" Situation ? " said the bold old man. " There is no situation ! Nothing remains, General Lee, but to put your poor men on your poor mules and send them home in time for spring ploughing. This army is hopelessly whipped, and is fast becoming demoralized. These men have already endured more than I believed flesh and blood could stand, and I say to you, sir, emphatically, that to prolong the struggle is murder, and the blood of every man who is killed from this time forth is on your head, General Lee."

This last expression seemed to cause General Lee great pain. With a gesture of remonstrance, and even of impatience, he protested : " Oh, general, do not talk so wildly. My burdens are heavy enough. What would the country think of me, if I did what you suggest ? "

" Country be d——d ! " was the quick reply. " There is no country. There has been no country, general, for a year or more. You are the country to these men. They have fought for you. They have shivered through a long winter for you. Without pay or clothes, or care of any sort, their devotion to you and faith in you have been the only things which have held this army together. If you demand the sacrifice, there are still left thousands of us who will die for you. You know the game is desperate beyond redemption, and that, if you so announce, no man or government or people will gainsay your decision. That is why I repeat that the blood of any man killed hereafter is upon your head."

General Lee stood for some time at an open window, looking out at the throng now surging by upon the roads and in the fields, and made no response. Then, turning his attention to me, he said cheerfully that he was glad my father's plight was not so bad as he had thought it might be, at the time of our conversation the night before. After a pause, he wrote upon a piece of paper a few words to the effect that he had talked with me, and that I would make a verbal report. If occasion arose, he would give further advices. "This," said he, "you will deliver to the President. I fear to write, lest you be captured, for those people are already several miles above Farmville. You must keep on the north side to a ford eight miles above here, and be careful about crossing even there." He always referred to the enemy as "those people." Then he bade me adieu, and asked my father to come in and share his breakfast.

I hugged my father in the presence of General Lee, and I saw a kindly look in his eyes as he watched us. Remembering that my father had no horse, I said, "Take my mare. I can easily get another."

"What!" said he, laughing, "a dispatch-bearer giving away his horse! No, sir. That is too pretty a little animal to make a present to a Yankee. I know they will bag us all, horse, foot, and dragoons, before long. No.

I can walk as well as anybody.   Have you any chewing tobacco ? "

I was immensely flattered at this request, and gave him a plug of excellent tobacco.   It was the first time that he had recognized me as entitled to the possession of all the " modern improvements " of a soldier.

And so I left them.   As I rode along in search of the ford to which General Lee had directed me, I felt that I was in the midst of the wreck of that immortal army which, until now, I had believed to be invincible.

CHAPTER XXVI

THE END

EIGHT miles of brisk riding carried me beyond the flotsam and jetsam of the Army of Northern Virginia. I was alone in the meadows on the north of the Appomattox River. The sun shone brightly, and under the wooded bluffs upon the opposite bank of the narrow stream the little valley up which my route led was warm and still. The dogwood was beginning to bloom ; the grass near the river banks was showing the first verdure of spring ; the willows overhanging the stream were purpling and swelling with buds. A cock grouse among the laurels was drumming to his mate, and more than once I heard the gobble of the wild turkey. Behind me, in the distance, were sounds of artillery ; from time to time, our guns opened to hold the enemy in check, or he, pursuing, availed himself of some eminence to shell our retreating masses. In due season the designated ford was reached. The little mare, her neck and flanks warm but not heated with exercise, waded into the stream up to her knees, and, plunging her nose into the water, quenched her thirst. A gray squirrel, startled from a hickory near the ford, ran out upon a limb, swung himself to another tree, and scampered away through the sunlight and the shadows to gain his castle in the hollow oak upon the hillside. In a neighboring cedar, a redbird (cardinal grosbeak), warmed by the sunlight, uttered the soft call with which he wooes his mate in springtime.

How peaceful, how secluded, how inviting to repose, seemed this sheltered nook! It was hard to realize what a seething caldron of human life and human passion was boiling so near at hand. I needed rest. It was Friday, and since I left Clover Station, Wednesday night, I had slept but three hours. Oh, the heartache of those last eight miles of travel, with time to reflect in solitude upon what I had seen! The hopeless, quiet dignity of General Lee, the impassioned desperation of my father, were present like a nightmare. The shattered idols of boyish dreams lay strewn about me on the road along which I had been traveling. I had seen commands scattered and blasted which, until now, had represented victory or unbroken defiance. I had beheld officers who, until yesterday, had impersonated to my youthful ardor nothing but gallantry, demoralized, separated from their commands, and with all stomach gone for further fighting. Ever and again, my thoughts went back to the brave troops through whose ranks I had ridden the night previous in search of General Lee; and then my pride rose afresh. Yet in my heart I knew that they were but a handful to resist the armies of Grant; that the Army of Northern Virginia was a thing of the past; that its surrender was only a question of a few days at furthest; and that the war was virtually ended. Then would come the sickening thought, so eloquently expressed by my father, that every man thenceforth killed was a noble life literally thrown away. And, knowing my father as I did, I felt that it was more than likely he would be one of those to fall; for his counsel was not the counsel of a coward. His courage and spirit of defiance were still unbroken. His proudest testimonial is that recorded concerning his conduct on the retreat by Fitzhugh Lee, who in describing it declared that, until the order of surrender went forth at Appomattox,

he fought with the fervor of youth, and exposed himself
as unhesitatingly as when he was full of hope at the opening of the war.

Alone, torn by these bitter thoughts, patriotic and personal, exhausted by two days and nights of excitement
and fatigue, and contemplating with no pleasant anticipations seventy miles of hard riding before me, I gathered
my reins, touched the flank of my horse, and resumed
my journey. The country south of the Appomattox was
wooded and somewhat broken. The roads led between
" hogback " hills, as they are called. I drew out my
brierwood pipe and consoled myself with a smoke ; for
among my other military accomplishments I had acquired
the habit of smoking.

I was taking it easily, and was riding " woman fashion,"
to rest myself in the saddle. The mare moved quietly
forward at a fox trot. I felt sure I was well ahead of the
flanking column of the enemy. Of a sudden my ear
caught the sound of a human voice. It was distant, — a
singsong note, resembling the woodland " halloo " we often
hear. For a moment I thought it might be the voice of
a darkey singing as he drove his team along. But it
ceased, and in its place I heard, in a direction which I
could not determine, sounds like falling rain, with heavy
drops distinctly audible in the downpour. I recognized
the sound.

When we were studying Virgil, our tutor delighted to
take up those lines of the Æneid wherein the poet describes the footfall of many horses as the cavalry approaches : —

> " It clamor, et agmine facto
> Quadrupedante putrem sonitu quatit ungula campum."

After reading them he would look around and ask, " Eh ?
don't you hear the very sound of the horses' feet in the

words?" Well, of course we did not, and Parson Dudley thought we were trifling young cubs not to see the beauty of Virgil's verbal horseplay. Still, the words stuck, and I often repeated them afterward. Now, who would have imagined that the little Latin I had acquired, partly *a priori* and partly *a posteriori*, would one day serve to aid in escaping capture? I listened. I repeated: "Quadrupe — dantepu — tremsoni — tuquatit — ungula — campum." I said to myself: "That sound is the sound of cavalry. That voice was the voice of command. Which way shall I go?"

"Plague take you, be quiet!" I said to the mare, slapping her impatiently on the neck; for at that moment she lifted her head, pointed her ears, and, raising her ribs, gave a loud whinny. By good luck, almost at the same instant the sound of clashing cymbals and the music of a mounted band came through the forest. The hostile forces were but a few hundred yards away. As I soon learned, they were moving on a road leading to the ford, but entering the road that I was traveling just beyond the spot where I first heard them. The hill on my left ran down to a point where the advancing column was coming into the road on which I was. The summit of the hill was covered by a thick growth of laurel and pine. I sprang from the saddle, led the mare up the hillside, tied her, and, reflecting that she might whinny again, left her, ran along the hill-crest as near to the enemy as I dared go, lay down behind an old log, covered myself with leaves and bushes, and was within a hundred yards of the spot which the enemy passed. I could see them from behind the end of my log.

"Hurrah! hurrah!" they shouted, as the band played "Johnny Comes Marching Home." They were elated and full of enthusiasm, for the Johnnies were on the run, and the pursuit was now little more than a foot-race. The band struck up "Captain Jenks of the Horse Marines" as they swept on to the ford, walking, trotting, ambling, pacing, their guidons fluttering in the spring breeze. "Hurrah! hurrah! hurrah!" How different was the cheering from the wild yell to which I was accustomed! I lay there, with my pistol in my hand, watching them, really interested in contrasting their good equipment and their ardor with the wretched scenes that I had left behind. A wild turkey hen, startled from her nest near the roadside, came flying directly up the hill, alighted on the further side of the log behind which I was lying, and, squatting low, ran within three feet of my nose. Peering into my face with frightened eyes, she gave a "put!" of amazement and sheered off. I convulsively clutched my pistol to shoot her. No, I did not shoot. I had reasons for not shooting. But I am sure this was the only wild turkey that ever came within range of my weapon without receiving a salute.

The cavalcade swept by, and did not suspect my presence. When all was still again, hurrying back to the filly, I mounted, rode down to the forks of the road, took the one that led westward, and galloped away. I felt sure, from the rapidity with which I had traveled, that this must be the advance of the enemy, and I resolved to take no further risks. I was right, for I saw no more Union troops. Late that afternoon, in Charlotte County, I passed the plantation of Roanoke, once the home of John Randolph. It looked desolate and overgrown.

"Oh, John Randolph, John, John!" thought I, as I rode by, "you have gotten some other Johns, in fact the whole breed of Johnnies, into a peck of trouble by the governmental notions which you left to them as a legacy. By the way, John," changing into a merrier vein, "I wish some of those thoroughbreds you once owned were still in your stables ; my gallant animal is nearly done for by the murderous pace of the last six hours." Neither the spirit nor the horses of John Randolph responded, either to maintain his principles, or to supply me a fresh mount from the skeleton stables, and I rode on.

I reached the Episcopal rectory at Halifax Court House after midnight. My brother Henry was the minister. He was a glorious fellow, who, if he had not been a preacher, would have made a dashing soldier. I hammered upon the door, and he came down. I was now only twenty miles west of my post at Clover Station. I had visited him several times while I was quartered there, but since the evacuation of Richmond he had heard nothing from any of us, although he had made many inquiries, for me particularly.

When I told him of my last three adventures, he looked me over, and, seeing how red my eyes were, said that he was afraid I was drunk. " Not much," I replied ; " but if you have anything to eat and to drink, get it out quickly, for I am nearly famished. You may think I am drunk, Henry, but come out and look at the mare. Probably you will think she has the delirium tremens." He was soon dressed, and we went out to minister to the faithful brute.

She stood with head hung low, her red nostrils distending and contracting, her sides heaving, her knees trembling, her flanks roweled and red, the sweat dripping from her wet body. Poor little Tulip (that was her name), I had not done it wantonly. I was performing a duty of life and death.

" You cannot ride her to Danville," said Henry, who was a good horseman.

" No, of course not. I came after your bay horse."

Henry loved his mare, and under other circumstances he would not have listened to such a proposition; but patriotism overcame him, and he simply answered, with a sigh, "Very well."

I count it a creditable episode in my life that I took off my coat, tired as I was, and gave Tulip a good rubbing down, and fed her and bedded her, bless her game heart!

"You cannot go forward at once," Henry urged, when we returned to the house. He started a fire in the dining-room, and placed an abundance of cold victuals and drink upon the table, and his pretty young wife entered to hear the war news.

"Well, I thought I might, but blamed if I don't believe I'm forced to take a rest," I replied. "Will you have your mare saddled and me waked at daybreak?"

It was so arranged, and, after I had eaten like a glutton, I lit a pipe and tried to stay awake to answer Henry's eager questions; but I fell asleep in the chair, and the next I knew he was leading me by the arm up to a large bedroom, the like of which I had not seen for many a day. Tumbling into bed, I knew no more until he roused me at daybreak, fed me, put me on his mare, and said a "God bless you!" I went off sore and reluctant, but soon limbered up and grew willing, as his horse, fresh and almost as good as Tulip, strode gallantly on to Danville.

"Man never is, but always to be blest." I was envying preachers, and thinking what a good time Henry was having; and he, poor fellow, had spent the night striding up and down the floor, bemoaning the hard fate which had made him a non-combatant.

It was about eight o'clock in the evening of Saturday, April 8, 1865, when the hoofs of my horse resounded on the bridge which spans the Roanoke at Danville. I do not recall the exact distance traversed that day, but it was enough for man and beast. I had a good, comfortable ride. Henry had filled my saddle-pockets with excellent food, and two flasks of coffee made by him, while I slept, from a precious remnant that he had preserved for the sick of his congregation. He was a prince of hospitality and common sense. He had liquor, and was no blue-nose; but he said that he would give me none, for the double reason that I seemed to like it too well, and that, in case of protracted effort, it was not so reliable a stimulant as coffee.

The lights of Danville were a welcome sight. The town was crowded with people, the result of the recent influx from Richmond. Riding up Main Street to the principal hotel, I learned that President Davis was domiciled at the home of Major Sutherlin, and thither I directed my course. The house stands upon Main Street, near the crest of a steep hill. As I approached, I saw that it was brilliantly illuminated. A sentry at the yard gate challenged me. I announced my name, rank, and mission, and was admitted. At the door, a colored man, whom I recognized as the body servant of the President, received me. In a few moments, Burton Harrison appeared, giving me a kindly greeting, and saying that the President and his Cabinet were then holding a session in the dining-room, and desired me to enter and make my report. I laughed, drew forth the short note of General Lee to the President, and remarked that my dispatches were for the most part oral.

I felt rather embarrassed by such a distinguished audience, but Mr. Davis soon put me at ease. In his book he mentions my coming, but, after the long interval between 1865 and the time at which it was written, he had forgotten, if indeed he ever knew, that I had been

sent by him to General Lee. Probably he never learned
what name General Walker inserted in the blank order
sent, when he requested the detail of an officer to communicate with General Lee. At any rate, I was the first
person who had brought him any direct news from General Lee since his departure from Richmond.

Those present, as I remember them, were, besides the
President and Burton Harrison, Mr. Benjamin, General
Breckinridge, Secretary Mallory, Secretary Reagan, perhaps General Bragg, and several others whom I did not
know, or do not recall. They sat around a large dining-
table, and I stood at the end opposite Mr. Davis. He
was exceedingly considerate, requested me to make my
report, which I did as briefly as possible, and then asked
me a number of questions. When he had done examin-
ing me, several others of the party made inquiries. One
thing I remember vividly. Somebody inquired how
many efficient troops I thought General Lee had left.
I was prepared for this question to the extent of having
tried to conjecture. In doing so, I had assumed that at
the time he started from Petersburg he had nearly one
hundred thousand men. That was the popular impression. With this in my mind as a basic figure, I believed
that his army had dwindled to one third of its number
when it left Petersburg; and so I ventured the opinion
that he might still have thirty thousand effective men,
although I was cautious enough to add that Mahone's
and Field's divisions were the only two that I had seen
which seemed to be intact and to have preserved their
organization. When I said thirty thousand, I thought I
detected a smile of sad incredulity on several faces; and
I have often wondered since how much that statement
detracted from the weight attached to my report in other
respects.

One question I answered as I felt. "Do you think General Lee will be able to reach a point of safety with his army?"

"I regret to say, no. From what I saw and heard, I am satisfied that General Lee must surrender. It may be that he has done so to-day. In my opinion, Mr. President, it is only a question of a few days at furthest, and, if I may be permitted to add a word, I think the sooner the better; for, after seeing what I have seen of the two armies, I believe the result is inevitable, and postponing the day means only the useless effusion of noble, gallant blood."

I am sure none of them had heard such a plain statement of this unwelcome truth before. I remember the expression of face — almost a shudder — with which what I said was received. I saw that, however convinced they might be of the truth of it, it was not a popular speech to make.

Mr. Davis asked me to remain. He said that he wished to talk with me further. While I was waiting for him in the hallway, Major Sutherlin, who had known me from childhood, beckoned to me and asked, "Are n't you hungry after your ride?"

I grinned. I was always hungry then.

"Jim," quoth the major, "see if you can't get something for the lieutenant to eat."

Jim went out, but in a few minutes returned, and, bowing, invited me into a butler's pantry. He apologized for the place, and explained that the house was so crowded he had nowhere else to spread the repast. He had provided milk, corn-coffee, butter and rolls, and cold turkey. I said, "Jim, shut up. You know I am not used to as good as this." With that I tossed off a glass of milk, swallowed a cup of coffee, and, opening my haversack, tumbled the butter and rolls and turkey-legs into it, and buttoned it up. Jim stood there, highly amused at the short shrift I made of his feast, and remarked, "You 's a fust-class forager, ain't you, lieutenant?" "Yes," I responded. "You must keep fire in the box, Jim, if you want the engine to run. Now I 'm ready for the President."

I slipped back into the hallway, and sat down to wait until the President should call me. In a little while the conference broke up, and he came to the door. "Now, lieutenant, I 'll see you," and he led the way into the drawing-room; there we had a long talk, I going more into details.

At the close of our conversation, he sat for some time peering into the gloom outside, and finally broke the silence by saying, "You seem to know the roads. Do you feel equal to another trip?"

"Assuredly," I answered. "I now have a relay of horses, and am more than glad to serve in any way I can."

"Very well," said he. "Leave your horse in Major Sutherlin's stable, so that it will be well fed, and report for orders to-morrow morning at eight o'clock."

I took the mare to the stable. It looked so inviting that I clambered up a ladder to the loft, opened my haversack, enjoyed Major Sutherlin's food, placed some hay under me and drew some over me, and had a glorious night's rest.

When I reported next morning, the President did not ask at what hotel I was stopping. I received my return dispatches, and I set forth to rejoin General Lee. Apprehending the probability of my capture, Mr. Davis gave me a brief letter of credentials, and said that I would explain his wishes.

Upon the same day that General Lee surrendered at Appomattox (April 9), I reached Halifax Court House on the return trip. My brother Richard was there, with his own horse and the horse that my father had lent the wounded man. They had been cut off at Sailors' Creek and forced southward. The enemy, flanking General Lee, had advanced by moving at least ten miles beyond Sailors' Creek, thus rendering it impossible for them to rejoin General Lee except by going through the Union lines. My brother was greatly perplexed concerning the course he should pursue, and after we had discussed the matter, he resolved to leave one of the horses and to go back with me. Monday morning we resumed the journey; and that afternoon we met the first of our men, who, paroled at Appomattox the day before, were mournfully wending their way homeward.

Upon hearing of the surrender, we turned back toward Danville to report to President Davis the failure of my mission. On arriving there, we learned that he had left the place, and gone to Greensboro, North Carolina. From the paroled men we met, we ascertained that our father was safe. We resolved to join Johnston's army. After leaving Danville, two days' ride brought us to Greensboro, and there we found Johnston's forces. We reported to Major-General Carter Stevenson, commanding a division of infantry. General Stevenson was a Virginian, one of the few in that army. A cousin of ours was on his staff. The army was bivouacked in and about the town of Greensboro, awaiting the result of negotiations for its surrender. Men and officers alike understood this, and there was a general relaxation of discipline.

We were among the first to arrive from Lee's army. General Stevenson gave us a cordial welcome. We told him we had not been captured, and had come to serve

under him. He asked us what we wished to do. We replied that we were ready to serve in any capacity in which
we could be useful ; I added facetiously that I was not
much of a lieutenant anyhow, and none too good for a
private. On our way, we had seriously discussed the formation of a command composed of officers of Lee's army
who had escaped from the surrender. Inviting us to
make his headquarters our home until something definite
was concluded, General Stevenson said, with a smile, that
he feared we had jumped out of the frying-pan into the
fire, and that Sherman and Johnston were already conferring about a cessation of hostilities. I must describe one
of the conferences as General Johnston himself narrated
it many years afterward.

One cold winter night about 1880, Captain Edwin
Harvie, of General Johnston's staff, invited me to join
him in a call upon the general, who was then living in
Richmond. Harvie was one of his pets, and we were
promptly admitted to his presence. He sat in an arm-
chair in his library, dressed in a flannel wrapper, and was
suffering from an influenza. By his side, upon a low
stool, stood a tray with whiskey, glasses, spoons, sugar,
lemon, spice, and eggs. At the grate a footman held a
brass teakettle of boiling water. Mrs. Johnston was preparing hot Tom-and-Jerry for the old gentleman, and he
took it from time to time with no sign of objection or
resistance. It was snowing outside, and the scene within
was very cosy. As I had seen him in public, General
Johnston was a stiff, uncommunicative man, punctilious
and peppery, as little fellows like him are apt to be. He
reminded me of a cock sparrow, full of self-consciousness,
and rather enjoying a peck at his neighbor.

That night he was as warm, comfortable, and commu-
nicative as the kettle singing on the hob. He had been

lonesome, and he greatly enjoyed both the Tom-and-
Jerry and the visitors. Harvie knew how to draw him
out on reminiscences, and we spent a most delightful
evening. Among other things, he told us an episode of
the surrender, under promise that we should not publish
it until after his death.

Johnston had known Sherman well in the United States
army. Their first interview near Greensboro resulted in
an engagement to meet for further discussion the following day. As they were parting, Johnston remarked: "By
the way, Cumps, Breckinridge, our Secretary of War, is
with me. He is a very able fellow, and a better lawyer
than any of us. If there is no objection, I will fetch him
along to-morrow."

Bristling up, General Sherman exclaimed, "Secretary
of War! No, no; we don't recognize any civil government among you fellows, Joe. No, I don't want any
Secretary of War."

"Well," said General Johnston, "he is also a major-
general in the Confederate army. Is there any objection
to his presence in the capacity of major-general?"

"Oh!" quoth Sherman, in his characteristic way,
"major-general! Well, any major-general you may bring,
I shall be glad to meet. But recollect, Johnston, no Secretary of War. Do you understand?"

The next day, General Johnston, accompanied by
Major-General Breckinridge and others, was at the rendezvous before Sherman.

"You know how fond of his liquor Breckinridge was?"
added General Johnston, as he went on with his story.
"Well, nearly everything to drink had been absorbed.
For several days, Breckinridge had found it difficult, if
not impossible, to procure liquor. He showed the effect
of his enforced abstinence. He was rather dull and

heavy that morning. Somebody in Danville had given
him a plug of very fine chewing tobacco, and he chewed
vigorously while we were awaiting Sherman's coming.
After a while, the latter arrived. He bustled in with a
pair of saddlebags over his arm, and apologized for being
late. He placed the saddlebags carefully upon a chair.
Introductions followed, and for a while General Sherman
made himself exceedingly agreeable. Finally, some one
suggested that we had better take up the matter in hand.

" ' Yes,' said Sherman ; ' but, gentlemen, it occurred
to me that perhaps you were not overstocked with liquor,
and I procured some medical stores on my way over.
Will you join me before we begin work ? ' "

General Johnston said he watched the expression of
Breckinridge at this announcement, and it was beatific.
Tossing his quid into the fire, he rinsed his mouth, and
when the bottle and the glass were passed to him, he
poured out a tremendous drink, which he swallowed with
great satisfaction. With an air of content, he stroked his
mustache and took a fresh chew of tobacco.

Then they settled down to business, and Breckinridge
never shone more brilliantly than he did in the discussions which followed. He seemed to have at his tongue's
end every rule and maxim of international and constitutional law, and of the laws of war, — international wars,
civil wars, and wars of rebellion. In fact, he was so resourceful, cogent, persuasive, learned, that, at one stage
of the proceedings, General Sherman, when confronted
by the authority, but not convinced by the eloquence
or learning of Breckinridge, pushed back his chair and
exclaimed : " See here, gentlemen, who is doing this sur-
rendering anyhow ? If this thing goes on, you 'll have
me sending a letter of apology to Jeff Davis."

Afterward, when they were nearing the close of the

conference, Sherman sat for some time absorbed in deep thought. Then he arose, went to the saddlebags, and fumbled for the bottle. Breckinridge saw the movement. Again he took his quid from his mouth and tossed it into the fireplace. His eye brightened, and he gave every evidence of intense interest in what Sherman seemed about to do.

The latter, preoccupied, perhaps unconscious of his action, poured out some liquor, shoved the bottle back into the saddle-pocket, walked to the window, and stood there, looking out abstractedly, while he sipped his grog.

From pleasant hope and expectation the expression on Breckinridge's face changed successively to uncertainty, disgust, and deep depression. At last his hand sought the plug of tobacco, and, with an injured, sorrowful look, he cut off another chew. Upon this he ruminated during the remainder of the interview, taking little part in what was said.

After silent reflections at the window, General Sherman bustled back, gathered up his papers, and said: "These terms are too generous, but I must hurry away before you make me sign a capitulation. I will submit them to the authorities at Washington, and let you hear how they are received." With that he bade the assembled officers adieu, took his saddlebags upon his arm, and went off as he had come.

General Johnston took occasion, as they left the house and were drawing on their gloves, to ask General Breckinridge how he had been impressed by Sherman.

"Sherman is a bright man, and a man of great force," replied Breckinridge, speaking with deliberation, "but," raising his voice and with a look of great intensity, "General Johnston, General Sherman is a hog. Yes, sir, a *hog*. Did you see him take that drink by himself?"

General Johnston tried to assure General Breckinridge that General Sherman was a royal good fellow, but the most absent-minded man in the world. He told him that the failure to offer him a drink was the highest compliment that could have been paid to the masterly arguments with which he had pressed the Union commander to that state of abstraction.

"Ah!" protested the big Kentuckian, half sighing, half grieving, "no Kentucky gentleman would ever have taken away that bottle. He knew we needed it, and needed it badly."

The story was well told, and I did not make it public until after General Johnston's death. On one occasion, being intimate with General Sherman, I repeated it to him. Laughing heartily, he said: "I don't remember it. But if Joe Johnston told it, it's so. Those fellows hustled me so that day, I was sorry for the drink I did give them," and with that sally he broke out into fresh laughter.

While these scenes were being enacted, Johnston's army lay about Greensboro, and I saw a great deal of the men and the officers. I will not attempt a comparison between its personnel and that of Lee's army. I was a prejudiced observer, and such comparisons can produce no good results. But I am free to say, from what I saw, then and thereafter, of Sherman's army, that I believe it was a better army than that of General Grant. If Lee's army and Sherman's had come together when they were at their best, the world would have witnessed some very memorable fighting. The spirit of General Johnston's men was much finer than, under the circumstances, anybody would have expected. They were defiant, and more than ready to try conclusions with Sherman in a pitched battle. Many expressed disgust and indignation when the sur-

render of the army was announced. An epidemic of
drunkenness, gambling, and fighting prevailed while we
were waiting for our final orders. Whatever difficulty
General Breckinridge may have experienced in procuring
liquor, the soldiers seemed to have an abundance of color-
less corn-whiskey and applejack, and the roadsides were
lined with " chuck-a-luck " games. The amount of Confederate money displayed was marvelous. Men had it
by the haversackful, and bet it recklessly upon anything.
The ill-temper begotten by drinking and gambling manifested itself almost hourly in free fights.

During this period of waiting came the news of the
assassination of Mr. Lincoln. Perhaps I ought to chronicle that the announcement was received with demonstrations of sorrow. If I did, I should be lying for sentiment's sake. Among the higher officers and the most
intelligent and conservative men, the assassination caused
a shudder of horror at the heinousness of the act, and at
the thought of its possible consequences ; but among the
thoughtless, the desperate, and the ignorant, it was hailed
as a sort of retributive justice. In maturer years I have
been ashamed of what I felt and said when I heard of
that awful calamity. However, men ought to be judged
for their feelings and their speech by the circumstances
of their surroundings. For four years we had been fighting. In that struggle, all we loved had been lost. Lincoln incarnated to us the idea of oppression and conquest.
We had seen his face over the coffins of our brothers and
relatives and friends, in the flames of Richmond, in the
disaster at Appomattox. In blood and flame and torture
the temples of our lives were tumbling about our heads.
We were desperate and vindictive, and whosoever denies
it forgets or is false. We greeted his death in a spirit of
reckless hate, and hailed it as bringing agony and bitter-

ness to those who were the cause of our own agony and bitterness. To us, Lincoln was an inhuman monster, Grant a butcher, and Sherman a fiend.

Time taught us that Lincoln was a man of marvelous humanity, Appomattox and what followed revealed Grant in his matchless magnanimity, and the bitterness toward Sherman was softened in subsequent years. But, with our feelings then, if the news had come that all three of these had been engulfed in a common disaster with ourselves, we should have felt satisfaction in the fact, and should not have questioned too closely how it had been brought about. We were poor, starved, conquered, despairing; and to expect men to have no malice and no vindictiveness at such a time is to look for angels in human form. Thank God, such feelings do not last long, at least in their fiercest intensity.

The army moved westward to a place named Jimtown, since dignified as Jamestown. There we were all paroled. We received one dollar and fifteen cents each. Of this, one dollar was in Mexican coin. I cut my initials upon my dollar, but it was stolen from my pocket the next day. We were ready to disperse to our homes. Our headquarters were in a tent.

That night we had our last army fright. By some means, a rumor had become prevalent that certain officers had distributed among themselves bolts of valuable cloth far beyond their own needs, leaving the soldiers ragged. The men formed bands, declaring they would ransack the officers' wagons and have this cloth. A friendly fellow brought us the news that one of these parties was approaching to search General Stevenson's headquarters wagon. Major Reeve, of the staff, indignant at such an accusation, but more indignant at the proposed insult to his commanding officer, swore he would die rather than

submit to such ignominy. He called upon us to defend
our manhood. Of course we were ready. Armed only
with our swords and revolvers, we were deployed by him
behind trees. It was moonlight. We could see the raiders coming through the woods. When within thirty yards.
they halted. Major Reeve, who was as gallant as he was
impetuous, challenged, and asked what they wanted. A
leader replied. "Are you men soldiers of Stevenson's
division?" inquired Reeve. On learning that they were,
he proceeded to deliver an address which, for eloquence,
pathos, and defiance, was as fine as anything I ever
heard.

He reproached them for thinking for an instant that
such a base rumor could be true. He reminded them of
the days when he had led them, and they were touched
by his references to their common struggles and common
sufferings. He asked them what General Stevenson or
any of his staff had ever done to deserve this distrust or
justify this degrading search. Finally, he told them that if
they still persisted, but one course was left to us, and that
was to die at the hands of our own men rather than submit tamely to such dishonor. We who were deployed
behind the trees felt that we were in a ticklish place.
Reeve was exalted by his own oratory. We were trying
to count the number of our assailants. For a moment
after he finished speaking there was a dead silence, a very
awkward silence. Then a voice shouted, "Three cheers
for Major Reeve!" They were given with a hearty good-
will, followed by cheers for everybody. The marauders
broke, crowded around Reeve, and hugged and wept over
him, and we sneaked back to the tent, much relieved that
this particular phase of the war was over.

The next day, the Army of the Tennessee dissolved. To
every point of the compass its officers and men dispersed.

Our course was directed to Danville. We did not encounter any Union forces until we approached that place.
Then we saw mounted Union pickets outlined against the
sky, at the top of the hill. They looked just as we had
often seen them before. It was hard to realize that they
would not fire upon us, and gallop away to give the alarm.
It was equally hard to realize that we soon should pass
them and be within the Union lines. In we went, giving
and receiving salutes. For the first time, we were in the
midst of a body of Union soldiers. What we felt then is
not important.

A week later, having been to Halifax to return to her
owner the finest mare I ever bestrode, I boarded a train
for Richmond, the brass buttons on my uniform covered
with black, a fit badge of mourning for the dead Confederacy. The cars were crowded with Union soldiers and
negroes flocking to the towns. The bearing of the Union
officers and soldiers toward Confederates was, with few
exceptions, extremely civil and conciliatory. One fellow
was so kind that, after he had offered me money, which I
refused, he slipped it into my pocket with a card saying,
" This is not a gift, but a loan, and when you are able
you can return it to me." I did subsequently return it,
but never forgot his delicate attention.

The bridges across the James at Richmond had all been
destroyed. Our train stopped at Manchester, opposite
Richmond. Thence we were compelled to proceed to the
city by way of a pontoon bridge thrown across the river
at the lower end of Mayo's Island. At the Manchester
terminus, we found a number of improvised vehicles, —
wagons, ambulances, etc., — with improvised drivers, too,
seeking passengers to carry over the bridge. These drivers were in many instances my old army comrades. One
of them was Colonel George ——, a former schoolmate,

not five years older than myself, a man of the highest social standing, a young soldier of distinguished gallantry,
who a month before had commanded one of the best regiments in Lee's army. It was pathetic, the sight of those
army boys, with their war-horses converted into teams,
trying to earn an honest penny to feed the folks at home.
I saw George stand at the rear of the ambulance that
he drove, open the door, collect the fares from the sleek
Union commissaries and quartermasters who patronized
him, mount his box, and drive away as humbly as if that
business had been, and was to be, his lifelong occupation.

It was fortunate for our boys that the negroes, who
until now had done this class of work, were so elated by
their freedom that they had performed no sort of labor
since the evacuation. They had thronged the city, but
not for work. The weather was warm, and they were
living in all kinds of makeshift habitations, ofttimes in
the ruins of burned buildings, procuring food from the
Freedmen's Bureau, and spending their time in the Capitol Square, where the older ones shouted and sang for
hours, and the children played at games.

I was too poor to indulge in the luxury of a ride, and
young and strong enough to walk to town. Slinging our
knapsacks, a party of us walked across the pontoon, lift-
ing our eyes from time to time to the grinning ruins before
us. It was past noon ; the day was warm, and the sun
was bright. It revealed, without concealing anything
from us, the complete destruction of the business portion
of the town. Through these ruins we wended our way.

The hand of reconstruction was already stretched forth.
Men were engaged in pulling down walls and cleaning
bricks. Already mortar beds had been built in the
streets, puddlers were at work, and, where work had progressed far enough, foundations were being laid anew.

The streets were already burdened with lumber for joists and woodwork, and every evidence was given of a rebuilding of the town. Nearly all the laborers were white men. Many of them I knew well, — men of as good social position as my own ; soldiers come home and resolved not to be idle, but to work for an honest living in any way in which they could make it. Sitting in the sun with their trowels, jabbing away in awkward fashion at their new and unaccustomed tasks, covered with dust and plaster, they were the same bright, cheerful fellows who had learned to labor in that state of life to which it had pleased God to call them, just as they had been willing followers, in sunshine and in storm, of their beloved Lee. At night, with their day's wages in their pockets, they would go home, change their clothing, take a bath, and associate with their families, — not at all ashamed of their labors, but making a joke of their newly discovered method of earning a sustenance. With all the hardship of such unaccustomed work, it was the best and most comfortable and least dangerous employment that they had been engaged in for years. Richmond rose from her ashes, and soon became, in great part by their efforts, a more beautiful city than ever before.

Passing through the business portion of the town, we reached the residential section, which was still intact. The trees were in full leaf. They cast their deep shadows everywhere, and a Sabbath stillness pervaded the streets, strangely in contrast with the air of busy life always presented when Richmond was the crowded and beleaguered capital. Few men and no women were upon the streets. Business had not been resumed, and the presence of Union soldiers and great numbers of negroes made women cautious about venturing forth unattended.

I had no home. The nearest approach to one was that

of my brother-in-law, Dr. Garnett. There my mother
and an unmarried sister were, and thither I repaired.
My father, as I learned, had not returned to Richmond.
Eliza, our faithful servant, whose kinspeople resided in
Philadelphia, had made a short visit to that place, and
among other things had brought back civilian clothes for
me. They had been bought by Philadelphia relatives,
who knew me only as an eighteen-year-old boy, and the
clothes were of the style worn by Philadelphia cousins of
my own age. In my room I found a civilian's attire laid
out for me, and I proceeded to divest myself of my uniform. For the first time in two years and eight months,
I appeared in citizen's dress. The sensation was peculiar.
The lightness and softness of the cloth was delightful, but
the sack coat and the straw hat made me feel bobtailed
and bareheaded ; and when I looked in the glass, instead
of confronting a striking young officer, I beheld a mere
insignificant chit of an eighteen-year-old boy. Nothing
brought home to me more vividly the fact that the stunning events of the last month had ended the career on
which I had started, and that I had received a great set-
back in manhood. This feeling was emphasized when
some one startled me by asking where I was going to
school.

The house had a broad veranda. That evening we sat
upon it, after tea, quiet and sad, but enjoying the refresh-
ing air and sense of peace. On the opposite side of the
street lived a family consisting of a mother and several
handsome daughters. They had been such ardent Confederates that they had been sent out of Alexandria into
the Confederate lines by the Union commander. That
they were still loyal Confederates we never had reason to
doubt until we saw a party of young Union officers ride
up, followed by their orderlies. We felt sure they had

come to arrest the occupants of that house. Imagine our
surprise, therefore, when, in a few moments, we saw the
lights go up in the drawing-rooms, and discovered that
this was a social call. One of the girls was soon banging
away on the piano and singing to her admirers. The
voices of hilarity, the sounds of mirth and music, horrified
us. We looked upon the conduct of those girls, in making merry, singing, playing, and receiving the attentions
of Union officers, as grossly indelicate, heartless to our
dead and to us, and treason to their Confederate comrades.
It was years before they regained social recognition in the
community. Their faithlessness to the lost cause chilled
my heart, and was a fresh reminder that the cause was
dead.

That night I tossed upon my bed, reflecting on the
past, contemplating the present, speculating as to the
future. The next morning I arose, and before breakfast
I wrote my will, as follows : —

I, J. Reb., being of unsound mind and bitter memory,
and aware that I am dead, do make, publish, and declare
the following to be my political last will and testament.

1. I give, devise, and bequeath all my slaves to Harriet
Beecher Stowe.

2. My rights in the territories I direct shall be assigned
and set over, together with the bricabrac known as State
Sovereignty, to the Hon. J—— R—— T——, to play
with for the remainder of his life, and remainder to his
son after his death.

3. I direct that all my shares in the venture of secession shall be canceled, provided I am released from my
unpaid subscription to the stock of said enterprise.

4. My interest in the civil government of the Confederacy I bequeath to any freak museum that may hereafter be established.

5. My sword, my veneration for General Robert E. Lee, his subordinate commanders and his peerless soldiers, and my undying love for my old comrades, living and dead, I set apart as the best I have, or shall ever have, to bequeath to my heirs forever.

6. And now, being dead, having experienced a death to Confederate ideas and a new birth unto allegiance to the Union, I depart, with a vague but not definite hope of a joyful resurrection, and of a new life, upon lines somewhat different from those of the last eighteen years. I see what has been pulled down very clearly. What is to be built up in its place I know not. It is a mystery; but death is always mysterious. AMEN.

I read this will at the breakfast-table. It amused the family, but with me it was no joke. I was dead. Everything that I had ever believed in politically was dead. Everybody that I had ever trusted or relied upon politically was dead. My beloved State of Virginia was dismembered, and a new State had been erected out of a part of her, against her will. Every hope that I had ever indulged was dead. Even the manhood I had attained was dead. I was a boy again, a mere child, — precocious, ignorant, conceited, and unformed. I had set my heart and soul on the career of a soldier. What hope was left for that? The night's reflections had made all these things clear as never before. Boy as I was, I felt it as keenly as did the embittered Moor when, in his agony, he exclaimed : —

> " Farewell the plumed troop, and the big wars,
>   That make ambition virtue ! O, farewell !
>   Farewell the neighing steed, and the shrill trump,
>   The spirit-stirring drum, the ear-piercing fife,
>   The royal banner, and all quality,
>   Pride, pomp, and circumstance of glorious war !

And, O you mortal engines, whose rude throats
The immortal Jove's dread clamours counterfeit,
Farewell! Othello's occupation 's gone ! "

In hopelessness I scanned the wreck, and then — I went back to school.

In June, 1865, a boy named John Sergeant Wise, a visitor at the home of his uncle, General Meade, in Philadelphia, was a witness of the triumphant return of the armies of the Union. He was regarded as such a mere child that he was not invited to the table when company came, but dined with the other children in the nursery. A little later, he sat in overalls and a straw hat fishing near the shores of the blue Chesapeake. In September, he was sent to school. In October, he was playing furiously on the scrub nine of his college baseball team. Two years later, he was admitted to the practice of law, and even then he had not attained his majority.

It is incredible that this stripling was the same person as the young officer whose observations and career have been chronicled in these pages. Nor is it more difficult now for the reader than for the writer to realize that this narrative is aught but a dream.

INDEX

Lee, General W. H. F., 328, 330, 333, 425.
Lee, Light Horse Harry, 334.
Lee family, 10, 69.
Lee's army, 59, 161, 260, 297, 330.
Legare, Sidney, 92.
Lewis, Andrew, 98.
Lewis, John, 238.
Lexington, Va., 100, 231, 233, 234, 310.
Liberty Hall Academy, 238.
Libraries, private, in Virginia, 64.
Lincoln, Abraham, 75, 116, 118, 131, 134, 144, 157–160, 454.
Lincoln, news of assassination of, 454, 455.
Littleton family, 17.
Logan, Governor, of Pennsylvania, 236.
Logans of Dungeness, 139, 279, 283.
Lomax, Colonel, 161.
Lomonizoff, Baron, 6.
Long, General, 339.
Longfellow, H. W., 134.
Longstreet, General James, 327.
Louis Napoleon, 92.
Luray Gap, 295.
Lynch, Commander, 182.
Lynchburg, Va., 137, 313, 416.
Lynnhaven Bay, 167.
Lyons, Mary Power, 69.
Lyons, Mr. and Mrs. James, 69, 70, 75.

McCabe, Captain W. Gordon, 354.
McCausland, General John, 268, 310.
McClellan, General George B., 170, 171, 177, 214.
McClungs, The, 239.
McDowell, Cadet, killed, 306.
McDowells, The, 239.
McFarland, Mr. and Mrs., 69, 70.
McKinley, President William, 239.
McLaughlin, Major, 296, 300.
McLaughlins, The, 239.
Mahone, General William, 268, 319–327, 330, 361, 372, 428.
Mahone's brigade, 364.
Male attire in 1856–60, 66.
Mallory, Colonel Francis, 322.
Mallory, Hon. Stephen, Secretary of the Navy, 402, 445.
Malvern Hill, 214.
Manassas, 162, 168, 178.
Manchester, Va., 457.
Marshall, Chief Justice John, 99.
Marshall, Colonel Charles, 342, 428.
Marshall, General Humphrey, 403, 404.
Mary Anne, a slave, 39.

Maryland, State of, 11, 18, 29, 30, 119.
Mason, George, 99, 334.
Mason, Hon. John Y., 92.
Massachusetts and John Brown, 133.
Massanutten Mountains, 295.
Meade, General George G., 353, 356, 358, 360, 463.
Mechanicsville, Va., 214.
Mecklenburg Resolutions, 238.
Meherrin, Va., 417, 419, 422.
Merrimac, the ship, 160, 172, 191, 193, 206, 209, 212.
Merrimac and Monitor, 191–205.
Merritt, Cadet, wounded, 299.
Methodists, 16.
Mexican War, 2, 4, 6, 30, 31, 268.
Michaux, of Michaux's Ferry, the, 139.
Milford Station, 308.
Minnegerode, Rev. Charles, 70.
Minnesota, the ship, 198, 201.
Minor, Lieutenant R. D., 195, 201, 202.
Mobile, Ala., 161.
Mohawk valley, 138.
Monacon country, 235.
Monitor, appearance of, 202, 205.
Monroe, President, 104, 112, 199.
Montgomery, Ala., 161.
Montgomery Guard, 110.
Moores of Rockbridge, 239.
Morson family, 69.
Morsons of Dover, the, 139, 143.
Moseley family, 152.
Mott, General, 324.
Mount Airy, 304.
Mount Custis, 29.
Mount Jackson, 302.
Mount Prospect, 29.
Mules used for equipage, 67.
Munford, Rev. William, 69.
Music, at entertainments in South, 68.
Myers, Major William B., 402.

Nag's Head, N. C., 180, 181, 189.
Nandua Creek, Va., 18, 26.
Nansemond River, Va., 167, 196.
Napoleon III., 92.
National patriotism in Virginia in 1858, 98.
"Navy Hill Cats," Richmond, 59.
Navy Yard at Norfolk, evacuation and burning of, 162, 164.
Negro troops, first encounter with, 366; enlisted by Confederacy, 394, 395.
Nelson, Captain, of the Phœnix, 10.
Nelson, General Thomas, 99.

*Notes, Appendices, and
Bibliography*

Notes to the text of
The End of an Era

Page 32, line 9: The poet, editor, lawyer, and Confederate veteran, James Barron Hope (1829–1887). For a sketch see Paul C. Wermuth, "An Ode to Reconciliation," *Virginia Cavalcade*, VII (Autumn, 1957), 14–17.

Page 53, line 13: This was Mary Elizabeth Lyons, of Richmond, whom he married in November, 1853. Part of their honeymoon was spent at "The Hermitage," near Nashville, as the guests of Andrew Jackson. Wise's first marriage had been in Nashville in 1838 to a local girl, Ann Eliza Jennings, on whom see Clayton Torrence (ed.), "Letters of Mrs. Ann (Jennings) Wise to Her Husband, Henry A. Wise," *Virginia Magazine of History & Biography*, LVIII (Oct., 1950), 492–515.

Page 57, line 13: For background see Edwin P. Adkins, "Henry A. Wise in Sectional Politics, 1833–1860," doctoral dissertation, Dept. of History, Ohio State University (Columbus, O., 1948).

Page 89, line 2: See William M. Adkins, "Obadiah Jennings Wise, '50: A Sketch of His Life," *Indiana University Alumni Quarterly*, XXXIV–XXXV (Winter, 1937–Winter, 1938).

Page 92, line 1: John Sydney Algernon Ashe Legaré

(1835–1907), of Adam's Run, S. C. A copy of his "Memories from the Life of a Ne'er do Weal" is in the Southern Historical Collection, University of North Carolina Library.

Pages 95–6: Wise elaborated on the subject of duels in his "The Fire-Eaters: 'Gentlemen's Battles' under the Code of Honor," *Sat. Eve. Post,* June 2, June 23, 1906 (pp. 6–7, 28; pp. 8–9, 24–25, respectively).

Page 100, line 31: In 1858 the maximum enrollment at V.M.I. was 158, of whom 142 made the journey to Richmond for the unveiling ceremonies of the Washington monument. William Couper, Lexington, Va., March 14, 1959, to Curtis Carroll Davis.

Page 102, para. 2: "Stonewall" Jackson was never Commandant of the Virginia Military Institute; he taught artillery, not infantry. The Commandant was Gilham, whole militia *Manual of Instruction* . . . , released only by December, 1860, is here cited anachronistically. See also Wise's "Stonewall Jackson As I Knew Him," *Circle,* III (March, 1908), 143–45.

Page 122, para. 2: Wise enlarged on the conditions of Virginia slavery in his "An Extinct Race: Master and Man—Owner and Friend," *Sat. Eve. Post,* Jan. 27, 1906 (p. 25).

Page 139, line 25: Wise aided his sister Ellen ("Néné," as the family called her, from the Portuguese for "baby"), Mrs. William Carrington Mayo of Richmond, in selling her reminiscences of Goochland County to the *Cosmopolitan Magazine,* where her article appeared in June, 1896, as "A War-Time Aurora Borealis." This piece, which features Gov. Henry A. Wise's visit to the Hobson family and his near-capture by Dahlgren's raiders, is note-worthy as an evocation of James River Canal life rivalling that of Dr. George W. Bagby's better-known essay.

Page 142, last para: Wise writes notably of the Seddon children in his "The Faithful Legion: The Slave Who Was Servant and Friend," *Sat. Eve. Post,* Feb. 17, 1906 (pp. 2–3, 15). Thomas Nelson Page must have had in mind just such a family, said Wise, when he wrote his poem about "Uncle Gabe's White Folks."

Page 152, line 7: For a view of "Rolleston," by J. R. Hamilton, see *Harper's Weekly,* X (Jan. 6, 1866), 4.

Page 208, line 30: Herring's *Blacksmith* had been ob-tained for Gov. Wise by his friend, the Virginia artist John Gadsby Chapman (1808–1889). For a biographical sketch, with many illustrations, see the exhibition cata-logue by William P, Campbell, *John Gadsby Chapman: Painter and Illustrator—December 16, 1962 through Janu-ary 13, 1963* (Washington: National Gallery of Art, [1962]).

Page 210, line 32: This officer was one Bolles, of Massa-chusetts—probably Brig. Gen. John A. Bolles, on whom see *Massachusetts Soldiers, Sailors and Marines in the Civil War* (Norwood, Mass., 1933), VI, 756.

Pages 227–28: According to his son Henry, Wise de-tested Early on political, personal, and military grounds. Ironically enough the same son, as a cadet officer at V.M.I. in 1894, commanded the rifle squad that fired a salute over Early's grave. Henry A. Wise, Washington, D.C., August 5, 1959, to Curtis Carroll Davis.

Page 247, line 9: "Duck" Colonna (1845–1924) stood for the original model of the young soldier in John P. Walker's painting, *A Typical Cadet of the V.M.I. New*

Market Corps (1912), now hanging in Stonewall Jackson Memorial Hall on the Institute grounds at Lexington.

Page **260**, line 34: On this cousin (1842–1918) see Warren U. Ober, "Noise in the Guard Room," *Virginia Cavalcade*, IX (Winter, 1959), 39–47.

Page **285** ff: Of Wise's several evocations of this paramount event in V.M.I. annals the widest-read was probably "The West Point of the Confederacy: Boys in Battle at New Market, Virginia, May 15, 1864," *Century Magazine*, XXXVIII (Jan. 1889), 461–71. Reprinted in *Confederate Veteran*, XXIII (May, 1915), 212–18.

Page **290**, lines 11–12: Effie I. Canning Carlton did not write this famous song until 1871. See William Couper, *History of the Shenandoah Valley* (3 vols., York 1952), II, 927.

Page **307**, line 6: Wise's note of condolence to Stanard's mother, sent from Staunton, May 19, 1864, is printed in *Letters of a New Market Cadet: Beverly Stanard*, ed. John G. Barrett and Robert K. Turner, Jr. (Chapel Hill, N.C., 1961), pp. 67–8. Reproduced as frontispiece to this volume is Benjamin W. Clinedinst's *Charge of V.M.I. Cadets at New Market* (1914), hanging in Jackson Memorial Hall at the Institute in Lexington.

Page **312**, lines 21–2: The date being June 11, 1864, the burning of the Institute did not occur till the next day; and there is no "high point" at the alleged distance south of Lexington. For a well illustrated discussion see Cecil D. Eby, Jr., "David Hunter: Villain of the Valley—the Sack of the Virginia Military Institute," *The Iron Worker* (Lynchburg, Va.), XXVIII (Spring, 1964), 1–9.

Page 313, line 16: "Early's division" should read, Breck-inridge's division of Early's corps.

Page 334 ff: Despite a post-war bitterness with Fitz Lee, engendered by their political differences, the two men were at last reconciled during a chance encounter at his friend John Chamberlin's bar in Washington, D.C., and Wise eventually wrote his sympathetic "Major-General Fitzhugh Lee, United States Volunteers," in *The Criterion*, July 9, 1896.

Page 339, line 5: See also Wise's "Two Great Confederates. General John B. Gordon and General James Longstreet: Characterisations by a Friend of Both," *American Monthly Review of Reviews*, XXIX (Feb., 1904), 199–208.

Page 402, line 27: Wise remembered as a boy seeing Thackeray on a visit to Richmond, and recalled that he "sweated his spectacles." See his remarks "At the Dinner to Anthony Hope Hawkins (Anthony Hope), October 23, 1897," in *Speeches at the Lotos Club*, eds. John Elderkin, Chester S. Lord, and Horatio N. Fraser (New York, 1901), pp. 239–41. This probably occurred during Thackeray's second visit to America, when he appeared in Richmond in January, 1856, shortly after Gov. Wise's inauguration. See Gordon N. Ray, ed., *The Letters and Private Papers of William Makepeace Thackeray* (4 vols., Cambridge, Mass., 1945–46), III, 547–51. Ray has, however, uncovered no evidence that Thackeray ever met the Wises.

Page 424, line 24: "I do want to ask you on my own account, however," Joseph Bryan wrote to Wise from Richmond, April 12, 1899—during their tiff over the editorial hostile to Wise in the Richmond *Times*—"because I have done some scouting myself, are you sure that Curtis (of whom I have often heard) had a *carbine*. I never knew a scout to carry a carbine, but always Army pistols—a carbine is a cumbersome article for the quick work that a scout has to do." From New York, April 13, Wise replied he wouldn't take oath it was a carbine: from where he stood, it looked like a cannon.

Page **428**, line 29: In 1867, when Wise was arraigned at Baltimore for his assault on Edward A. Pollard, Reverdy Johnson and Col. Marshall served as his local defense counsel. "We moved the case to Towsontown, where it died a natural death," Wise reminisced in his speech, "Centralization by Construction," Maryland State Bar Association *Transactions* (1907), pp. 23–24.

Page **432**, lines 19–20: Henry A. Wise's battlefield promotion to Major General took place on April 6, 1865.

Page **445**, line 7: For a detailed discussion of this Danville rendezvous, with photographs of all concerned (including young Wise), see Robert L. Scribner, "Seven Days in a Quandary," *Virginia Cavalcade*, XIII (Winter, 1963–64), 5–15.

Page **449**, line 13: Wise also did a brief reminiscence, "Joseph E. Johnston," *Circle*, III (May, 1908), 287–88.

Page **461**, line 26: The assignee was the prominent lawyer and future Congressman from Virginia, John Randolph Tucker (1823–1897), whom Wise would place among the Fire-Eaters in his *The Lion's Skin: A Historical Novel and a Novel History* (New York, 1905), p. 85.

Appendix 1.

A CHAPTER GLOSS TO *The End of an Era*

Over the years certain readers have been heard to murmur against the witness value of *The End of an Era* because of its author's admission in his Preface that he did not personally participate in all the events narrated. This is a legitimate criticism, though it has perhaps been leaned upon too ponderously. In order to lay the ghosts of scholarly complaint—or at least direct them where to wail the loudest—Wise's most knowledgeable offspring was consulted. This is Mr. Henry A. Wise, who, following partnership in his father's law firm, succeeded Henry L. Stimson as United States Attorney for the Southern District of New York. Mr. Wise was asked to give a chapter-by-chapter assessment of *The End of an Era*. Writing from Washington, D.C., April 26, 1958, Mr. Wise reports as follows. . . .

You have asked that I tell you "those portions of *The End of an Era* he did not personally witness." I, of course, cannot personally give any information concerning any of the events embraced in the book; and as I have read it I have found difficulty in surmising in which he did and in which he did not participate. However, I will give you my best guess:

Chapter I	Of course this is all hearsay. My Father was born December 27th, 1846, and his family returned from Brazil in 1847. He certainly could have no memory of Brazil. He never returned to Brazil at any time.
Chapter II	This is all description and calls for no comment.
Chapter III	The same may be said of this.
Chapters IV–VII	I think these call for no comment. During the period covered by these chapters he was moving through the period when he was less than four years of age to the time when he was hardly eleven. So, I conclude that while his narrative is quite accurate he has attributed to himself thoughts as of then that certainly were not as distinct at that time as he portrays them to have been.
Chapter VIII	I have no comment other than to say that the story as therein recorded corresponds with all that I ever heard of this event.
Chapter IX	Is quite accurate. He, of course, was not at Harper's Ferry. But he has quite accurately reported the events, and much of it is of record, and a

great deal of it was told to him by his Father and Brothers who were participants.

Chapters X–XII

Are quite accurate. He, of course, was not in any of the military operations. His knowledge of these came from what he was told by participants, and what he read concerning these events.

Chapter XIII

I do not think he was at Rolleston at the time of the battle between the *Monitor* and the *Merrimac*. It is my recollection that he then was at school in Goochland County. However his stepmother, his brother and other members of the family did witness the battle and he had reported that he learned from them and from other sources.

Chapter XIV

I do not think and am quite positive that he was not at Rolleston at the time it was overrun by the Federal Army. His brother and other members of the family were there, but departed before the army (U.S.) took the place.

Chapter XV

Is quite accurate. But I never heard that he went to Rocky Mount before going to V. M. I.

Chapters XVI–XVIII   Are accurate.

Chapter XIX   Is accurate up to the time he was shot. The subsequent events concerning the battle of New Market are what he learned from others.

Chapter XX   Is accurate and calls for no comment.

Chapter XXI–XXII   I do not think my Father was in Petersburg during all of the occurrences he records. I am quite positive he was not there when the Crater explosion occurred. What he reports is largely what his brothers, cousins and Father may have told him. I also very well remember hearing Col. Haskell tell my Father of his, Haskell's participation. And my Father and Mahone subsequently were most intimate. I personally went over the battle field with my Father and Mahone when I was about ten or twelve years of age. My Father did know practically all the principal actors in that event; and he knew every Confederate whose picture he painted in this chapter. It also must be remembered that General Meade, who was the field commander of the

Federal forces, was my Father's uncle-in-law; and my Father and his brother visited General Meade's home shortly after the surrender at Appomattox.

Chapter XXIII–XXVI He did participate in the events narrated, but was not in any of the fighting from Petersburg to Appomattox. I don't think and am very positive that he was not present on the occasion when my Grandfather told General Lee that the jig was up and that thereafter the blood of every man killed would be on his hands. However, it is true that my Grandfather did so inform General Lee. I am inclined to think that there is some exaggeration in the reported interviews he had with President Davis and General Lee. However the fact is that he did carry the last communications that took place between them.

Appendix 2.

1846
December 27: Born at American Legation, Rio de Janeiro, second son and third child of Henry Alexander Wise (1806–76), Envoy Extraordinary and Minister Plenipotentiary to Brazil, by his second wife, Sarah (Sergeant) Wise of Philadelphia.

November 1847–December 1855
Lives at the family plantation, "Only," on Onancock Creek, Accomack County, eastern shore of Virginia.

January 1856–December 1859
Resides at Government House on Capitol Square, Richmond, during his father's term as Governor of Virginia.

January–June, 1860
Lives at "Eastwood," Goochland County, with his sister, Annie Jennings Wise, and her husband, Frederick Plumer Hobson.

1862
July–April: Removes to "Rolleston" plantation, new home of his father and stepmother, Mary Elizabeth (Lyons) Wise, on Deep Creek, an eastern arm of the Elizabeth River, Princess Anne County, just south of Norfolk.

July: Refugees with family to Richmond, to Goochland County, to Rocky Mount (Franklin County), under supervision of older brother, Rev. Henry A. Wise.

September 1: Leaves Rocky Mount for Lexington, where he enrolls as plebe in Virginia Military Institute, Class of 1866.

1864

May 15: Is among those cadets wounded at Battle of New Market, Shenandoah County, during Confederate victory over Federals under Gen. Sigel.

June: Leaves Lexington to volunteer for Confederate States Army, having risen to Sergeant in Corps of Cadets.

1865

September–April 18: Serves in C.S.A., rising to rank of full Lieutenant, first as drillmaster with Col. Robert Preston's regiment of Reserves, last as adjutant to Maj. Francis J. Boggs, commanding artillery defenses of the Richmond & Danville R.R.

April 6 carries final dispatch from Gen. Lee near Farmville to President Davis at Danville.

Surrenders with elements of Gen. Joseph E. Johnston's army at Jamestown, northeast of High Point, North Carolina.

1866

September–June 29: Enters the University of Virginia at Charlottesville. Pledges Beta Theta Pi fraternity. Graduates from School of Moral Philosophy.

1867

June 29: Graduates from School of Law, winning Washington Society gold medal for debate.

November 14: In pistol combat at Baltimore wounds journalist Edward A. Pollard for an allegedly insulting communication to former Gov. Wise.

1869–1888
Practices law at Richmond (in partnership with father until latter's death September 12th, 1876).

1869
November 3: Marries Evelyn Byrd Beverley Douglas (1851–1925) at Nashville, Tenn., daughter of Hugh Douglas of Nashville. In due course the couple have "a baseball team" of seven sons and two daughters.

1875
January 29: Qualifies to practice before the Supreme Court of the United States.

1876
July 1: Appointed by Gov. Kemper to the Board of Visitors of the Virginia Military Institute, one-year term.

1877
February 20: Elected Captain of the Richmond Light Infantry Blues (founded 1793), at its reorganization. Serves until June 28, 1882.

1880
August: Challenges George Ben Johnston, M.D., of Richmond to a duel. Authorities arrest both men.

November 2: Nominated for the U. S. Congress, Third District, by the Readjuster wing of the Democratic Party. Defeated by cousin George D. Wise, running on the Funder wing.

1882
May: Appointed by President Arthur as U. S. District Attorney for Eastern District of Virginia; serves until March, 1883, before resigning to enter politics.

With seven others, appointed by Gov. Cameron to the

Board of Visitors of the University of Virginia, serving until 1886.

July 25: Near Christiansburg, Montgomery County, engages in pistol duel with John S. Crockett, Commonwealth's Attorney for Wythe County: the next-to-last duel in Virginia.

1883 and 1885

March: Elected to the 48th Congress as Congressman at Large (Republican) from Virginia.

1884

March 5–6: Publishes open letter renouncing the principle and practice of duelling in the Richmond *Whig* and *State*, respectively (triggering end of the "code" in Virginia).

1885

November 3: Nominated for Governor on the Republican-Readjuster coalition ticket, is narrowly defeated by Democratic nominee, Maj. Gen. Fitzhugh Lee, in controversial election attracting national attention.

1888

June: Serves as chairman of the anti-Mahone delegation from Virginia to the Republican National Convention, Chicago, which nominates Benjamin Harrison for the Presidency.

September: Removes with family to New York City, settling eventually at 154 West 76th St. Engages in corporate, then general law work—until *ca.* 1894 as General Counsel for the Sprague Electric Railway & Motor Co., becoming the Edison General Electric Co., with offices at 44 Broad St; in private practice until 1898 with Dallas Flannagan, thereafter with son Henry A. Wise, with offices at 20 Broad St.

1889

July 4: With other surviving New Market cadets, awarded an honorary A.B. degree in the Arts, Sciences, and Literature by the Virginia Military Institute at Lexington.

1891

March 20: Admitted to the New York Society, Sons of the American Revolution, by right of descent from Gerard Spencer of Lynn, Mass.

1893

January: Visits England with Oscar T. Crosby as advisory counsel for British branch of the Edison General Electric Co., consulting with Solicitor General and Queen's Counsel. Makes brief trip to Paris.

February 17: Joins Union League Club of New York City, sponsored by Chauncey M. Depew and seconded by William H. Lee (resigns December 31, 1910).

1896

June: Delegate to the Repblican National Convention, St. Louis, which nominates William McKinley for the Presidency.

1898

May 31: Admitted to the Confederate Veterans Camp of New York (resigns March, 1912).

1899

October: Acquires "Kiptopeke" on the point of Cape Charles, Northampton County, Virginia, as summer home, naming it for local Indian chief who welcomed John Smith in 1608.

1900

June: Delegate to the Republican National Convention,

Philadelphia, which nominates McKinley for the Presidency.

1903

January 1: Elected president of the West Side Republican Club of New York City.

1907

Health begins to fail, with attack of angina pectoris. Settles at "Kiptopeke."

1908

October 19: Admitted to the Virginia Society of the Cincinnati by right of descent from maternal great grandfather, Lt. Col. John Cropper, of the Eleventh and Seventh Virginia Continental Lines.

1911

August: Formally dissolves New York City law firm of Wise & Wise.

1913

May 12: Dies of pneumonia aged sixty-six years, five months, at summer home of son Henry A. Wise near Princess Anne, Somerset County, Maryland.

May 15: Burial in family plot at Hollywood Cemetery, Richmond, Virginia.

Bibliography

1. SELECTED WORKS DISCUSSING JOHN S. WISE

Biographical Directory of the American Congress: 1774–1949. Government Printing Office, 1950; p. 2,035.

Bryan, John Stewart. *Joseph Bryan: His Times, His Family, His Friends*. Richmond, 1935.

Carpenter, Frank G. *Carp's Washington*. Intro. Cleveland Amory. New York, Toronto, and London, 1960.

Chesterman, Evan R. "Duels and Duelists of Bygone Virginia Days: John S. Wise Declines a Fight with Page McCarty," *Richmond Evening Journal* (26 Nov. 1908), p. 5.

Copeland, W. S. "Danville Reminiscences," *Danville Register* (12 Oct. 1911), p. 2.

Couper, William. *One Hundred Years at V.M.I.* 4 vols., Richmond, 1939.

———, *The V.M.I. New Market Cadets: Biographical Sketches. . . .* Charlottesville, Va., 1933.

Cutchins, John A. *A Famous Command: The Richmond Light Infantry Blues*. Richmond, 1934.

Davis, Curtis Carroll. "A Legend at Full-Length: Mr. Chapman Paints Colonel Crockett—and Tells about It," *Proceedings of the American Antiquarian Society*, LXIX, Part 2 (Oct. 21, 1959), 155–74. Illustrated.

————. "His Name was Diomed," *Virginia Cavalcade*, X (Autumn, 1960), 42–47. Illustrated. The composition and critical reception of the first dog book by an American.

————. "Wise Words from Virginia: The Published Writings of John S. Wise, of the Eastern Shore and New York City," *Papers of the Bibliographical Society of America*, LIV (4th Quarter, 1960), 273–85. The introduction stresses Wise as man of letters.

————. "The Small Bang at Bangs," *Virginia Cavalcade*, XI (Autumn, 1961), 4–9. Illustrated. Wise as duellist, with emphasis on encounter with John S. Crockett.

————. "Very Well-Rounded Republican: The Several Lives of John S. Wise," *Virginia Magazine of History & Biography*, LXXI (Oct., 1963), 461–87. Illustrated. Biographical essay, stressing Wise as politician and as lawyer.

Dictionary of American Biography, XX (1936), 429. By Prof. Robert D. Meade, Randolph-Macon Woman's College.

Encyclopedia Americana (1957 Edition) XXIX, 427.

Harrison, Mrs. Burton. *Recollections Grave and Gay.* New York, 1911.

"John S. Wise—A Man of Genius," *The Galaxy: A Magazine of Literature*, II (Nov. 1908), 13–14.

La Rue, George, "J. S. and Otherwise," *American Field*, XLIV (20 July 1895), 49–50.

Library of Southern Literature, XIII (1929), 5,937–40, plus sixteen-page selection from *Diomed, End of Era,*

Lion's Skin, and *Recollections*. By James H. Lindsay, editor of the Charlottesville, Va., *Daily Progress* (erroneously identified in XV, 258, as the Rev. John H. Lindsay).

Likenesses:

1885 Aug. 1: *Harper's Weekly*, XXIX, 488.

1901: White's *National Cyclopaedia*, XI, 320.

1902 Dec. 2: Richmond, Va., *Dispatch* (p. 2).

1905 Oct. 12: Baltimore, Md., *Sun* (12/5).

1913 May 13: Baltimore, Md. *Sun* (p. 2).

1913 May 13: Richmond, Va., *Times-Dispatch* (p. 1).

1918: Jennings C. Wise, *Col. John Wise* . . . , p. 245.

Massey, John E. *Autobiography*. Ed. Elizabeth H. Hancock. New York and Washington, 1909.

National Cyclopaedia of American Biography, White's, XI (1901), 319–20.

Pennypacker, Samuel W. *The Autobiography of a Pennsylvanian*. Philadelphia, 1918.

"Sketch of John S. Wise, Republican Candidate for Governor of Virginia. . . ." N.p., *ca.* 1885. Broadside, Southern Historical Collection, University of North Carolina Library.

"Sons of the Law" (Talk of the Town), *The New Yorker*, XXXI (April 9, 1955), 23–24.

Squires, W[illiam] H. T. *Unleashed at Long Last: Reconstruction in Virginia*. . . . Portsmouth, Va., 1939.

Weaver, Richard M. "The Confederate South, 1865–1910; a Study in the Survival of a Mind and a Culture." Unpublished Doctoral dissertation, Dept. of English, Louisiana State University (Baton Rouge, 1943). See pp. 16, 294–95.

Wilder, Marshall P. *The People I've Smiled With.* New York, Akron, and Chicago, 1899.

Wise, Barton Haxall, *The Life of Henry A. Wise of Virginia: 1806–1876. By His Grandson* . . . New York, 1899.

Wise, Jennings Cropper. *Col. John Wise of England and Virginia (1617–1695): His Ancestors and Descendants.* Richmond, 1918.

Withers, Robert Enoch, M.D. *Autobiography of an Octogenarian.* Roanoke, Va., 1907.

Young, John Russell. *Men and Memories: Personal Reminiscences.* Ed. May D. Russell Young. New York and London, 1901.

2. SELECTED WORKS TREATING "THE END OF AN ERA"

REVIEWS

1899 July   Southern History Association *Publications*, III, 230

       Nov. 16   *The Nation*, LXIX, 379–80.

       Dec.   *American Monthly Review of Reviews*, XX, 747.

       Dec. 1   *The Dial*, XXVII, 418–20. By Francis W. Shepardson.

       Dec. 20   *Home Journal*, No. 51 (2/6). By William C. Bamburgh.

1900 Feb.   *Book Buyer*, XX, 58–59. By Mary Tracy Earle.

Feb.   *Wake Forest Student*, XIX, 440–41. By
            G. A. Foote.

Apr.   *American Historical Review*, V, 604–
            605.

EXCERPTS

1900 Jan. 17   "Presbyterian Lexington," in Richmond,
                Va., *Central Presbyterian*, XXXV (No. 3),
                pp. 2–3.

1903 June 21   "The Charge of the Boy Battalion," in
                Baltimore, Md., *Sunday Sun* (p. 11).

1909 Aug. 2   Col. Haskell at The Crater, in Columbia,
                S.C., *State* (3/1–2).

1910 June 16   Chapter I, in E. J. Edwards' column,
                "New News of Yesterday," New York
                Evening Mail (8/5).

1913 May 13   Cadets at New Market; Sayler's Creek
                dialogue with Lee, in New York *Evening
                Post* (6/1–2).

1959   "Lee Sends His Last Message to Jeffer-
                son Davis," in Philip Van Doren Stern,
                Secret Missions of the Civil War . . . Chi-
                cago and New York, pp. 282–96.

1961   "John S. Wise's Will [the "J. Reb."
                document], in *A Civil War Treasury of
                Tales, Legends and Folklore*. Ed. B. A.
                Botkin. New York, pp. 542–43.

Jan. 6   Bruce Catton, "Gallant Men in Deeds of
                Glory," *Life*, L. 64, 66.